GROLIER'S
MASTERPLOTS
1990 ANNUAL

GROLIER'S MASTERPLOTS

1990 ANNUAL

GROLIER'S LITERARY ANNUAL
*Essay-Reviews of 100 Outstanding
Books Published in the United States
During 1989*

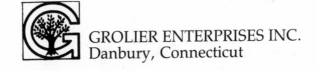

GROLIER ENTERPRISES INC.
Danbury, Connecticut

Grolier Enterprises Inc.

ISSN 0194-0503
ISBN 0-7172-8243-0

Prepared by
Sachem Publishing Associates, Inc.
Guilford, Connecticut

*Grolier Enterprises Inc. offers
customized Harvard Classics
bookplates. For details on ordering,
please write:*

Grolier Enterprises Inc.
Sherman Turnpike
Danbury, CT 06816

Printed in the United States of America

LIST OF TITLES

———

CONTRIBUTING REVIEWERS FOR 1990 ANNUAL

CHARLES AGVENT
DAVID ALVAREZ
MARIA BRAZILL
GARY BROCKMAN
CONSTANCE CLYDE
LISA M. CLYDE
WENDY DUBOIS
DAN DUFFY
LESLIE M. FRENCH
ESTHER M. FRIESNER
ROBERT F. GISH
NANCY E. HENRY
DEBORAH IRONSON
SHERYL JEAN
ELIZABETH J. JEWELL
DAVID M. KENNERLEY
RICHARD LACHMANN
JEANNE LARRIVEE

DEIRDRE L. MENCHACA
LYN MILLER-LACHMANN
KARIN A. NOBILE
EDWARD B. ROWE
LOUIS SASSO
CHRISTINE BRENDEL SCRIABINI
NANCY M. SEYBOLD
JOHN SOKOLNICKI
ELIZABETH BOUVIER SPENCER
WILLIAM SPENCER
CHRISTINE LINDBERG STEVENS
JANELLE STEVENSON
JOHN E. STEVENSON
HANK STEWART
ADRIENNE SUDDARD
BERTIE SWEET
E. P. TISCHER
ELLEN S. WILSON

PREFACE

As 1989 drew to a close, a new era was being heralded. The materialism, personal gratification, and empty values revealed in Tom Wolfe's 1988 work *Bonfire of the Vanities*, which characterized the spirit of the 1980s, were to be a thing of the past. The 1990s, it was proclaimed, would be the "real" decade, marked by a new appreciation for tradition, relatedness, and involvement. Whether this fresh wind would continue to blow throughout the decade has yet to be determined, but the books published in the United States in 1989 do reveal signs of a transition.

The power of cultural identity was a recurring theme in 1989. One of the most acclaimed works of the year, *The Joy Luck Club*, a first novel by Amy Tan, explores the generational and cultural gulf that separates four Chinese-born mothers and their American-born daughters, a gap that is ultimately bridged by love. Another outstanding novel, in which a Cuban-American musician's Latin heritage is the key to both his success and eventual destruction, is Oscar Hijuelos's *The Mambo Kings Play Songs of Love*. Surely one of the most controversial novels of the century, Salman Rushdie's *The Satanic Verses* draws heavily on Eastern religion and the Eastern literary tradition of the nested fable, on magic and mysticism, to tell a classical story of the struggle of good against evil. That the Muslim world reacted to this work with such outrage was shocking to many in the West, only serving to underscore the significance of the cultural differences. In *The Storyteller*, Mario Vargas Llosa also focuses on the encounter of two very different and seemingly incompatible cultures, those of a Western intellectual and a small Amazonian Indian tribe.

Russian emigré Sergei Dovlatov's delightful *Ours: A Russian Family Album* brings to life four generations of his colorful relatives to give the author's American-born son a feel for his Russian heritage. Native American writer Michael Dorris, in *The Broken Cord*, recounts the poignant story of his adopted son Adam who was afflicted with fetal alcohol syndrome, a condition that is exploding among the Native American population as cultural prohibitions against women's drinking have altered along with other perceptions about feminine roles. Alice Walker, in *The Temple of My Familiar*, weaves a magical tale of how three generations of black Americans acknowledge their connections to each other and to their collective pasts.

The recipient of the National Book Award for nonfiction, Thomas Friedman's *From Beirut to Jerusalem*, is an American reporter's account of nine years on assignment in the Middle East, in which he clarifies many cultural differences that have contributed to the conflict there. Few authors are able to capture and convey the marvels of ethnic diversity as successfully as the late travel writer Bruce Chatwin, whose collection of essays and short stories *What Am I Doing Here* sheds light on such diverse subjects as African politics, Chinese geomancers, and the sacred aspects of walking as practiced by the Aboriginals. Le Ly Hayslip's memoir, *When Heaven and Earth Changed Places*, describes her peasant origins in war-ravaged Vietnam, her escape to the United States, and a return visit to the country of her birth, portraying with painful honesty the pull of two cultures. German novelist Günter Grass tried his hand at travel writing in *Show Your Tongue*, a reflection in essays, drawings, and poetry of a sojourn in Calcutta, India, that chronicles suffering and misery. Another outstanding travel writer, V. S. Naipaul, journeyed to the southern United States to investigate the complexities and contradictions inherent in that region, detailing in *A Turn in the South* his experiences with a cross section of black and white Americans.

A frequent theme in 1989 was a character's reassessment of his own identity as a response to a change in circumstances or environment. In John Casey's *Spartina*, the fiction winner of the National Book Award, a man resolves to change the course of his life, allowing himself to achieve his dream. Ironically, one of the finest novels to investigate British manners, particularly the traditional master-servant relationship, was *The Remains of the Day* by Japanese-born author Kazuo Ishiguro, whose poignant depiction of an English butler's identity crisis when faced with a most untraditional employer won England's prestigious Booker Prize. John Irving's *A Prayer for Owen Meany* is a contemporary allegory in which the protagonist learns about fate, faith, and miracles through his ongoing relationship with a small boy. Another novel focusing on the clash of the past and the present is *Baumgartner's Bombay* by Anita Desai, about an elderly Jew who fled Nazi Germany to settle in Bombay. The successful, middle-aged artist in Margaret Atwood's *Cat's Eye* must reevaluate a destructive childhood relationship. The narrator of Christa Wolf's *Accident/A Day's News* attempts to come to terms with a personal crisis (her brother's life-threatening illness) and terrifying world events (the Chernobyl disaster). In *To Asmara* by Thomas Keneally, an Australian journalist embarks on a fact-finding journey to the Eritrea region of Ethiopia but discovers more about himself. Anita Brookner's *Latecomers* dissects the connection between two dissimilar childhood friends whose early life as Jewish refugees from Nazi Germany has left one of them with unresolved conflicts. *The Shawl* by Cynthia Ozick is another evocation of the pain of the Holocaust.

In more than one novel, characters learned significant lessons about life in the fast lane. In E. L. Doctorow's *Billy Bathgate*, a young boy who passes a summer's apprenticeship in mobster Dutch Schultz's gang is irrevocably changed by the experience. In Paul West's *Lord Byron's Doctor*, the impressionable young protagonist's experiences with the dissolute poet are devastating. The sexual exploits of the unprincipled college professor of Anne Bernays's *Professor Romeo* cost him his wife, his girlfriend, and his job, leaving the reader satisfied that this reprobate has gotten what he deserved. Joyce Carol Oates's *American Appetites* concerns successful, attractive people for whom boredom and meaninglessness are constant companions. Few collections of short stories have portrayed the emptiness of contemporary life as successfully as Mavis Gallant's *In Transit: Twenty Stories* or T. Coraghessan Boyle's *If the River Was Whiskey*.

For many writers, the impact of early experiences on the course of their lives was a matter for examination. Historian Jill Ker Conway in *The Road from Coorain* describes her agonizing struggle to break free of her dependent mother and the constraints of Australian society. Journalist Russell Baker's autobiography *The Good Times* examines the influence that his desire to win his mother's approval had upon his success, while novelist John Updike's *Self-Consciousness: Memoirs* reveals the anxieties, insecurities, and physical afflictions that have plagued him throughout his life.

Several novelists employed their creative talents to recast or reinvent history. Julian Barnes's *A History of the World in 10½ Chapters* is a jumble of the real and imagined in a postmodern novel. *Oldest Living Confederate Widow Tells All* by Allan Gurganus explores the memories of a ninety-nine-year-old survivor. The complex *Foucault's Pendulum* by Umberto Eco brings the 14th-century Knights Templar into the modern world.

Historians also were engaging in reflection and reevaluation. Paul Fussell's *Wartime: Understanding and Behavior in the Second World War* is an attempt to redefine World War II in more realistic and less glorified terms than those in which it is typically portrayed. A second significant book that focuses on the same period is *How War Came: The Immediate Origins of the Second World War 1938–1939* by Donald Cameron Watt. Another much-examined topic, the Holocaust, is reappraised in Arno Mayer's *Why Did the Heavens Not Darken?: The "Final Solution" in History*. In the year of the French Revolution's bicentennial anniversary, Simon Schama brings a startlingly fresh per-

spective in *Citizens: A Chronicle of the French Revolution.*
American foreign policy also deserved another look. Two experts in the field shared their views: George F. Kennan in his memoirs *Sketches from a Life*, and J. William Fulbright, in a collection of essays, *The Price of Empire*. Stanley Karnow's *In Our Image: America's Empire in the Philippines* assesses U.S. relations with that country.

A number of biographies that appeared in 1989 centered on the reconsideration of a misunderstood or ignored figure. Martin Bauml Duberman's *Paul Robeson* sheds considerable light on the real accomplishments of a controversial man who has been largely forgotten. Sheldon M. Novick chose as his subject one of the United States' best known and most intelligent and capable legal minds in *Honorable Justice: The Life of Oliver Wendell Holmes*, about whom no full biography has been written. Ian Gibson's *Federico García Lorca* is a classic biography of the gifted and complex Spanish poet and dramatist.

The 1990 *Grolier's Masterplots* contains 100 exciting and diverse works, each one carefully selected to represent the best of those books published in the United States in 1989. Although fewer than half have been mentioned here, this edition contains 44 volumes of fiction, 8 memoirs and journals, 17 biographies and autobiographies, 6 collections of essays, 11 works of history and current affairs, 4 of social science, 3 of science, 3 of travel, 3 of social criticism, and 1 of literary criticism.

Susan Carter Elliott

ACCIDENT/A DAY'S NEWS

Author: Christa Wolf (1929–   )
Publisher: Farrar, Straus and Giroux (New York). 113 pp. $15.95
Type of work: Novel
Time: April 1988
Locale: East Germany

*An excursion into the mind of a woman as she describes a day of crisis and
waiting, the day her beloved brother undergoes surgery for a brain tumor, a
day just following the Chernobyl disaster*

Principal character:
AN EAST GERMAN WOMAN, a writer

Christa Wolf's *Accident/A Day's News* is not a novel in the conventional sense. It is a first-person narrative that is, more than anything
else, a meditation on what it means to be human. It is an intense
multilayered investigation and recollection of the thoughts and feelings
of an East German writer regarding the events of a particular day.

The book opens early on a beautiful spring day as she is realizing
that the fire in the Chernobyl reactor and the radioactive cloud that
has been released have changed the fabric of existence. True to her
vocation as a writer, she thinks first of the accident's impact on language. She will avoid the word "exploded" in relation to the cherry
blossoms, although such a day only a year ago would have found her
thinking and saying, "The green is exploding." Later, she thinks of
the "radiant sky" and realizes that "Now one can't think that anymore, either." And even later, while musing about the deadly cloud of
radiation, she thinks it would be "interesting to see which poet would
be the first to dare sing the praises of a white cloud." For this new
horrifying cloud has "knocked the white cloud of poetry into the archives."

On this day when minds around the world are focused on Chernobyl,
the woman is also living under the strain of a more personal crisis. Her
brother, whom she addresses as "brother heart," and who obviously
is very close to her, is undergoing surgery for a brain tumor. The two
important events are juxtaposed in her thoughts throughout the day.
She has an almost symbiotic relationship with her brother and sends
him messages as the operation progresses, using beams of energy that
"traverse the poisoned layers of air without becoming infected." She
imagines each step of the operation and speaks to him, cautioning,
scolding, or soothing as necessary. Concentrating on the very finger-
tips of the surgeon in order to guide them, she tells her brother, "In
the deepening wells of your unconsciousness, you shall be soothed."

While she takes her morning shower, the woman listens to the news and hears a young expert advising against giving children fresh milk, spinach, or salad or allowing them to play in the park or a sandbox. She moves on to her breakfast and recognizes in the preparation—the measuring of coffee and the savoring of its aroma, the boiling of an egg —the "imperishable pleasures" of life. And yet, her next thought is that these are the last of the eggs from before the accident.

She goes to the post office, stopping on the way to talk with some neighbors. As they speak to her, her interior monologue continues, in which she picks up on things that they say and associates freely from bits and pieces of information. She tells her brother that, after almost two hours in surgery, "it is beginning to become strenuous." She stops suddenly and thinks, "What's going on? Are you letting yourself go?" She proceeds to rally him by bullying and encouraging, "Don't let go, brother! Hang on. Yes, that's right. I'm going to pull a little bit now. . . . Don't try that again." She is his lifeline and is determined to keep him alive.

Upon arriving home, she makes a phone call to her youngest daughter in Berlin and finds her fearful for her children and angry at the perpetrators of the accident: "They'll never ever learn. . . . They're all sick." After listening to anecdotes about her grandchildren, the woman tells her daughter, "Shakespeare and Greek tragedy wouldn't do a thing for me now compared with your children's stories." The monumental is dwarfed by simple and small pleasures.

Working in her garden, her thoughts turn to her brother and the complexity of the operation. One slip could result in changes to his personality or damage to his very consciousness. She is feverishly and angrily pulling nettles and weeds with her bare hands, in spite of the warnings on the radio about wearing gloves when gardening and thinking about the surgeons "peeling out from its healthy environment the tumor which was nestled very, very snugly up against the pituitary gland—root and branch, indeed down to the last cell."

One of the book's epigraphs, two sentences by Carl Sagan, sums up a central issue occupying the protagonists's thoughts on this day: "The connection between murder and invention has been with us ever since. Both derive from agriculture and civilization." At one point in her commentary to her brother, the woman asks, "What do people want?" and concludes, "People want to experience strong emotions and they want to be loved." If these desires are left unfulfilled, they create a substitute, "the entire breathlessly expanding monstrous technological creation, a substitute for love." "They," the young scientists and men in white coats, are responsible for the disaster at Chernobyl. The surgeons too, "like all specialists," have lost the "holy terror" and the "reverend fear" of delving into spheres of mystery. They are driven to take apart and experiment without thought of the consequences by their desire to find a substitute.

She recalls a conversation with her brother in which he had accused her of being equally compelled to write even when she had recognized the power of words to wound or destroy. Recognizing her complexity as a human being in this dark and deep desire to invent or create in spite of the outcome humbles and angers her but ultimately makes her no less unforgiving of the scientists. This is the turning point of the day for her, and she seeks release from her feelings by hurling utensils again and again across the room and eventually crying.

At one o'clock in the afternoon, a phone call informs her that the operation was a success. She can relax and enjoy her lunch. While doing the dishes she is surprised to find herself singing the "Ode to Joy" at the top of her lungs. She discovers later that it was at this moment that her brother woke from the anesthetic.

Exhausted from the strain of the day, she lies down for a nap but begins to read an article on the scientists of Star Wars. She thinks of these "highly gifted, very young men" with overdeveloped brains and believes that they have no need for human relationships because they have formed pseudorelationships with their computers to absorb their emotions. And she wonders what mistake in human evolution led to the human propensity for linking the satisfaction of one's desires with the urge to destroy. She also questions where her own responsibility lies and what personal "blind spot" she harbors.

Feeling a need to move, she gets her bicycle and rides into the woods, where she thinks of her brother and, knowing now that he has lost the sense of smell as a result of the operation, hopes that the "fragrance of the woods in springtime is firmly anchored" in his memory. She recalls a discussion with her brother in which she asserted that the stark choice between "living with radioactivity or with the dying woods" is one of false alternatives. Her brother, more of a realist, responds that failure to make the choice means the loss of creature comforts. She does not want to believe that it is man's wishes that lead to self-destruction.

> Has the idle, oversized part of our brain fled into manic-destructive hyperactivity, faster and faster and, finally—today—at breakneck speed, hurling out ever new fantasies, which we, unable to stop ourselves, have turned into objectives of desire and entrusted to our machine world in the form of production tasks?

During dinner her oldest daughter calls, and the narrator discusses the "blind spot" with her daughter, questioning whether entire civilizations might not somehow find the courage to penetrate to the heart of darkness, the blind spot that allows them to destroy. Later, she watches a television show in which a scientist admits that the development of any new technology involves risks, and she composes an imaginary letter stating that the "risk of nuclear technology was not comparable to any other risk and that one absolutely had to renounce this technology if there was even the slightest element of uncertainty." Finally, she settles into bed with Conrad's *Heart of Darkness*, which seems to speak directly to the thoughts that have preoccupied her mind on this day.

Accident, like many of Christa Wolf's books, has a strong autobiographical element to it, in spite of her disclaimer that all the characters in the novel were invented by her. It seems fair to say that the issues and questions are ones with which she has wrestled. This is not an easy book to read, for the free-association style demands close attention and, occasionally, some rereading in order to determine where one is in time, or to whom or what is being referred. It is also demanding because its issues are important and complex.

Accident is a small book, but one that is replete with abstract concerns. The urgent philosophical narrative, however, is frequently relieved, lightened, and enlightened by moments of simple, domestic everyday activities. Work in the garden, the preparation of meals, visiting with neighbors, and opening the mail interrupt and deflect abstruse thought, sending it in new directions.

Thoughts about the two events, memories of childhood games and fairy tales, and recollections from the war are all interwoven in a lyrical, at times highly poetic, prose. *Accident* is disturbing, inspiring, and thought provoking. It is, finally, life affirming, moving the reader to agree with the narrator's closing thought: "How difficult it would be, brother, to take leave of this earth."

Maria Brazill

AFFLICTION

Author: Russell Banks (1940–   )
Publisher: Harper & Row (New York). 355 pp. $18.95
Type of work: Novel
Time: The present
Locale: Lawford, New Hampshire

Within the space of a week, Wade Whitehouse's troubled life reaches a terrible climax with far-reaching effects for his family, several of his friends, and his neighbors in a small New Hampshire town

> *Principal characters:*
> WADE WHITEHOUSE, a well driller and part-time police officer
> LILLIAN HORNER, his former wife
> JILL WHITEHOUSE, Wade and Lillian's daughter
> GLENN WHITEHOUSE, Wade's father
> ROLFE WHITEHOUSE, Wade's brother
> MARGIE FOGG, Wade's lover
> JACK HEWITT, one of Wade's coworkers
> GORDON LaRIVIERE, Wade's employer and a town selectman

Wade Whitehouse and his former wife, Lillian, have been divorced for nearly three years. Remarried, Lillian lives in Concord, New Hampshire, about a two-hour drive south of Lawford, the town where Wade lives. Wade and Lillian were high-school sweethearts who saw in one another the potential to be something more than the other men and women around them in Lawford. In fact, Wade and Lillian have been married to and divorced from one another twice; Lillian has custody of their ten-year-old daughter, and Wade has limited visiting rights, a situation that rankles him. Wade's parents still live in Lawford, and he has a younger brother, Rolfe, a history teacher, who makes his home in a Massachusetts suburb.

Wade is Lawford's part-time police officer. He also works full-time drilling wells for Gordon LaRiviere, a town selectman. Because of the divorce, Wade gave up the house that he and Lillian built and now lives in a trailer on the outskirts of town. Margie Fogg, who works as a waitress, is Wade's sometime confidant and lover.

The novel's immediate events span the annual week-long hunting season, at the end of October into November. Jack Hewitt, one of Wade's coworkers, acts as a guide for Evan Twombley, a labor leader from Boston, who is killed while they are out hunting. Everyone but Wade is sure that the shooting is an accident, and his feeling is reinforced when Rolfe tells Wade that he thinks the labor leader may have been murdered in some sort of cover-up.

Against the backdrop of the shooting, Wade's relationship with Lillian becomes even more strained. Wade wants custody of Jill and goes to see a lawyer in Concord. While in Concord, Wade, by pure luck, discovers that Lillian is having an affair with the lawyer who represented her in the divorce. Wade decides to use this information to discredit Lillian in a custody battle.

Back in Lawford, winter sets in early. Wade and Margie visit Wade's parents and find that Wade's father, Glenn, has been drinking; the furnace is not working; and Wade's mother has died during the night, frozen to death. Despite the fact that Glenn Whitehouse is an alcoholic who beat his wife and children, Wade plans to move into his parents' home and asks Margie to move in with him. It is Wade's hope that this new arrangement will aid him in gaining custody of Jill.

After Mrs. Whitehouse's funeral, Gordon LaRiviere gives Wade an inside job with his company, and Wade is suspicious of this unsolicited move. It reinforces his feelings about the hunting accident and the part that LaRiviere, Hewitt, and the labor leader's son-in-law may have had in the presumed accident. By Thursday of that week, Wade's emotions have been on something of a roller-coaster ride. He is frustrated in his relationship with Lillian, ambivalent toward his mean-spirited and violent father, and angry thinking about what may be behind the death of Evan Twombley—so angry that he wants to strike someone with his fists.

That night, Wade sees Jack Hewitt drive by his house, and Wade follows him, driving a truck that Gordon LaRiviere has loaned him. The two race along a lumber trail through the woods and onto a frozen lake. Holding Wade off with a rifle, Hewitt drives off the ice. Before Wade can get LaRiviere's truck off the ice, it breaks through and sinks into the lake.

Wade hitches back to town and goes to the restaurant where Margie works. She has taken Wade's father there rather than leave him alone at the house. She is angry with Wade; Wade and his father argue and nearly come to blows in the restaurant.

The next day, Wade finds out from the town clerk that a corporation headed by LaRiviere and Twombley's son-in-law has been buying up property around the town at low prices, with the exception of the land owned by Wade's father. This information strengthens Wade's notion that Twombley's death was not accidental. When Wade reports to work, LaRiviere fires him because of what happened to the truck; he is also replaced as the town's police officer by Jack Hewitt. In addition to this, Margie realizes that she has made a mistake joining Wade in his family's house and decides to move out. At this point things really begin to unravel for Wade; a toothache that has been bothering him off and on for weeks flares up and, unable to find a dentist who will extract the tooth, he pulls it out himself. On Saturday of that week, Wade meets again with his lawyer and is told that despite Lillian's liaison there probably will not be a substantive change in the custody arrangement. Lillian has agreed to some liberalization of the visitation rights, but Wade is not happy with the outcome. After meeting with the lawyer, Wade picks up Jill and returns to Lawford.

As Wade arrives home, he finds Margie moving her things out of the house. Wade tries to hold Margie, asking her to stay. But Margie pushes him away. Jill starts hitting Wade, and Wade strikes his daughter. Wade is stunned by what he has done. Margie takes Jill back to Concord. Meanwhile, Wade's father has seen his son hit Jill and begins taunting Wade. Wade goes into the barn; his father follows and attacks him with a whiskey bottle. Wade strikes out at the old man with the butt end of a shotgun, killing him. He then sets fire to the body and the barn.

As the fire rages, Wade heads for the woods and for Jack Hewitt who is hunting deer on the last day of the season. Wade follows Jack's trail, finds him, and kills him. Wade then departs—his whereabouts unknown. In the years following Wade's disappearance, Lawford changes: a ski resort is built there, but the Whitehouse property remains in the family; Margie Fogg moves to Littleton, New Hampshire, to be near her parents; Lillian and Jill move to Seattle, Washington. Rolfe Whitehouse is left to try to piece together the events that led to his brother's disappearance.

This novel, finely written and well crafted, is the story of one man's disintegration and of the legacy that alcohol and physical abuse engender. In a sense it is polemical, for it deals with the effects of physical violence by fathers toward their sons. The novel is also a tragedy. Wade Whitehouse's fate was sealed early on in his life. There was one brief time when he might have made his escape as his younger brother had done: when Wade and Lillian were first married—when they recognized their individuality, they could have, should have, broken free. Lillian eventually was able to escape, but Wade seemed to live his life a step or two behind everyone else.

Wade's story is told by his brother, Rolfe, who pieces together what happened to his brother during the one significant week. Rolfe is Ishmael, left alone to tell the tale of Wade Whitehouse's life. As Rolfe discovers, Wade did not leave Lawford because he loved the town; he was not able to leave his father because he loved him, too. Yet Wade's character, as Russell Banks draws him, is that of a man incapable of showing love, incapable of opening up to anyone. He is alcoholic, belligerent, lonely, poor, and violent. The only person with whom he shares any intimacy (after Lillian) is Margie, but he can never bring himself to love her openly. Lillian was the only person whom Wade had told about the way his father treated him and his mother, and ultimately Wade repeated the pattern.

This Russell Banks novel is a marvelous achievement. The author takes a disturbing and haunting story and makes it entirely acceptable to the reader. Banks accomplishes this by the sheer power of his writing skill and by infusing the novel's events, places, and descriptions with a lyricism that is unexpected in what is essentially a Gothic tale.

With each of his novels, Banks's skill as a writer becomes more apparent. On the surface, *Affliction* is a distressing, brutal story, but that is not the reason it gets beneath the reader's skin. Its effectiveness lies in the way that Banks makes one conscious of roads not taken; of choices not made; of the delicacy of the relationship between parents and children, between husbands and wives; and of the need for love in the time that people spend together.

Perhaps Banks says it best using Rolfe as a spokesperson:

". . . our stories . . . describe the lives of boys and men for thousands of years, boys who were beaten by their fathers, whose capacity for love and trust was crippled almost at birth and whose best hope for a connection to other human beings lay in elaborating for themselves an elegiac mode of relatedness, as if everyone's life were already over."

Louis Sasso

AMERICAN APPETITES

Author: Joyce Carol Oates (1938–)
Publisher: E. P. Dutton (New York). 340 pp. $18.95
Type of work: Novel
Time: The late 1980s
Locale: The northeastern United States

> *Small misperceptions and deceits among educated and well-behaved people lead to melancholy, anguish, and even death*

> *Principal characters:*
> IAN MCCULLOUGH, a respected, middle-aged political scientist
> GLYNNIS MCCULLOUGH, Ian's wife, a writer and "collector" of people
> SIGRID HUNT, a former model and dancer, Glynnis's acquaintance
> DENIS GRINNELL, Ian's best friend
> ROBERTA GRINNELL, Denis's wife and Glynnis's friend
> BIANCA MCCULLOUGH, Ian and Glynnis's nineteen-year-old daughter

Ian and Glynnis McCullough live and work in the cozy, well-heeled community of Hazelton-on-Hudson, New York. Their tight circle of friends considers them an ideal couple. Professionally successful—he as a political scientist and she as a food expert and cookbook writer—they live vigorously and well.

Ian studies demographics. He is fascinated by collective destiny, by finding connections among apparently unrelated factors. Indeed, he theorizes that only a statistical study could unravel the social, domestic, and professional tangle of married life. Glynnis is currently writing a cookbook, *American Appetites*. (She is a woman who enjoys what she does, at least while she is doing it.) Their nineteen-year-old daughter, Bianca, attends Wesleyan University. Many years ago, their son died just days after his birth, and Ian is surprised by the rage that he still feels—a rage not unlike that which he feels at his father, who committed suicide when Ian was young.

Glynnis, ever social, "collects" people. She is known to take up, cultivate, and casually drop vulnerable, unattached women in the arts. One such woman, Sigrid Hunt, a flame-haired former model and dancer, telephones Ian in near hysteria. Although Ian barely remembers meeting her, he braves a snowstorm to drive to her shabby garage apartment in Poughkeepsie. Living in squalor, Sigrid is six weeks pregnant by her jealous Egyptian boyfriend who has threatened to kill her if she seeks an abortion. Both repulsed and attracted by this "unanticipated intimacy," Ian does not know what to do. He is sexually stirred, for Sigrid reminds him of Glynnis before babies, before resentment, sorrow, and loss. He remembers his own daughter as a small child, utterly helpless and as needy as Sigrid is now. Impulsively he writes the woman a check for $1,000.

As Glynnis cooks for Ian's surprise fiftieth-birthday party, she gloats over her reflection in the copper pans. In spite of an underlying malaise, she is satisfied with her life. She loves Ian like a "twin." She has even had an affair for eight months with his best friend, Denis Grinnell. Glynnis never allows her casual affairs to get too messy. Ultimately, she gives up her men, she believes, as sacrifices for Ian and "for us." Now she and Ian are alone for the first time in nineteen years. Willful Bianca is away at college, and a certain strain has been lifted. Still, something seems unsettled between Glynnis and Ian, and despite the party's success that evening, her melancholy remains.

Ian works hard, plays squash, and dines with friends. During twenty-six years of marriage, he and Glynnis, never considering therapy, have learned to accommodate his periods of impotence. But he worries about Glynnis's increasing contempt for his "abstractedness" and "cold-bloodedness." The day after the party they argue over what he terms its excessiveness—"us celebrating us." Preoccupied with thoughts of Sigrid, he tries in vain to reach her. Although he had planned to, Ian has never told Glynnis about his brief, chaste afternoon with the younger woman.

Late one evening, Glynnis, bitter and drunk, sets an exquisite table and serves Ian an overcooked meal. She has found the canceled check to Sigrid. In a baiting, taunting rage she accuses him of having an affair, discloses her own, and regales him with old grievances. When she attacks him with a knife, he frantically pushes her back. Stumbling, she falls through a glass door and blacks out.

For three weeks, Ian and Bianca keep vigil at Glynnis's bedside as she lies comatose in the hospital with multiple skull fractures. Although neighbors had called the police and reported screams coming from the McCulloughs' house, father and daughter speak of "the accident," the dangers of plate glass, and that his sixty-five stitches came from trying to "save" Mommy.

When Glynnis dies suddenly, friends and coworkers express their sorrow to Ian and help him arrange a memorial service at the Unitarian church. Glynnis was never religious but always wanted to believe that there was a little more than "just us, just here." Ian is stupefied with shock and humiliation. Bianca shifts from rage to withdrawal and becomes obsessed with the *Tibetan Book of the Dead*. Loyal friends are perplexed.

Weeks pass. Roberta, Denis's wife, visits Ian and reports that the police are questioning all his friends. She told the police that Glynnis had called her one evening before the accident and accused her and Denis of covering up Ian's affair with Sigrid. When two detectives meet with Ian, he appears vague and confused. Feeling protective of Glynnis and Sigrid, he refuses to defend or explain his actions on the night of the accident.

The police arrest Ian on second-degree murder charges. He hires a social acquaintance, the shrewd and expensive criminal lawyer Nicholas Ottinger. Privately, Ian wonders if Ottinger has been Glynnis's lover; he begins to speculate about other men as well. Believing that his life is over, Ian thinks of himself as a "posthumous man." He refuses to testify. Surely if he is guilty the scientific process of the legal system will find him guilty in spite of his defense. But Ottinger steadfastly maintains that since the prosecution can produce no witnesses, no evidence, and no motive, it has no case. He repeatedly postpones the trial through legal maneuverings. Bianca wants to quit school, teach in Thailand, and become more than "just us."

Ian asks Denis if he and Glynnis were lovers, and Denis says no. Later, visiting the Grinnells in Cape Cod, Ian learns that the couple is heading for a divorce. During an awkward moment alone with Roberta, Ian confesses his love for her and asks her to marry him. Although tempted, she is wary and evasive.

When the trial begins, Ian retreats inward. As the story of the events surrounding Glynnis's death unfolds, he senses shifting sentiments among the jurors. Information is factual but breeds ambivalency.

After a casual dinner with his old friends Meika and Vaughn Cassity, Ian finds himself alone with Meika, who shamelessly flirts with him and confesses that she has loved him for years. During their ensuing short-lived affair, he pleads with her to marry him. She says she will marry him—someday—and then tells him that Vaughn and Glynnis were once lovers.

A detective locates Sigrid, who has been missing since the trial began. Testifying for the defense, she swears that she was never Ian's lover, that the $1,000 check was for an abortion, and that she has been hiding only to avoid publicity. For the first time since the accident, Ian wishes to live. On the stand he admits to killing Glynnis during a drunken fight—a fight from which he should have walked away. Believing that they were irresistibly pulled together that night by mutual fury and pain, he submits that she would still be alive were it not for him.

As he awaits the verdict, Ian thinks, "I will blow my brains out or I will marry." Four months after the acquittal, Ian and Sigrid are living together in Maine, not yet married. Now tanned and relaxed, Ian wonders if he will kill himself by fall. He has resigned from his institutional post and plans to write. His is now a bookish, unshackled existence much like that of his college days. Bianca, who remained loyal to her father while he was on trial for murder, has been estranged from him since the verdict and is now living in Bangkok. Roberta and Denis are separated. Meika and Ottinger are lovers. One evening, Sigrid serves a picnic-style meal to Ian and his friends. She smiles and cheerfully offers more pie all around. But, despite the comfort, she wonders, as it was Glynnis's habit to wonder, why she feels so alone and so melancholy.

Joyce Carol Oates begins this slim novel with a breezy, whimsically written tale of love, courtship, and marriage. Her characters are attractive, well bred, and successful. Their world seems a healthy and comfortable place. But, subtly and ironically, Oates reveals lives fraught with anguish. Petty lies and deceits come to light as tiny cracks in otherwise stable relationships. Innocent moments—Sigrid and Ian's meeting, Bianca's dancing at the birthday party—appear darkly foreboding. Nonetheless, the world Oates creates, however ominous, remains a civilized one. Ian and Glynnis's despair and disillusionment are neither insoluble nor unique. Indeed, feelings of emptiness and ennui are the unspoken norm in their own social set. Yet, sadly, real intimacy seems either impossible or too painful. "Small" infidelities and deceptions form the very fabric of the characters' lives. For them, reality is based more on what they think and feel, or on what they wish to think and feel, than on what is. In a sense, they are people for whom the unexamined life is the only comfortable life—although for them the price proves high.

The story ends as it begins—in apparent harmony and festivity. Broken hearts are on the mend. Time has healed some wounds. Loyalties have shifted and partners have recombined, but the small circle of friends remains intact. Lives have been reinvented to alleviate the discomfort of loneliness and despair—once again. *American Appetites* is a provocative and insightful look at marriage and manners among educated and narcissistic Americans.

Wendy DuBois

AMONG SCHOOLCHILDREN

Author: Tracy Kidder (1945–   )
Publisher: Houghton Mifflin (Boston). 340 pp. $19.95
Type of work: Social criticism
Time: The present
Locale: Holyoke, Massachusetts

    A year in the life of Chris Zajac, a teacher who endeavors to enrich her pupils' lives within a faulty educational system

        Principal personages:
            Chris Zajac, a fifth-grade teacher
            CLARENCE, her sweetest and most troublesome student
            ROBERT, one of her most emotionally deprived students
            JUDITH, her prettiest and smartest student

Among Schoolchildren follows Chris Zajac, a teacher at Kelly School in Holyoke, Massachusetts, through an academic year as she endeavored to expand the minds and horizons of her fifth-grade pupils. Mrs. Zajac's task was not an easy one; many of the children achieved well below grade level and were unruly. But, as author Tracy Kidder demonstrates, the fault lay more in their situation than in the children themselves. Holyoke is a depressed paper-mill town, the birthplace of both volleyball and the household cleaner Lestoil. Many parents, from disadvantaged backgrounds, live in poverty. Chris is a native of Holyoke who would not consider living anywhere else.

At thirty-four years of age, with two children of her own, Mrs. Zajac referred to herself as an "old-lady teacher." With a reputation for being a "witch," she was firm but fair. She assigned homework daily and accepted only her pupils' best effort. Her heart is in teaching.

The first day of school, Mrs. Zajac laid down rules of conduct, making sure to establish her superiority from the start. There were about twenty students in her class, representing a range of racial diversity. Over half were eligible for free lunches. She let them choose their own desks, but on the second day it became clear that some needed to be separated and placed near positive influences.

Chris soon identified a boy named Clarence as a potential source of problems. He refused to do work and provoked other students. She kept him after school, but instead of punishment, she tried to reason with him, explaining that being good is really best for him.

Robert, also, was a troublemaker. He often spoke out of turn and slapped himself in the face repeatedly after being reprimanded. Felipe was the most imaginative story writer in the class and was often the first to raise his hand. But he too tended to get into trouble. Judith, a beautiful Puerto Rican girl, quickly proved to be the brightest and often was Mrs. Zajac's savior. Unassuming about her extraordinary intelligence, she was very popular. There were also Claude, Henrietta, Jimmy, Ashley, Pedro, and more.

Chris taught other students besides her homeroom class, which mingled with others during reading and math and were divided into groups according to ability. She was not afraid to digress or bend a schedule if she felt that she was reaching the students. Often Chris took time for "self evaluation," whereby she tried to think of ways to enliven her lessons, and kept a list of things to do each day. She found refuge in the teachers' lounge and at home with her husband, Billy.

Mrs. Zajac had her work cut out for her. In a lesson on American history, half the students did not know the name of their country. When she asked what the word "abroad" meant, Robert replied "a woman." She had to contend with sleepy students who watched television until midnight. As the weeks unfolded, Chris learned more about her students. Every day the children wrote essays in their personal journals about whatever subject they wished.

Clarence continued to be a source of frustration. Not only did he refuse to do the work, he distracted the rest of the class. On the third day of school, he threw an eraser at one classmate and punched another. Chris strove to be fair: "Children get dealt grossly unequal hands, but that is all the more reason to treat them equally in school." She refused to expect less from Clarence because he was poor, but unfortunately, the after-school detentions were ineffective.

Mrs. Zajac had plenty of tricks to reach the children. She invented games to make lessons more fun, such as a contest to review for a test. Once, when the entire class seemed sluggish, she had a student go to the board and pretend to be the teacher. Sitting at his tiny desk, Chris did a silly imitation of his previous behavior, which made them laugh. In minutes they were revitalized and engaged in the lessons.

Their parents did not want to get involved in their formal education. In fact, they seemed to expect Chris to do her job and theirs as well in the six hours she had their children each day. It was a struggle to get parents to attend conferences or reply to her notes.

Kidder offers a brief history of teaching to put Chris, and the Kelly School, in perspective. He notes that the United States has put a great deal of faith in education but has invested little in teachers. Chris earned only $25,532 a year, the top of the local salary scale. Many good teachers choose to leave teaching for jobs in administration.

The Flats, the neighborhood where Kelly School is located, consists mainly of decrepit residential and industrial buildings. Since the population in Holyoke is declining, many buildings are abandoned or burned out. Attempts at urban renewal are evident, but no one is sure if the neighborhood will really come back.

Grading history tests at home, Chris was haunted by visions of her students. There was Jimmy, a drowsy boy who was frequently absent and prone to bringing in homework done by his mother. He was lazy but not stupid. Chris vowed to "wake him up." Pedro, a Puerto Rican boy who rarely spoke, seemed remotely cheerful but was barely doing second-grade work. Once, after reviewing a disturbing note from his mother, the guidance counselor visited his home. He lived on a crumbling block with a suicidal grandmother and a transvestite uncle.

Judith was a pleasure. From a strict Puerto Rican household, she was the first to finish assignments. Chris did everything she could to keep Judith from losing interest. She wanted Judith to go to college, and not become pregnant, although that was common in Holyoke.

Robert, with his black, crew-cut hair and heavy pot belly, seemed always searching for approbation. "Where had Robert learned that the best way to deal with failure is to embrace it?" Chris wondered. He certainly was capable—sometimes he did get an A.

Clarence was Mrs. Zajac's biggest problem. He stole pens, cards, and candy and beat up a boy, yet he could be very sweet. Once he wrote to her: "I love Mrs. Zajac." Chris liked him despite his faults. Rumors that he was beaten at home disturbed her, but she saw no evidence: "Let's face it. I as a teacher have to deal with things as they are in the classroom, whatever the situation is at home."

Chris took pains to translate her lessons into language relevant to fifth-graders. To help illustrate the causes of the American Revolution, she explained, "All a war is, is a gigantic argument, and how many of you have been in an argument with someone?" This sparked a lively discussion. She drove home the plight of the slaves by holding an auction where some class members were slaves and others buyers.

In early spring, Clarence's behavior worsened. He fought daily with Chris and refused to do his work. It was serious enough that he was placed in Alpha, a special class for disciplinary problems. Chris was ambivalent over his departure. While it was probably better for her class, it did not seem best for him. This situation took its toll. Her students' progress slowed, and they often needed scolding. Chris feared that she might be reaching the point of burn-out.

With Clarence gone, she devoted her attention to other needy students, like Robert and Claude. She was disgusted at herself for letting their behavior get out of hand. When she had to isolate Robert for a few days, steps were taken to enable him to see a psychiatrist.

After Easter, life in the classroom grew brighter. Tiny glimmers of promise appeared, as when Chris praised Robert for doing all his homework and answering the questions correctly. She decided that the class was indeed accomplishing more without the disruptions of Clarence. The class took a trip to Old Sturbridge Village, and it was a delight. On the bus ride home, Chris led the children in singing songs.

Kidder describes the homes of Judith and Felipe in a Puerto Rican section of Holyoke. To gain a better insight into the background of her Hispanic students, Chris and her husband visited Puerto Rico.

Kidder points out that U.S. schools fall short of Horace Mann's vision of "great equalizers." Many schools are internally segregated, keeping children of various abilities (and socioeconomic levels) on separate tracks.

Finally June arrived. The heat made it difficult to concentrate on schoolwork. Clarence came back for a visit; he was doing fairly well in his Alpha class. Chris faced year's end with regrets about lessons never completed and expectations of progress dashed. But Kidder explains that teachers have little way of knowing how profoundly they can redirect a child's life.

In order to maintain an exuberant outlook, Chris arranged to teach sixth grade the next year. On the final day of school, when the children learned who their next year's teacher would be, the ones slated to have Mrs. Zajac seemed happy. The others, however, showed their disappointment.

As with his widely acclaimed *House* and *Soul of a New Machine*, Tracy Kidder has taken a somewhat mundane subject, embraced it, and created a story as riveting as any suspense novel. Yet this is not simply a tale of an isolated schoolteacher and her class, but a portrait of the American condition, revealing all its serious social problems.

It is obvious that Kidder took great care to gather his facts. He observed the class in session, read the students' journals, conducted interviews, toured the town, and made personal visits to children's homes. While sections on the history of American education and the trip to Puerto Rico are not as engaging as the classroom scenes, they are valuable in rounding out the story.

Since most people have encountered a teacher like Mrs. Zajac somewhere in their childhoods, it is interesting finally to see the classroom through her eyes. *Among Schoolchildren* frequently sparks childhood memories of spelling bees and recess. The picture Kidder paints is both moving and unsettling. If American education is in such a tired state, one wonders how—or if—it can be repaired.

David M. Kennerley

AND THE WALLS CAME TUMBLING DOWN:
AN AUTOBIOGRAPHY

Author: Ralph David Abernathy (1926–)
Publisher: Harper and Row (New York). 638 pp. $25.00
Type of work: Autobiography
Time: 1926–1988
Locale: The United States, primarily the South

> *Ralph David Abernathy played a significant role in planning and carrying out the nonviolent protest strategies and goals of the civil rights movement of the 1960s and 1970s*

> *Principal personages:*
> RALPH DAVID ABERNATHY, a Baptist minister and civil rights leader
> JUANITA ODESSA JONES ABERNATHY, his wife
> MARTIN LUTHER KING, JR., his friend, a fellow minister
> CORETTA SCOTT KING, his wife

At his birth in Linden, Alabama, in the spring of 1926, Abernathy, the youngest child in a large family, was named David. But one of his sisters began calling him Ralph David. The name stuck, and when Abernathy enlisted in the army in 1944, he used that name. He regrets consenting to the name change and prefers to think of himself as a namesake of David, the shepherd boy who killed Goliath; Abernathy's decision to become a Baptist minister and to improve the spiritual, social, and political conditions of blacks follows the outlines of David's calling to oppose the tyrannies of King Saul. Abernathy's prosperous farmer father, W. L. Abernathy, was a righteous, hard-working man. Abernathy's mother, Louivery Valentine Bell, guided him toward the ministry.

The Abernathy name was conferred on Ralph David's great grandfather by a white plantation owner, but the respect accorded the name came from the efforts of black Abernathy ancestors. His grandfather related many stories about slavery, but young Ralph David did not comprehend racism, segregation, and the Jim Crow system until he was accosted as a "nigger" and ordered by a white man to drink a bottle of soda. His refusal was almost met by a beating until the store owner identified the boy, and the fury of the white man was tamed by the reputation of Abernathy's father. Abernathy resolved to challenge the injustices of segregation, a resolve that would find him in Montgomery, Atlanta, Albany, Birmingham, St. Augustine, Selma, Chicago, Memphis, Washington, and Charleston over three decades of confrontation and struggle for racial equality.

During his time in the army during World War II, Abernathy gained more sophistication in dealing with segregation and new motifs of slavery. He enlisted in 1944 and at age eighteen was a platoon sergeant. His army friendships solidified in France and Germany at the end of the war. Rheumatic fever prevented Abernathy from joining his unit in the invasion of Japanese-held islands. All members of his unit were killed in combat, and he was sent home, to ponder his fate.

Enrolled at Alabama State University in Montgomery, Abernathy led a hunger strike to improve the quality of food. His mother died in 1947, and he resolved to announce his call to preach on Mother's Day 1948. After graduation in 1950, he enrolled in the graduate program at Atlanta University. That summer, he first met Martin Luther King, Jr., at Ebenezer Baptist Church.

Abernathy returned to Montgomery to become dean of men at Alabama State and accept a call to preach at the First Baptist Church. He met and married Juanita Odessa Jones, who attended Tennessee State University and grew up in the same Alabama county as Coretta Scott King. The wedding took place August 31, 1952, and brought Abernathy and Juanita three (surviving) children and thirty years of mutual support.

Abernathy and King first combined forces during the historic Montgomery boycott. By the Supreme Court's 1954 decision in *Brown* vs. *Board of Education*, racial segregation in schools was declared unconstitutional. Sparked by the decision of Rosa Parks to remain seated on a Montgomery bus in December 1955, King and Abernathy became involved in civil rights protests. The formation of the Montgomery Improvement Association, with King as president and Abernathy as program chair, and the strategies of nonviolent protest modeled after Thoreau and Gandhi, led to success in Montgomery and a method of operation for future campaigns.

Nonviolence and Christian principles were soon met with violence. King's house was bombed and later blasted by a shotgun. Buses were fired on by snipers. Individuals were harassed. Churches were bombed —including First Baptist. Victory in Montgomery, however, came in 1957. King accepted a call from Ebenezer Baptist Church, back in Atlanta. Abernathy remained in Montgomery for a time and then accepted a call from the West Hunter Baptist Church in Atlanta. In their mutual dedication to advancing civil rights, the move to Atlanta served to strengthen their liaison, out of which the Southern Christian Leadership Conference (SCLC) was formed. That organization was headed by King until his assassination in 1968, whereupon Abernathy took the helm.

The success of the Montgomery campaign was matched by the failure of the Albany, Georgia, campaign in 1961. Attorney General Robert Kennedy had seen to it that segregation in public transportation was illegal, and the Interstate Commerce Commission issued such a ruling on September 22. The Student Nonviolent Coordination Committee (SNCC), led by Stokley Carmichael, tested the ruling, and members were arrested. Abernathy and King became involved, in part, to reconcile internal differences in the local and national black community among radical SNCC and moderate NAACP (National Association for the Advancement of Colored People) members. Abernathy and King were arrested, tried, convicted, and sentenced to two months in jail, the first of many such jail terms—one of which led to King's classic "Letter from a Birmingham Jail" in 1963. As Albany arrests increased, President John F. Kennedy heightened his attentions to civil rights. Although victory in Albany was postponed until 1962, the larger battles were won more dramatically, resulting in a Public Accommodations Act in Birmingham and a Voting Rights Act in Selma.

The following year, 1963, was one of the most dramatic and moving times in the civil rights movement. In Birmingham the adversary was "Bull" Connor. Abernathy and King rallied to the support of black activist Fred Shuttlesworth. The resulting violence in Birmingham caused the federal government to take notice. Marchers having to contest with guard dogs, billy clubs, water hoses, and house bombers (all recorded by national television news coverage) and the eloquence of King, awakened the nation. The Birmingham campaign culminated in King's ringing "I Have a Dream" speech in Washington, D.C., on August 28, 1963, before a crowd of 250,000 people. Hubert Humphrey judged it "a good thing . . . for the nation and the world." When President Kennedy was shot on November 22, King's own fears increased that he might be killed.

In the year of passage of the 1964 Civil Rights Act, the SCLC focused its attentions on St. Augustine—site of numerous open Ku Klux Klan meetings—by protesting federal assistance to the city and by attempting to integrate public swimming pools. In 1965 the SCLC was working for voting rights in Selma and mounting voter registration drives. Here, Abernathy and King locked horns with Governor George Wallace, the Klan, and the persistent surveillance attempts of J. Edgar Hoover. President Lyndon Johnson's support for civil rights took more tangible form, and although murders of civil rights workers increased, the vote was obtained.

In 1966, the SCLC ventured north to Chicago where Jesse Jackson headed the organization's Operation Breadbasket. The machinations of Chicago mayor Richard J. Daley were too much for the SCLC's familiar strategies for integrating schools and redressing the economic inequities in the city's slums. Frustrated, King and Abernathy left Chicago. Seventeen years later the Daley machine was defeated by black candidate Harold Washington.

King's assassination occurred on the balcony of a Memphis motel on April 4, 1968. Abernathy was in his room in the Lorraine Motel when he saw King fall. He rushed to his aid and held him while an ambulance was called—and stayed with him until all measures to save King failed. Abernathy continued to support the King family through autopsy, funeral, burial, and relocation of the body to a tomb at the King Center for Nonviolent Social Change.

Abernathy followed King as leader of SCLC, carrying out the Poor People's March and the creation of Resurrection City in Washington, D.C., in May. The civil rights movement peaked with Robert Kennedy's assassination. An era had ended, and Abernathy, although he staged one more major protest in Charleston in 1969, could not duplicate King's charisma and following.

In his accounting of the fascinating forces and personalities that made up the histories of the civil rights movement during the 1960s and 1970s, Abernathy draws many biblical analogies. As Martin Luther King's lieutenant in the SCLC and in their mutual attempts to shatter racism and prejudice—through nonviolent protest—Abernathy compares himself to Joshua shouting down the walls of Jericho.

And the Walls Came Tumbling Down is Abernathy's narrative of how it really was in the times leading up to, during, and following the wrenching events of 20th-century America, of assassinations, Vietnam, urban riots, and campus chaos. Faced by the same larger issues surrounding all historians' quest for fact and truth, Abernathy presents only his "version," his recollections of those tumultuous times as seen by one man, a black man, but a man very much in the center of events.

His recollections and descriptions alternate between the significant and the trivial. His portrayal of his own role, particularly in relation to Jesse Jackson and King, often seems self-serving rather than objective or hortatory. His choice and manner of describing some of King's relationships with women and the details of his death and the posthumous condition of his body border on the tasteless.

Notwithstanding such choices on Abernathy's part, *And the Walls Came Tumbling Down* is an indispensable version of one of the most triumphant and tragic times in modern American history—and of an obscure youth's rise to manhood and national prominence.

Robert F. Gish

ANY OLD IRON

Author: Anthony Burgess (1917–   )
Publisher: Random House (New York). 360 pp. $19.95
Type of work: Novel
Time: Before, during, and after the two world wars
Locale: Wales; England; Israel; the Soviet Union; and the world-war battle-fields

Two families live through the world wars, becoming involved with nation-alist movements, with each other, and with what may be Excalibur, King Arthur's sword

> Principal characters:
> THE NARRATOR, unnamed in the book, a Jew from Manchester, philosophy student, and trainer of terrorists
> ZIPPORAH, the narrator's sister, a percussionist
> REGINALD "REG" MORROW JONES, a soldier and sword stealer
> BEATRIX JONES, Reg's sister
> DAN JONES, Reg's slow-witted brother
> DAVID JONES, Reg's Welsh father
> LUDMILA JONES, Reg's Russian mother

As *Any Old Iron* opens, the narrator is speculating on the possibility that a weapon seen in London and in Wales is the sword Excalibur. The blade, preserved in oil and inscribed with an "A," allegedly had belonged to King Arthur and Attila the Hun. The skeptical narrator then begins the story of Reginald Jones, who brought the sword back from Russia, and Reg's Welsh father, David, and Russian mother, Ludmila.

David Jones ran away to sea at age fifteen and became a cook. An assistant cook on the *Titanic*, he later tells the narrator about the night the liner sank and how he managed to get aboard a lifeboat. Rescued, he landed in New York and went to work at a Russian restaurant. There David fell in love with Ludmila, the daughter of the owner, and the couple soon married.

As World War I began, David heard that his father was dying, and he and Ludmila went to Wales, luckily missing their scheduled passage on the *Lusitania*. Before dying, David's father gave him a large nugget of unrefined gold and an encyclopedia. David then joined the army, where he heard more about Welsh nationalism, while Ludmila studied the language. Reading the encyclopedia, he discovered that Benedic-tine monks of the 1st century had taken British royal treasures for safekeeping.

Following a leave, David was shipped across the Channel to the war zone, where he came down with pneumonia. After another leave at home, he was sent to Ireland to help quell the Easter Rising of 1916 and was shot. In the hospital, he met Reginald Morrow, who had written a book about Welsh history and Arthur's sword. Posted to the Isle of Wight and then to France, David was hit by bomb fragments. Ludmila, who was notified that David was dead, went to Petrograd to stay with her cousin Yura.

In Petrograd, Ludmila witnessed the beginnings of the Russian Revolution and was wounded during a demonstration. Recuperating, she received a letter from David, alive after all. Following their reunion, David became an army cook, and they had three children: Beatrix, Reginald Morrow, and Daniel Tetlow Jones. Offered a share in a restaurant, David moved the family to Manchester.

The narrator, now describing himself as a Jew, is the son of a civil engineer, who grew up in different parts of the world. He meets Reg Jones in Manchester, where they are both studying at the university. When the narrator goes to a party given by one of his professors, it is also attended by Reg's sister, Beatrix. Beatrix, with whom the narrator falls in love, is an independent woman and devotee of free love. The narrator, who lives with his sister, Zipporah, at his aunt's house, goes to tea with Beatrix a week later and ends up making love to her.

Afterward they go to hear Zipporah (Zip), a singer and percussionist, in a concert. The three of them then attend a farewell party for Reg, who is leaving to fight in the Spanish Civil War. On the way, they stop to see Reg's brother, Dan, who is slightly mentally handicapped. At the party Beatrix, discovering that Reg has stolen their father's gold nugget, takes it away and orders Dan to hit Reg. The narrator escorts Beatrix home while Reg accompanies Zip, with whom he falls in love. When Reg returns from Spain, he and Zip marry.

Beatrix takes a job in the Foreign Office just before World War II begins. The narrator joins the Army Physical Training Corps, Zip joins a professional orchestra, and Reg joins the Intelligence Corps and begins to show signs of deranged jealousy over Zip. Posted to Gibraltar, he becomes involved with the Sons of Arthur, a Welsh nationalist group. Dan, too, finds himself a soldier.

Meanwhile, a German bomb exposes some Roman ruins near Abergavenny, the Welsh town in which Ludmila and David operate a pub. A stele with "GLAD ART REG" and an opening for a sword is found in the ruins. During a visit with Zip, the narrator discusses Reg's growing madness. Later, in London, the narrator proposes unsuccessfully to Beatrix. On leave from training recruits, the narrator visits the ruins before stopping at David and Ludmila's pub, where he is received suspiciously by the couple.

Dan Jones, now a prisoner of war in Italy, is put on a train in Rome that also carries treasures from a Benedictine monastery at Monte Cassino. On Gibraltar, the Welsh nationalists meet. Reg reports that he has killed a German in civilian clothes in La Linea. The incident is hushed up and Reg sent away in custody. In Portsmouth, Reg changes his uniform and escapes. Unable to reach Beatrix, he returns home and walks in on Zip making love to another man. He turns himself in to the authorities, but Beatrix helps him get a post as an interpreter in a Russian camp for displaced persons.

In the camp, Reg sleeps with one of the Russian women, Maria Sokolova. The KGB and SMERSH are monitoring the supposedly free Russians. A visiting official turns out to be Ludmila's cousin Yura. Maria, who is married, sleeps with Reg again. Dan, meanwhile, is in a POW camp in Poland. One morning, the prisoners wake to the sound of gunfire to find the Germans gone and themselves free to leave. While searching for food, they see a sword among the treasures taken by the Soviets from the camp storeroom.

At the Russian camp in England, the Russians are readied for the trip home, where Reg fears they will be killed. He is sent away to keep him quiet, but he jumps from the ship taking him back to Gibraltar. The narrator, on a pass in London, meets Beatrix and Irwin Roth, an American writer with whom she is involved. Reg visits Beatrix, leaving the next day for the port from which the Russians are to sail. While looking for Maria, he is mistaken for a Russian and put in the hold, to be let out after the ship has sailed. On board ship, Reg finds that Maria is sleeping with a Soviet officer. Reg, stealing a coat, leaves the ship at Odessa to find his suspicions of slaughter confirmed. Knocked out, he is taken to a hospital in England, where he is reconciled with Zip despite his murderous thoughts.

Meanwhile, Dan and his party are trudging through Poland, fighting hunger and gangrene. Dan continues to march south, believing that he has seen Arthur's sword, as one of the party dies. When Dan has finally made his way home, Zip and Reg return to Abergavenny and a dying David. The bank is robbed by the Sons of Arthur as Dan and Reg are making a deposit. The brothers visit the ruins while the Sons plan strategy. After David's death, the family, including Irwin, now married to Beatrix, talks of the future. Ludmila returns to Russia.

After the war, the narrator earns his degree in philosophy, then looks for a teaching job. Reg and Zip are managing the pub. The Sons of Arthur commit terrorist acts. The narrator, having found a job, receives a cable from his father summoning him to Israel, where he finds that his mother has been killed by a bomb. He reluctantly agrees to stay and help his old instructors teach terrorism.

Reg, now a translator for an exchange orchestra Zip is with, visits his mother in Petrograd. At Beatrix's request, he is asked to assist in the defection of cousin Yura, a high Soviet official. Reg agrees to help if Yura steals the sword from the Hermitage. Returning to Wales with the sword, Reg tries to fit it in the stone plinth, otherwise keeping it under his pillow despite his wife's urging that he give it back. Zip tells the narrator of Reg's madness, while the narrator informs her of their mother's death. The Sons of Arthur hear of the sword and forcibly take it.

Beatrix, in New York with Irwin, leaves him. Although the Soviets demand the sword's return, the Sons keep it and continue kidnapping and bombing. At a Welsh liberation meeting in London, Reg steals the sword as bombs explode and, fighting, escapes.

Meanwhile, the narrator accompanies the president of Israel to New York, where the narrator finds Beatrix, now a chef in a Russian restaurant. She joins their party, and upon landing in Manchester, throws her body between the president and an assassin's bullet. Reg, beaten by the Sons of Arthur, sells the pub, moves to Israel with a pregnant Zip, and meets the narrator, who is giving up training terrorists.

Reg explains how he retrieved the sword from Dan, and together they made a nightmarish journey to a pond. There, they ceremonially threw in the gold nugget and the sword, which Dan claimed had glowed and spoken to him. As the novel ends, the narrator and Reg are discussing the past and the future, justice and injustice, as the narrator smells the orange trees.

Any Old Iron is a powerfully written novel about the struggle of surviving in a modern world filled with war, coldness, and cruelty, a struggle Burgess has explored in other works such as *A Clockwork Orange*. Each of the families has its own way of coping with events. The Joneses appear to rely on luck and a grounding in the past, symbolized by the gold nugget and the sword, while the narrator's family views life philosophically, yet struggles to shape the world. They make bridges, teach, and play music. Burgess asks his readers to examine their thoughts about race and nation as he chronicles the emergence of the Soviet Union and Israel taking modern form while Wales endeavors to recapture its ancient form. In the end, life is shown to be a battle in which everyone needs to fight. If Excalibur is not available in the modern world, any old iron will do.

Deirdre L. Menchaca

BARBARIAN SENTIMENTS:
HOW THE AMERICAN CENTURY ENDS

Author: William Pfaff (1926–   )
Publisher: Hill and Wang (New York). 198 pp. $19.95
Type of work: Social science
Time: The 20th century

> *Political columnist William Pfaff's provocative examination of the ideals*
> *that have shaped, and impeded, America's post–World War II foreign policy*
> *—a policy largely based on the unwillingness of the United States to reassess*
> *its self-imposed role of "model" to the rest of the world*

Chapter 1 of *Barbarian Sentiments: How the American Century Ends*, is entitled "Dead Stars," a metaphor suggesting the "exhausted ideas . . . in the American political atmosphere." This is the essential premise of William Pfaff's examination of the condition of America's foreign affairs.

The United States, having "enjoyed a relatively happy history," possesses an innate disregard for the past and the accountability that history demands. It is an American characteristic to think of its past in terms of inevitability, a philosophy self-justified by the existence of democracy. "Democracy" justifies every American conviction, including, quite significantly, America's international relationships: ". . . the American insistence that human freedom implies history's malleability has engendered an activist foreign policy which presumes that [other] nations . . . can be changed into something more acceptable to Americans." History itself, therefore (according to American doctrine), "has been achieving its democratic fulfillment." Pfaff numbers such precepts among the "dead stars" of American political culture.

Democracy, at its responsible best, must not preclude the relevance of history. It is unreasonable to label the past "inevitable." And it is politically, strategically, and morally unsound to designate the United States as the social yardstick upon which all nations are to be measured. Nevertheless, in its dogmatic self-appraisal, America holds up its own socioeconomic system as an example to all. "Americans will usually claim that free enterprise and free political institutions are mutually indispensable," but in Western Europe, for instance, this credo is historically inappropriate and is readily rejected not only by the European left but by most conservatives and a good percentage of the right as well. Pfaff fears that the "liberating marketplace liberalism" professed by the Reagan administration expresses "a lasting fac-

tor in the alienation of the United States from Continental Europe—
and indeed, from nearly all of the rest of the world."

Many of the post–World War II assumptions made by the United
States concerning Western Europe have remained largely unanalyzed
and as such are in critical need of reassessment. The primary American assumption—the one that has dominated the American outlook on
Europe for forty-five years—is that all Western societies are moving
in the same direction, mindful of the same goals; furthermore, the
uncontested vanguard of the "movement" is the United States. Un-
derstandably, Europeans (and perhaps especially the French) resent
this assumption.

The single greatest arena of conflict for the United States and the
Soviet Union has been, and continues to be, Central Europe, the geopolitical entity most responsible for the cold war. The Central European front is vital to Soviet security, and the recent upheavals in
Eastern Europe present an ongoing threat to that security. It is becoming increasingly clearer to Americans and Soviets alike that "nothing
is going to be settled if the Central European problem is not settled."

Pfaff foresees the complete withdrawal and/or expulsion of Soviet
power from Eastern and Central Europe as the "only . . . eventual
outcome imaginable . . . given the endurance and power of European
civilization and the inevitable transience of Communism." In so saying, Pfaff reiterates his position that the future is the manifest product
of the past. Underestimating the fertility of history is a political short-
coming traditionally shared by the United States and the Soviet Union.

To introduce his chapter "The Soviet Union," Pfaff quotes from a
passionate article written for the Winter 1944–1945 issue of *Partisan
Review*. Analogically likening the totalitarian principles of Stalinism to
a profound, incarnate evil, it is an excellent example of a common
perception of the times. In the 1940s, Soviet power was viewed by
many as both invasive and irresistible. That opinion has remained
popular; in fact, many modern observers of global politics continue to
write similar sentiments about Soviet power, especially in terms of its
extent, expansion, foreign influence, and even its irresistibility. Of this
power, Pfaff, however, contends that "it was not irresistible in the
1940s and 1950s, nor has it been since."

In examining the etymology of the word "totalitarianism"—a term
born of a need to describe a regime "making a 'total' claim upon a
people's allegiances"—he is able to distinguish between the inherent
depravity of Stalin's totalitarian nation and the distinctly different Soviet Union of the 1960s and 1970s. Such distinctions must be considered central to any evenhanded political (or even ethical) judgment.
It is unfortunate that this is a point on which Americans tend to be

weak, especially since the history of the 20th century alone bears out the value—even the necessity—of possessing a more accurate understanding of other regimes:

> The radical possibilities of political evil demonstrated in Russia from the 1930s into the 1950s, and in Germany between 1933 and 1945, need to be remembered for what they really were if we are to continue to avoid them. The nature of Soviet totalitarianism under Stalin cannot be appreciated if the U.S.S.R. of Khrushchev and Brezhnev is treated as if it were the same thing. If reactionary regimes in Chile, Greece, Argentina, or Iran—or a racialist government in South Africa—are routinely described as Fascist, then we lose a grasp of what Nazism and Fascism really were.

Pfaff believes that the United States has jeopardized its ability to create a reasonable defense strategy because its appraisal of the Soviet Union is so unrealistic. Furthermore, there has been a rift between Western Europe and the United States, a rift that was especially aggravated during the eight Reagan years. The crux of the controversy, Pfaff asserts, is the American failure seriously to "define the changing nature of the threat and the moral proportionality of the chosen means of defense."

The United States has always failed to grasp fully the workings of the Asian and African societies with which it has concerned itself. Americans, in general, equate "development" with Western technology. Such a philosophy functions well within the framework of industry and capitalism but accommodates poorly the religious, moral, and social values of Eastern culture. It is difficult for the United States to believe that the price of Westernization could ever be too high. But even in modern Japan, an exemplary success in its "intelligent but discriminating adoption of Western ideas and practices," there are those who recognize, regretfully, the great cost to Japanese civilization.

In conclusion, Pfaff discusses the once predominant image of America as truly "the New World." That image was essentially a series of favorable myths enjoyed and perpetuated by the rest of the world, primarily Europeans. The myths were fairly safe until 1917, when Woodrow Wilson's internationalism thrust the United States into visible contact with foreign societies that ever since (especially since World War II) have expected "American action . . . to redeem the myth." American fact and fantasy have often clashed, but the belief in the ultimate inviolability of the United States has sustained many a European throughout the latter half of the 20th century.

America's self-image, however, underwent a dramatic reexamination. During the 1960s and 1970s, the future of the United States rested unsteadily on questioned political principles, rejected social mores, and challenged moral standards. This "rebellion" was quelled by the aggressive rallying efforts of a neoconservative faction whose objective it was to reaffirm "American worth and American primacy." The effects came quickly and deliberately:

> In successive elections in the late 1970s and the 1980s, Americans elected
> . . . Presidents whose principal, even sole, qualification . . . was their ability to make Americans feel better about themselves and about their country. There was a competition in reassurances . . . that the country was still a "good" country, . . . its leadership intact. This very insistence suggested, however, that doubt about these things persisted . . . .

So the doubts, as they should, remain. The dynamics behind "the American Century"—forced upon and invited by the United States—may no longer be preserved within reason. In fact, it is not unthinkable "that the United States revert to its natural condition, which is isolationism."

William Pfaff has shared his insight as an experienced foreign-affairs columnist and in so doing has generated a number of original analyses, perspectives, and speculations regarding the role of the United States in an ever-changing world. A responsible work of modern history, Pfaff's book thoughtfully appraises the politically significant issues and events that have shaped the 20th century.

Published in 1989, *Barbarian Sentiments* takes the reader to the end of a decade. But does it? Between the time the book was published and the time the 1980s actually ended, the world did anything but stand still. With but a few weeks remaining, 1989 added to its legacy the fall of Panamanian dictator and suspected drug czar Manuel Noriega, the political and physical dismantling of the Berlin Wall, and the execution of Romania's tyrant, Nicolae Ceauşescu.

Such consequential events—events that change history, make history, are history—do not render *Barbarian Sentiments* outdated; rather, they validate the germane and intuitive messages of Pfaff's work. Current world affairs are indeed complex and far-reaching, and to quote historian Tad Szulc, "*Barbarian Sentiments* brings together the strands of contemporary history in the most brilliant fashion."

Christine Lindberg Stevens

BATTLE FOR JUSTICE: HOW THE BORK NOMINATION SHOOK AMERICA

Author: Ethan Bronner
Publisher: W. W. Norton & Company (New York). 399 pp. $22.50
Type of work: Current affairs
Time: June-October 1987
Locale: Washington, D.C.

A national power struggle over Robert H. Bork's nomination to the Supreme Court raises questions about the Constitution in daily life, and the impact of the personal philosophies of Supreme Court justices on civil liberties

> *Principal personages:*
> ROBERT H. BORK, a federal appeals judge for the District of Columbia
> EDWARD KENNEDY, the Democratic senator from Massachusetts who played a key role in opposing Bork's Supreme Court nomination
> LAURENCE TRIBE, a Harvard Law School professor and Bork opponent
> RALPH G. NEAS, the executive director of the Leadership Conference on Civil Rights, a grouping of 180 organizations

The retirement of any Supreme Court justice, appointed for life, is an event. But the retirement, during the Constitution's bicentennial year of 1987, of Justice Lewis F. Powell, Jr., a flexible conservative and often the "swing vote on a polarized bench," was especially significant. Powell provided the decisive vote for the Court's liberal wing on such issues as abortion, separation of church and state, and affirmative action. Yet he also voted with conservatives on protecting business issues, the death penalty, and aiding the prosecution in criminal cases. Thus, with Powell's retirement, the entire future of the institution came under question. Consequently, Robert H. Bork, federal appeals judge for the District of Columbia and the Reagan administration's first choice as Powell's replacement, fell under close scrutiny. As the administration attempted to nominate Bork quickly, interest groups such as the National Association for the Advancement of Colored People (NAACP), the Leadership Conference on Civil Rights, led by Executive Director Ralph Neas, and many other civil rights groups moved to block the nomination.

Essentially, Powell's retirement meant that conservatives could gain Supreme Court control and with it the nation's moral and legal agenda. From the day Reagan took office in 1981, he made it clear that government policies of the previous two decades toward race, sex, and religion would change dramatically. Reagan's administration clearly stated that its view of justice diverged from that of the established civil rights community. For these reasons, the battle over a Supreme Court justice and personal justice began when Reagan nominated Robert Bork.

Immediately following Powell's resignation, Laurence Tribe, a Harvard law professor, appeared via national satellite news and announced that Bork's nomination would endanger the right to abortion and even birth control. The main issue of the nomination, he said, was the danger Bork posed to the evolving right of personal privacy. During that same weekend, Edward Kennedy of Massachusetts drafted a powerful anti-Bork statement. Collectively, Neas, Tribe, and Kennedy, along with the rest of the nation's civil rights and liberal establishment, were prepared to challenge the president and the Justice Department over the Constitution's interpretation and the direction of law and justice in America.

This was no small challenge, for the power of the Court has grown considerably in the past half century, and today justices are among the nation's most prestigious and powerful individuals. However, the author raises many pertinent questions regarding the Constitution's own role and power. Bronner asks, "Is the nation's charter analogous to a slab of Carrara marble and the nation like Michelangelo, searching for the splendid form hidden inside? Or is the document's meaning more fixed?" Bronner reminds his audience that anyone attempting to answer these questions must consider the framing fathers' ambiguous words, such as "liberty" and "due process," while answering a still larger question: "Does the nation have license to reinterpret those terms in the light of its own changing standards?"

Bork's opposition questioned his beliefs on these issues. They examined his book *The Antitrust Paradox*, related writings and lectures about antitrust law, his teachings at Yale University, and his record in private law practice. They also searched for clues in Bork's professional and political career that would reveal his soundness for decision making as well as his regard of the Constitution and his views on how justices should apply it.

They considered an article Bork wrote at age forty-one for *Fortune* entitled "The Supreme Court Needs a New Philosophy," which held that the Bill of Rights was an incomplete, open-ended document, and the work of its completion fell to the Supreme Court. Three years later, in the *Indiana Law Journal*, Bork let his constitutional views be known again. This article, which stipulated "that only those liberties made explicit by the Constitution could be legally defended," later became Exhibit 2 in Bork's Senate confirmation hearing and served as evidence for his rejection.

In 1972, Bork advised Richard Nixon on legislation to limit busing in school desegregation cases. During Nixon's presidency Bork became involved in many delicate political matters that required his legal expertise and personal resolve. Bork's political activities slowed down between 1976 and 1980 when he suffered the losses of a close colleague and his beloved wife, Claire. Uncertain about what to do next, he returned to his former Washington, D.C., law firm as senior partner. Shortly after, recently elected President Reagan announced Bork as his choice for the District of Columbia Court of Appeals.

Although Bork was not eager to fill this post, he saw it as a clear signal: "If he wanted to join the Supreme Court, he would have to go on the appeals court first." He spent five years on the bench, where he was a powerful voice of conservatism. His liberal colleagues often accused him of activism. During this period, Bork married Mary Ellen Pohl, a former nun belonging to the Society of the Sacred Heart, a religious society that had undergone radical changes. As Pohl mourned a loss of religious tradition, Bork concurrently lamented the course of the law. Both abhorred sudden, seemingly mindless rejection of old traditions as substitutes for egalitarian and utopian impulses.

Like Reagan, Bork believed that the emphasis on individual rights and equality had ventured too far and had led to permissiveness and increased crime. In short, he was sure that the nation had lost its "moral compass." He felt that a muscular conservatism would help to fight the expansion of individual and minority rights, which he believed were illegitimate. He therefore opposed busing and affirmative action with the rationale that they were intrusive regulations; he opposed homosexual rights and abortion because they were not upheld in the Constitution; he favored the death penalty and advocated greater firmness in dealing with criminals; he supported increased religion in public life so as to restore morality; he promoted a return to more states' rights, regardless of what majorities might do to those who would not conform; and he condemned the intrusiveness of the Democratic Congress. Bork backed up these positions with a narrow view of the Constitution and praised a return to "original principles." In Bork's estimation, there was little room for judges to give meaning to the charter's broad phrases.

Bork's rigid ideologies were vigorously attacked during the more than thirty hours of questioning his confirmation hearing entailed. Senator Kennedy hotly warned, "Robert Bork's America is a land in which women would be forced into back alley abortions, [and] blacks would sit at segregated lunch counters. . . ." Kennedy's was a landmark speech, for it defied the Senate tradition of examining the nominee's personal character or integrity by focusing instead on Bork's vision for society.

Meanwhile, the White House ironically portrayed Bork to be a natural judicial successor to Justice Powell, a most inaccurate comparison. Whereas Bork spoke constantly of the need for an overarching theory for the Court, Powell believed that law should develop case by case. However, since Powell was the centrist model, the administration was determined to make Bork fit the mold. However, Bork failed to convince a frightened public to trust his judgment. Thus, on October 23, 1989, the Senate defeated Bork's nomination by a vote of 58 to 42.

Reagan's next nominee, Douglas Ginsburg, a young judge on the District of Columbia Circuit Court of Appeals, had a short-lived nomination, from which he withdrew when his business practices and use of marijuana were called into question. Finally, Anthony Kennedy, fifty-one years old, a judge on the Ninth Circuit Court of Appeals in California, won the approval of the public and the Senate after displaying a markedly more moderate constitutional view than Bork. When asked in the committee questionnaire what qualities a judge should have, Kennedy answered, "Compassion, warmth, sensitivity, and an unyielding insistence on justice." He spoke of the Constitution as having a capacity for growth and of its framers as having made "a covenant with the future." For the many who fought the Bork nomination long and hard, these words were the harbingers of artful justice.

The interplay of power among those advocating liberal and conservative interpretations of the Constitution, which would have a profound influence on future generations, is the central theme of Bronner's *Battle for Justice: How the Bork Nomination Shook America*. The battle that Bronner describes was not over an individual, but rather what that individual represented for America's future. One need not be a historian to be engaged in this political drama, which masterfully unfolds through the personal profiles of the individuals involved. Bronner's book is heavily skewed toward the Bork opposition. The reader feels the energy—and downright fury at times—of those trying to block Bork, but gains little insight into those working with the Reagan Administration to promote the nominee. Yet, as he is portrayed by Ethan Bronner, Robert Bork, the object of the opposition, embodies the powerful political forces of the event while conveying his own unique human intellect and emotion.

Karin A. Nobile

BAUMGARTNER'S BOMBAY

Author: Anita Desai (1937–   )
Publisher: Alfred A. Knopf (New York). 230 pp. $18.95
Type of work: Novel
Time: 1933 to the present
Locale: Bombay; Calcutta; the Himalayas; Berlin; Venice

Hugo Baumgartner confronts his childhood as a Jew in Nazi Germany when
he meets and attempts to help a German drug addict in present-day Bombay

> *Principal characters:*
> HUGO BAUMGARTNER, a Jew who had lived in Bombay for
>   more than forty years since fleeing Nazi Germany
> FARROKH, the proprietor of the Café de Paris in Bombay
> LOTTE, a former cabaret performer, now an elderly alcoholic
>   and friend of Baumgartner
> JULIUS ROTH, a furniture builder in Delhi, who met Baumgart-
>   ner in a detention camp
> KURT, a young Aryan drug addict from Germany
> JAGU, a drunkard who lives in a shack with his family outside
>   Baumgartner's apartment building
> CHIMANLAL, Baumgartner's business partner and co-owner of
>   a successful racehorse

Hugo Baumgartner is an elderly German exile who has lived in India for over forty years since he fled Nazi Germany in the 1930s. Baumgartner lives alone in a dingy apartment near the famous Taj Hotel. His only companions are numerous stray cats he feeds and cares for in his one-room apartment. Baumgartner spends his days visiting restaurants to request leftover food for his cats. Baumgartner's favorite resting spot, and the source of much free food, is the Café de Paris, run by Farrokh. Baumgartner's only other social contact is with Lotte, a retired cabaret performer, with whom he can speak German.

One morning, Farrokh complains that his café is being disturbed by another foreigner, a drug addict who orders food without paying and then falls asleep at his table. The foreigner, a blond Aryan, reminds Baumgartner of his childhood in Germany. In a series of chapters, Anita Desai weaves together a remembrance of Baumgartner's life and the circumstances that brought him to an impoverished old age in Bombay with an account of Baumgartner's brief encounters with the young drug addict.

Baumgartner grew up in Berlin, the son of a prosperous furniture maker who enjoyed visiting the racetrack and betting on horses. One of Baumgartner's principal memories is of his disappointment at never being allowed to accompany his father to the track. Through a series of telling details, the author describes the effect of the Nazis upon

Baumgartner and his family. Baumgartner's father loses most of his customers because "wealthy Jews . . . no longer were interested in anything so difficult to transport as furniture." Non-Jews refused to patronize the father's business, and the family was forced to economize. The father gave up betting on horses, the mother dismissed her maid, and young Hugo no longer was given chocolates for dessert.

Later the father was arrested and taken to Dachau concentration camp for a fortnight. When he returned, he refused to talk with anyone and shortly thereafter killed himself. Hugo's mother was forced to sell the family business and then her furniture and apartment to a man from Hamburg in order to support herself and Hugo. The man from Hamburg arranged for Hugo to move to India and work as an exporter of wood to Europe. Hugo's mother refused to leave Berlin. Hugo first traveled to Venice, his only encounter with Europe outside his hometown. He continued by ship to India, settling in Calcutta, where he became a prosperous wood exporter.

Baumgartner's life was shattered when the British rulers of India placed him in a detention camp for enemy aliens during the six years of World War II. The British did not distinguish between German supporters of the Nazis and Jewish exiles such as Baumgartner. The camp was controlled by pro-Nazi Germans, who celebrated Hitler's early victories. Baumgartner befriended the other Jews in the camp, especially Julius Roth, who, like Hugo's father, was a designer of elegant furniture.

After the war, Baumgartner was released from detention and returned to a Calcutta devastated by Japanese bombing attacks and by the eruption of violence between Hindus and Moslems in anticipation of India's independence from Britain. Baumgartner's business went bankrupt during the war. He did manage to retrieve a set of postcards mailed to him by his mother and never forwarded to the camp. The cards were short and cryptic, and ended in 1941. For the rest of his life, Hugo keeps the postcards as his only remembrance of his mother.

Hugo settled in Bombay, once again becoming prosperous in partnership with Chimanlal. The two men bought racehorses, allowing Hugo to imitate his father and finally spend time at a racetrack. When Chimanlal died, his son forced Baumgartner into retirement. It was then that Baumgartner severed his few ties with other people and devoted himself to caring for stray cats. His only remaining friend is Lotte, who also suffered financial losses when her lover, a prosperous Indian merchant, died and his family cut her off. Hugo visits Lotte after his encounter with the young German. She consoles him with gin and and invites him to sleep with her.

Baumgartner awakens sickened by the gin and returns to the Café de Paris. Farrokh is frantic over the German's continued presence in his café. He convinces Hugo to talk with the addict. Baumgartner discovers that the young man is German when he replies to Hugo's words. Farrokh begs Baumgartner to take the German home with him. Baumgartner does so, even though he is not sure why he should befriend a German after those people forced him into exile and murdered his family. Baumgartner argues with himself, deciding that this young man was born well after World War II and has no connection with the Nazis.

Upon reaching Baumgartner's apartment, the young German is revolted by the stench from the cats and from the scraps of food Baumgartner has brought to feed his pets. Baumgartner learns that the young man's name is Kurt, "or some such name—abrupt, like a blow, or a slash." Hugo prepares a meal and opens a rare beer for the young man, who meanwhile has locked himself in the bathroom to take drugs. Kurt emerges reenergized and tosses the beer and food on the floor. He notices some tarnished silver bowls on a shelf. Baumgartner tells Kurt that the bowls were prizes won by his racehorses. The young German cannot believe that the elderly and impoverished Baumgartner could have been an owner of racehorses.

After Kurt leaves the apartment, Baumgartner locks the door, rereads the postcards from his mother, and falls asleep. Hours later, Kurt picks the lock, enters Baumgartner's apartment, stabs the old man to death, steals the silver bowls, and disappears. Kurt's actions are noticed only by Jagu, a man living with his family in a shack made of paper bags and tin cans in front of Baumgartner's apartment building. Every day, Baumgartner had passed by Jagu's shack as he entered and left on his daily rounds. The two men never spoke, but Baumgartner had looked on Jagu with fear. Baumgartner worried that the street dweller would want to kill him in order to steal what little he had. Baumgartner also saw Jagu as a symbol of utter poverty, the condition toward which Baumgartner was descending.

Jagu observes Kurt's trail of bloody footprints and calls the night watchman, who alerts the police. The police arrest Jagu for the murder, assuming that the homeless man was the most likely to commit such a crime. Lotte is alerted and runs to Baumgartner's apartment. She and Farrokh weep for the death of their friend and for his lack of importance in the eyes of the police and neighbors. Lotte takes the postcards from Baumgartner's mother home with her, "as if they provided her with clues to a puzzle, a meaning to the meaningless."

Baumgartner's Bombay captures the flavor of life in the two very different worlds of Germany and India. Anita Desai, whose mother is

German and father is Indian, makes use of accurate and telling details to convey Baumgartner's memories of a German childhood and his years as an adult in Calcutta and Bombay. By interweaving chapters of Baumgartner's past with ones telling of his constricted old age, Desai is able to show how Hugo's isolation and fears in old age were prefigured by the loss of his rich and secure early childhood. Baumgartner's only good fortune was to survive the Nazis and then to prosper in India. However, his prosperity, and Lotte's, were lost by the chance death of their Indian friends. Finally, Baumgartner's own life is lost through a chance encounter with a German, not a Nazi but a banal drug addict.

Desai conveys the dignity and sadness of Hugo Baumgartner's life, allowing the reader to empathize with the main character. The longings and essential goodness of Hugo and his friends emerge through the details of their lives. The harsh circumstances of Baumgartner's life, the fading memories of his mother, and his brief encounters with other humans and his love for stray cats will sadden the reader. However bleak his life or pathetic his death, Baumgartner will command the reader's attention and respect.

Richard Lachmann

BERNARD SHAW: VOLUME TWO, 1898-1918: THE PURSUIT OF POWER

Author: Michael Holroyd (1935–   )
Publisher: Random House (New York). 420 pp. $24.95
Type of work: Biography
Time: 1898-1918
Locale: England and Ireland

The evolution of Bernard Shaw from age forty-two to sixty-two into a sought-after celebrity playwright, yet one who is unable to shape public opinion, politics, and social history

> *Principal personages:*
> (GEORGE) BERNARD SHAW, playwright and Fabian propagandist
> CHARLOTTE SHAW, his wealthy, worrisome wife
> SIDNEY and BEATRICE WEBB, husband and wife, together the guiding force of the Fabians
> HARLEY GRANVILLE-BARKER, a brilliant theatrical protégé of Shaw
> H. G. WELLS, a popular novelist, friend and antagonist of Shaw
> MRS. PATRICK CAMPBELL (STELLA), an actress friend beloved by Shaw

In June of 1898, George Bernard and Charlotte Shaw commence their honeymoon. On crutches following foot surgery, he tumbles and breaks an arm. Working hard despite Charlotte's intrusive anxieties and imposed holidays, Shaw writes *The Perfect Wagnerite*, a book showing a pessimistic shift in his philosophy—his hope transferred from rationality to irrationality. He deifies the life force evident in paradoxically powerful "supermen" such as the genial Caesar in his historical play *Caesar and Cleopatra* and even the irresistibly polite Lady Cicely in his adventure-comedy *Captain Brassbound's Conversion*. The Shaws' unconsummated marriage meets reciprocal needs but tries them both. Resentfully, he joins her ambitious travels, and she supports his ambitious projects, including the book *Fabianism and the Empire*, his attempt to clarify and unite diverse Fabian opinion about the Boer War.

Charlotte (part secretary, part mother to Shaw) prefers politics to plays, but Shaw cheerfully loses his run for a county council seat. Still largely unknown to London audiences, Shaw manipulates inept if earnest translators and bewildered foreign disciples who successfully publicize his work abroad. In 1901, Shaw renders his old prizefighting novel, *Cashel Byron's Profession*, into a mock-Elizabethan blank-verse romp called *The Admirable Bashville*. In 1907 his romantic comedy *Man and Superman* is staged. Its *Don Juan in Hell* dream sequence showcases Shaw's new philosophy of "Creative Evolution": the Life Force blindly works through conflicting human wills to produce "God." At Yeats's invitation, Shaw writes *John Bull's Other Island* for Dublin's Abbey Theatre, which rejects it. To Shaw's surprise, London audiences delight in his partly mystical Irish play.

When Shaw becomes the fatherly collaborator of actor-playwright-director Harley Granville-Barker at the avant-garde Court Theatre, rumors circulate that Granville-Barker is Shaw's natural son. Written for the Court, *Major Barbara*, Shaw's first "religious" work, costs him more birth travails than any other script. Despite rewrites, the "evil" character of Undershaft takes control of the play, subverting the "good" characters and Shaw's original scheme. The ambiguous ending unsettles even its author.

Rising Liberal and Labour parties confound the strategies of Fabians Sidney and Beatrice Webb. Having "permeated" the Conservatives, must they now oppose them? Hoping to recruit new leadership, the Webbs and Shaw befriend H. G. Wells, a young novelist with unorthodox views. Wells joins the Fabian Society but, bored, is impatient to leave—preferably after vanquishing and extinguishing it. Shaw encourages Wells's criticisms while deftly disarming the younger man's ploys to oust him and the Webbs. Although *Major Barbara* proves controversial, even detractors admire the Court's ensemble acting. More in love with Shavianism than each other, Granville-Barker and actress Lillah McCarthy launch a doomed marriage. Shaw becomes friends with Dr. Almroth Wright, whose supposed medical discovery (at which Shaw scoffs) becomes the premise of *The Doctor's Dilemma*, a black comedy of self-delusion. Granville-Barker meanwhile uses his years of directing and acting at the Court to test his ideas for a national theater.

In Paris, Shaw poses for a bust by Rodin, as he will pose nude or eccentrically costumed for countless Shavian icons in every artistic medium. Charlotte moves the Shaws to the rectory at Ayot St. Lawrence, and Shaw participates in the Webbs' Fabian summer school. For years, the Shaws' motorcar occasions nearly fatal comedy in desert and mountain. Back in England, Shaw's *Getting Married*—a comedy without scenes, acts, or action—fills the stage with stock farce characters trapped in *talk*, making playgoers and critics alike uncomfortable.

Archibald Henderson, a young North Carolinian math teacher, becomes Shaw's compliant biographer, filling volume upon volume with Shaw-supplied "facts." With his affectionate friend G. K. Chesterton, Shaw publicly debates for decades. Amid Shaw's labors for authors' rights, his biggest campaign is against stage censorship. In a laughably wholesome play, *The Shewing-up of Blanco Posnet,* he includes words from the censor's list, guaranteeing the play's suppression in England even while a courageous Abbey Theatre production of the Western parable makes observers wonder what the fuss is about. By publishing the inoffensive "offending" words in the newspaper, Shaw further ridicules the censor. However, the irritated authorities ignore his testimony at a high-level inquiry, refusing to publish his written report.

For a West End repertory season in 1909, Shaw composes *Misalliance,* portraying destructive parent-child relations. Critics dislike the play's odd style, a forerunner to that of Eugene Ionesco and Joe Orton. Meanwhile, Beatrice Webb enters public life as a crusading suffragette, partly compensating for the absence of Wells, who (to everyone's relief) left the Fabian leadership in 1908. (Although Wells and Shaw drew new members, chiefly female, their amusing but sterile debates pained both men—and Wells's scandalous philanderings threatened Fabian respectability.)

Shaw finishes *Fanny's First Play* in March of 1911. This play-within-a-play, staged with a teasing mystery as to its authorship, is Shaw's first long-running hit. In 1912 his religious-parable play, *Androcles and the Lion,* confuses and annoys those who see it. (In these prewar years, Shaw will dash off several experimental one-act plays and clownish skits that not only anticipate later dramatic forms but express his private fears and obsessions.) Exhausted by mutual irritation, the Shaws endure their first separate holidays, followed by their most serious crisis. Having always been enamored of Mrs. Patrick Campbell's stage presence, Shaw devises for her the part of Eliza Doolittle in *Pygmalion.* In person the ailing Stella ("Mrs. Pat") mesmerizes him with her charm; he falls wildly in love. They exchange passionate letters, and he pays chaste, secret visits to her sickbed. Charlotte, finding out, is wounded yet unyielding. After evading Shaw's one pathetic attempt to consummate their affair, Stella marries a man who is willing to leave his wife. Shaw is crushed. Although *Pygmalion* is a theatrical masterpiece, the blithely absent-minded Beerbohm Tree as Higgins and the middle-aged, unstable Stella as teenaged Eliza nearly endanger Shaw's sanity. Still, the outrageously un-Shavian production is a crowd-pleaser.

With Shaw's financial backing and Clifford Sharp's editing, the Webbs launch the socialist periodical *The New Statesman.* The playwright starts following international politics—and correctly foresees the approaching war. When the conflict erupts, England seethes with chauvinist, German-hating hysteria. For sneering at such emotional excesses, Shaw is socially ostracized as a traitor. Neither pacifist nor jingoist, his books *Common Sense about the War* and *More Common Sense about the War* at first alienate most of his public and friends. But as the carnage and horror mount, a bereaved and battered Britain finds war less glorious and the Shavian view of it less treasonous. Himself an intimate witness of death and destruction domestically, Shaw officially tours the front. Charlotte retreats from politics into a numb, smiling spiritualism. The dark, ironic humor of Shaw's recruitment and propaganda plays disturbs officials but appeals to common soldiers. He begins a long, paradoxical involvement with Ireland, mocking nationalism while advocating home rule, and quietly endowing Irish cultural enterprises while noisily refusing to return "home." By Armistice, his friends dead or mourning, Shaw feels emptily old. He, too, mourns the loss of his sister Lucy, who dies with her hand in his. In the same crematorium where their mother burned, Lucy flames "with a steady white light, like a wax candle."

So voluminous and labyrinthine are the documents by and about the busy Bernard Shaw that not even a three-volume biography could contain a full sequential narrative of his crowded days. To trace the network of sources and influences connected to the incidents and arguments that occupied him would be the work of more than even a Shavian life span. The responsible biographer of "G.B.S." can only hope to select and distill the salient themes of the Irishman's life and character, presenting the reader with a condensed map of a vast, complex terrain. Volume II of *Bernard Shaw*, like Volume I, charmingly crystallizes what Michael Holroyd has learned and guessed about his verbose yet elusive subject. Although hardly the last word on Shaw, this biography's remarkable photographs, crisply focused facts, and wittily compressed prose provide more than one lens through which to begin examining the character and art of the man who remains one of the greatest English-language playwrights.

As the middle volume of a trilogy, this book necessarily lacks the drama of overture or finale. And Holroyd's obligatory analyses of play after play can sometimes grow routine, even psychoanalytically glib. But his few lapses of inspiration are far outweighed by the coiled compactness and hard-earned insight of nearly every sentence in the book. The reader's appetite is whetted for Volume III: *The Lure of Fantasy*, due in 1991.

Gary Brockman

BILLY BATHGATE

Author: E. L. Doctorow (1931–)
Publisher: Random House (New York). 323 pp. $19.95
Type of work: Novel
Time: 1935
Locale: New York City; Onondaga; and Saratoga Springs, New York

Billy Bathgate's reminiscence of a summer in his youth when he served as a mobster's apprentice in the gang of the legendary Dutch Schultz

Principal characters:
> BILLY BEHAN BATHGATE, an aspiring gangster and precocious factotum for Dutch Schultz
> MARY BEHAN, Billy's aging and eccentric mother
> ARNOLD GARBAGE, Billy's pack-rat friend
> REBECCA, Billy's girlfriend
> DUTCH SCHULTZ, the leader of a major New York gang
> BO WEINBERG and LULU ROSENKRANTZ, members of Schultz's gang
> OTTO ABBADABBA BERMAN, Schultz's lieutenant and financial wizard
> DIXIE DAVIS, Schultz's attorney
> DREW PRESTON, a socialite and moll to Weinberg and Schultz
> HARVEY PRESTON, her husband

When he was fifteen, in the summer of 1935, Billy Behan, alias Billy Bathgate, sought and gained the attention of mob boss Arthur Flegenheimer, alias Dutch Schultz ("the Dutchman"), the historic Prohibition mobster. Now an adult, Billy looks back on that time, a time that helps explain his current wealth and the reason for keeping his real identity a secret.

Billy's neighborhood, along Bathgate Avenue in a poorer part of the Bronx, and his father's desertion and mother's disheveled person and forsaken life serve as partial motive for his ambitions for and acceptance into the "good life" of gangsterdom. The main allure, however, is the aura of adventure surrounding Schultz and his gang, and Billy's own innate propensity for life outside the law.

Billy knows nothing about his father. His mother, Mary Behan, is on an observably seedy decline toward forgetfulness, insanity, and oblivion as a bagwoman. Billy is almost as much an orphan and street urchin as his friends Arnold Garbage and Rebecca, a libidinous resident of the nearby Max and Dora Diamond Home for Children. A mix of Jewish and Irish bloodlines, Billy inherits an innate dexterity and has considerable talent, literally and figuratively, as a juggler. It is during one of his juggling demonstrations outside Schultz's beer drop in the Bronx that Billy gains the attention of the notorious, hot-tempered killer and gang leader. Schultz's awareness that Billy's dexterity of hand as an entertainer extends to quick-mindedness and native wit, prompts a gratuity that soon leads to employment as errand boy and informant.

In his persistent attempts to gain acceptance by Schultz and his stooges, Billy learns early on that certain torture and possible death (often combined) await anyone who betrays Schultz. Bo Weinberg, one of Schultz's best gunmen (along with Lulu Rosenkrantz and a man known only as Irving) provides shocking evidence of this one night on a tugboat in the dark waters of the Atlantic when Bo's feet are cemented into a tub and he is pushed alive into the ocean.

Bo's brief talk with Billy that night and Billy's memory of the song Bo sings in the face of death, "Bye bye blackbird . . .," stay with Billy long beyond that night and serve as a kind of soundtrack to his own fear of what Schultz might do to him—and to Bo's girlfriend, Lola (Drew Preston). That very night on the tug, Schultz appropriates Drew as his own mistress and sends her, with Billy, back to a hotel where Billy watches her undress and dress and prepare, chameleonlike, for her new role as Dutch's moll. She says a quick goodbye to her wealthy husband, Harvey—involved at that very moment on the couch in a homosexual liaison.

Thus begins a series of eye-opening, on-the-alert adventures and misadventures with Dutch and his gang that call for a monumental juggling act on Billy's part, an act as both voyeur and participant, where the payoffs are money, women, travel, a broken nose, a beating, and always the worry about a potential bullet in the head or knife across the throat. Billy, moving up in the neighborhood, obtains a gun from Arnold Garbage, buys new clothes, pays Rebecca for sexual favors, throws a party for all his old Bathgate Avenue friends, and gives money and gifts to his mother. He is soon, however, caught up in a different social network, much beyond his neighborhood, that leads to intriguing and dangerous situations in other areas of the city and upstate in rural Onondaga, where Schultz, with the aid of his egregious attorney, Dixie Davis, buys out the town and ostentatiously converts to Catholicism in preparation for a trial on federal tax charges; and in Saratoga Springs, where Billy is sent as a monitor for and companion to Drew Preston, removed from the attentions of the press and Dutch's growing obsession on orders from Dutch's accountant and numbers king, Abbadabba Berman.

It is Berman who takes special charge of Billy in his induction into the gang. And it is Berman who, in protecting Schultz (and his own well-being), orders Lulu to break Billy's nose as a ruse for explaining the blood-covered hotel carpet resulting from Schultz's cold-blooded murder of restaurateur Julie Martin. Berman, too, notes the special attraction Billy has for Drew Preston, only twenty-one. Few, however, including Billy, realize the full erotic nature of Drew and her animal appetite for raw experience. On their drive to Saratoga Springs, Drew soon seduces a very willing Billy who promised both Bo Weinberg and, more implicitly, Schultz, to look after her in an entirely different sense. Meanwhile, during the murder trial, the gang moves to an abandoned house outside of town.

Schultz is soon acquitted in the Onondaga trial. Drew Preston, with Billy's assistance and a tip to Harvey Preston, hurries to the Saratoga airport, escaping harm at the hands of Berman and assorted thugs and, eventually, ending further involvement with Schultz, who has a new set of troubles.

Upon his return to New York City, Schultz faces two threats: Special Prosecuting Attorney Thomas E. Dewey, who indicts him on state tax-evasion charges; and Tammany district leader James J. Hines, who rejects further Schultz payoffs (in part because of Weinberg's murder) and tells Billy, sent as emissary, that business with Schultz has ended. Without Hines there is no fix, and just as Schultz's assassination of Dewey is planned, Schultz, Berman, Irving, and Lulu are gunned down in gangland war as Mafia elements encroach. Bo Weinberg, among others, is avenged.

Schultz dies on October 24, 1935, and only wily Billy Bathgate escapes and lives into the future on a gigantic stash of Schultz's millions that he cleverly and clandestinely recovered. From a vantage point of wealth and a successful business partnership (of an unidentified nature) with Arnold Garbage, Billy looks back on the most formative and memorable summer of his youth.

Billy poetically describes his life as a walk through the bazaar of life in the age of Dutch Schultz. Certainly Bathgate, and Doctorow behind him, speak in voices and sensibilities much beyond those of a fifteen-year-old hood. Doctorow's persona shines brightly through Billy (young and old), making him seem more the poet than the criminal. But much of the power of this novel and of Doctorow's artistry as a storyteller is that in Billy's characterization and consciousness the novelist makes eminently credible the madness and brilliance of the criminal mind and of civilized society sliding once again into atavistic violence, cruelty, and corruption—but still, like humanity at large, on the edge of some kind of redemption.

Doctorow attains some of this pervasive thematic ambivalence of innocence edging into experience through tapping the traditions of the oldest of novel forms—the maturation or initiation narrative. But such a tightly textured novel as this weaves plot and theme closely with characterization, setting, and, indeed, prophecy.

American mythology reverberates time and again with bad boys. Billy observes at one point that Schultz seemed his father, a part of— one infers—the old romantic destiny of the hero as child being father to the man and the father continuing his cyclical, generational legacy. Thus Billy Bathgate takes his place, along with Billy the Kid, Jesse James, Dutch Schultz, and other outlaws, as something of an American icon—the individual, the loner, the rebel, the fallen American Adam resolved to seek again and restore that once-known and always dreamed-of brave new world, now on the frontier between ideal and real. For Schultz and his heir Billy, America's once new wilderness world, now urbanized, must be rescued from laws, government, and bureaucratic "justice" and restored to a more localized and indivi- dualized world. Although *Billy Bathgate* is a gangster novel, it resem- bles the Western novel, a form Doctorow explores more directly in *Welcome to Hard Times*.

For Drew Preston to fit into such a mythology, the stereotype has been modified to reflect an emerging feminism. Drew Preston is the American Eve recrafted as a lusting cameo shaped by 20th-century angst, mindless to the consequences or even the motives of gender and the politics of sex other than sheer willfulness and being.

Billy finds pleasure and peril in his stroll through such a monstrously and grotesquely beautiful American bazaar. He also finds himself, his destiny as a doer and a taker, a builder, and, ultimately, a ravager. Finally occupying the catbird's seat of criminal acquisition with a le- gitimate cover, he can make his "confession" of how he made it Amer- ican-style, how he succeeded via the American adaptations of social Darwinism. In the American version of poetic justice, the "bad," too, have a chance of success, however brief.

Doctorow's *Billy Bathgate*, with its special blending of historical novel and Bildungsroman, amounts to a modern illustration of the role and power of fiction itself, and of history as the supreme, inspirational fiction known as the American Dream, its fame and shame, imagined and made manifest. Certainly Billy's is one American boy's story of his quest for manhood and maleness, for approval as a "capable boy" in the land of the free and the home of the brave. But *Billy Bathgate* as novel is also the story of "everyman," another fascinating telling of the various ways and devices of the fall—its fortunate and unfortunate endings and beginnings, and the epic, anguished sweetness of remem- bering the glory days and their turning.

Robert F. Gish

THE BROKEN CORD

Author: Michael Dorris (1945–   )
Publisher: Harper & Row (New York). 300 pp. $18.95
Type of work: Autobiography
Time: 1971 to the present
Locale: The United States

Native American writer Michael Dorris recounts his family's struggle with the effects of his adopted eldest son's fetal alcohol syndrome

Principal personages:
MICHAEL DORRIS, a Native American professor and writer
ADAM DORRIS, his first son, adopted at the age of three
DENIS DAIGLE, the social worker who helped to place Adam
BEATRICE MEDICINE, a Native American colleague of Dorris's at Dartmouth
JEANEEN GREY EAGLE, the director of a drug and alcohol rehabilitation center on a reservation in South Dakota
PHIL MAY, a sociologist researching fetal alcohol syndrome among Native Americans
LOUISE ERDRICH, Michael Dorris's wife, also a Native American writer

In 1971, Michael Dorris became one of the first single men to adopt a child legally. An anthropologist of Native American heritage and a professor at Franconia College, he was given a three-year-old Sioux boy from South Dakota whom he named Adam. He knew little about Adam at the time. The child had been born prematurely to an alcoholic mother. After almost dying of pneumonia and general neglect, he had been removed to a foster home. Two years after the adoption, Adam's biological mother died of acute alcohol poisoning.

Adam's development was somewhat behind that of other children, but Dorris attributed it to his slow start in life and the deprivations he had suffered. Yet shortly after arriving in his new home in New Hampshire, Adam suffered a seizure and almost died. His epilepsy proved difficult to control, even with medication. It was the first sign of far more severe problems.

The following fall, Dorris started a new, more demanding job as a professor of anthropology at Dartmouth College. There he met a number of Native American students and faculty and helped to establish a Native American Studies program. One of his colleagues was Beatrice Medicine, who invited him to visit the Sioux reservation in South Dakota where she had grown up. There, the Dorrises, father and son, received Lakota names in a traditional ceremony. The idyllic summer they shared gave way to difficulties in the fall, when Adam fell further and further behind in his day-care center. Dorris blamed racism and a lack of understanding of his child's special circumstances. When Adam was rejected by a private-school kindergarten because of "learning difficulties," Dorris had him tested by specialists. Instead of showing him as gifted, as Dorris had expected, the tests revealed "borderline" developmental disabilities. Yet it took the adoption of a second son, when Adam was six, for the full truth to sink in. Adam's younger brother mastered tasks far more quickly and soon surpassed his older brother in intellectual skills.

To understand Adam's limitations and their cause, Dorris began to investigate Adam's background. Having already known about the mother's alcoholism, he found that Adam's father (who had been beaten to death in a brawl) and maternal grandmother had been alcoholics as well. He became aware of the extent of alcoholism on reservations throughout the country and particularly among the Sioux. Among the factors responsible were the use of alcohol as a means of exchange between whites and Native Americans in past centuries, the economic and social conditions of a conquered and humiliated population, prohibitions that made drinking seem attractive and encouraged binge drinking, and an attitude of tolerance for drinking on the reservation. Also, there were genetic and psychological factors that predisposed the children of alcoholics to become alcoholics themselves.

During the 1970s, scientists were just beginning to understand the phenomenon of fetal alcohol syndrome (FAS), which affects the offspring of women who drink liquor during pregnancy. Adam's mother was one of those women, and Adam exhibited most of the classic signs —facial abnormalities, a small head circumference, premature birth, developmental disabilities, and other neurological impairments. Dorris recalled similar facial abnormalities among youngsters he had seen on the reservation, and he journeyed to the Pine Ridge Reservation in South Dakota to talk with Jeaneen Grey Eagle, the director of a drug and alcohol rehabilitation center there.

Grey Eagle painted a bleak picture of alcohol abuse in her community. Most of the young people in the rehabilitation program suffered from FAS or from fetal alcohol effect (FAE), the milder form of the syndrome. Even youngsters who were not impaired intellectually suffered emotional disabilities that Dorris characterized as "bad judgment," an inability to see beyond the immediate reality. Grey Eagle estimated that one-quarter of the children on her reservation were victims of FAS or FAE; at least half of the adults were problem drinkers.

Dorris received a grant to study FAS among Native Americans, and in the course of his research he discovered that most of the mothers of

FAS children were in their late twenties or thirties. According to Phil May, a sociologist in New Mexico whom Dorris interviewed, a woman's body gradually loses its ability to process alcohol quickly enough to protect her unborn child. Many of the FAS mothers had more than one child affected with the syndrome, and some women had given birth to four or five impaired children. The explosion of FAS babies was a relatively recent phenomenon, for historically, Native American culture had frowned on female drinking. The women's movement helped to change people's attitudes, and women began to be perceived as equals in the bar as well as in the workplace.

Both Grey Eagle and May outlined for Dorris the catastrophic consequences of FAS. A new generation of impaired children was reaching childbearing age. Without much sense of the future and of the consequences of their actions, these children were at high risk for alcoholism, drug abuse, and promiscuity. The number of FAS children would increase exponentially. May, a white sociologist, proposed more government programs to educate young people about the effects of alcohol abuse during pregnancy. Grey Eagle, a Native American, went even further, arguing for the incarceration of pregnant women to guarantee their abstinence and "the survival of Indian people." Alcoholism is not a victimless crime, as Adam's existence testified. That left the question of the government's role. Should the government engage in draconian measures, such as forced sterilization, the licensing of parents, or the incarceration of pregnant women? Was it a woman's right to determine what she could do with her own body, even if inside that body was a new and fragile life?

In 1981, Dorris married Louise Erdrich, a former student in the Native American Studies program at Dartmouth and an aspiring fiction writer. She adopted Dorris's three children. Adam accepted her as his new mother, but in the book's foreword, which she authored, Erdrich questioned the extent to which Adam understood what being a mother meant. Adam attended a special high school for developmentally disabled youngsters and worked in supervised settings, but had difficulty holding down a job. His coworkers took advantage of his simple and trusting nature, and he often became the victim of cruel jokes. Dorris recalls the agony he and Louise experienced trying to decide whether Adam should be sterilized and how their son could be persuaded to accept the operation. He concludes his story with a conversation he had with Adam on his son's twenty-first birthday. Adam said he was now old enough to drink legally. Dorris had to convince him not to drink, but he knew that nothing he said would be sufficient for a young man who had virtually no comprehension of the results of his actions.

The final chapter of *The Broken Cord* is Adam's own version of his story. It is an account of the facts of his life, as he remembers them. They are a mass of details without any organizing theme or sense of awareness of his situation. At the same time, it is an impressive effort, showing a great deal of persistence and determination on the part of a severely impaired teenager.

The Broken Cord is a moving, emotionally draining work that raises many troubling issues and provides few answers. In telling his family's story, Dorris employs the techniques of a good novelist, using vivid detail to help the reader understand what Adam is really like. The tender moments between a father and his eldest son are revealed as they travel through South Dakota in search of their common heritage. Evident also is Dorris's frustration as he refuses to accept his son's limitations and tries to make him into something he will never be. Finally, the reader empathizes with his profound sadness when he comes to realize that the boy he loves will never love fully or enjoy what is most beautiful in life, but will instead "forever travel through a moonless night with only the roar of wind for company."

Dorris is also a social scientist, and in presenting the results of his investigations, he helps his readers to understand the phenomenon of fetal alcohol syndrome and its effects upon the Native American community. Here he raises important questions. To what extent are an oppressed community and its members responsible for their actions? What obligation do those in the majority have, given policies in the past that encouraged alcohol abuse among Native Americans? At a time when the Supreme Court is debating the right of a woman to abort her fetus, Dorris adds another dimension—that the fetus's "right to life" is the right to a full and healthy life. Should women's rights be restricted to guarantee the full rights of unborn children? Should women who do drink be encouraged to abort or accept sterilization rather than give birth to children whose quality of life will be severely diminished? Some of these questions Dorris raises; others are raised by the reader of this thought-provoking work. There are no easy answers.

Lyn Miller-Lachmann

A CARELESS WIDOW AND OTHER STORIES

Author: V. S. Pritchett (1900–   )
Publisher: Random House (New York). 164 pp. $16.95
Type of work: Short stories
Time: The present and recent past
Locale: London and various locations outside the city

Six stories that recount the foibles and desires of people in their everyday lives—lives sometimes tinged with the unusual and the oddly mystifying

Lionel Frazier, a hairdresser, is on a holiday at a resort hotel on the English coast. As "A Careless Widow" opens, Lionel, a man who prefers to be alone, meets Mrs. Morris, the widow who lives in the apartment below his. Mrs. Morris and her son are staying at one of the villas in the town but taking their meals at the hotel. Lionel is put off by encountering Mrs. Morris because he likes his privacy—he spends most of his time on holiday walking the countryside and the cliffs nearby. Mrs. Morris, a woman who talks too much, has become chummy with Lionel because he does her a favor from time to time. As far as Lionel is concerned, women arrive at his shop tousled and complaining, and they leave transformed, equipped for the hunt once again; this is all they are to him. But despite himself, Lionel begins to tell Mrs. Morris things about himself. He finds that he would like to talk with Mrs. Morris and her son about the terror he experienced walking along "the Coffin," a large rock jutting out from a cliff, with a steep path to the sea. At one point, Lionel considers climbing down the path but is afraid. When Lionel meets Mrs. Morris and her son, the young man tells Lionel that when he was a child he and his mother climbed the path by the Coffin. Lionel is truly surprised by this bit of information. The next day, Lionel and Mrs. Morris meet at the hotel; she has had her hair cut, and Lionel sees her with different eyes. She tells him that she may be moving from her flat, and Lionel is bothered by the news. He does not like change, even when it means that Mrs. Morris will be out of his life. As Mrs. Morris leaves him, Lionel sees her as another garrulous fragment of ordinary life going about its business. He is afloat in space, and beneath his feet he begins to feel the cold of an empty flat.

In "Cocky Olly," Sarah, a teacher, reflects on a time when she was fourteen and met the Shorts: Major Glanville Short; his wife, Emma; and their son, Benedict. The Shorts live next to Sarah's family in the country outside of London. Sarah's father claims that on weekends, guests at the Shorts' swim naked in the swimming pool. Sarah decides to find out for herself about the Shorts and their guests. She climbs through the hedge between the properties, something she has done before, but never on a weekend. Getting through the hedge has always excited Sarah—somehow the air seemed freer, the smells different. All that Sarah sees, however, are several men and women sitting in chairs on a long veranda or on the lawn—no sign of naked people or a swimming pool. One summer afternoon, while Sarah is in the Shorts' meadow, she hears a gunshot, and Benedict Short, about Sarah's age, asks Sarah for her help with a bird he has shot but that is still alive. Shortly after they get to it, the bird dies and they bury it. A storm comes up, and the two take shelter at Benedict's house. Sarah changes her wet clothes for some of Benedict's, is invited to tea, and spends time with the Shorts' guests. To pass the time indoors, everyone plays a game of hide-and-seek called "Cocky Olly." Sarah, who has never seen so many people at one time talking their heads off, is flabbergasted. She and her family keep to themselves; doors are always shut at Sarah's home. At the Shorts', all doors are open and names fly about. On purpose, Sarah leaves her wet clothes behind so that she will be able to return. The next day, Sarah is back, and she and Benedict go out to the meadow; on impulse, Sarah kisses Benedict. Sarah and Benedict ride the train together to and from school. One day, some of Benedict's schoolmates start taunting him, and he and Sarah jump on a train as it leaves the station. The train is an express train and will not make their usual stop. Once the conductor finds them, he arranges to put them off at the first available stop and notifies their parents of their eventual return. While Benedict and Sarah are waiting for a return train, a detective makes Benedict prove his identity because they are looking for a boy about Benedict's age who sent his parents over a cliff in an automobile.

In "A Trip to the Seaside," Alfred Morton Andrews, a widower of sixty-five, retired from the carpet trade, is looking for a wife. His search takes him to a seaside town, home of his former secretary, Louisa Browder, whom he has not seen since she walked out after they had a row five years ago. When he arrives at her address, Andrews encounters her sister, Sarah, who does not like him in the least. When Andrews finally gets to see Louisa, he finds that she is different yet the same. Louisa tells him that she is married, with a stepson. She rejects Andrews's notion of their getting together, telling him that he missed his chance five years ago when, together at a trade show, Louisa wanted something to happen between them, but Andrews dropped the ball. The next day when he went to Louisa's hotel room to tell her that her sister had been trying to reach her by phone, he found her with another man. Angry and hurt by this discovery, he called Sarah back and made an excuse for Louisa's not being able to call her sister. Sarah called him a liar, and Andrews blurted out that she was with a man. Now, five years later, Sarah tells him that she is glad that nothing ever happened between him and Louisa. Sarah drives Andrews to the train station, and Louisa goes off to meet her husband.

Miranda and Philip, two of the main characters in "Things," lead quiet, settled lives. Philip is a semiretired engineer. For years he and Miranda lived abroad without a home of their own. Now, in the southwest of England, they love their own home. One day, Miranda's sister, Rhoda, who has lived in Italy for years with her lover, Sammy, arrives in a car loaded with her things. She and Sammy are thinking about settling in England and going into the antiques business. After their parents died, Rhoda and Miranda divided their parents' possessions. Rhoda (and Sammy) sold all of their things except one painting. Miranda and Philip proudly display their possessions in their home. Rhoda announces that she plans to sell the painting to start her antiques business and would like to have them sell a painting they own along with hers. Miranda and Philip refuse. Rhoda says that she will be off early the next morning on an antique-scouting trip. When Philip gets up after Rhoda has left, he checks to be sure that she has not taken the other painting with her. Miranda thinks of her sister as one of those old village people who seem to be made of weather rather than flesh and blood—now here, now gone.

In "A Change of Policy," Paula, a woman of taste who is prudent about money, is visited by George Southey, who wants to find out why Paula no longer works at their former company. Paula tells George that new management pushed her aside, and rather than take ill treatment, she left. Now she does a bit of translating and reads to an old woman who is blind. Southey tells Paula that his wife, Ethel, had a stroke and has been in a coma for two years; his son, Harry, is away at school. At dinner, George confesses that he wants to be Paula's lover. Paula refuses, despite the fact that she is tempted. Paula considers taking a job in Munich, and when she mentions this to an elderly woman who had spent time there, she tells Paula that Paula's sister had an affair with a German, the same man with whom Paula had been in love years before and had hoped to marry. Paula visits George's wife at the hospital, then agrees to George's proposal. They spend a few months together as lovers, and Paula is liberated by the experience. Then, suddenly, George is killed in an automobile accident while on a business trip to Frankfurt. Paula, when she gets the news, feels as though her life has been torn out of her. In time, George's wife comes out of her coma, and she and Paula share a house in Sussex, with their memories of George.

In "The Image Trade," Pearson, a writer, is having his photograph taken by Zut, a famous photographer. Zut arrives at Pearson's home. A man of few words, he sets Pearson up in the book-clogged room where Pearson works. Pearson would prefer one of the more smartly decorated rooms in the house. As the photographer focuses, the writer ponders whether the photographer has got him. His soul, he feels, spreads all over his body; his face is nothing. The only time Pearson and his face exchange a word is when he shaves. Eventually, when Pearson sees his portrait, he realizes that monosyllabic Zut has the touch of Bosch about his work.

It is easy to be deceived by the seeming effortlessness of V. S. Pritchett's stories. They appear to be trifles, but they all resonate with a fission, an iciness, an edge. In "Things," Rhoda is a strange bird, and one does not know which way she will jump. People act in odd and yet beguiling ways. Lionel, in "A Careless Widow," is both repelled and attracted by Mrs. Morris. In "A Change of Policy," Paula, a woman of probity, realizes that her last chance for freedom may lie in an affair with George Southey, a man who pops in on her after an extended absence and wants to be her lover. In "A Trip to the Seaside," Alfred Andrews's hubris is quite amazing when he wants to take up with a woman whom he has not seen in five years. But these characters are not losers in the conventional sense—they are people trying to get on with their lives. They may consider taking short cuts, but their malice is at a minimum.

Perhaps Pritchett's tenderest story is "Cocky Olly," in which a mature woman reflects on the central experience that awakens her to the variegated texture in life. Sarah's contact with the Shorts helps her to realize that there are lives in which doors are open and names do indeed fly about. And even as these stories are filled with a sense of life's joys, there is a quality of fear and sadness to most of them. George dies in an auto accident, and Paula's happiness ends; she then befriends her lover's wife. Lionel is terrified by the cliffs and the sheerness of the drop to the ocean, yet he walks above the sea continually. The complacency of Miranda and Philip's life is shaken by Rhoda's brief and unsettling visit. Pearson, the writer, has to give himself over to the strange, hulking photographer, who will not be denied in truly capturing the writer's soul. At this point in his long and distinguished career, V. S. Pritchett is unnerving in his ability to draw deft vignettes that reveal much about human motivation.

Louis Sasso

CARIBBEAN

Author: James Michener (1907–   )
Publisher: Random House (New York). 672 pp. $22.95
Type of work: Novel
Time: The pre-Columbian era to the present
Locale: The Caribbean Sea

The political, racial, and economic history of the Caribbean as seen through a mix of historic and fictional characters

> *Principal characters:*
> Don Hernán Ocampo, the emissary of the king of Spain, sent to the Caribbean to investigate Christopher Columbus's rule in Hispaniola
> Sir Francis Drake, the fiery English naval commander and foe of the Spanish presence in the Caribbean
> Henry Morgan, the famous leader of the Caribbean's buccaneers
> Sir Hugh Pembroke, the scion of a family of wealthy Jamaican plantation owners and leader of that island's sugar interest
> Horatio Nelson, the famous English naval hero as a young man
> Toussaint L'ouverture, the leader of Haiti's revolutionary movement

Caribbean, James Michener's latest panoramic historical novel and his thirty-first book, begins with the island of Dominica and the destruction of the peaceful Arawaks by the warring Carib tribes. From there the scene moves swiftly westward, to the Maya outpost on the coastal island of Cozumel. Ix Zubin, widow of the high priest who served the Temple of Fertility and a learned woman in her own right, is determined to teach her sixteen-year-old son, Bolón, the history of his people's former greatness. Embarking on a perilous journey, they arrive first at the abandoned city of Tulúm, traveling eastward to the sacred land of Chichén Itzá. Learning of the chaos in their destination city of Mayapan, they join with a group of fellow wanderers and travel through the jungle to the great ruins of Palenque. It is there that Bolón sees for himself the great wonders of his Mayan ancestors. Returning with his mother to Cozumel, he is offered as a human sacrifice before he can realize his dream of reviving that greatness.

It is but a few years later that Christopher Columbus, searching for a route to the Far East, finds himself on the island of Hispaniola (Haiti and the Dominican Republic today). Many years later, upon hearing rumors of corruption and persecution by the great explorer, King Ferdinand orders an emissary, Don Hernán Ocampo, to Hispaniola to investigate. There, listening to the often conflicting testimony of the island's residents, he begins to understand the complicated, and sometimes tortured, life of Admiral Columbus. In the end, although absolving Columbus in his report, the king becomes aware of the dangerous precedent the Spanish have established in Hispaniola and the Caribbean.

In the chapter "The Spanish Lake," Michener blends real and imagined personalities to chronicle the details of the incessant feud between the Spanish and the English for control of the Caribbean. In this duel, which takes place from 1567 to 1597, the Spanish governor Don Diego Ledesma battles the English commander Francis Drake on the isthmus of Panamá, on ports along the coast of South America, and at the huge harbor of San Juan in Puerto Rico. Their most climactic battles, however, are waged at Cartagena, the walled capital of the Caribbean Spanish empire. The long conflict, which ultimately consumes both of these gallant opponents, marks the beginning of the end of the Spanish influence in the Caribbean.

The story shifts to the island of Barbados and the fortunes of the Tatum brothers. Isaac and Will Tatum, inheritors of a small parcel of land, are a study in contrasts. Isaac, ambitious, hardworking, and greedy, rises steadily as a farmer, accumulating land and slaves and investing in the soon-to-be profitable sugar trade. Will, on the other hand, is unpredictable, adventurous, and honorable. Following a slave revolt and a falling out with his brother, Will leaves the island and its accelerating troubles for a life of adventure and pirating on the high seas. Upon his return he takes his nephew, Ned Pennyfeather, under his wing, and the two join up with Henry Morgan's infamous buccaneers. Will develops and sustains a hatred of all things Spanish, whereas young Ned is married and becomes an innkeeper in Port Royal, Jamaica. Will, meanwhile, after several brushes with death, eventually settles down in the Spanish city of Cartagena where, ironically, he becomes the companion of a handsome Spanish widow.

By the 1730s, sugarcane is the dominant and most profitable crop in the Caribbean. Jamaica is the center of sugar production, and the Pembroke family the controllers of what, in England, is known as the "Sugar Interest." The Pembrokes, like many plantation families, are represented in Parliament, thus ensuring the continuation of their very profitable business. The youngest of the Pembrokes, John, is eventually assigned to a Danish plantation in St. John, but that island is destroyed by a murderous slave rebellion. Returning to England, he defends, with the rest of his family, the plantation owners' Sugar Interest before an increasingly hostile public. In the end, it is the powerful plantation owners who are victorious.

(

"A Wedding in Nevis" tells the sad and often frustrating tale of Horatio Nelson's younger years. Although he would one day gain heroic distinction at Trafalgar, his formidable abilities as a commander are overlooked as he gains a reputation for meanness and intractability. Constantly seeking a wealthy wife, he eventually blunders into an ill-advised marriage; unable to secure a seagoing assignment, Nelson reluctantly turns to farming. It is only years later, when England is once more at war, that his abilities are called upon again.

With "The Creoles" Michener explores the profound implications of the revolution in France for the Caribbean in general and for the island of Guadeloupe in particular. Paul Lanzerac, a French colonist, is the center of the tale, and it is his peculiar fortune to be loved by two beautiful Creole women, both of whom he loves in turn. The developing romances are left unresolved as he travels to France to continue his education. It is there that he learns of the turbulent passions that are about to plunge his country into turmoil. Returning to Guadeloupe, still undecided as to which girl he will eventually marry, he adopts the side of the French monarchy. When the monarchy is overturned, the envoys of revolution, led by Victor Hugues, extend their reign of terror to Guadeloupe. Lanzerac has made his choice by now, the other love of his life going on to lead the Creole rebellion. Lanzerac and his wife are eventually guillotined, as are a number of the wealthy landowners throughout the island.

By the end of the eighteenth century, France's portion of Hispaniola —St. Domingue—is the world's most profitable, and beautiful, colony. For the free coloreds, caught between the disadvantaged blacks and the wealthy whites, the events in distant France portend the possibility of new freedoms. The island's whites, meanwhile, are fearful of such prospects. By 1791 the island is convulsed by rebellion as contradictory edicts are issued from France. The emergence of General Toussaint L'Ouverture as a powerful black leader heightens the tensions, and despite the efforts of Napoleon's generals to return the slaves to their plantations, the eventual black victory proves inevitable.

"Martial Law" continues the story of the black man's struggle for equality in Jamaica. Here, despite the great advances in abolishing slavery throughout the world, the imposition of martial law in the mid-1860s, following rebellions in cities throughout the island, results in the mass slaughter of innumerable blacks. As was the case in Haiti years before, a seeming paradise is turned into a living hell. It is in this chapter that Michener reveals the ugly attitudes held, and written about, by Alfred Tennyson and Thomas Carlyle.

In the last four chapters, Michener explores the Caribbean through the eyes of a Trinidad scholar, a Detroit newspaperman, a fervent

Rastafarian, and a contemporary black academic who unwittingly stumbles upon a strange world where zombies walk. Throughout, it is always the Caribbean Sea itself, and its chain of island jewels, that emerge as the novel's most central, and enduring, character.

Given the vast number, size, and popularity of James Michener's books, it is remarkable that he did not decide upon a writing career until he was past forty; equally intriguing is the fact that, at age eighty-two, he is still producing compelling works of both breadth and quality. As is often the case with Michener's sprawling historical novels, *Caribbean* opens in the distant past, employs a diverse range of characters, and continues into the present. While never a literary stylist, Michener employs a consistent, workmanlike brand of prose throughout, the resultant narrative carrying the reader across a vivid landscape covering more than 500 years. Meticulous with his research, Michener employs a considerable number of historical personalities along with his fictional characters, including compelling portraits of Sir Francis Drake and Horatio Nelson. Once again, this particular type of novel employs characters who are propelled through history by their sometimes indistinguishable descendants, the resulting continuity serving to link major events. It is only in the later chapters, where ordinary people are used to relate more contemporary events, that the story begins to wane. As he has proved so many times previously, Michener is at his best when describing great people engaged in great events or quests. With his effective dramatization of one of the world's most bitterly contested, and culturally diverse, regions, Michener, with *Caribbean*, has produced a work that will stand with his very best.

Bertie Sweet

CAT'S EYE

Author: Margaret Atwood (1939–   )
Publisher: Doubleday and Company (Garden City, N.Y.). 446 pp. $18.95
Type of work: Novel
Time: 1950s to the present
Locale: Toronto

A successful, middle-aged artist who returns to her hometown of Toronto for a retrospective of her work, reassesses her childhood and her passionate, destructive relationship with a friend

Principal characters:
ELAINE RISLEY, a successful artist
CORDELIA, her childhood friend and tormentor
GRACE, another childhood friend whose life Elaine admires
CAROL, Elaine's first girlfriend
JON, Elaine's first husband

Elaine Risley hates Toronto. She hated it when she was young for its puritanism and its emphasis on rituals and traditions that left her, and her unorthodox family, out. She hates it now, as an adult, in all its glittery superficiality. And her feelings for her childhood home are, she recognizes as she walks the streets as an adult, colored by a year or so when she was nine and lost some part of herself to Cordelia, the girlfriend she was destined then to obey and try to please. "That bad time you had," her mother calls it many years later, a vague reference to something neither understood.

Before the family moves to Toronto, Elaine is happy. She, her mother, and her brother travel around the Canadian woods with her father, an entomologist who gathers data on insect infestations. When he receives a university appointment, the family settles in the suburbs and Elaine and her brother, Stephen, start school. Stephen, as unsocialized as Elaine, nevertheless fits right in with the simpler, less conniving boys. Elaine has different standards to meet. In the world of little girls, a best friend is necessary to survive, and there are rules and allegiances that are all unspoken and quite incomprehensible to a thoughtful and naive child such as Elaine.

Elaine's first acquaintance is Carol Campbell, who latches on to Elaine because they ride the same bus to school. Elaine never particularly likes Carol, but she has longed to live like other little girls, her ideal drawn from school readers, and Carol will do. She has clothes, toys, and what Elaine considers a proper life.

Carol's other friend, who unhesitatingly adopts Elaine, is Grace Smeath. Grace is a year older, with long braids, and has a mother with a heart ailment, who must spend part of every afternoon lying on a couch while the girls play quietly in the basement. The threesome works well enough for a while, and as she learns to play little-girl games, Elaine assesses what she had missed before:

> I see that there's a whole world of girls and their doings that has been unknown to me, and that I can be part of it without making any effort at all. I don't have to keep up with anyone, run as fast, aim as well. . . . I don't have to think about whether I've done these things well, as well as a boy. All I have to do is sit on the floor and cut frying pans out of the *Eaton's Catalogue* with embroidery scissors, and say I've done it badly. Partly this is a relief.

This acceptable if boring pattern changes with the arrival of Cordelia, a wealthier child who seems more knowledgeable than the other three. Cordelia is the boss, and immediately Elaine is completely in her thrall. Before long Elaine becomes the victim.

Elaine's "bad time" begins one afternoon when the girls are pretending that Elaine is Mary, Queen of Scots, and they bury her in Cordelia's backyard. There are boards over the hole, which Cordelia has been digging for some time, and as they shovel the dirt on top of the boards Elaine can hear them talking. After a while, Elaine realizes they have gone away. "When I was put into the hole, I knew it was a game; now I know it is not one. I feel sadness, a sense of betrayal. . . . When I remember back to this time in the hole, I can't really remember what happened to me while I was in it. I can't remember what I really felt." The episode is never referred to again, but afterward Cordelia and the other girls begin trying to "improve" Elaine, devising elaborate punishments for her and explaining that she is simply not measuring up. The instigator is always Cordelia—Carol and Grace never do anything but follow her lead.

For the next year or so, Elaine's "punishments" grow progressively more severe. Elaine has taken to going to church with Grace, searching for some elusive quality of goodness that she thinks Grace has, and having Sunday dinner with the Smeaths. Two key events finally bring her dependence on Cordelia and the discipline to an end.

One Sunday, Elaine overhears Mrs. Smeath and her sister Mildred discussing her. They too, Elaine learns, find faults in her that she is unaware of. Even worse, they know the girls are finding ways to punish her. " 'You don't think they're being too hard on her?' says Aunt Mildred. Her voice is relishing. She wants to know how hard. 'It's God's punishment,' says Mrs. Smeath. 'It serves her right.' "

Instantly, Elaine hates Mrs. Smeath, whom she used to admire for her orderly household and mysterious heart condition. She had thought that what was going on was secret, but Mrs. Smeath has known and approved all along. Elaine stops praying in church with Grace. She has lost confidence in God, and once again feels excluded.

Shortly after this episode, as Elaine and the girls are walking home from school, Elaine commits the sin of laughing when Cordelia falls down in the snow. It was not a malicious laugh, because Cordelia had been playing, and Elaine thinks the fall is a play fall. Explanations are useless, and in any event she is given no time to explain. Her punishment this time is to fetch her hat, which Cordelia has snatched from her head and thrown into the ravine.

There is an old wooden bridge over the ravine, which the girls cross on their way home from school. The ravine is legendary, deep, dark and supposedly full of unspecified bad men who do undescribed violence to little girls, and they are forbidden to go down into it. Even worse, the water in the ravine flows out of the cemetery. It has dead people in it, Cordelia had announced earlier.

Elaine considers disobeying Cordelia this time. For an instant, they are both aware of that possibility. She goes down into the ravine after all, because if she goes home without her hat, she will have to explain why. Moreover, she is afraid of making Cordelia angry. Once in the ravine, she slips through the ice into the frigid, waist-high water, and when she looks up at the bridge the heads of her friends, visible over the railing, have vanished. The reader learns, much later, that they ran to Elaine's house and told her mother she was being kept late at school as punishment for rudeness.

It is clear to the reader that Elaine comes close to freezing to death in the ravine, although to the adult Elaine the episode is still mysterious. Elaine as a child has a vision that she decides is the Virgin Mary, in a black robe with her heart visible, glowing like a coal, outside of her body. The vision floats down from the bridge and tells Elaine she can go home, that it will be all right, and Elaine manages to pull herself out. The next time she sees her friends, as they try to find some new punishment for her, she walks away. "It's like stepping off a cliff, believing the air will hold you up. And it does. I see that I don't have to do what she says, and, worse and better, I've never had to do what she says."

From the point on, Elaine's life proceeds on a course she would consider ordinary. She makes new friends, goes through puberty, dates boys. And she renews her friendship with Cordelia, who has undergone some metamorphosis, become sloppy, sullen, with poor grades and an emotional instability that has finally come to the attention of her fashionable family. Now, Elaine is in charge of the relationship. They go where she wants to go. It is clear that Carol and Grace never really mattered to either one of them.

Elaine moves away from Toronto in her late twenties, leaving her failed marriage and taking her young daughter. She has become a moderately successful artist and has been adopted by the women's movement, whose proponents find their own interpretations of her surrealist paintings. But the paintings, in truth, are all of Elaine's personal icons. There is a series of Mrs. Smeath on her couch, sometimes naked, sometimes wearing only an apron, sometimes ascending to heaven. There are three women falling off a bridge. And there is a mysterious, black-robed figure floating high above a ravine.

A retrospective of Elaine's paintings allows them to be viewed as a whole, and permits art critics to draw conclusions about the pattern of her work. Elaine's own personal retrospective as she walks through Toronto, sees her ex-husband, and peers down from the bridge into the ravine, awakens repressed memories. There is no pattern that makes sense, however. There is only the knowledge of something lost.

Cordelia, who became a pitiful figure and then disappeared from Elaine's life altogether, made her believe she, Elaine, was nothing. There are blocks of her childhood she cannot remember. Cordelia inflicted damage that Elaine's well-meaning parents could never have prevented. As an adult, Elaine lives a comfortable, happy life. But Cordelia taught her to hold herself apart. This is the cross that she bears as an adult.

Margaret Atwood's disturbing look at childhood covers much more than just little girls' cruelty or how single incidents form adult character. Her approach is more metaphysical. As she explains at the opening of the novel, time is "a series of liquid transparencies, one laid on top of another. You don't look back along time but down through it, like water. Sometimes this comes to the surface, sometimes that, sometimes nothing. Nothing goes away." The reader comes to understand that Elaine's life as a successful, content adult is just one stage. She will always be the little girl buried and betrayed by her girlfriends, the young mother who attempts suicide in her kitchen, the arrogant young artist who tells off her older, manipulative lover.

Atwood's vision is, on the whole, dark. In *Cat's Eye* she manages to convey something profound about the nature of existence in a story that is deeply moving and, surprisingly, funny. The humor arises not out of any lightheartedness, but out of the recognition of common experience. Readers will care about Elaine, however aloof she manages to be, and this novel will help them understand themselves, and in Atwood's world, understanding is enough.

Ellen S. Wilson

CHRISTOPHER UNBORN

Author: Carlos Fuentes (1928–   )
Publisher: Farrar, Straus and Giroux (New York). 531 pp. $22.95
Type of Work: Novel
Time: 1992
Locale: Mexico

The recounting of the amazing things that happen in Mexico during Christopher Unborn's nine-month gestation in his mother's womb

> *Principal characters:*
> CHRISTOPHER UNBORN, the narrator, an unborn child
> ANGEL PALOMAR Y FAGOAGA, Christopher's gypsylike father
> ANGELES, Christopher's long-suffering mother
> DON FERNANDO BENÍTEZ, Angel's uncle, who argues that "only a miracle like the reappearance of the Virgin can save Mexico"
> DON HOMERO FAGOAGA, Angel's uncle, a running-scared member of the long-ruling Revolutionary Institutional Party (PRI)
> CAPITOLINA and FARNESIA FAGOAGA, Angel's cracked old-maid aunts
> THE FOUR FUCKUPS, members of a rockaztec band, friends of Angel and his family
> FEDERICO ROBLES CHACÓN, a young cabinet minister
> MAMADOC, a new virgin symbol created to give Mexicans hope
> ULISES LÓPEZ, a minister-for-life and rival of Robles Chacón
> PENNY LÓPEZ, Ulises's unattainable daughter
> LUCHA PLANCARTE DE LÓPEZ, Ulises's lustful wife
> MATAMOROS "THE AYATOLLAH" MORENO, a writer frustrated by his envy of Angel
> COLASA SÁNCHEZ, a doelike girl
> CONCHA TORO (AKA DOLLY LAMA), an aging Chilean entertainer, Matamoros's lover

It is 1992 in Mexico. The country's foreign debt has reached "$1,492 billion—a pretty sum to celebrate the five centuries since Columbus's arrival and our division and conquest." There live (miserably) 30 million souls in Makesicko—that is, Mexico—City. The air is so foul that the government talks of constructing a massive, purifying dome over the entire place. ("The pulverized shit of three million human beings who have no latrines. The pulverized excrement of ten million animals that defecate wherever they happen to be. Eleven thousand tons per day of chemical waste. The mortal breath of three million motors endlessly vomiting puffs of pure poison. . . .") Of course, anyone who has seen fireworks knows that this—a dome—is impossible.

Mexico is "a narrow, skeletal, and decapitated nation. . . ." To pay the interest on its external debt, it has had to mortgage itself to the foreign tourist and oil industries (the territory of the Yucatán has been ceded to Club Méditerranée). Mexico, then, is "only a kind of ghost of its ancient cornucopia-shaped self."

Into this "world beyond anarchy" is conceived Christopher, who is more than just precocious: He is observing and perceiving even before he is a gleam in his parents' eyes. His day of conception is memorable. As his parents roll together on the sands of a private beach in Acapulco, "from the heavens it rains. . . . Over their heads flew a pair of buttocks like the trembling wings of an uncertain bat. . . ." It was Angel's Uncle Homero Fagoaga, fleeing by parasail from the guerrillas, defecating in his terror. From this incident alone, Christopher knows he is a special kid.

His parents, Angel and Angeles, have decided to make him on this day in January 1992 particularly, for on October 12, Mexico will celebrate the 500th anniversary of Columbus's discovery of the Americas. And the first male child born at midnight on that day—and whose surname most closely resembles Columbus—will be named the Prodigal Son of the Nation. This honor will bring the child every advantage and power in Mexico.

Why is such a contest—which undoubtedly will spur massive human spawning—being held in a country already spilling its guts with overpopulation? Because *something* must be done to distract the people from their grotesque conditions. It is for this reason also that Federico Robles Chacón, the youngest cabinet minister, created the phenomenon known as Mamadoc. Mamadoc, once a lowly secretary, is the official sponsor of the contest. She has been transformed surgically back into a virgin; she now belongs to no one but belongs to all. She will start an artificial dynasty for Mexico. Never mind that the poor girl only wants to go back to her boyfriend!

It is a while before Angel and Angeles are sure they have made a baby for the Christopher Contest, but in the meantime, Christopher is alive and kicking (albeit minutely) in Angeles's womb and is full of insights about the people swirling in and out of his budding life. His mother is golden; she can do no wrong. She is soft-spoken, and she is tolerant and loving of Angel. She even helps him to foment a mass uprising in Acapulco against the ruling Revolutionary Institutional Party (or, they later wonder, was it the government that did it?); and she moves with Angel after this debacle to Makesicko City.

But Angel, although trying to be a good man to her, cannot help but lust after Penny, the sweet-sixteen-year-old daughter of Minister-for-Life Ulises López, the archrival of Robles Chacón. Angel abandons Angeles in the middle of her pregnancy to live with the Lópezes, sleeping with Lucha, Ulises's wife, in order to try to spend even one night with Penny. He never succeeds in bedding Penny but becomes embroiled in the insurgency of the homeless and downtrodden masses, who go on a rampage to avenge their hatred of those—like the Lópezes —who have "forced into submission or defeated the savage majority, that majority without direction. . . ."

This event, which becomes known as "the night of the Ayatollah," is led by (and named for) Matamoros Moreno, a fearsome writer of a scholarly book who has nursed an envy of Angel that knows no bounds. With this revolution, "Mexico City once again witnessed everything it could bear: only the memory (extinct) of the fall of the Aztec capital or the forgetting (voluntary) of the memory of the earthquake of September 19, 1985, could be compared to this new disaster."

Matamoros, leading the people who surge into the López home and kill Ulises and Lucha, becomes the victorious defiler of Penny, as Angel looks on: "sex was part of the passion and the hope of the revolution for all, in which the perennially frustrated desires of Mexicans would be gloriously brought to fruition: Screw the boss's daughter! Fuck the unreachable princess! Nail Don Ulises López's daughter! Bring the impossible close to the possible in one ferocious and vibrant blow!" Because "the Mexican Ayatollah" has interrupted Minister Robles Chacón's national-morale project, Robles Chacón has Matamoros executed. Despite the removal of this impediment, however, Robles Chacón is learning that one cannot beat the system; something always goes wrong. His problem now? The National Virgin Mamadoc has encircled his knees and said that she is dying of love for him. His long-engineered plans are in jeopardy again!

Angeles now becomes the focus. Angel's aunts Capitolina and Farnesia try to find her, in order to claim her baby for themselves, but she has disappeared! Christopher realizes that a friend of his parents, Hipi Toltec, one of the Four Fuckups, has taken Angeles to a place where, Hipi says, Angel is waiting. Angel, in the meantime, has absconded with his late enemy Matamoros's bastard daughter. They "feel that being a loving couple is more difficult but also more important than having no ties." But he comes to realize how much he needs Angeles.

Christopher Unborn's parents are finally reunited, just in time for his birth on the beach in Acapulco as October 12, 1992, begins. As Christopher experiences "each maternal shake," he forgets more of what he has been telling the reader. He pleads, "READERS, RESOLVE MY DILEMMA: Is it worth it to be born in Mexico in 1992?" As his precognition fades, Christopher, now born, answers his own question: it is "a country of sad men and happy children."

This stream-of-consciousness novel is not just an entertaining story (and a very well-translated one at that). Carlos Fuentes's profane and sly tale of *Christopher Unborn* is also a biting political and moral indictment, not only of the powerful industrialized nations that have facilitated Mexico's slide but also Mexico itself, a country where personal corruption has supplanted the common good. Although the wicked humor, surrealism, and mysticism (common elements of Latin American literature) blunt the sting, Fuentes's anger and frustration are living and breathing to the reader, just as is Christopher Unborn.

Lisa M. Clyde

CITIZENS: A CHRONICLE OF THE FRENCH REVOLUTION

Author: Simon Schama (1945–   )
Publisher: Alfred A. Knopf (New York). 948 pp. $29.95
Type of work: History
Time: The late 18th century
Locale: France

The last days of the reign of Louis Capet on the throne of France, the ensuing violence of the revolution, and its failure

> *Principal personages:*
> LOUIS XVI, the king of France
> MARIE-ANTOINETTE, the Queen of France
> MARQUIS DE LAFAYETTE, a hero of the American Revolution and commandant of the National Guard
> JEAN-PAUL MARAT, a Jacobin regicide
> MALESHERBES, the defender of the King at his trial
> MAXIMILIEN DE ROBESPIERRE, a Jacobin regicide, member of the Committee of Public Safety, and leader behind the Terror

Simon Schama's long history of the French Revolution represents "a deliberate turning away from analytical history towards Events and Persons, both long forbidden, or dismissed as mere froth on the great waves of history." Schama does not see the revolution as preordained by inexorable forces of social change, or as historically determined by impersonal scientific or sociological laws that demote events and persons to anecdotal unimportance. Taking the story out of the hands of sociologists and historical determinists and following the precedent of 19th-century narratives, Schama tells the story as political and personal experience, even at "the risk of being seen as a mischievously old-fashioned piece of storytelling."

Challenging the familiar theory that the revolution marked the painful transition of France from a feudal, bankrupt old regime to "some great change in the balance of social power," and choosing to present his argument in the form of a narrative, Schama claims that there was nothing structurally wrong with the government of the old regime and that the revolution was the result of tensions among the elite on how best to reinvigorate a France that had run up a huge national debt through its many wars with England, including the American Revolution. Schama's narrative argues that the old regime, drowning in oceans of debt and creaking under the weight of the growing cult of Sensibility, with its dramatic emphasis on the natural rather than the tutored, and on freedom rather than discipline, its preference for liberty over authority, spontaneity over calculation, candor over artifice, and heart over head, was unable to create representative institutions that could execute its programs of reform.

In fact, Schama's Louis XVI, an incoherently amiable character wanting to be loved, addicted to the hunt, was an eager but indecisive reformist. "So he got rid of those ministers identified with the muscular absolutism of his grandfather and replaced them with reformers who would somehow conjure up changes that might be both politically liberal and fiscally copious." His wife, the Habsburg princess from Austria, Marie-Antoinette, whom the regicidal Jacobins vilified, visited in 1782 the grave of Jean-Jacques Rousseau, twenty-five miles out of Paris, at Ermenonville, the most hallowed shrine of the Cult of Sensibility.

A procession of reformist governments, one after the other, failed to come to grips with the superabundant institutionalized problems that beset the nation in the days before the storming of the Bastille in 1789, an event that marked the beginning of the end for the monarchy. Schama rejects the idea that French society was so encrusted with anachronisms that it became incapable of modernity, and that the revolution was necessary to smash the old regime to pave the way for the new world. He argues instead that the revolution—with its resulting abolition of space and privacy, its patriotic militarism that was to last for more than twenty years, and its Draconian, coercive egalitarianism, enforced by the guillotine—was an interruption of modernity. Drawing an alarming parallel with contemporary society, Schama writes that "literacy rates in late eighteenth-century France were much higher than in the late twentieth-century United States."

In a brilliant example of the prerevolutionary age that made heroes of scientists and saw the birth of aviation, the steam engine, and the electric battery, Schama tells of a visit Louis made to a special school for the blind the day after Christmas 1786. The king saw twenty pupils, all of whom were blind at birth or in early infancy, reading aloud from books printed in raised relief-print. They identified places and features on maps, sang songs, and played musical instruments. Impressed, the reformist king endowed the school with special funds and scholarships. The Jacobin Terror attacked this school, and others, as "infamous relics of absolutist charity and clerical superstition." The blind children were returned to the streets to become beggars and cursed pariahs.

> The "old regime," then, was not a society doddering its way to the grave. Far from appearing moribund, signs of dynamism and energy may be found wherever the historian looks. From the King downward, the elite were less

obsessed with tradition than with novelty, and less preoccupied with feu-
dalism than with science.

As long as the nation was not beset with an industrial slump and a
disastrous harvest, the monarchy had reasons for optimism about the
prospects of the economy and its future. Those reasons for monarchi-
cal optimism ended when the nightmarish forces of nature devastated
the agricultural sections of the nation in 1788. The cruelties of weather,
combined with internal political dialectics about the direction and failures of the national reforms, unloosed the worst passions. Inflationary
bread prices spelled destitution. As many as one-fifth of the Paris
population received some sort of relief. Schama writes, "The calamity
touched different groups of the population in different ways, dragging
each down to a level of subsistence from which it thought it had safely
escaped."

To add to the difficulties of the paralytic monarchy, the queen fell
into complete disfavor with the French population. She ultimately became involved through the plotting of court intriguers in the infamous
Diamond Necklace Affair.

The violence that characterized the revolution in its later stages
actually, according to Schama, emerged early in the proceedings.
Even after the storming of the Bastille on July 14, 1789, and the lynch-
ing of its governor, whose decapitated head was carried on the end of
a pike about the streets of Paris by the mob, the king remained personally popular, and much of the random violence was done in his name,
albeit without his approval, and for patriotic pride.

From 1789 to the King's failed flight to Varennes in 1791, the revolution underwent a constitutionalist phase. This constitutional phase
sought a new monarchy popularly endorsed, a king energetically working on behalf of his people and not on behalf of the privileged and
aristocratic classes. This constitutional phase of the revolution was no
more successful in setting up representative institutions that would
execute the needed reforms than the old regime had been, or, for the
record, the regicidal Jacobin regime that would come later.

After the king's ill-fated flight to the Austrian border, revolutionary
passion took over completely from revolutionary reason. Louis Capet
was no more the father of his country, but a traitor to France. This
act, done mostly out of concern for the safety of his family, unloosed
a terrible cycle of violence that soon saw all of France besieged with
guillotines.

With the monarchy in disgrace, and the king soon to be guillotined,
the violence escalated. The most violent of the political opposition,
the Jacobins, led by Robespierre, Danton, Hébert, Marat, and Saint-

Just, rose to power and decided to crush the political opposition. Some two thousand citizens, mostly clerics, were executed in a single month in the city of Lyon. When civil war broke out in the provinces, the Jacobin government carried out a scorched earth policy. The worst and most atrocious fighting occurred in the province of Vendée. Paris answered the Vendéan resistance with systematic genocide. Whole populations were exterminated, and the countryside razed, under the rubric of liberty, equality, and fraternity.

In Paris, Charlotte Corday assassinated Jean-Paul Marat, the most violent of the Jacobin leaders. She blamed him for the bloodshed that washed over the nation. Her action did no good. Soon the Jacobins fought among themselves. Ironically, those who had sent so many others to die by the guillotine, were themselves decapitated. Danton, Hébert, Saint-Just, and Robespierre, after a failed suicide attempt that blew off half his jaw, all went to the knife.

The instability of the government and the revolutionary violence continued, to a lesser degree, until the rise of Napoleon. After a complete decade of revolutionary government, the rural poor were no better off than they had been under the old order. In fact, all the progress in industry and commerce that had developed was stopped dead in its tracks by the revolution.

Schama writes, "The French Revolution had, from 1788 onward, been made possible by force of arms, by violence and riot. At each stage of its progress those who had profited from its force sought to disarm those who had put them in power."

Citizens: A Chronicle of the French Revolution is an impressive book, perhaps a touch too long, that challenges much of the popular and conventional wisdom about the French Revolution. For this break with the traditional ways of telling the story of the last days of Louis Capet, Schama should be praised. He has written an interesting book that can only provoke thought and discussion among those who take the time to read it.

John Stevenson

THE CONTROL OF NATURE

Author: John McPhee (1931–   )
Publisher: Farrar, Straus and Giroux (New York). 272 pp. $17.95
Type of work: Essays
Time: The present
Locale: Louisiana; Iceland and Hawaii; Los Angeles

Three essays documenting examples of man's attempts to control the destructive forces in nature

A major theme in fiction is humankind's struggle against the forces of nature. In *The Control of Nature*, John McPhee documents humankind's real-life efforts to triumph over nature in order to preserve home and livelihood. In three essays McPhee describes stunning examples of the ongoing conflict. He first tells of the efforts of the U.S. Army Corps of Engineers to prevent the Mississippi River from changing course; next, how residents of Iceland and Hawaii cope with the lava flow from volcanic eruptions; and last, the steps taken by Los Angeles to prevent its disintegrating mountains from burying its residents.

In the essay "Atchafalaya," McPhee introduces the reader to the Mississippi River in Louisiana through its history. "The river's purpose [is] to get to the Gulf by the shortest and steepest gradient." Over time, the shape of the river naturally changes as silt is carried in the water. The mouth advances; the current slows in certain sections. Before humans were present on the delta, major changes would occur roughly once a millennium. By the 1950s, the flow of water from the Mississippi was ready to shift to the Atchafalaya, a small distributary.

If the Mississippi were to be allowed to shift, however, a large, developed civilization would be destroyed. Baton Rouge and New Orleans, thriving port cities, would no longer be on a major river. The major industrial companies located between them would die or relocate without the river as infrastructure. "The Sixth World War would do less damage. . . . Nature . . . had become an enemy of the state."

To fight mother nature, in 1963, the U.S. Army Corps of Engineers built a navigation lock and a series of complex associated structures. At a site known as Old River, where the water from the Mississippi was most likely to be diverted to the Atchafalaya, a lock was built to attempt to control the flow. But the water constantly threatens to break out of the complex system, either at Old River or in countless other places. Only constant surveillance by the Corps prevents the Mississippi from diverting. To this day, the lock system has weathered many close calls. Floods from the contributing rivers often send threatening vibrations through the system. When McPhee asked a geologist if it is inevitable that the Mississippi will swing to the Atchafalaya, the answer was yes, but this view differs from that of the Corps. So far, the Corps has triumphed.

In "Cooling the Lava," McPhee describes how residents on islands in Iceland and Hawaii marshal their forces to counter the lava flow from volcanic eruptions. The traditional response to an eruption is to get out of the path of flow. The residents of an Icelandic island in the chain called Vestmannaeyjar would not respond traditionally. They waged a war against nature to prevent the destruction of Heimaey, an important port town and a major fishing center for Iceland. The volcanic eruption threatened not only the town, but also the Icelandic economy. They decided to cool the lava with water to stop its flow.

At first the cooling was confined to the lava front; they watered the flow "like a garden" hoping to reduce the heat to "create a wall of chilled lava to dam the flow behind." Unfortunately, the wall needed to be thicker than the one ordinary hoses could create. Bulldozers were needed to flatten the apalhraun, the jagged glass surface of the lava, and make roads for crews to install heavy pipe to carry huge quantities of water to the lava dam. The crust was cool and thick enough—1.5 feet—to support the bulldozers. Inside, the lava still burned red-hot. Water was channeled by the pipes from the ocean to the front of the flow. Many workers came from Iceland, served for forty-eight hours, and returned home. It would take several days to cool the red lava and blacken the lava front. The atmosphere was combatlike. People sustained injuries ranging from afflictions of the throat to severe burns. Helmets were worn for protection from falling ash and volcanic bombs (ejections of molten lava).

While the army pumped water for the advancing flow, the volcano continued a series of violent eruptions. Bombs fell, and ash covered the town. The harbor was threatened by lava that squeezed through a dislodged mountainside. The flow would fill the harbor. The army marshaled its pumps with those of a commercial ship and a local boat. Ship- and land-based pumps battled the flow for five days until a cool lava wall was created.

Other battles were also fought, some won by human beings and some won by the volcano. In the end, the harbor was preserved, although much of the town was destroyed. Previously, "many other possibilities were studied for diverting, slowing, or stopping lava, but, with minor exceptions, they were hypothetical. . . . The Battle of Heimaey was without precedent."

In Hawaii, the state and federal governments also declared war on volcanos. The efforts to do battle, few in number, were unsuccessful. Inspired by the success in Iceland in 1973, the U.S. Army Corps of

Engineers considered building a dam between the volatile Mauna Kea and Mauna Loa volcanos. The dam was intended to create a reservoir where the lava could be cooled before it destroyed property or killed residents. But after evaluation, the Corps decided that Iceland had not won. Too many homes had been destroyed in the fight; they diverted the flow, but did not stop it. The officials opted for a different treatment of the volcanos. The Hawaiian eruptions are studied, but not fought.

In the last essay, "Los Angeles against the Mountains," McPhee describes a third seemingly unstoppable force of nature—debris flows. Los Angeles is situated at the base of the San Gabriel Mountains. From the flat, semidesert area near the ocean, this large, old mountain range rises. At least in part due to the expanding population of the city and in part due to the natural beauty of the area, people choose to live at the base of that mountain range. But the San Gabriels are rising and disintegrating as quickly as any mountains in the world. When a fire and flood occur, the culmination is often descending rocks that threaten property and lives.

The city has attempted to cope with the threatening flow of rocks by digging a series of "one hundred and twenty bowl-shaped excavations that resemble football stadiums and are often as large." Through a system of lined channels and basins, the city hopes to guide and catch the rock flow away from its residents. The basins are amazingly close to populated areas. "Like the freeways, the debris-control system ordinarily functions but occasionally jams." When something gets away, homes are inundated and sometimes people die. A debris flow can almost be predicted. Heavy rainfall is only one contributing factor. At the lower levels of the steep mountains grows chaparral, an impenetrable brush that has a "vital necessity to burst into flame." The seeds that fall from the plant will not germinate except after a fire. The plant is highly flammable with oils and resins that can explode into flame after a long dry season. After a fire there is nothing left but a blanket of fine ash. Fine material from the mountain slides downhill and collects in dry stream beds. The oil from the chaparral makes the hillside water resistant. In the rains after a fire, water collects into a permeable layer of mud and tumbles down. As more water collects, a major debris flow becomes more likely.

Usually, the debris basins work. However, people move to canyons in the mountains where basins are not large enough to accommodate a flow that will be greater due to land development, or they move where there is no basin at all. Amazingly, after a debris flood, the area is rebuilt, often with more expensive homes. Longtime residents become accustomed to the possibility of a flood. If they do not, other people are ready to buy their homes. The collective memory is dimmed by the beauty of the area and the growing population's need for housing. The cycle continues; people rebuild after the mountains slide downhill.

In his three essays, McPhee succeeds in documenting a detailed intimate account of humankind's struggle against the ever-stronger forces of nature. The author succeeds through examples, but also through his personalization of the fight. His use of battle imagery draws the reader into the struggle. He also describes individuals in the midst of battle, revealing how and why they continue to protect their lives and property from nature.

McPhee's prose is clear and concise. His images seem to be taken from the everyday conversation of the local residents. The prose is ordered and matter-of-fact in the description of destruction, mirroring the residents who order their lives for the unpredictable battle.

Often he interjects himself into the essay to further personalize the larger-than-life struggle. His anecdotes reinforce the impression of the individual working against and with nature. He describes his curiosity about and awe of the events. Through his own thoughts he helps the reader to appreciate why people continue to live or work in precarious locations and the spirit that enables them to continue to strive to triumph.

Finally, the book is well researched. McPhee gives historic or geologic perspective to the situations he documents. He places the individuals involved on a time line of events that contributes to an atmosphere of tension and excitement. In the end, *The Control of Nature* is a thought-provoking and exciting collection of essays. McPhee documents the traditional theme of humanity against continuing real-life struggles.

Deborah Ironson

DANGER AND SURVIVAL:
CHOICES ABOUT THE BOMB
IN THE FIRST FIFTY YEARS

Author: McGeorge Bundy (1919–   )
Publisher: Random House (New York). 735 pp. $24.95
Type of work: History
Time: 1938–1988
Locale: The United States and Europe

A retrospective analysis of the events and political decisions that have shaped nuclear policy worldwide in the years since the first atomic bomb portended devastation of the planet

> *Principal personages:*
> NIELS BOHR, a nuclear physicist
> DWIGHT D. EISENHOWER, U.S. president, 1953–1961
> JOHN F. KENNEDY, U.S. president, 1961–1963
> NIKITA KHRUSHCHEV, Soviet premier, 1958–1964
> J. ROBERT OPPENHEIMER, a nuclear physicist
> FRANKLIN D. ROOSEVELT, U.S. president, 1933–1945
> HARRY S. TRUMAN, U.S. president, 1945–1953

The only atomic bombs ever used in warfare were the two dropped three days apart in August 1945 on Hiroshima and Nagasaki. Yet fear of a cataclysmic nuclear war has been the major determinant of international politics ever since and changed forever the way people see their world. Twice in the intervening years, the "unthinkable" veered close to reality: in Berlin beginning in 1958 and in Cuba in 1962. McGeorge Bundy was special assistant for national security affairs at the White House during both crises and so brings to this political history of the atomic bomb a particularly knowledgeable and personal perspective.

Bundy begins with the discovery of nuclear fission in 1938 by two German radiochemists, Otto Hahn and Fritz Strassmann. Credit for interpreting their experimental findings belongs, however, to the physicists Lise Meitner and Otto Frisch, who supplied the theoretical explanation. By their calculations, a uranium nucleus split into two new nuclei would release 200 million electron volts of kinetic energy. Upon hearing this, Niels Bohr, the foremost nuclear physicist of his day, exclaimed, "Oh what idiots we all have been! Oh but this is wonderful! This is just as it must be!"

Scientists around the world hailed the momentous discovery and quickly made a further discovery: the fission of the uranium-235 isotope produced a "chain reaction" of nuclear fission, thus promising a new source of almost limitless energy. Here, also, was the potential for a bomb of hitherto unheard of power.

Why, Bundy asks, did the United States alone develop the bomb? The answer lay in the differing national consensus, political as well as scientific, from country to country. In France, before the Germans invaded in 1940, research was spurred solely by the quest for a way to make a controllable "reactor" for producing energy. German physicists continued to advance theoretical knowledge of nuclear fission but, like the French, focused practical research on useful energy production. Germany's failure to pursue development of a bomb as World War II enveloped Europe seems strange but had several underlying causes, such as an already overextended war effort, Hitler's fixation on World War I weaponry, and the reluctance of the scientific community to hazard the delicate status of Jewish members by closer government relations.

A persistent legend traces America's decision to make the bomb to a letter Albert Einstein wrote to Franklin Roosevelt. Bundy spells out a far more complex process in which British interest in a collaborative effort weighed heavily. The British possessed a secret paper by two German refugees, Frisch and Rudolf Peierls, setting forth an elegant theoretical demonstration of how a uranium bomb could be made. But such a project required the safe location and resources only their American allies could provide.

Roosevelt authorized production of the bomb on October 9, 1941, and by 1942 the famous Manhattan Project was in full swing. Bundy sees the gradual evolution of a politics of nuclear weaponry as having begun with the debates over where to use this awesome weapon. Japan became the target by the coincidence of readiness of the bomb in 1945 and perception of a way to end the war quickly, but there had been agonizing deliberations over the morality of destroying cities. Agreement was finally reached on the military necessity of acting without warning, and Tokyo and Kyoto were ruled out as possible targets for their unifying value in postwar recovery as political and cultural symbols.

Looking back on America's brief monopoly of nuclear power, Bundy deplores the lost opportunity to initiate an international arms control pact. By 1957, when the Soviet Union startled the world by launching the satellite *Sputnik*, the arms race was far advanced and the American public was told of a "missile gap" vis-à-vis the Soviets. Dire predictions of nuclear war came from every quarter, as in the warning from the commanding general of the Strategic Air Command that a Soviet missile attack "could virtually wipe out our entire nuclear strike capability within a span of thirty minutes." In this atmosphere

Nikita Khrushchev launched an effort to end the four-power Berlin occupation, which would eliminate the irritant of American, British, and French troops deep inside Soviet East Germany. His initial demand for a new peace treaty with Germany in six months was deflected by agreement to negotiate (primarily between the two nuclear powers), but Khrushchev continued for four years to exploit the ostensible Soviet nuclear advantage. The end came with the confrontation over missiles in Cuba in 1962, preceded by exposure in Washington in 1961 of the myth of a missile gap. While the superpowers were thus engaged, Britain, France, and Israel were developing their own nuclear capabilities. China became the fifth nuclear power in 1964. Three of these—France, Israel, and China—refused to sign the Non-Proliferation Treaty of 1968 on peaceful uses of atomic energy. This was, Bundy points out, to keep their options open, although it was also indicative of the growing disparities among national nuclear policies.

The years of the Berlin and Cuban crises, a pivotal phase in the formation of U.S. nuclear policy, found two quite different presidents successively in the White House, Dwight D. Eisenhower and John F. Kennedy. Both accepted the crucial importance of the nuclear option in dealing with Khrushchev, but their handling of the crises reflected dissimilar approaches. Aware of Khrushchev's thirst for world stature, Eisenhower sought negotiations but relied for direction on his own cool assessment as former general of the military realities. Sending more troops to Europe was, in his view, hardly the solution—like throwing hand grenades into the streets to protect people from thugs. A nuclear attack was overkill. His guiding principle was, in fact, to stall for time to defuse the situation. His confidence in such a course arose from his firm belief that there was "nothing in the world that the Communists want badly enough to risk losing the Kremlin."

Kennedy took a more adversarial approach, one of his first moves being to increase conventional forces in Europe. Then, in 1962, nuclear war suddenly became an imminent possibility with the discovery by U.S. spy planes of Soviet missiles in Cuba. Thirteen days later, Khrushchev agreed to their removal. Bundy, as national security advisor to Kennedy, worked around the clock at the White House with the president and top administration officials in the feverish race to head off catastrophe. His day-by-day account of those thirteen days is a gripping story of how the successful U.S. strategy was forged and how Kennedy, sometimes with humor, reconciled conflicting advice.

Bundy regards the Berlin and Cuban crises as the evolutionary point at which nuclear *danger* superseded nuclear *balance* (his emphases) in political calculations East and West. The vulnerability of both sides in any nuclear exchange put too high a price on such action. But the place of nuclear capability in deterrence strategies continues to be argued by everyone from government leaders to political activists. Bundy notes three "called bluffs" since 1962 where nuclear force was apparently contemplated—the Sino-Soviet border dispute of 1969, the Yom Kippur War of 1973, and the Vietnam War—taking courage from their nonnuclear outcomes. Indeed, concludes Bundy, the tradition of nonuse of nuclear weapons after 1945 "is the most important single legacy of the first half century of fission."

Danger and Survival: Choices about the Bomb in the First Fifty Years covers a period of worldwide fear without precedent in the history of civilization. For the first time, humankind has had the power to obliterate life on earth. It is hardly surprising to find the political reverberations a still unfolding story, and McGeorge Bundy cautions the reader to accept his account as partly research of public records, partly firsthand knowledge of one critical phase, and partly his personal conclusions to date.

His research is impeccable and exhaustive, assuring *Danger and Survival* a place as durable history. There is also the historical value of his firsthand version of events, but it bears the marks of his predilections. J. Robert Oppenheimer and John F. Kennedy, for example, both receive admiring coverage by an erstwhile White House staffer, and Barry Goldwater gets dismissed at one point as "a genuinely special case among politicians." Of course, such bias adds piquancy.

Some readers may find the au courant nature of the concluding chapters, a virtue in other circumstances, slightly jarring because the ends in 1988. Would Bundy have been less confident of the future progress of arms control if he were writing after the precipitate collapse of Communist rule in Eastern Europe in 1989? Although one might well ponder the answer to this question, among others, the reader is nevertheless grateful for Bundy's brilliant encapsulation of the first fifty years of the nuclear age.

Adrienne Suddard

A DIVIDED LIFE: A PERSONAL PORTRAIT OF THE SPY DONALD MACLEAN

Author: Robert Cecil (1913–   )
Publisher: William Morrow & Co. (New York). 212 pp. $18.95
Type of work: Biography
Time: 1913-1983
Locale: Primarily England; Washington, D.C.; Cairo, Egypt

A university acquaintance and diplomatic colleague relates and analyzes Donald Maclean's background and duplicitous career in the British diplomatic service

> *Principal personages:*
> DONALD MACLEAN, an ideological spy
> SIR DONALD MACLEAN, Donald's father, a Liberal member of Parliament
> MELINDA, Donald's American wife
> GUY BURGESS, a British traitor who disappeared with Maclean
> KIM PHILBY, a British intelligence agent who spied for the Soviets
> ANTHONY BLUNT, a respected member of British society until he was revealed as a spy

Donald Maclean disappeared from sight on Friday, May 25, 1951, throwing the British intelligence world into a panic: for a decade and a half Maclean had had access to some of the highest-level British intelligence information, including nuclear secrets. The conclusion that Maclean had defected to the Soviet Union was naturally horrifying to his superiors, particularly since for some months they had realized that he had been passing information to the Soviets but had not yet moved to pin him down.

Biographer Robert Cecil remains vague on the nature and true import of the secrets Maclean conveyed to the Soviet Union. This vagueness is probably deliberate, for several reasons: there is little proof of exactly what Maclean passed to the Soviets, and Cecil's main interest and major focus in his book *A Divided Life* are to examine why Maclean did what he did. Why would a privileged member of Britain's upper class become an undercover Soviet agent?

For fifteen years Maclean had been granted rapid promotion in the British intelligence machinery. Intelligent, witty, and attractive, he gained diplomatic postings to some of the most coveted embassies in the world: London, Paris, Washington, and Cairo. The British diplomatic service was more than generous in forgiving Maclean a number of indiscretions—social, personal, and professional—during his tenure, failing to realize the serious anger, conflict, and emotional angst in which they were rooted. It is hard to imagine that anyone could get away with as much in the diplomatic corps in this more cynical time. In Maclean's era, loyalty to class and nation was simply presumed; even a measure of Communist sympathy was not considered too provocative.

Maclean's abrupt defection to the Soviet Union in 1951 severely strained Anglo-American relations during the Cold War era. (The British reaction to the event exacerbated the problem: "British reticence in the immediate aftermath of the defection was one of the factors that most exasperated American opinion.") That period in British history has had far-reaching effects on Britain's national psyche and the country's relations with the United States; in fact, it can be argued that U.S.-British diplomatic and intelligence relations have been tainted ever since.

Maclean was one of the group that has come to be called the "Cambridge Comintern," including the now-notorious spies Kim Philby, Guy Burgess, and Anthony Blunt. This affiliation has formed the bulk of the attention paid to Maclean and the others, but author Cecil notes that such individuals' interest in exploring alternative political philosophies and methods of governance had been sparked earlier in their childhood. Indeed, "many undergraduates reached university ripe for recruitment" by Communist agents. Cecil explains that for this inter-war generation, there was none of the sense of security and certainty that governed the early lives of their parents. Massive unemployment and social and political turmoil were everywhere visible; in that more innocent time, then, it is not too surprising that despair and cynicism were common among the members of the elite class coming of age in the 1930s.

Cecil does not discount the importance of Maclean's university experience, but his writings indicate that probably the most pivotal influence in Maclean's political and ideological development was his father, Sir Donald Maclean, a Liberal member of Parliament: ". . . there can be no doubt that the relationship had an important bearing on the son's development and thus in his conversion to communism and recruitment into Soviet espionage." Forty-nine years old at the time of his son Donald's birth, Sir Donald was a busy, powerful lawyer and public figure, bound to be intimidating to children well versed in respect for their elders. He expected big things from his sons and brooked no argument from them, even in light of the changing social and political times.

> [Young Donald] had a loving relationship with his mother, but as his interest in politics increased and his views diverged more and more from those of his father, some tension was inescapable. His eldest brother, Ian, was

more easy-going than Donald and less politically orientated, but even he found his father self-righteous and intolerant of disagreement. Regular church- or chapel-going, family prayers and bans on Sunday games, and on alcohol and tobacco on all days, had been familiar features of life in nonconformist households before 1914. Such restrictions in the freer atmosphere of the 1920s, however, were less easily tolerated by the younger generation.

Maclean eventually becomes what Cecil characterizes as an "ideological spy." Donald was not seduced into spying for the Soviet Union by greed for money, by thrill seeking, or by blackmail—common reasons today. In the 1930s, when he was at Cambridge and then joined the British diplomatic service, the Soviet Union represented a new hope, a new way of life. Its political philosophy gradually became, in a way, almost a religious ideology for Donald. "Maclean with his ambivalent attitude towards his stern father and his Presbyterian upbringing, was both repelled and attracted by the discipline implicit in [the Soviet] creed. Attainment of his ideals required discipline, but he also had bodily needs, connected with sex and alcohol, which were in conflict. This tension exacerbated the split in his personality. . . ."

Maclean inflicted hideous damage during his life, not only to himself and his country, but also to his friends and family. The individual to suffer the most tangible effects and psychological ramifications of his double life was Melinda, his wife. A young American, she met Donald in Paris in 1939, early in his career, and married him in 1940, even though she was already aware of his temper, sexual ambiguity, and difficulty with alcohol. Despite indifference and numerous separations, until his death in 1983 Melinda remained caught up in Maclean's agonized and agonizing orbit.

As a so-called political refugee in the Soviet Union, Maclean assimilated to an unusual degree, working, learning Russian, and hoping to "instill into advanced students a clearer grasp of the realities of international relations." His relationships with other British defectors, his wife, and his children occasionally fell into shambles. Maclean, however, never abandoned his Marxism, despite the inefficiencies and inadequacies of the Soviet system, which he, always a clear-headed and objective observer, could not have helped but notice. He was, after all, an ideological spy.

Author Robert Cecil attended Cambridge University about the same time as Donald Maclean and worked with him at various times in the diplomatic service. Their similar backgrounds and long acquaintanceship serve great value in *A Divided Life*, for at the heart of the book is a close, knowledgeable analysis of Maclean's childhood and his personal and class values. While Cecil's natural, easy familiarity with the ins and outs of the British intelligence world and diplomatic service may prove difficult to those readers who have not previously explored this era in British history, his surprising empathy—even sympathy— for Maclean is very affecting. In this thoughtful and insightful biography, Donald Maclean is portrayed not only as a self-absorbed, amoral political tool—a spy—but also as a victim of a confusing time, a rigid class, and a private mental torment.

Lisa M. Clyde

THE EMPEROR'S NEW MIND: CONCERNING COMPUTERS, MINDS, AND THE LAWS OF PHYSICS

Author: Roger Penrose
Publisher: Oxford University Press (New York). 466 pp. $24.95
Type of work: Science

If flexible human brains indeed incorporate nondeterministic quantum-level activity in producing insights that transcend the limits of systematic computation, computers can never possess "minds" capable of conscious thoughts and feelings

Following Martin Gardner's foreword, mathematical physicist Roger Penrose asks, "Can a computer have a mind?" Although he provisionally accepts British mathematician Alan Turing's proposed "thinking" test, he flinches when artificial intelligence (AI) extremists say that computers will someday not only mimic but possess consciousness. American philosopher John Searle's "Chinese Room" thought-experiment dramatizes the difference between manipulating symbols and understanding them—in contrast to the "strong AI" view of individual human consciousness as only a software program running on the brain's hardware.

Early in this century, German mathematician David Hilbert wondered whether there is a universal algorithm (a series of predetermined procedures for performing a computation) for solving *all* mathematical questions. In response, Turing imagined an infinite number of rudimentary machines, each performing one from a list of every conceivable algorithm. His hypothetical "Universal Turing Machine" can, given the right instructions, duplicate the output of *any* Turing machine. American logician Alonzo Church worked on Hilbert's problem more abstractly and numerically, but both Turing and Church showed that Hilbert's problem is insoluble: no algorithm can be so universal as to include all algorithms that include *it*.

Examining the relation of mathematics to reality, Penrose presents black-and-white maps of a set of mathematical points discovered by Benoit Mandelbrot. The author distinguishes "real numbers" (at least intuitively associated with real-world measurements) from "complex numbers" (mathematical constructs, such as the square root of negative one, unrelated to human experience). He considers mathematical discoveries such as the Mandelbrot set (constructed using complex numbers) "real" in the Platonic sense.

Austrian logician Kurt Gödel's theorem proved that any thorough and consistent formal mathematical system must generate some systemically true statements unprovable within the system. For Penrose, insight transcends and precedes formulation, even as eternal mathematical truth exists independently of discovery or verification. After discussing Gödel-type theorems implied by Turing's result, the author pictures recursively enumerable and recursive sets as algorithmically definable points on either side of a boundary. The Mandelbrot set's curlicued outline may be indeterminate, like certain examples of non-recursive mathematics that require infinite computation to define intricate borders with infinitely greater precision. Complexity theory addresses multiple-variable problems (such as mazes) whose exponentially increased complexity renders them algorithmically incomputable in reasonable time.

In reviewing the development of classical (prequantum) physical theory, Penrose dubs Euclidean geometry, notwithstanding its status as pure mathematics, a "SUPERB" scientific theory describing the physical world of static objects. The dynamics of Galileo and Isaac Newton expanded Euclid's principles to spell out laws governing objects at rest *and* in motion. Unfortunately, in the mechanistic "billiard-ball" world of Newtonian dynamics, predicting the effects of even three balls colliding in a void is incalculably complex. The equations of Hamiltonian mechanics and the multiple dimensions of phase space are ingenious tools for managing the complex data needed to track particle movements. In the 19th century, newly detected and measured forces and effects demanded extensions (such as Maxwell's electromagnetic theory, the wave equation, and the Lorentz equations of motion) to Newtonian mechanics. But new formulations exposed new problems—such as Dutch physicist Hendrick Antoon Lorentz's "runaway particles." To reconcile new observations with Galileo's relativity, physicist Albert Einstein and French mathematician Henri Poincaré developed "special" relativity theory. Einstein's "general" relativity theory combined *curved* Minkowskian four-dimensional "space-time" with Galileo's insights into gravity, yet generated seeming time paradoxes incompatible with classical determinism. Despite such puzzles, the author believes that classical physics is theoretically computable—although demonstrably untrue for quantum phenomena.

Although provocative philosophically, quantum theory arose pragmatically in response to baffling discrepancies between classical physics and experimental results. Each photon of light passing through one of two slits, for example, behaves as a wave (as if it "foreknew" all possible routes)—unless it is "observed" or "measured," in which case it behaves classically as a particle. In the quantum state, an "unobserved" particle seems to exist in two (or more) places at once, occupying every possible location in branching probability amplitudes.

Mysteriously and magically, "detection" at classical scale makes the particle "jump" from its quantum state to a single probabilistic outcome. Quantum behavior is calculated in the complex vector space known as Hilbert space, determining particle spin and mapping Argand-plane vectors on a Riemann sphere. Speed-of-light photon spin is called "polarization." Analyzing objects with larger spin or systems with many particles is extremely complicated. Einstein, Boris Podolsky, and Nathan Rosen intended their "EPR paradox" to underline unsatisfactory features of quantum theory—whose real-world accuracy is nonetheless confirmed experimentally. Having explained Erwin Schrödinger's equation, Paul Dirac's equation, and quantum field theory, Penrose describes Schrödinger's thought-experiment involving a dead-*and*-alive cat. By defying realist and "objective" interpretations, quantum behavior makes some physicists (but not the author) doubt objective reality altogether.

The laws of physics are time-symmetrical, with the seeming exception of the second law of thermodynamics, which dictates a relentless increase in entropy (the randomized "disorder" of a state of thermal equilibrium). Penrose traces low entropy in humans first to plant foods, then to the sun, and ultimately to the initial state of the universe after the "big bang." With all that cosmologists describe about the primordial fireball from which the universe has cooled, still no one knows *why* the second law exists or if it might somehow be time-symmetric. The space-time singularities called "black holes" are inevitable by-products of entropy, and the Weyl curvature hypothesis charts a possible "big-crunch" ending to the cosmos. After computing the rarefied "specialness" (given all possible universes) of this entropic cosmos, the author concludes that many mysteries remain.

Such mysteries, he believes, relate to the mystery of consciousness. He suspects that a much-needed theory of quantum gravity will be time-*asymmetric*. As few physicists appreciate, the state-vector reduction (or quantum leap) *is* time-asymmetric. Discerning a relation between the implications of the "Hawking's box" thought-experiment and the Weyl curvature hypothesis, he speculates that the state-vector reduces when there is a one-graviton difference between superimposed gravitational fields.

Penrose next describes the basic makeup of the human brain, suggesting that consciousness is probably located primarily in the cerebral cortex. Split-brain experiments seem to produce split (double) consciousness. Given the way the visual cortex and single neurons process input, Penrose shows how computers could model the behavior of neurons—were it not for the fact that the brain's ever-changing "wiring" cannot reduce to "logic gates." Dismissing parallel processing as a model for consciousness, he proposes a role for quantum mechanics in brain functions.

Wondering how a self-aware mind aids evolutionary survival, Penrose doubts that a purely algorithmic consciousness could arise by natural selection or lead to nonalgorithmic insights. Inspiration seems to arise whole from the unconscious, then to be judged by the conscious mind. Some thoughts (such as mathematical and musical) are nonverbal, as if in direct contact with a Platonic reality. Here the author touches on philosophical questions of reality, determinism, strong determinism, and the anthropic principle. If the formation of certain quasicrystals requires quantum-level input, he argues, might not thought? Indeed, experiments show that conscious acts and perceptions take a fraction of a second longer than unconscious ones. Science may one day validate man's childlike intuition that consciousness involves something much more than mere algorithmic processing.

In his prologue and epilogue, Roger Penrose recasts the tale of "The Emperor's New Clothes" in the future when a "thinking" supercomputer is unveiled. A puzzled boy asks the computer how it feels—a question the computer cannot even comprehend.

An award-winning physicist and the Rouse Ball Professor of Mathematics at Oxford University, the author of this idea-crammed book is ostensibly arguing for just such a child's-eye view of human consciousness, as opposed to the reductive, mechanistic views of artificial-intelligence zealots. His true subject, however, seems to be the thrill of exploring, chiefly mathematically, the infinite mysteries of physical and Platonic reality. With tireless coaxings and reassurances, as well as his own sometimes whimsical drawings, the congenial author guides readers through hundreds of equation-studded pages devoted to mathematical theory, computer science, physics, cosmology, and neurology.

The persevering reader comes to share Penrose's vision of a surprisingly "magical" universe whose secrets people have scarcely begun to glimpse. Whether or not his specific guesses about time-asymmetric quantum gravity and quantum-level brain activity prove prescient, the author insists that a deeper, unknown reality underlies incomplete theories—and that algorithmic machines can almost certainly never possess self-awareness, emotion, insight, or will. Cosmic yet humane, *The Emperor's New Mind* is a timely call for scientists and philosophers to regain both common sense and a sense of wonder.

Gary Brockman

FARM: A YEAR IN THE LIFE OF AN AMERICAN FARMER

Author: Richard Rhodes (1937–)
Publisher: Simon & Schuster (New York). 336 pp. $19.95
Type of work: Current affairs
Time: The late 1980s
Locale: Crevecoeur County, Missouri

A season-by-season chronicle of one year in the life of an American farming family

> Principal personages (pseudonymous):
> TOM BAUER, the owner of the 337-acre Bauer farm
> SALLY BAUER, Tom's wife, the mother of three, and the book-keeper
> WAYNE BAUER, the Bauers' eldest son, troubled by poor eyesight
> BRETT BAUER, the middle Bauer child, who has difficulty in school
> SAMMI BAUER, the youngest, already involved with the farm

There is perhaps no human endeavor as myth shrouded, romanticized, misunderstood, or just plain difficult as humankind's oldest occupation: farming. It is an occupation that demands a formidable range of skills and experience; not only must modern farmers be familiar with such ancient skills as land reading, crop rotation, animal husbandry, and weather forecasting, they must also possess a daunting mastery of high-tech machinery, chemicals, and genetics. Also, they must be able to wade successfully through an increasingly complicated bureaucracy regarding farm laws and programs. Assuming that one possesses all these qualities, and a good deal of luck besides, the reward—after endless labor and disappointment—is what, in most circles, would be considered little more than a marginal profit. Indeed, despite the best efforts and planning, many farmers are forced either to go out of business or to sharply curtail their planting. In one year alone, in the mid-1980s, 240,000 people left their farms. In Missouri, site of the Bauer farm, 15,000 farmers went out of business from 1984 to 1987. Only shrewd planning, sound investments, and prudent diversification allowed the Bauer farm not only to survive, but also to show a profit of some $20,000 a year.

Tom and Sally Bauer use the six o'clock farm report as an alarm clock. They also use its information—hog, cattle, and grain prices—to plan the day's business. Now, with the harvest season approaching, Tom's principal concern is how to store what promises to be an unusually large crop. Commercial elevators, farm grain bins, river barges, and other facilities nationwide are expected to be filled to capacity. So Tom begins his day at the Comstock Grain Company, hoping that by making early arrangements, he can beat the crowd. He is able to negotiate some space, but at substantial cost, reinforcing the age-old suspicion between farmers and grain dealers. As a precaution, he arranges backup space with one of his brothers.

Once home, Tom begins getting his combine in shape. This is his most important machine; over the next three months, he and his wife will spend more than 200 hours driving the combine day and night through clouds of blowing chaff, mold, insects, and dust, in 90° F heat and 20° F cold. The survival of his crop, and his livelihood, will depend on this machine being in as near perfect working order as possible.

Late in the afternoon, Tom discovers a problem with his hogs. Hog farming is an extremely profitable business, and one that demands constant attention and state-of-the-art equipment. One of his pregnant sows has a prolapsed rectum, a condition that, in the absence of a veterinarian, he must repair himself. On other occasions, he must trim teeth, castrate males, and treat any number of minor ailments. He must also do the same with his cattle, as well as be able to tell which animals are ready at which time for sale.

With corn having to meet federal standards for moisture content, harvest time is a time to be concerned about the weather. A lengthy stretch of rain might not harm the bulk of the corn crop, but it could be devastating for soybeans; the year before, in response to the worldwide emergency resulting from the disaster in Chernobyl, Tom had sold his soybeans—at a substantial profit—before they were even in the ground. These he calls his "Chernobyl beans." If he loses these, he stands to lose a major portion of his yearly income. Waiting out the rain means catching up on the innumerable chores and supply needs of the farm. As the rain continues and the crop begins to deteriorate, the prospects of a bumper crop diminish. As Tom's best friend, Clarence, tells him: "Mother Nature has a way of taking care of surpluses."

Tom begins combining the bottomland corn first, moving on gradually to his other fields. The corn that he and Sally pick is a native American invention, first domesticated some 5,000 years ago in Central America. Today, this "grass distorted to biological monstrosity" is harvested at the rate of 14 billion bushels a year. Unlike most other crops, corn is unable, in its present state, to propagate naturally; without humans to shell and disperse the kernels, the seedlings growing from a fallen ear would smother each other. As a result, corn depends on people as much as people depend on corn.

The harvest is moving along smoothly, despite the rain, when Sally and her daughter, Sammi, hit a terrace with the combine. Tom fixes the machine, refuses to assign blame, and continues. Running a combine over rows of corn requires both brute strength and dexterity. Unlike many farmer's wives, Sally is adept with large machinery. Slick spots, holes, sharp turns, and sudden descents are just a few of the hazards in running a combine, any of which can cause wear or a potentially disastrous breakdown. It is only when Tom has converted the machine to sow soybeans that he experiences his first major breakdown. The repair takes several days and costs over $2,000. Naturally, it occurs at the worst possible time. Philosophically, Tom remembers how his grandfather had said that "machines don't break down when they're sitting in the shed."

Despite the time, rain, and expensive repairs, the harvest is a success. Likewise, the hogs have farrowed, and the best cattle have fetched a good price. Tom has time to think about his children. His oldest, Wayne, wants badly to be a farmer, but suffers from a congenital eye condition that severely limits his vision. Much as he yearns for a son to follow in his footsteps, Tom privately doubts that Wayne's resolve will be enough. His other son, Brett, is having difficulty in school. Tom and Sally attend a parent-teacher conference in which strategies are discussed. Tom knows that the times have changed, that farmers today have to be educated in order to understand the complexities of ever-changing government regulation, chemicals, and genetic breakthroughs. Tom takes it hard when Brett announces that he is giving up farming to join the air force.

Winter on the farm is a time of catching up and mending fences. Animals are tended to, machinery fixed, and days are devoted to attending meetings around the county to learn about the new farm programs. It is also a time for books and taxes. Measuring their crop and animal returns against utilities, fuel, storage, repairs, livestock feed, depreciation, and new equipment, the Bauer family clears a little over $19,000. Farming may be a good life, but it does not make one rich.

Tom knows that spring is coming; there are dead skunks and possums on the roads, and the pastures are turning greener by the week and starting to fill up with calves. He can also sense the new season by the way the chisel plow bites the earth. "The ground's chewy, rubbery." Once chiseling is completed, the drain tiles have to be cleared of obstructing roots. Finally, it is time to plant. Tom plants corn first, because corn has the longer growing season. Soybeans are last. This year, Tom has a new planter, a computerized machine that eliminates waste and provides an accurate count of how many seeds and rows are planted. When he is not planting, he is tending to the calves that are born each spring. This is a dangerous time, for it is not uncommon for cows to have birthing difficulties. With the help of the veterinarian, Tom manages to save both a calf and a cow from certain death, an act that gives him great satisfaction. "I like spring and fall best," he says out of the blue. "You can see where you're going."

Farm is Richard Rhodes's ninth book, and his first since winning the 1988 Pulitzer Prize for his history *The Making of the Atomic Bomb*. By closely examining the day-to-day trials and triumphs of an ordinary farming family, he vividly re-creates the relentless toil, doubt, and rewards inherent to the agriculture industry. It is an industry in which the old mixes with the new, and one in which everyone—no matter how skilled, prepared, or equipped—is at the constant mercy of the elements. Seeds, crops, and animals are living things, as is the soil itself, and the cycles through which the farmer works are not so very different from the ones that govern life itself. Such rewards, however trivial-seeming at the moment, are pointed out, celebrated even, throughout Rhodes's warmly evocative narrative. There are no dull days in a farmer's life, and few restful ones either. And yet, as complicated as it has become, there is always a direction, a goal—seed time and harvest, over and over. It is the endless cycle, the constant renewal in spite of sometimes seemingly hopeless obstacles, that gives this book, and the family it portrays, its power both to instruct and to inspire.

David Alvarez

FEDERICO GARCÍA LORCA: A LIFE

Author: Ian Gibson
Publisher: Pantheon Books (New York). 551 pp. $29.95
Type of work: Biography
Time: 1898–1936
Locale: Spain; the United States; Cuba; Argentina

A biography detailing the life, personality, relationships, and works of the greatest of Spain's poets and dramatists

> Principal personage:
> FEDERICO GARCÍA LORCA, Spanish poet, playwright, musician, artist

Federico del Sagrado Corazón de Jesús García Lorca was born in the village of Fuente Vaqueros on the Andalusian plain ten miles from Granada. His father, Federico García Rodriguez, was a wealthy beet farmer. His mother, Vicenta Lorca Romero, a former schoolteacher, was from a humbler background. Although Federico played with his younger siblings, Francisco and Concha (Isabel arrived later), and numerous cousins, he was not very physically active, due to having extremely flat feet and one leg shorter than the other. Consequently, he developed into an observant, imaginative child. Fascinated by ritual, he would "say Mass" in the backyard; after having been enthralled by a traveling puppet show, he began putting on his own shows. The sensitive boy also noted the contrast between his own family's wealth and the poverty of the other villagers. Lorca's memories of Fuente Vaqueros would inspire much of his writing.

Federico's primary education was dull. He was never to be a good student, but in 1909 the family moved to Granada, which, with its romantic Alhambra, was an education in itself. There Federico began studying the piano, at which he excelled. At ten he entered secondary school, which he later remembered with pain, especially incidents such as the other boys calling him "Federica."

At the University of Granada, two professors were to have a profound influence on the future poet. They were Fernando de los Ríos Urruti, whose socialist idealism inspired Lorca up to the end of his life, and Martín Domínguez Berrueta, who broadened the future writer's appreciation of Spain by taking him, with other students, on study trips throughout the country. Lorca also joined a group of young intellectuals called the *Rinconcillo*, where he made lifelong friends of prominent poets, musicians, artists, and journalists.

When his parents would not allow him to leave the university to study music in Paris, Lorca "turned his creative urges to poetry." In

February 1917, the eighteen-year-old published a short, dramatic piece of poetic prose about Granada called "Fantasía simbólica." That summer with Berrueta, he wrote an article for the local press spelling out his philosophy of art, that "the true artist works by intuition." Lorca's relationship with Berrueta ended when, in April 1918, Lorca published his book *Impressions and Landscapes*, about trips he had taken with Berrueta without crediting the professor with having organized the trips.

In Burgos, Lorca fell hopelessly in love with a María Luisa Egea González. His poems from the following months reveal an obsession with sexual frustration as well as a growing hatred of the repressiveness of the church. He seemed to think that he was unattractive to women, and his letters indicate a new awareness (alluded to in obscure metaphors) of his "difference" from other men.

In the summer of 1919 the impresario Gregorio Martínez Sierra, deeply moved by the young poet's reading of his works, persuaded Lorca to rewrite one of the poems as a play. Martínez Sierra's production of the play, *The Butterfly's Evil Spell*, was not a success. In the fall of 1919, Lorca moved to Madrid, where he was exposed to a rich culture. He was well received in the capital, as evidenced by an early biographer's remark that "the minstrel's success was devastating."

Studying flamenco guitar revived Lorca's interest in gypsy *cante jondo* (or deep song), and in 1922, with the composer Manuel de Falla, he organized a *cante jondo* festival in Granada. Lorca, rediscovering his Andalusian soul, believed that, like the gypsy singers, he possessed *duende*, a "form of Dionysian inspiration always related to anguish, mystery, and death." His involvement with *cante jondo* led to his writing *Gypsy Ballads*, published in 1928 and considered "the most celebrated book of poems in the whole of Spanish literature." In the puppet farce *The Tragicomedy of Don Cristóbal and Señorita Rosita* and *The Shoemaker's Prodigious Wife*, the Lorca play most performed during his lifetime, Lorca used the rich, metaphorical language of the common Andalusians that he had heard as a child.

At twenty-four, having finally completed his law degree to please his parents, Lorca met the eccentric genius Salvador Dalí. The two were immediately attracted to each other, and with the future film director Luis Buñuel and others, they formed a brilliant circle. The friendship between artist and poet deepened and influenced the work of both. During his "Lorca" period, Dalí included the poet's head in numerous paintings, and Lorca wrote his excellent "Ode to Salvador Dalí." Dalí also nurtured the poet's talent for drawing. Fully aware now of his own homosexuality, Lorca sought a sexual relationship with the artist, who repelled Lorca's advances. Lorca, greatly depressed, later felt that Dalí and Buñuel together betrayed him when they made the film *Un Chien Andalou* (An Andalusian Dog), supposedly about the poet. Lorca and Dalí were finally reconciled shortly before the poet's death.

In 1927, after he had tried for years to get it produced, Lorca's historical drama *Mariana Pineda* was a great success in both Madrid and Barcelona, with the famous Margarita Xirgu in the title role. That same year Lorca met the renowned bullfighter Ignacio Sánchez Mejías. Years later Lorca would write his famous elegy for the bullfighter, who was fatally gored in the ring.

In February 1929, Lorca's play *The Love of Don Perlimplín for Belisa in His Garden*, an extraordinary work on the theme of sexual impotence, was suppressed by the dictatorship of Miguel Primo de Rivera. Lorca was depressed about the play, and feeling abandoned by both his lover, Emilio Aladrén, and Dalí, he decided to go abroad, and his father agreed to finance a trip to New York. There he was welcomed by many Spanish friends. At parties Lorca dazzled Americans with his "magic personality," piano playing, and Spanish songs. Lorca also felt an affinity for Harlem blacks, another oppressed minority. Witnessing the great stock market crash strengthened his feelings against capitalism. Although letters home were cheerful, poems that Lorca wrote in the United States reveal a still-profound depression. From New York, Lorca went to Cuba. There he gave lectures to large, receptive audiences and wrote his "Ode to Walt Whitman" and the play *The Public*, an exploration of homosexual love.

Back in Spain, under the Republic, Lorca became the enthusiastic artistic director of La Barraca, a traveling university theater that brought classic Spanish plays to rural villages. To discredit the new government, conservatives depicted La Barraca as a Communist propaganda vehicle. In 1931, Lorca gave a speech in Fuente Vaqueros expounding his belief in freedom of ideas and the coming of a "classless society." Such remarks made him a target for the fascists.

Inspired by an actual event, *Blood Wedding*, premiering in 1933, was the "great work" everyone had anticipated. In the play, a bride runs off with her former lover during the wedding festivities, and the lover and the groom kill each other. The enormous financial success in Argentina of this powerful, dark tragedy at last gave Lorca independence from his parents. The poet himself was also popular in Argentina, where he became good friends with the Chilean poet Pablo Neruda.

Lorca's next play, *Yerma*, dealt with the controversial topic of sterility. Like other Lorca plays, *Yerma* makes the point that the only road to happiness in love is to follow one's instincts. Catholic conservatives found the play "immoral" and "anti-Spanish," while liberals thought it was a refreshingly realistic and moving drama. Lorca had intended his next work, *Doña Rosita the Spinster*, to be a comedy, but according to one critic, it "induced the lips to smile and the heart to grieve." *Doña Rosita* drew on Lorca's own background more than any of his other plays.

The House of Bernarda Alba, Lorca's last play, was a masterpiece. The name of the matriarch of the household was borrowed from a former neighbor of the García Lorcas, and other characters were based on real people. The violent plot, however, was wholly an invention.

In interviews in 1935 and 1936, Lorca was increasingly critical of fascism and more sympathetic to communism. In early summer 1936, reluctant to leave his lover, Rafael Rodríguez Rapún, Lorca resisted Margarita Xirgu's invitations to join her in Mexico, where she was performing his plays. By midsummer it was too late, for the war had begun. To escape the violence in Madrid, Lorca went home to Granada, against his friends' advice. There he was put under house arrest by the Falangists. Frightened, he hid at the house of a poet friend, Luis Rosales, but was apprehended. Federico García Lorca was shot to death as a "red" by order of Commandant José Valdés Guzmán at the village of Víznar on August 19, 1936, exactly two months after he had completed *The House of Bernarda Alba*. The magnitude of the tragedy was expressed by a young friend of Lorca who happened to see him being transferred from the police station in Granada to Víznar. The young man cried out to the soldiers, "You are going to kill a genius! A genius!"

Federico García Lorca: A Life is an extraordinary book about an extraordinary person. Researched over twenty years, it brings to life the odd-looking little poet with his awkward gait, large head, and sad, dark eyes; and the reader comes under the spell of Lorca's *duende*. The reader also shares Ian Gibson's own frustration that Lorca never kept a diary and that more information about his homosexual relationships is not available. The complex soul of the poet remains elusive. Through Gibson's vivid depiction of conditions in Spain in the early decades of this century, the reader gradually becomes aware that Garcia Lorca, the champion of freedom and equality, and his talented, idealistic friends were on a collision course with the implacable conservative elements in the country. Ian Gibson has rendered a fascinating portrait of a poet who created great dramas, the greatest of which was his own life.

Leslie M. French

FELLOW PASSENGERS: A NOVEL IN PORTRAITS

Author: Louis Auchincloss (1917–   )
Publisher: Houghton Mifflin (Boston). 223 pp. $18.95
Type of work: Short stories
Time: 1930s to the present
Locale: Maine; Virginia; New York

A series of character sketches of people who influenced the life of Dan Ruggles, a lawyer and part-time writer, from his childhood, through his school years, and into his law career

> Principal characters:
> DAN RUGGLES, the narrator, a Wall Street lawyer
> AUNT MABEL, his father's sister
> UNCLE THEO, his mother's brother
> LEONARD ARMSTER, Dan's college roommate
> ORLANDO HATCH, a law-school and business colleague
> ALTHEA SARTORIS, a writer
> ADRIAN SCHMUCK, Althea's associate
> GUY HALLOWELL, a scholar
> MOLLY HALLOWELL, Guy's wife
> CLEMENT LUDLOW, a partner in Dan's law firm
> ABEL DONNER, another law partner

Aunt Mabel was the sister of Dan Ruggles's father. As a boy, Dan enjoyed her company and admired her as she interrupted her nursing career to care for family members. She supervised Dan's cousin, Cynthia, as she recovered from pneumonia, and Grandmother Ruggles's recuperation from a stroke, a period prolonged by Grandfather Ruggles's senility. Although she was able to restart her career, other relatives enjoyed her professional services without professional fees. Finally, she nursed Uncle Jonathan until his death, only a year before her own.

Uncle Theo was twelve years younger than his sister, Dan's mother, who was overprotective, especially of her younger brother, never expecting him to do well on his own. Uncle Theo believed in success, however, and went to Argentina, where he made his fortune in cattle ranching. In Argentina, Uncle Theo decided that he wanted to marry Laura, who was already married. When Uncle Theo and Laura did marry, Dan's mother, although she disapproved, gave a cocktail party to introduce the bride to family friends. Laura drank too much, perhaps to embarrass the "stuffy" Ruggleses. Yet Uncle Theo never showed any sign of regretting his choice.

When Dan went to Yale, he roomed with Leonard Armster. Leonard was not from "society," but "by the sheer power of his intellect" he was accepted. Leonard was gifted with words, and Dan wanted to become a writer, so the two tacitly agreed to exchange benefits. Leonard received introductions, and Dan received an education in beauty, Leonard's passion. After Dan left Yale to attend law school in Virginia, the two friends met less often but kept in touch. They met again when Dan went to New York for the engagement party of his cousin Clover and her fiance, Munroe (both friends of Leonard's). Leonard was drinking more than usual and was moody. Dan and Leonard talked and Leonard admitted to being in love with both Clover and Munroe. That same night Leonard died following a fall from a window. When Dan received a suicide letter, he understood that Leonard had chosen to escape a life he did not wish to live, because he did not see it as beautiful.

Dan met Orlando Hatch at Virginia Law School. He was a thorough Southerner—handsome, friendly, and so completely honest he could not understand temptation. Dan and Orlando graduated from law school in 1941 and went into the navy. After the war, Orlando became very successful. Dan introduced him to Zoe, and she and Orlando married. Their only disagreements, as far as Dan knew, were over their only son, Tommy. Orlando felt compelled to protect Tommy from failure. Zoe did not believe Tommy should be so protected. When Tommy came to Dan with the news that he had embezzled, he asked Dan to break the news to his father. Dan was too late; Orlando had known for years that Tommy was a compulsive thief and had made his son take a position in his firm so he could watch him. Zoe also had known and had agreed to let Orlando take responsibility for Tommy's life. Orlando was proud that he had kept Tommy honest for as long as he did.

When Dan met them, Althea Sartoris was a successful writer of short stories and Adrian Schmuck was her self-appointed protector. Adrian admired Althea's work, accompanied her to parties and meetings, stood by when she overindulged in alcohol, and tried to talk her out of changing her style to imitate that of her dead husband, who had written one novel. When Althea married a publisher who thought she could write a great novel, she discarded Adrian. When her novel never materialized, her marriage broke up, and her drinking worsened, Adrian found her in Bellevue Hospital. He rescued her, nursed her, and sold her new works without commission. Ultimately Althea decided that Adrian had been stealing from her, and she broke with him again. Adrian was not hurt by her attitude. He was pleased to have had a part in developing the genius that was "on loan" to her.

Guy Hallowell had a passion for Murray Ogden, an early statesman from Virginia. He lived in Ogden's former home and published "an endless succession" of Ogden's works. Molly, Guy's wife, was a cousin of Dan's mother, and Dan was often a guest at the Ogden-Hallowell house while attending law school. Later, the Hallowells asked Dan to handle their legal business, including Molly's fortune and "elaborate posthumous plans" for an Ogden Foundation. Over the next several years, Dan saw Molly growing alarmed over Guy's identification with Murray Ogden. She was especially hurt at hearing Ogden's views on slavery justified by Guy. Finally, Molly, knowing that she had a heart condition, asked Dan to set up her will to sell the estate at her death, so that Guy would not live there alone, but she died before the new will was completed. When Guy learned of Molly's intentions, he decided to sell the house in accordance with her wishes, yet he was miserable about it. Dan, at the urging of his wife, made sure that the business was postponed. A year later, Guy discovered a tiny hint that Mrs. Ogden disapproved of slavery, and he decided to remain in the Ogden house, issuing the joint papers of Murray and Sophia Ogden.

Clement Ludlow was a partner in the firm of Arnold & Degener with whom Dan worked at a critical time in Ludlow's life. Ludlow was a fifty-year-old bachelor, living with his mother. When he invited Dan to dinner, the conversation stumbled over Mrs. Ludlow's wish that her son would marry. Ann, a charming young girl who had been coming to read to her, would be perfect. Mrs. Ludlow made it too clear for Clement to bear that she talked about this subject to the girl. Alone with Dan, Clement talked about his wish to marry, but he felt he could not act on his wish because "Mother comes smashing in . . . making it so crudely obvious . . . ." Dan urged Clement not to let that stop him, and Clement called Ann that same evening and asked her to marry him. Ann accepted him, but she did not feel comfortable in his world. She acted in ways that he could not understand. She embarrassed Clement by calling him and clinging to him and by her frank statements. At a party given by a senior partner of the firm, Ann was asked to speak. She issued a warning to all present that she intended to get her proper share of Clement Ludlow's life. After their marriage, Dan was less in Clement Ludlow's confidence, but he thought that Ann had gained her end.

Abel Donner was another partner at Arnold & Degener. To Dan, he had "no detectable interest in people or . . . books" or anything other than the law. He represented various members of the Thorne family. Donner had disapproved when Jason Parrish, a young but very successful writer had married into the Thorne family. Jason had first encountered Donner when the lawyer refused to accommodate Mr. Thorne by having a paper notarized without his presence. Fascinated by Donner's rectitude, Jason found a chance to test the lawyer by sending an unnotarized document into a business meeting. Donner suggested that Dan could notarize it, but Dan remembered the first time Jason met Donner and would not allow him this victory. Jason was called in to attest the document.

Fellow Passengers is a collection of short stories as well as "A Novel in Portraits." Each story is a carefully constructed study of a particular character, and each should be read for itself. From each of the unique individuals in Dan Ruggles's life, readers can learn something about themselves and the world. Aunt Mabel accepts her world, even as she exerts herself to overcome the obstacles it places in her path. Uncle Theo places his goals before him and is satisfied with what he achieves. In contrast, Leonard Armster can neither accept nor be satisfied. Orlando Hatch, Althea Sartoris, and Adrian Schmuck are too possessive, Orlando to his own ruin, Althea and Adrian both to Althea's disadvantage.

On the other hand, these stories are woven together around the life of Dan Ruggles. Dan is a man pulled by apparently opposite impulses, some of which lead him to write, others bringing him to study and practice law. As he learns the personal stories of the people around him, he also grows and develops. Eventually, Dan reconciles himself to the two parts of his life, striking a balance that everyone must find for one's own self. This balance is what Guy and Molly had at first, but as Guy became more and more obsessed, the balance was lost, until he found it again in a chance note by Sophia Ogden. Whether Clement Ludlow ever found the right balance in his life, the reader is left to wonder.

Janelle Stevenson

A FIRST-CLASS TEMPERAMENT: THE EMERGENCE OF FRANKLIN ROOSEVELT

Author: Geoffrey C. Ward
Publisher: Harper and Row (New York). 889 pp. $27.95
Type of work: Biography
Time: 1905–1928
Locale: Campobello Island; Hyde Park and Albany, New York; Washington, D.C.

A vivid, unsentimental, sometimes startling biography of the young lawyer and public official who became president

> *Principal personages:*
> FRANKLIN DELANO ROOSEVELT, lawyer and politician
> ELEANOR ROOSEVELT, his wife
> SARA DELANO ROOSEVELT, Franklin's mother
> LOUIS HOWE, campaign director, secretary, friend, strategist of the Roosevelts

On June 7, 1905, Eleanor and Franklin Roosevelt boarded the liner *Oceanic* for a delayed honeymoon in England and on the Continent. Eleanor was the niece of President Theodore Roosevelt (who had given her away at her wedding); Franklin was the son of James Roosevelt, a distant cousin of Theodore. They had been married for nearly three months but had postponed their honeymoon so that Franklin could complete his first year at Columbia Law School.

Theirs was clearly a marriage of opposites. Eleanor, the orphaned daughter of an alcoholic father and a distant, self-absorbed mother, was raised by various relatives. She was extremely insecure, afraid to trust her handsome young husband's constancy, and yearned for emotional intimacy, which her husband was unable to provide. Franklin was exuberant and self-assured, an outgoing, flirtatious young man, who was cut off from his feelings. He had been taught, by his overprotective mother, that unpleasantness of any kind—fear, failure, humiliation, envy, anger—was to be laughed off.

Upon the newlyweds' arrival in Paris, a letter was waiting from Columbia Law School; Franklin had not passed two of his courses. He cabled his mother to have his law books sent to him, without explaining why he needed them. A few days later, in a letter to her "new mother," Eleanor unwittingly noted that Franklin was sad at having failed two exams and would retake them in the fall if possible. When he finally got around to telling his mother (two weeks later), he coupled it with protestations of bewilderment and hints of injustice.

Their first child, Anna, was born in 1906. Eleanor felt inept at housekeeping, and now she felt the same confusion with child-rearing. She hired nurses and relied on a fashionable pediatrician who believed one must "control" babies until they adjust to rigorous schedules. Sara argued with the doctor's severity and told the nurses that, of course, they must comfort a crying child. So began the struggle between Eleanor and Sara over child-rearing. Franklin had an easy relationship with Anna and loved to play with her. Eleanor found a role she could comfortably fill in Franklin's life: she could become his helpmate, taking over the tasks his mother had always performed.

In June 1907, Franklin passed the New York bar exam and joined a Wall Street law firm. All in all, he did not enjoy practicing law. What he learned mostly was that breeding counted less than cunning and that good manners could be enhanced by aggressiveness and the ability to maneuver. He did, however, enjoy the contact with people—many kinds of people he would never have met otherwise—and he became interested in politics.

In 1910, Franklin decided to run for a state senate seat in Pough-keepsie. Eleanor, pregnant again, agreed with him, although Sara was not pleased. The Democratic party wanted him because he was a Roosevelt, his mother had money, and he could swing some Republican votes. His race for the senate was successful, making him only the second Democrat elected from the 26th district since 1856.

Although voters would remember FDR for an early stand as a reformer opposed to the Tammany Hall machine, he was not well liked among fellow politicians, developing a reputation for shiftiness. Over the next three years, the new New York Factory Commission produced a flood of reform bills that would serve as future national models. Franklin voted for them but with little apparent enthusiasm. The needs of his constituents were alien to him. He did, however, support conservation, particularly of forests.

In 1912 he was renominated for the state senate. He hired Louis Howe to manage his campaign and won by a larger margin, running ahead of presidential candidate Woodrow Wilson. President-elect Wilson offered Franklin several federal positions, which he declined until the position of assistant secretary of the navy was offered. (This thrilled him; he was following Teddy Roosevelt's route to the presidency.)

He was sworn in on March 17, 1913, his eighth wedding anniversary, and imported Louis Howe, who became his special assistant. By this time, his sons James and Elliott had been born and another had died in infancy. Eleanor and the children summered at Campobello during these years. Eleanor was unhappy because she saw Franklin only briefly through the summer, and his short stays allowed them little private time together. His mother hovered, the children clamored, and he often brought guests. When the family moved to Washington, Eleanor began an exhausting social whirl. Franklin, however, never tired of it; he was well-liked, and with his charm and self-confidence, he overshadowed her.

After the sinking of the *Lusitania* (with the loss of 128 Americans) in 1915 by a German submarine, prowar advocates called for U.S. intervention in World War I, but President Wilson wanted America to remain neutral. Theodore Roosevelt and others called for greatly increased American armaments and mounted an all-out assault on the administration's military posture. FDR supplied them with ammunition with which to back these charges; he issued a shrewdly worded statement to the press that seemed to support Wilson's stand, but hinted that because the navy was short 18,000 men, thirteen of its second-line battleships were out of commission. He displayed for the first time in public his extraordinary ability to overwhelm his questioners with facts and figures, absorbed through intensive last-minute briefings and retained just long enough to disarm potential antagonists.

Strain between Franklin and Eleanor began to show during the war years. Eleanor was tired of the yachting stories he and his friends always told. He showed irritation when she slipped into his mother's too familiar role of earnest exhorter. The Roosevelts' last child, John, was born in 1916 (Franklin, Jr., had arrived in 1914). Hereafter, Eleanor and FDR would have separate rooms.

Meanwhile, the prospect of U.S. involvement in the war grew. Wilson, buoyed by his 1916 reelection, received congressional approval to bolster U.S. forces, including a fully equipped navy.

That summer, Eleanor was reluctant to go to Campobello, afraid to leave Franklin. She had let go her secretary, Lucy Mercer, suspicious of FDR's interest in her. Lucy then joined the navy and was assigned to work in the same building as FDR. Lucy and Franklin were not always discreet—many seemed to know of their affair, including Eleanor's cousin Alice. In October 1917, Lucy was "relieved of her duties" at the Navy Department by order of the secretary of the navy. She moved, but she and Franklin still saw one another. In September 1918, Franklin, after a summer tour of Europe, became ill with pneumonia. When Eleanor was unpacking his things, she found love letters from Lucy. Eleanor then told FDR that she would willingly grant him a divorce but that he must consider its effects on the children. His mother threatened to cut him off from funds, and Howe reminded him that divorce would end his political career.

Franklin decided to stay with Eleanor, but on November 9, 1918, he tried to resign as assistant secretary in order to serve on active duty. The president refused to accept his resignation, and two days later the war was over. In 1920, still serving in the Navy Department, FDR was nominated to run on the Democratic ticket as vice-president with James Cox, but they were defeated by the Harding-Coolidge ticket in a landslide.

In July 1921, on an expedition to Bear Mountain, New York, with the Boy Scouts, Franklin apparently picked up the polio virus he was to battle for the next seven years. The illness was diagnosed at Campobello, and he remained there for the summer, extremely ill and unable to get out of bed. He returned in great pain to New York in September 1921. He exhibited a stoicism about his condition that continued until his death and a determinedly cheerful attitude toward both his family and outsiders. His limited recovery was slow (he did not stand—in steel braces—until February 1922), but as he made slow progress through the 1920s he resumed his interest and involvement in New York state politics.

Franklin supported Al Smith for governor in 1922 and U.S. senator in 1926 and nominated him for president at the Democratic convention in 1928. With Smith leaving the governorship, the party nominated Franklin for governor. Unexpectedly, he won a narrow victory in the face of Herbert Hoover's triumph over Smith, becoming a major Democratic force.

This fascinating, well-written, enormously detailed chronicle explores twenty-three years in the life of a famous American, and presents both the myths of his career and the facts of his personal and political lives. He was rich, handsome, democratic, and a family man; he was also conniving, a devious politician, and an adulterer. Publicly, he was a young hero, stricken by polio in the prime of his life. But it was his seven-year battle with excruciating pain, his determination to walk again, that mellowed and honed him into the man who became the thirty-second president. Geoffrey Ward has captured the pain and confusion of Franklin Delano Roosevelt and those who were closest to him—Sara, Eleanor, and others.

Jeanne Larrivee

FIVE SEASONS

Author: A. B. Yehoshua (1936–   )
Publisher: Doubleday and Company (Garden City, N.Y.). 359 pp. $19.95
Type of work: Novel
Time: The present
Locale: Israel; East and West Berlin; Paris; Vienna

A man makes the slow recovery from his wife's death to the true beginning of his new life

>Principal characters:
>MOLKHO, an Israeli government employee
>ENAT, his daughter, a soldier
>OMRI, his elder son, a college student
>GABI, his younger son, a high-school student
>MOLKHO'S MOTHER-IN-LAW, a German refugee
>THE LEGAL ADVISOR, a widow from Molkho's office
>THE INDIAN GIRL, an eleven-year-old child
>URI ADLER, Molkho's former youth counselor
>YA'ARA, Uri's wife
>NINA ZAND, a homesick Russian émigré

After a long and unsuccessful bout with cancer, Molkho's wife dies in early autumn. The end comes peacefully, in the night, and Molkho sets about the business of informing the relatives, making funeral arrangements, and ridding the house of all paraphernalia associated with his wife's life, illness, and death. He goes about these tasks with an oddly commercial attitude, pondering how he may best achieve some financial advantage. For example, he agonizes over arrangements for the resale of a large supply of Talwin—a drug that was first prescribed, then contraindicated, for his wife's case. He also makes every effort to resell symphony tickets that he cannot use during the prescribed period of mourning. When this comes to nothing, the thought of all that money going to waste compels him to attend a performance despite the proprieties.

His wife's death was drawn out over several years. Now that it is finally over, Molkho considers what to do about his own life, his sex life in particular. After her initial diagnosis, his wife refused to sleep with him, and she had been the only woman with whom he ever had sex.

Molkho's voyage of self-examination and discovery really begins that winter, with a trip from his home in Israel to Europe. Initially, he visits his wife's cousins in Paris. He then heads for West Berlin, where he has signed up for an opera tour that was the suggestion of a widowed legal advisor from the government office where he works. They

will be staying at the same hotel. Molkho reads this as an invitation to
a love affair, about which he does not seem to have clear-cut feelings.

The legal advisor arrives, but almost immediately falls down the
opera-house steps and sprains her ankle. Molkho falls back into the
role with which he is most comfortable: caring for an invalid woman.
He even manages to buy her some Talwin for the pain, but she takes
one pill too many and falls into a long, deep sleep. Molkho is virtually
widowered a second time. He walks the wintry streets of West Berlin
alone to pass the hours. Molkho's wife was born in Berlin, leaving
Germany with her mother after her father committed suicide, just before World War II.

When the legal advisor does recover, she goes off by herself. When
he tracks her down in a beer hall, she charges Molkho with having in
effect killed his wife little by little. He does not understand her malice
but knows that any chance for an amorous liaison is gone.

In the spring, official business takes Molkho to the small village of
Zeru'a, to investigate incidents of possible financial malfeasance.
There he meets the most incongruous object of his desire imaginable,
an eleven-year-old Indian girl. His fixation allows him to treat the
affairs of the village more tolerantly than otherwise. Like his abortive
encounter with the legal advisor, his passion for the Indian girl goes
unspoken and unconsummated. Almost as fascinating to him as the
girl herself is her father, who is obviously ill when Molkho first calls.

Molkho's obsession sees him through the runaround he gets trying
to track down Ben-Ya'ish, the young man responsible for the village's
convoluted finances. Even though he relishes the opportunity to make
repeated visits to Zeru'a, nothing distracts him from the exacting calculations involved in maximizing his expense account.

Finally he manages to meet with Ben-Ya'ish, and Molkho's sympathetic disposal toward the village glosses over the juggling that the
former has been doing to keep things going there through some bad
times. Certain items for which Zeru'a received government funds—
the construction of a park, for instance—have been deferred in favor
of using the money for more immediate community needs, such as
support for those members temporarily unemployed. Business settled
and the girl none the wiser, Molkho departs.

Summer brings Molkho a bizarre offer. He is contacted by Uri
Adler, his old youth-group counselor. Uri has become an Orthodox
Jew, and as such has been encouraged by his rabbi's group to divorce
his wife, Ya'ara. Ya'ara has had one miscarriage after another, and
tradition demands that Uri have children. What Uri proposes is that
Molkho marry Ya'ara after the divorce.

Molkho tries to remember Ya'ara and whether he was ever in love with her. He convinces himself that this was indeed the case and agrees to go along with Uri's idea that the two of them spend a weekend together, just to see whether they ought to go ahead with the divorce/marriage plan.

Ya'ara comes to stay on a weekend when Molkho's three children —Omri the college student, Enat the soldier, and Gabi the high-school boy—are all away. Ya'ara is a remarkably passive person, taking the initiative in nothing. Molkho is equally reticent, not wishing to rush things.

He continues to justify his lack of action to himself as the weekend drags on, although in his mind he is already taking command of the new wife he has had wished upon him. He decides that he will get her to dye her hair, use makeup, learn to drive, get herself a better job. Still obsessed with sickness, he considers that a woman of her type does not easily succumb. Unrealized fantasies, however, do nothing to advance him with Ya'ara. They do not sleep together, and in the end she goes back to her husband. The episode leaves feelings of uneasiness and lack of fulfillment on both sides.

Autumn returns, and with it a mission for Molkho, at his mother-in-law's behest. A friend of hers from the old-age home where she lives is a Russian émigré. The woman's daughter, Nina Zand, had accompanied her mother out of Russia. Now, however, she has found herself unable to adjust to life in Israel and is miserable. She wishes to be repatriated. As a favor to his mother-in-law and her friend, Molkho agrees to travel to Vienna with the young woman in an attempt to get her readmitted to the Soviet Union.

Molkho is highly critical of Nina, privately annoyed by everything about her, from her plump, rabbitlike appearance to the fact that she can barely speak a word of Hebrew. As she is equally unversed in any of the other languages Molkho speaks, theirs is a very silent partnership.

The official whom Molkho contacts in Vienna about Miss Zand's problem is not very encouraging. Legal channels offer her no hope for repatriation, despite the fact that her old employers in the Soviet Union have sent word that she can have her former position back. In an uncharacteristic burst of initiative, Molkho formulates a plan.

He takes Miss Zand to West Berlin, intending to get her back into Russian-occupied territory via East Berlin. Once more Molkho finds himself staying in the same hotel in West Berlin that almost a year ago witnessed his romantic debacle with the legal advisor. There is an added complication this time, for the hotel is so solidly booked that Molkho and Nina must share a room and, therefore, a bed. Even this enforced intimacy does nothing to break Molkho out of his celibate mold. The only effect it has is to make him feel all the more uncomfortable.

Eager to set his plan in motion, he escorts Miss Zand through to East Berlin, where they go to the Anti-Fascist War Memorial. Inside, she approaches a middle-aged couple and begins to speak to them, probably explaining her plight. Molkho removes himself, afraid of becoming involved. He slips into the street and eventually goes back to the West Berlin hotel to await word. None comes for a long time, so he returns to East Berlin where he at last tracks down his wife's old house. It is an incomplete pilgrimage that brings back the familiar malaise that seems to dog Molkho's every initiative. Even as he stands on her street, he wonders what ever possessed him to seek it out.

He returns to the war memorial and then to the West Berlin hotel where a vague message from Miss Zand tells him that they have taken her. He arranges for the storage of her trunk at the hotel and flies home.

He is met at the airport by his daughter, Enat, who tells him that his mother-in-law has broken her arm and is hospitalized. The prognosis is not good—once lively and intellectually active, the older woman has sunk into a definite decline—but here at least Molkho is back on the most familiar territory of his life. He goes to the hospital and despite his recent journey insists on sitting up all night beside his mother-in-law's bed. When he does leave, in the early hours of the morning, he reflects that memories of his dead wife seem to have gone. If nothing has replaced them, if he has failed to find another significant woman in his life, he realizes that this is because a man needs to be in love.

Five Seasons skillfully plots the geography of loss. Even though Molkho's loss was long anticipated—the sort of death conventionally considered a relief to the survivors—he must still work himself through an even longer process of letting go. While at first glance it is hard for the reader to think of the petty, penny-pinching Molkho as a vessel for grand passions, this in no way detracts from the reality of his grief. Perhaps, the author suggests, those losses which are more dramatic are those from which one recovers more quickly. Nor is it enough to make a rational decision to get on with the business of living: the heart, too, must consent.

Esther M. Friesner

FOR LOVE & MONEY: A WRITING LIFE, 1969-1989

Author: Jonathan Raban (1942–   )
Publisher: Harper & Row (New York). 344 pp. $22.50
Type of work: Literary criticism
Time: The present
Locale: England, with short jaunts to other countries

Jonathan Raban describes how he became a writer and how he maintains himself as a writer, and includes previously uncollected fiction, portraits of family life, literary criticism and book reviews, and travel pieces

For Love & Money, divided into five sections, is partly Jonathan Raban's account of his rise as a professional writer and partly a collection of pieces documenting that rise. It begins, as it must, in childhood with the inevitable mistake of the young, and sometimes not so young, whose dreams have little grounding in reality. "I was a writer. More precisely, I was an author. For writers, or so I supposed, actually did quite a bit of writing, moving fast from one piece of paper to the next. Authors were as immobile as waxworks. They sat at desks in photographs." In this world Raban invents an alter ego, Jim, and reinvents his childhood experiences in more dramatic and glamorous terms.

Raban's pitiful, unrealistic, and quite ordinary notions of writing and being a writer were shattered when he read, at sixteen, Joyce's *Portrait of the Artist as a Young Man*. That book, and the many to follow, including William Empson's *Seven Types of Ambiguity*, made him realize that his previous notions of reading and writing were doomed with the bathwater. In his early twenties, Raban began teaching and published his first book, a textbook called *The Technique of Modern Fiction*. He took a lectureship at the University of East Anglia, where he was appointed junior to novelist Malcolm Bradbury, who told Raban that the way to overcome the difficulties of free-lancing for a living was to diversify. Raban took the words to heart and soon began writing television plays and book reviews for the *New Statesman*. In his late twenties, Raban gave up teaching after he had "had a six-month run of lucky flukes, and times were flush. The idea of living in London and writing for a living—writing *anything* for a living—possessed me completely."

Section II describes Raban's life in London in 1969 when book reviews paid his rent. Raban discusses how the reviewer, with his license to read more freely and widely than the academic, is in a position to gain a sense of the broad proportions of things that few academics can rival. The difficult task of the reviewer is "to capture a good likeness in as few strokes as possible, with the stamp of his own style in every line, to be vivid, intelligent and impossibly concise." Raban speaks incisively and authoritatively about how the reviewer must accomplish this task and still do justice to the book being reviewed despite the trend toward shorter reviews and fewer review pages in newspapers and magazines.

The greatest part of Section II consists of Raban's own literary reviews of books by and about such writers as Lord Byron; Henry Mayhew; and William Makepeace Thackeray, whom he calls "the cleverest (which is not to say the most intelligent, by any means) novelist in English" and whose "strongest talent was for impersonation." Of Anthony Trollope's relationship with the reader, Raban says "he is a chronic flirt, trading on with flattery, professions of intimacy, hints of secret collusion. Then, the trap is sprung, and the reader finds himself left cruelly alone, with only brute paradoxes for company, in a world as morally icy as any in English fiction."

Mark Twain is the only 19th-century American writer examined by Raban. In discussing Twain's great travel book *Innocents Abroad*, Raban highlights "Twain's genius as a writer for mocking what he revered and for maintaining a sneaking reverence for what he mocked" and "his continuous verbal playfulness, his somersaults of tone, his implicit trust in the contradiction as the most truthful sort of utterance." Raban has more difficulty expressing critical insights with *Huckleberry Finn*, which he calls "incomparable." Despite the presence of establishments such as the Huck Finn Shopping Center and the Mark Twain Pet Center in Hannibal, Missouri, Raban is still able to recover some of the magic landscape he discovered when he first read the American classic at age seven. Raban's best-known book, *Old Glory: An American Voyage*, recounts a journey on the same grand river that flows through Twain's book.

Evelyn Waugh, whom Raban compares to the American cinematic artist Harold Lloyd, is one of the modern writers discussed. "Lloyd's simplicity, his air of being an inexpressive waif at large in a monstrous world, comes very close to Waugh's characteristic posture in his novels." Another is Anthony Powell, of whose chef-d'oeuvre Raban says, "For all its charm as an epic of beautifully orchestrated gossip, there is a shallowness at the heart of *The Music of Time*, an absence of anything that could be called a moral intelligence."

Raban seems to find modern American writers more interesting than their 19th-century counterparts. In reviewing her *Collected Stories*, he says that Eudora Welty "is the one Southern writer whose gifts are comparable to those of Faulkner. Her imaginative concerns run in close parallel to his. If she lacks Faulkner's unapproachable stature, she far outreaches him in humour, tenderness and exactitude." While he says nothing of great interest about Saul Bellow or John Updike, Raban is insightful about Tom Wolfe, whom he calls "the crowned king of fabrics, prices, status symbols and class manners," and Robert Lowell. In panning Steven Gould Axelrod's *Robert Lowell: Life and Art*, Raban describes the difficulties of writing a biography of one whose life was so much a part of his poetry and goes on to say that "we can all count ourselves lucky that Lowell happened to be around in our messy stretch of history; more than any other writer he has got down on paper what it feels like to be morally alive in our particular snakepit."

Section III consists of only a few pages and describes Raban's experience writing plays for radio, television, and the stage. The attraction of playwriting is the addition of society to the usual solitude experienced by the writer. But that society—actors, directors, and producers—was also in part responsible for Raban's disillusionment with this form of writing. When one of his plays is produced and bombs, Raban can admit to himself that the play was bad, but the actors "had the much harder job of keeping themselves persuaded that it wasn't."

Raban's entry into journalism is depicted in Section IV, starting with small magazines and working his way to *Radio Times*, the BBC program guide, which he could always count on for an assignment that would send him away from writing troubles at home for a few days and allow him a taste of life he would otherwise not encounter. The seductive promise of instant distraction, publication, and payment had its downside, however:

> The most damaging aspect of feature journalism is the way it turns life into a series of larks. A few days spent in someone else's world (however dismal, violent, pretty or even boring that world may be) is simply not enough to experience it as real. It is too tightly framed by one's own domestic normality. Wherever you are today, you know that next Monday you'll be home, and from the perspective of home today will seem too exaggerated, too highly coloured, too remote to take quite seriously. So the writer slips into a style of mechanical facetious irony as he deals with this wrong-end-of-the-telescope view of the world.

What follows in Section IV are samples of Raban's pieces for magazines. "Living on Capital" is an account of his childhood, particularly his messy relationship with his father, who became an Anglican priest and with whom he now has an easy relationship. "Living with Loose Ends" is about marriage and the family and how they figure into the British novel. In "Fishing," Raban reflects that "the deepest pleasure in going fishing is the discovery that what the pool really holds isn't fish at all but visions, dreams, the stirred-up mud of a life." This piece also contains a marvelous and funny account of fly-fishing with

Robert Lowell, whom Raban calls perhaps the worst fisherman in the world.

Section V is concerned with travel and writing and how unlike a story is a journey. "For travelling is inherently a plotless, disordered, chaotic affair, where writing insists on connection, order, plot, signification." In "The Journey and the Book," Raban argues for the vitality of the English travel book, despite its image of the intruding privileged observer. He says that the one essential condition for travel books, which he calls the supreme improvisatory form, is the experience of living among strangers.

Among the classic travel accounts he discusses is *Eothen* by Kinglake who, "more than anyone, established the voice of the modern English literary traveller." He calls Robert Louis Stevenson's *The Amateur Emigrant* "the best account ever written of the great European adventure in the 19th century, the passage to America, the New World." Modern writers covered by Raban include Hilaire Belloc; J. B. Priestley; and Edmund Wilson, whose depiction of the snobbery, hypocrisy, and insensitivity of the English in *Europe without Baedeker* Raban admits still stings today. Gavin Young's *Slow Boats to China* allows Raban to discuss the pitfalls in writing a travel book, mainly the balance between invention and assertion. Travel books cannot "afford to be simple inventories of everything that happened on the trip. Too many of the events and people in *Slow Boats to China* have earned their place in the book merely because they happened to be there in life."

The book ends, fittingly enough, with Raban's discovery of the *Gosfield Maid*, the 31-foot ketch on which he coasted around Britain and Europe for five years. It is stranded by the tide, unsightly, when he finds it. Much of what Raban describes in this book was stranded, often unsightly, and the reader can be grateful for his retrieval. The pleasure in reading such a book from such a writer is that one is constantly surprised. At one moment the reader is getting "inside dope" about writing book reviews, the next he is watching Robert Lowell flop into a brook while fly-fishing, the next he is watching novelist John D. MacDonald install a "cat-flap" on his bathroom door, and then he is leaning out the window of Raban's London apartment with a sextant and a jeering audience below. Each turn of the page has the potential for the unexpected, and all is described with a precise and often elegant prose.

Charles Agvent

FOUCAULT'S PENDULUM

Author: Umberto Eco (1932–   )
Publisher: Harcourt Brace Jovanovich (San Diego). 641 pp. $22.95
Type of work: Novel
Time: The present
Locale: Brazil; Milan; and Paris

A complex novel of philosophical speculation and occult lore focusing on the quest of a group of editors to discover the secret of a Templar plot to take over the world

> *Principal characters:*
> CASAUBON, the narrator, an editor and expert on the Templars
> BELBO, also an editor, who becomes obsessed with the plot
> DIOTALLEVI, another editor, who finds the Hebrew connection to all things

Umberto Eco, professor of semiotics, philosopher, historian, literary critic, aesthetician, and author of the best-selling medieval mystery *The Name of the Rose*, has presented the world's readers with another complex mystery strewn with nuggets of medieval esoterica and laden with philosophical speculations. *Foucault's Pendulum* is a book that provides the reader not only with an interesting story but also with an education on the occult and a multitude of intellectual diversions. Few will be able to absorb it all in a single reading.

In the first chapters of the book the reader is introduced to the narrator, Casaubon, and to the home of Foucault's pendulum, the Conservatoire des Arts et Métiers in Paris, where the dramatic plot will culminate. Most of the rest of the book goes back over the events that have compelled Casaubon to hide himself in the museum to observe the pendulum for the duration of a night. From the beginning, the reader is told that the story about to be read will be elusive and complex. It will be played out on many different levels, and these levels will not be confined to the strictly rational: "The Salle Lavoisier in the Conservatoire is actually a confession, a confession in code, and an emblem of the whole museum, for it mocks the arrogance of the Age of Reason and murmurs of other mysteries. Jacopo Belbo was reasonably right; Reason was wrong." The reader will be challenged with both symbols and unique modes of thought that are both historic and psychotic.

While waiting in the museum, Casaubon begins to recount mentally the events of the recent past. Two days before, at home in Milan, he had received a phone call from Paris from his colleague Belbo. Belbo announces that he is in trouble and that "the Plan" they had been speculating about and creating over the past years is "real." While on the phone, Belbo is grabbed by others, and the phone goes dead. Casaubon then goes to Belbo's apartment to learn more about why Belbo came to Paris and what has happened to him. First he must discover the password to get into the computer files. It turns out to be "No," which is both a practical response to the computer's question of "Do you have the password?" and Belbo's lifelong philosophical position.

Casaubon and Belbo first became acquainted when Belbo, an editor with the publishing company Garamond, asks Casaubon, a graduate student writing a thesis on the Knights Templar, for his opinion on a manuscript about them. The Templars were a medieval crusading order that rapidly became rich and powerful through their conquests in the Holy Land. In the early 14th century they were accused of homosexuality, heresy, and idolatry. They were disbanded by the king of France, persecuted, and their leader hanged. Since then there have been rumors that they knew many occult secrets, such as how to make gold, and that underground vestiges of the group still survive.

At Garamond, Casaubon is presented to Colonel Ardenti, who claims that his book on the Templars is based on a recently discovered document, incomplete and in code. He claims that not only have the Templars survived, but they also have a secret directorate and are planning world conquest to be realized in the year 2000. According to this document, the Templars, before their public elimination in the 14th century, put in place a plan that would stretch over most of Europe and span six centuries. Until this complex scheme is ready to be put into motion, no one would know the complete plan or who the other conspirators were. After leaving the document with Garamond, Ardenti is apparently murdered.

A few years pass following Ardenti's death. During this time, Casaubon is living in South America, learning about non-Western occultism and the Rosicrucians, themes that will be woven into the unfolding of the plot. When he returns to Italy, Casaubon opens a cultural investigation agency and eventually begins to work closely with Garamond, after being hired to write a history of metals.

It is at this point that Casaubon is introduced to the role that Foucault's pendulum plays in Belbo's imagination. While there are examples of the pendulum in many places, the one at the Conservatoire des Arts et Métiers is special to Belbo, probably because it is in an old church:

> "For those who have no faith, it's a way of finding God again, and without challenging their unbelief, because it is a null pole. . . . Wherever you put it, Foucault's Pendulum swings from a motionless point while the earth

rotates beneath it. Every point of the universe is a fixed point: all you have
to do is hang the Pendulum from it." "God is everywhere?" "In a sense,
yes. That's why the Pendulum disturbs me. It promises the infinite, but
where to put the infinite is left to me."

Belbo's feeling about the pendulum will determine the outcome of the
story.

Besides publishing respectable books, like the illustrated history of
metals, Garamond also functioned, under a different name, as a vanity
press. Given the number of potential authors who believe that they
have been made privy to the secrets of the occult or to secret plots,
the owner of the press decides to publish scholarly books on the occult
and mysterious. These books will, in turn, lure the paying authors
willing to spend a great deal to document their favorite obsessions in
print.

In the process of dealing with all of these hermetic texts, the editors
—Belbo, Diotallevi, and Casaubon—become intrigued with the logic
and the various rites involved with the occult. They meet modern
Druids and many others. As their lives become more and more infused
with the knowledge of the occult, they begin to experience difficulty
remaining strictly rational and to have mystical experiences. They also
turn their attention to unraveling the Templar plot that came so dramatically to their attention years before.

Working on the code in the Templar document begins as an intellectual challenge and soon becomes an obsession. They begin with the
fundamental axiom: "the Templars have something to do with everything," and with the first tenet of hermetic thought, that in the whole
universe there is not a single fact that does not reveal a mystery. From
these two propositions they build and refine in elaborate detail the
outlines of the Templar plan to take over the world in the year 2000.
Into this plan, they work most of the historical events of the last 600
years and decide that the elaborate plan has been brought to a halt by
historical circumstance. The plotters cannot carry out the plan because
they lack the information needed to call the whole group together and
to learn the secret of the Templars that will enable them to control the
world.

Belbo, Casaubon, and Diotallevi then believe that they may have
uncovered the secret of the Templars. According to Belbo, the Templars had learned the critical point—"the Omphalos, the Umbilicus
Telluris, the Navel of the World, the Source of Command"—that
controls the telluric currents of the world. These magnetic currents
can be used to predict and control major weather and seismic events.
It is this secret that has been kept over the past six centuries. It is still
a secret because the map needed to locate the point has been missing.

In the interpretation put forth by Belbo, the hypothetical map has to be put under Foucault's pendulum in Paris at the specific time and date mentioned in the Templar document. The motion of the pendulum will then show where "the Umbilicus" is.

The trouble with the group is that they come to believe their own fantasy. They come to believe that one can arrive at the truth "through the painstaking reconstruction of a false text." Belbo rewrote history and becomes determined to make it come true.

Belbo is kidnapped by believers in the Templar plan who assume that he knows where the map is and that the plan as he has worked it out is true. Casaubon follows the kidnappers to Paris and hides in the museum to rescue his friend and to uncover the plotters. In the occult ceremony at the museum, Belbo is hanged on the pendulum and the kidnappers are frustrated in their search for the map.

The point that Umberto Eco wishes to make in this complex novel is that one cannot bow to the lust for power and to nonmeaning. Belbo ultimately knew that "fragile as our existence may be, however ineffectual our interrogation of the world, there is nevertheless something that has more meaning than the rest." That something is often touched in a single moment in each individual's life when he is at one with himself and his destiny.

Foucault's Pendulum can be rewarding on many different levels of meaning. To merely summarize the plot, which is not the strongest element in the book, is to do an injustice to both the book's wit and its philosophical insights. The ideal reader of the novel will not only leave himself time to savor each of the 641 densely packed pages but will also freely refer to a library of texts on occultism and medieval history. Other readers will enjoy the novel but will be left with the feeling that they have missed much. In summary, the book is difficult but will repay the efforts of the stout of heart and intellect.

Christine Brendel Scriabine

FROM BEIRUT TO JERUSALEM

Author: Thomas L. Friedman (1953–)
Publisher: Farrar, Straus and Giroux (New York). 525 pp. $22.95
Type of work: Current affairs
Time: 1979-1988
Locale: Lebanon and Israel

*A correspondent's "journey" between two neighboring Middle East coun-
tries uncovers similar origins for the Lebanese and Israeli-Palestinian conflicts and examines the obstacles that continue to impede solutions*

> Principal personages:
> MENACHEM BEGIN, Israeli prime minister
> ARIEL SHARON, Israeli foreign minister
> YITZHAK SHAMIR, Israeli prime minister
> SHIMON PERES, Israeli finance minister
> YASIR ARAFAT, the head of the Palestine Liberation Organiza-
>   tion (PLO)
> HAFEZ AL-ASSAD, Syrian president
> FOUAD AJAMI, a Lebanese Shiite scholar
> DAVID HARTMAN, an Israeli philosopher
> ZE'EV CHAFETS, an Israeli writer

From Beirut to Jerusalem can be read in simplest terms as a travel
book, an account of the somewhat picaresque journeys of an American
reporter in an area of the world that is seemingly familiar yet proves
to be totally different from the reader's expectations. In this respect
Thomas Friedman writes in the genre of 19th-century American travel
literature, a type made famous by writers such as Mark Twain. Indeed,
he quotes from Twain's *The Innocents Abroad* in his concluding chapter: "There is the Sea of Galilee and this Dead Sea—neither of them
twenty miles long or thirteen wide. And yet when I was in Sunday
school I thought they were sixty thousand miles in diameter." Like
Twain and other predecessors, Friedman has an eye for the absurd,
for the event or anecdote that vividly describes the life he sees around
him.

The resemblance ends there, however. Friedman is no ordinary observer concerned with conveying the sights and sounds of an exotic
region to American audiences whose knowledge of it differs little from
Twain's. He is a true reporter, committed not only to the clarification
of conflicts that defy explanation as well as solutions, but also to the
debunking of myths. His method is more surgical than analytical, as
he dissects the posturings of a Yasir Arafat, the illusions of Palestinians, the assumptions of omniscience of Israeli leaders, the deadly
power of Hafez al-Assad, the naïveté of American Marines in Leba-

non, and other elements in Middle Eastern situation. As he reports, with the candor that distinguishes this book, civil war in Lebanon and the civil revolt of Palestinians in the occupied West Bank and Gaza Strip bore "little resemblance to the bloodless, logical, and antiseptic descriptions he found in most of his textbooks."

The book is organized in two parts, corresponding to the author's assignments as *New York Times* correspondent first in Beirut and then in Jerusalem. Aside from the differences in legal status between the two, Beirut being Lebanon's true capital, while Jerusalem, spiritually the capital of Israel but unrecognized by other nations as such, the two assignments underline the enormous difference between civil war in Lebanon and civil disagreement in Israel. The first bids to destroy the fabric of a society, while the second seeks to establish the proper orientation and identity of a particular state.

The chapters on Lebanon plunge the reader headlong into the charnel house of modern Beirut, a place where nothing is fixed and coping with survival all but impossible. In good journalistic tradition Friedman begins his account with a graphic incident. A man is kidnapped before his very eyes, as he sits in a taxi caught in a traffic jam. A host of other incidents, anecdotes, and conversations vividly describe life in a city that has lost any semblance of order, with no political center, no rational form of behavior, and random unreasoning violence. (At one point, when the author wonders why Christian artillerymen are shelling a particular place that has no military value, he is told that it is because they have the ammunition!)

As such chapter titles as "Would You Like to Eat Now or Wait for the Ceasefire?" indicate, the Lebanese environment places its people under extraordinary stress. It is a stress that has been going on for fourteen years without letup. Yet the amazing coping ability of the Lebanese shines through the book, providing some hope that humanity can triumph over the worst kind of adversity: mindless violence. As the author notes, "the Lebanese figured out a way to profit from the vagaries of their own anarchy," inventing their own prescriptions to cope with the horrors of Beirut. Stress for them, he says, has become so normal that when peace finally arrives, as it surely must, it will drive them all crazy!

One of the most important chapters in the book is a digression of sorts, but a digression that serves to clarify the underlying sources of these seemingly obscure conflicts and how they have evolved. The chapter is entitled "Hama Rules." In 1982 the Syrian city of Hama was all but leveled by tanks and artillery of the army of its own government, and some 20,000 of its residents were killed. The attack had been ordered by Hafez al-Assad after the discovery of a plot to overthrow him organized by the Muslim Brotherhood, a fundamentalist Sunni Muslim organization opposed to the regime. The Brotherhood's main stronghold was in Hama.

Friedman's reflections upon this singular event provide a useful analysis of Middle Eastern conflicts in general and the Lebanese and Israeli-Palestinian conflicts in particular. Friedman finds three traditions operating simultaneously in the area: tribalism, authoritarianism, and the still-evolving tradition of the modern nation-state. Although it has disappeared nearly everywhere else in the world, tribalism survives in the modern Middle East because Lebanese, Palestinians, Israelis, and to some extent other peoples there have still not broken away from their long-established commitments to tribal unity and solidarity. Their attachment to the modern nation-state, as to whatever regime is in power, remains superficial at best. This fact explains the extreme intensity of conflict among the various Lebanese factions; each faction is essentially a tribe.

Similarly, authoritarianism survives because of the absence of either democratic or legitimate governing traditions. With rare exceptions, today's Middle Eastern rulers are insecure, suspicious of rivals, alert of necessity to threats to their rule. The modern nation-state system, which was imposed upon the region by the British and French after World War I, reinforces this instability. Rulers seek to confirm their authority by whatever means seem necessary, including extreme repression; thus "Hama Rules," which means, in fact, that there are no rules at all. "When the modern veneer of nation-statehood is stripped away . . . one man triumphs, the others weep."

Friedman deals forthrightly with the PLO and its raffish leader Yasir Arafat; with the PLO presence in Lebanon and the 1982 Israeli invasion that it generated; and with the abortive U.S. intervention, which, if nothing else, taught both Israel and the Reagan administration important lessons about involvement in a place they discovered they knew nothing about. The story is a grim and tragic one, but it bears repeating because of its implications for future U.S. policy. Yet the Israelis also misread the signs, assuming they had come with their military might to protect a Christian community surrounded by a Muslim sea, while their leaders, Menachem Begin and Ariel Sharon, sent them into battle out of an obsession with the "pornography" of Jewish power.

The author takes a different tack when he (and his assignment) are shifted to Israel. As an American Jew, he discovers a country very different from the one he visited as a teenager, or sent used clothing to, or thought about as he walked the streets of Minneapolis puffed up with pride over the defeat of Arab armies in the Six-Day War. Instead he finds a nation at war with itself, split over politics as well as its identity and proper mission as a Jewish state. The realities of internal disagreements between Orthodox Jewry and the secular Zionist movement that built the Israeli state are brought out through long conversations with secular Israelis such as Ze'ev Chafets; advocates of a Torah society such as Rabbi Schiller, who would restore liberal Judaism to the land; and redemptionists such as David Hartman.

Perhaps the Israeli tragedy is that, along with the search for their identity and its accompanying divisiveness, they must now deal with the problem of ownership of their national home. The *intifada* (correctly translated as a "shaking up, shaking the dust from oneself, breaking free from someone") has placed an enormous strain, not on the Israeli economy, but on the Israeli self-image, as if they had come under siege in their own home. Here Friedman offers at least some hope—only, however, if Palestinians and Israelis can somehow be brought together long enough to correct the misunderstandings that exist on both sides. The author feels that if any outside power can accomplish this it must be the United States. The naive but wonderful optimism, the bold outlook that still marks America, can be brought to bear in such a way as to jar both sides out of their fantasies. But to do this requires American policymakers to play several roles at the same time: they must be at once obstetrician, friend, grocer, and tough-as-nails hardball player, ready to play by "Hama Rules."

This is an excellent book, detailed and accurate yet constantly stimulating. A more detailed chronology than the cursory one at the beginning would have been useful, as well as maps of both countries and one of the UN Partition Plan for Palestine. But these minor criticisms do not detract significantly from the text.

William Spencer

GEEK LOVE

Author: Katherine Dunn (1945–   )
Publisher: Alfred A. Knopf (New York). 348 pp. $18.95
Type of work: Novel
Time: The 1950s to the present
Locale: The United States

In modern day Portland, Oregon, an incognito Olympia Binewski attempts to save her daughter, Miranda, while narrating the story of her remarkable family's twenty-year travels across the United States with Binewski's Carnival Fabulon

Principal characters:
 OLYMPIA "OLY" BINEWSKI, the narrator
 ALOYSIUS "AL" BINEWSKI, her father, owner of the Carnival Fabulon
 LILLIAN "LIL" HINCHCLIFF BINEWSKI, her mother
 ARTURO "ARTY" BINEWSKI, her older brother
 ELECTRA "ELLY" and IPHIGENIA "IPHY" BINEWSKI, her twin sisters
 FORTUNATO "CHICK" BINEWSKI, her younger brother
 MIRANDA BARKER, her daughter

Olympia "Oly" Binewski lives on the second floor of a boarding house in Portland, Oregon. Her identity is unknown to both her mother, Lil, elderly and insane in an apartment on the ground floor, and her daughter, Miranda, who lives upstairs having no idea that she is related to both her fellow tenants. It is from this venue that Oly recounts the bizarre story of the Binewski family, as she tries to save Miranda from the designs of the appalling Miss Lick in Katherine Dunn's unusual novel.

The Binewski family is a truly macabre creation. Al Binewski is the patriarch and owner of Binewski's Carnival Fabulon, a traveling carnival and freak show. He meets Lillian Hinchcliff during a weekend's stopover near Boston. Lil wins his heart when she volunteers to step in for the regular "geek," who has gone AWOL. A geek, for those uninitiated to sideshow terminology, is an individual who draws great crowds by biting the heads off of live chickens. Soon after Lil's generous and effective debut, the pair are married.

The Carnival Fabulon is facing hard times. Performers, especially freaks, are hard to find, and the number of top-drawing acts is shrinking. In a moment of inspiration, Al and Lil create a plan to literally repopulate the sideshow: they will ingest powerful and dangerous chemicals prior to conception and during pregnancy and breed themselves a family of monsters.

Their results exceed their twisted expectations. Their firstborn, Arturo, has hands and feet attached to his torso without the benefit of arms and legs. He is destined to swim in a gigantic aquarium and preach to the dazed public as "Arty the Aqua Boy." The next successful attempt provides them with the twins, Elly and Iphy, beautiful girls attached at the waist and sharing a single set of limbs and organs from there down. They will dazzle audiences and attract admirers as they sing and play duets at the piano. Olympia is next and is a disappointment to her parents: she is a bald, albino, hunchbacked dwarf with no noticeable talents or attributes. She is encouraged to develop her voice, so that she can succeed as a barker.

The youngest child appears to be the greatest disappointment of all. Shortly before his birth, the other children were shot at by a local named Vern Bogner, who spotted them in a parking lot and felt the need to eliminate them; the family is, therefore, already in an uproar when Lil delivers an apparently normal baby boy. They are on the verge of abandoning the child when he reveals powerful telekinetic talents. The baby is named Fortunato, and nicknamed "Chick." They decide to keep him.

As time passes and the children grow, the family dynamics develop into complex patterns. Arty has the most popular act, and his ego grows to match it. His "Aqua Boy" speeches become oracular, and he begins to include sermons on the benefits of his simpler means of life. He attracts a devout following of hangers-on. Iphy is devoted to Arty and thinks he can do no wrong; Elly is suspicious and watchful, leading to some tension between the twins. Oly worships Arty and is jealous of Iphy. As Chick's talents begin to develop, Arty resents the turn of attention away from himself. Chick is a sweet child who loves everyone equally. Al and Lil are proud of the children, pleased with the reborn success of the carnival, and oblivious to the familial undercurrents, especially the growth of Arty's power over everyone.

The traveling contingent is joined by a menagerie of unusual individuals: Dr. Phyllis, intent on studying the children for purposes of her own, most notable for having performed abdominal surgery on herself; Alma Witherspoon, an enormous woman who has decided that she wants to be "just like Arty," and who fundamentally changes the direction of the carnival; Norval Sanderson, a journalist who smells a Pulitzer Prize story in the making; and C. B. Ford, the fly-roper, whose act consists of lassoing flies with miniature lariats made of human hair.

With these additions, the family dynamics start to change subtly. Arty virtually takes control of the carnival from Al, and he removes Chick as a threat to his power by converting him to a devoted ally. The twins mature physically, and at the same time Oly discovers that

Arty has found ways of satisfying his sexual needs. And Chick's tele-kinetic abilities are refined to an exquisite level.

Two events now take place that will precipitate the downfall of the Carnival Fabulon. First, Alma Witherspoon takes steps to become "just like Arty": she has Dr. Phyllis amputate her limbs. Soon the carnival is followed by hundreds of "Arturan" converts, who start as novices—fingers and toes removed—and gradually build up to the limbs. Chick is able to use his power to assist in the operations. Second, the tour is joined by the "Bag Man," a mute hulk whose destroyed face is covered by a veil (except for the right eye), who becomes Arty's bodyguard.

As the Arturan disciples swell in number, the family tensions begin to crack. Arty learns that the twins have taken to entertaining male visitors. In furious jealousy, he gives them to the Bag Man, who wants to marry them. Lil finally recognizes the Bag Man as the crazed gun-man, Vern Bogner (Arty has known all along), and kills him, but not before he has the chance to impregnate the twins. Iphy wants the baby, Elly does not. Chick, meanwhile, has taken over for Dr. Phyllis, who has become a full Arturan convert. Arty has Chick lobotomize Elly. Oly has Chick telekinetically impregnate her with Arty's seed.

The babies are born. The twins deliver a twenty-six pound blob named Mumpo, who does nothing but eat voraciously, almost evilly. Oly gives birth to a little girl, Miranda, perfectly normal except for a little tail. Arty is contemptuous of such normalcy, and Oly sends Miranda to a convent to be raised as an orphan, out of fear for her safety. Her fears are well-justified. Elly regains enough consciousness to murder Mumpo, whereupon Iphy kills her. Poor Chick, who only wished to stop people's pain, is horrified by the chain of events and incinerates the carnival and almost everyone in it in a massive burst of flame. Only Oly and Lil survive.

Returning to the present, cotenants Oly and Miranda become friends. Miranda is not aware of their familial relationship, but as an art student is eager to have Oly pose for her. While Miranda draws, she tells Oly how she has been approached by the heiress Mary Lick. Miss Lick has an odd hobby: she tracks down women who, in her opinion, are impeded by appearance, and convinces them to have surgery to correct these flaws. Miss Lick has an extensive video li-brary of the women before, after, and especially during the various operations. She wants Miranda to have her tail amputated.

Oly is disturbed by the prospect and is determined to prevent it. Oly arranges to meet Miss Lick, who is fascinated by her deformities, and they become friends of sorts. Oly discovers that Miss Lick is basically just a lonely woman with a kinky hobby. Yet, despite her growing sympathy for the other woman, Oly is determined to protect Miranda. As the time for the proposed operation nears, Oly rigs a trap to poison Miss Lick. The plot goes awry, the women struggle, there is a gun, it goes off, and they both die. The novel ends with a note from Oly to Miranda telling her of her unique heritage.

A simple recounting of the plot of this most unusual novel must seem bizarre and possibly disgusting. Many readers will not get past the first chapter, in which Katherine Dunn begins immediately and shockingly to turn convention and normalcy topsy-turvy. Yet ultimately, *Geek Love* is an indescribable black comedy, using shock and the absurd to question standard concepts of normalcy and freakishness. The characters in this novel are as rich and human as anyone, despite exterior appearances. When their behavior is strange, shocking, and cruel or sweet and generous, it is a reflection of their internal selves and not their outward deformities.

This is an audacious, inventive, and disturbing book, with humor as black as it gets: one can imagine Horst, the cat trainer, and Sanderson, who breeds maggots for the fly-roper, squabbling over who gets the residual body parts from the Arturan converts, and see the level of both depravity and hilarity the book achieves. *Geek Love* is exquisitely, almost poetically, written. Structurally, it weaves the past and present in a highly suspenseful manner.

Where Dunn truly makes the book work, however, is with the characterizations. From the Binewski family members to the smallest supporting role, each character is indelibly etched in memory, with Oly, as narrator, the most fully realized and memorable. The reader who starts out aghast at her condition, quickly accepts it and finally begins to take Oly's own pride in her beautiful abnormality.

Geek Love is not an easy book, and it is not for the squeamish. Extremely graphic at times, it has the capacity to disturb the most hardened and unflappable reader, yet in the final analysis, like all successful black humor, it celebrates the human condition. Not everyone will like *Geek Love*—no one, however, will forget it.

Hank Stewart

GOLDWYN: A BIOGRAPHY

Author: A. Scott Berg (1949–)
Publisher: Alfred A. Knopf (New York). 579 pp. $24.95
Type of work: Biography
Time: 1879-1974
Locale: The United States

A biography of Samuel Goldwyn, a Polish immigrant glove cutter who, from an early fascination with the infant film industry, rose to become one of Hollywood's most famous independent film producers

> Principal personages:
> SAMUEL GOLDWYN, a film producer
> FRANCES GOLDWYN, his wife
> SAMUEL GOLDWYN, JR., their son
> LOUIS B. MAYER, Goldwyn's rival
> WILLIAM WYLER, one of Goldwyn's best directors

"Samuel Goldwyn was not born on August 27, 1882," A. Scott Berg notes at the very beginning of his biography of Goldwyn. He was actually born Schmuel Gelbfisz in Warsaw, Poland, probably in 1879. When he was fifteen his father died, and, as the young Schmuel saw few prospects around him, he decided to go to America. He made his way by stages, stopping in Hamburg, where he learned glovemaking before going on to London. Schmuel Gelbfisz became Samuel Goldfish before he embarked for New York. Years later, Berg notes, Goldwyn would "wax tearful about the vision of arriving in New York Harbor and seeing for the first time that Mother of Exiles welcoming the tired, the poor, and the huddled masses yearning to breathe free. But there is not a trace of his ever passing through Ellis Island. . . ." Berg speculates that Goldfish probably entered the United States through Canada, his first glimpse of the United States more likely the Maine border than the New York Harbor.

Discovering that New York City held slums as depressing as Europe's, Goldfish made his way upstate to Gloversville, New York. A poor glove cutter, he found success as a glove salesman. When his company moved to Manhattan, he met a brother-sister vaudeville team, Jesse and Blanche Lasky. At age thirty-one, Goldfish married Blanche; in 1912 they had a daughter, Ruth. The next year, Sam Goldfish walked into a nickelodeon, and when he walked out, he was determined to launch a career in motion pictures. With his brother-in-law, Goldfish formed the Jesse L. Lasky Feature Play Company; they brought in a man named Arthur Friend to handle the legal aspects of the business and a fledgling playwright, Cecil B. DeMille, as director. DeMille and a cast left for Arizona to film *The Squaw Man*, but the moment DeMille saw the scenery in Arizona, he decided it was not "Western" enough. They reboarded the train and continued on to Los Angeles, where *The Squaw Man* became the first feature-length film made in Hollywood.

The company enjoyed growing success, but it irked Goldfish that Lasky seemed to get all the credit for their accomplishments. Their relationship deteriorated further in 1915 when Blanche filed for divorce. In 1916 the company merged with Adolph Zukor's company and became Famous Players-Lasky Corporation. Between Zukor and Lasky, Goldfish felt he was being forced out of the company; he resigned and formed a partnership with two brothers named Selwyn. Pairing the syllables of their names, they formed Goldwyn Pictures. Shortly thereafter, Goldfish petitioned to change his name legally to Samuel Goldwyn.

The company moved from New York to California, as did a stage comedian Goldwyn had signed, Will Rogers. As various new partners joined the Goldwyn Company, Goldwyn was forced to resign. When the company that bore his name eventually joined with Metro Pictures Corporation and then independent producer Louis B. Mayer, Goldwyn's stock was bought out, ending his connection with the company that became known as MGM (Metro-Goldwyn-Mayer). Goldwyn had by then established himself as an independent producer, arranging with First National and then United Artists to distribute his films. Famous Players-Lasky, meanwhile, became Paramount Pictures.

In 1925, Goldwyn met and married Frances Howard, a cool, elegant woman twenty-four years his junior. Frances married him because she hoped he would provide the security her own family life had lacked. Their marriage, although not a warm one, endured because Frances became a supportive wife who entertained flawlessly and saw to Goldwyn's comfort. She became interested in his films, reading scripts and studying the budgets. She was terrified that the indebtedness that came with every picture in the early days would ruin them. She objected to his extramarital flings and threatened to leave him if she ever found out about another woman or if he gambled away any more money (Goldwyn had a weakness for cards). The threat worked. The Goldwyns presented a united front to the world. They had one child, Sammy, christened Samuel Goldwyn, Jr. (it was part of the couple's agreement that the boy be raised a Catholic).

Meanwhile, Goldwyn's relationship with his daughter, Ruth, had deteriorated badly. After his divorce from Blanche, he had often written to Ruth and told her that she was the person he loved most in the world, but he rarely saw her. After a trifling disagreement, they did not speak to each other for twelve years. Goldwyn refused to pay her allowance, and at the time of her marriage she hired a lawyer to sue for some of the support payments he had not made. Goldwyn delayed and bickered, finally settling for a lump-sum payment.

Goldwyn imported a Hungarian actress named Vilma Banky and starred her in a successful series of movies with Ronald Colman, his dashing leading man. When sound pictures came in, Banky's career was over. Goldwyn's next discovery was a Russian-born actress named Anna Sten. He was so taken with her beauty that he overlooked the fact that she barely spoke English. If Sten was a disappointment, Goldwyn fortunately could count on Eddie Cantor in the early 1930s. When Cantor left Goldwyn, angry that all his pictures seemed to follow the same formula, Goldwyn started looking for new talent. An exotic Indian-Irish beauty named Merle Oberon appeared on the scene, and Goldwyn soon signed Miriam Hopkins, Joel McCrea, and David Niven, who Goldwyn thought would never play more than supporting roles. Goldwyn also signed Lillian Hellman to write for him.

Goldwyn had early decided that because as an independent producer he could not make many films, his films needed to be of high quality. He had an instinct for finding talented writers (like Hellman and Ben Hecht), cameramen (Gregg Toland), and directors (including William Wyler). He was equally adept at enraging people and appropriating ideas and credit from whomever he pleased. He made outrageous demands and manipulated his actors, writers, and directors shamelessly.

Goldwyn made a string of fondly remembered classics, including *Stella Dallas* (1937), with Barbara Stanwyck; *Wuthering Heights* (1939), with Laurence Olivier and Merle Oberon; *The Little Foxes* (1941), with Herbert Marshall, Teresa Wright, and Bette Davis; and *The Pride of the Yankees* (1942), with Gary Cooper. However, winning an Academy Award eluded Goldwyn until he followed Frances's advice and made a story about the men returning from World War II—*The Best Years of Our Lives* (1946), with Dana Andrews, Fredric March, Myrna Loy, Teresa Wright, and a handicapped veteran named Harold Russell.

The film was an overwhelming financial and critical success, garnering Oscars for editing, score, screenplay, director, best supporting actor (Harold Russell), best actor (Fredric March), and best picture. Harold Russell was also awarded a special Oscar for the example he set in coping with his handicap (he had lost both hands). The highlight of the evening for Goldwyn was when he was presented the Irving Thalberg award as the "producer with 'the most consistent high quality of production' that year." After the Goldwyns had returned home and Frances had been in bed, she got up and went back downstairs to look for Sam. Berg notes that "she found him sitting on the edge of a couch in the dark living room, his Oscar in one hand, his Thalberg in the other. His head bowed down, he was sobbing.''

The problem for the future was that Goldwyn was unable to top, or even equal, *The Best Years of Our Lives*. He made a series of forgettable films over the next few years. In 1955, he released *Guys and Dolls*, a film based on a successful Broadway show. Although critics were not impressed with the film, it was the number-one box-office attraction of the year. Another movie based on a stage success, *Porgy and Bess*, was fraught with disasters both during the production (Stage 8, with sets and costumes ready to start filming, burned to the ground; Goldwyn fired the director, Rouben Mamoulian, just before filming started) and after the picture came out, when it failed to make enough at the box office even to cover its cost.

Goldwyn, a tough survivor, became a difficult and demanding patient after suffering several strokes. On January 31, 1974, at the age of ninety-four, he died. Two years later, the seventy-three-year-old Frances succumbed to cancer.

A. Scott Berg's work reflects his meticulous research and interviews with those who knew the maddening motion-picture mogul. Very often, Goldwyn's business machinations elicit from the reader admiration for his cunning even while one's sympathies lie with the actor, writer, or director who is being manipulated by him.

Although there are moments in this biography when one feels that the real Goldwyn—the inner man—will remain forever an enigma, the book is as much a story of the rise of the motion- picture industry as it is of the producer Samuel Goldwyn and, as such, is relentlessly fascinating. Hardly a page goes by without the mention of some famous movie star, director, or mogul, and to see the day-to-day activity of Goldwyn as he puts these people together to create a film is enthralling.

Elizabeth J. Jewell

THE GOOD TIMES

Author: Russell Baker (1925–   )
Publisher: William Morrow & Co. (New York). 351 pp. $19.95
Type of work: Autobiography
Time: 1937-1961
Locale: Baltimore; London; Washington, D.C.; New York City

Memories of the spectacular rise from newsboy to The New York Times
*editorial-page columnist by Russell Baker, who acknowledges his mother as
the motivating force behind his achievements*

> Principal personages:
> RUSSELL BAKER, newspaper reporter and columnist
> LUCY ELIZABETH BAKER, his mother
> MIMI BAKER, his wife
> BUCK DORSEY, managing editor of the *Baltimore Sun*; Baker's
> lifelong mentor

If it were not for the relentless goading of his mother, Russell Baker
might never have become the successful writer and social critic he is
today. In his first autobiography, *Growing Up*, Baker describes the
tribulations of his early childhood, when his mother would urge him to
"make something of himself." *The Good Times* picks up the story in
his early adolescent years.

Growing up had not been easy for Russell Baker. After his father
died in 1930, when he was five, his mother had to rely on aid from
relatives. It took seven years to save enough to move to Baltimore,
fulfilling her dream of owning a home of their own. At his mother's
insistence, Baker started working for the *Baltimore News-Post* as a
paperboy, his "start up the ladder of journalism."

The good times really began about 1939, after Baker's mother married Herb, a railroad man with a decent income. They moved to a
better section of Baltimore, which Baker likened to "paradise." In
1942, Baker entered Johns Hopkins University on full scholarship and
joined the weekly campus newspaper, the *News-Letter*. His first article reported details of an upcoming tea dance. After a two-year stint
in the navy interrupted his education, he returned to Johns Hopkins,
where he found his duties as managing editor of the *News-Letter* entertaining and stimulating. He enjoyed writing and it showed.

After graduation, Baker stumbled into a job as police reporter at the
Baltimore Sun for thirty dollars a week. He was dismayed to learn that
he had no desk—police reporters just called in their stories to the
rewrite desk. Working the night shift, he covered routine news of
Baltimore's seedy side: robberies, murders, shoplifting, fatal accidents. He learned the differences between "ho-hum," "good," and

"terrific" murders. Suicides were so common that they rarely counted as news.

It took Baker nearly two years to prove himself before he was allowed to do any newswriting. Initially, his assignments were unchallenging—banquets, club meetings, culling stories from press releases. The first opportunity he was given to shine was an interview with novelist Evelyn Waugh. Unfortunately, he was given no time for preparation and he "flopped with a dull thud."

The *Sun*'s low salaries actually gave Baker an advantage. Vacancies created by unhappy employees in search of better pay allowed rapid advancement. His typing skill, rare then, was an asset. By 1949 he had more interesting stories and was working the rewrite desk, quite a distinction for someone so young.

During his early years at the *Sun*, Baker developed a reverence for the man who had hired him, Buck Dorsey, the formidable managing editor. Baker viewed him as the quintessential newspaper man. Unfortunately, Dorsey rarely noticed him, except for the time he called Baker into his office to lecture him about "good taste."

Although Baker continued to live under his mother's roof, he felt uneasy about not being able to support himself. While he enjoyed the comforts of home, he also yearned for independence. In addition to his busy career and watchful mother's eye, another force was operating in Baker's life. Since his college years, he had been keeping company with Mimi, who helped him regain his strength at some moments, and sapped it at others. In 1950, earning only seventy dollars a week, he married her. The next year, they had a daughter. When they moved into a basement apartment, his mother viewed him as "moving down in the world, not up."

Under the leadership of new city editor Ed Young, big changes began to happen at the *Sun*. He recognized Baker's ability and promised him important work. Baker "loved him instantly." Young also managed to get him a raise. Finances were so strained that Baker devotes a whole chapter to "money." His three closest friends at the *Sun* were forced to leave because of money. Although he realized he would never get rich working at the *Sun*, Baker believed the experience was invaluable, and he stayed on.

His career reached a turning point at age twenty-seven, just weeks after the birth of his second child. Out of the blue, Dorsey invited him to become chief of the *Sun*'s London bureau for two years. He could not have dreamed of a better proposition—they would pay his family's expenses as well. This was proof for his mother that he finally was making something of himself.

On his journey to London, he was overcome with familiar self-doubt. He knew little of British politics, foreign policy, or economics. Curiosity and elation triumphed, however. After two months of writing a few minor stories, he was visited by Dorsey. At first nervous at being scrutinized by his idol, Baker was on a first-name footing with Dorsey by the end of the week. Dorsey praised him, leaving Baker puffed with self-confidence.

After his family joined him, he found time to explore the wonders of Britain, touring London's tangled streets and the English countryside. He also took trips to Normandy and Paris. The big story of Baker's London assignment was the coronation of Queen Elizabeth II, a "color story"—glitzy but lacking the hard news at which Baker excelled. Under great pressure to make the most of this very important but predictable story, he decided to cover the pageant with the same care and open, alert mind he would bring to a hard-news story. The results exceeded all expectations. The laudatory cable sent by Dorsey confirmed that he had "scored an absolute triumph."

Baker polished his reporting skills immeasurably during his first year in London. Although he felt that he had followed his mother's advice to work hard and make something of himself, he still was not completely satisfied. When Dorsey offered him a prestigious job as White House correspondent, he accepted. He was further flattered when Scotty Reston at *The New York Times* Washington bureau began courting him for a similar position. He decided to stick with the *Sun,* partly out of loyalty to Dorsey, a kind of father figure. Even after these amazing offers, Baker's mother urged her son not to rest on his laurels.

It did not take Baker long to discover that the *Sun* White House correspondent position was a bad move. There was little going on, and Baker felt claustrophobic. He read novels to keep his mind from atrophying. After an unbearably tedious job covering President Eisenhower's vacation, he decided to jump to *The New York Times* and Scotty Reston, whom he very much admired. Breaking the news to Buck Dorsey, his mentor for years, was painful.

The first weeks with the *Times* were disappointing. Stationed in the New York office to learn the ropes, he found the *Times* overstaffed and bureaucratic. He likened it to an "insurance office." Once in Washington, however, covering more than just the White House, he was happy. The status of the *Times* was much greater than that of the *Sun.* He began receiving calls from such politicos as Senator Lyndon B. Johnson.

The late 1950s and early 1960s were exciting times for Baker in Washington. He covered Eisenhower's heart attack, Robert Kennedy's early days as Senate committee counsel, and Estes Kefauver's doomed bid for the presidency. John Kennedy, Richard Nixon, Hubert

Humphrey, Eugene McCarthy, and Stuart Symington were all key political players who appeared in his stories. The Kennedy-Nixon presidential election was a career highlight for Baker. During this time he strove to remain impartial, refusing to "play the game" of becoming buddies with the candidates, unlike some of his less ethical colleagues.

By the early 1960s, Baker's enthusiasm for reporting had waned. He had grown tired of being a small fish in a big pond. Just as he was considering an end to his reporting days, his old mentor Buck Dorsey offered Baker a prize position as columnist on the *Sun*'s editorial page. He could write whatever he wanted and travel wherever he wanted. And the money was good. Scotty Reston and Orvil Dryfoos, publisher of the *Times*, could not accept his resignation. Instead, they offered him a similar column on the *Times*'s editorial page, where Baker's Pulitzer Prize-winning "Observer" column was born.

Years later at his mother's funeral, having established a golden reputation in journalism, Baker reflects upon the roots of his success, namely his mother. And although he has achieved his goal of "making something of himself" several times over, he still hears her reprimanding voice, telling him to try even harder.

More than a chronicle of events leading to Russell Baker's journalistic success, *The Good Times* is an engaging story of the boy in every man and his search for approval. Baker carefully explores possible motivation for his perseverance. Many times, it is his mother who is the driving force. Often he admits to fits of self-doubt, hardly characteristic of the stereotypical, hard-nosed journalist. He shows how the loss of his father when he was only five drove him to seek role models in his superiors. Proving his worth to them became almost as vital as proving his worth to his mother.

Baker is most successful when describing the wonder of his earlier, more innocent years. As he grows older, he is hardened by experience. Some descriptions of political events of later years, without the benefit of the young-boy perspective provided in the rest of the story, seem heavy by comparison, resembling one of his hard-news stories.

Baker plans to write a third autobiography covering his later years as a columnist. Judging from his ongoing journalistic success, the reader can expect that throughout the book he will continue to hear his mother's voice, spurring him on, loud and clear.

David M. Kennerley

GREAT PLAINS

Author: Ian Frazier (1951–   )
Publisher: Farrar, Straus and Giroux (New York). 290 pp. $17.95
Type of work: Travel
Time: The present and the historical past
Locale: The American Great Plains

*An account of one man's journey through the Great Plains and his attempt
to define and understand the area*

> *Principal personages:*
> IAN FRAZIER, an observer and recorder
> GERARD BAKER, a plainsman and park ranger
> JIM YELLOW EARRING, a Sioux hitchhiker
> GEORGE SCOTT, a Wyoming rancher
> KATHLEEN CLAAR, a museum curator
> LE WAR LANCE, the Sioux heir to Crazy Horse

In the fall of 1982 writer and journalist Ian Frazier decided to move
from New York to Montana. He resolved to explore by van that vast
body of American landscape and history known as the Great American
Desert and later as the Great Plains—that portion of the American
heartland typified in much current public perception as merely the void
between New York and Los Angeles.

Frazier's residence in Kalispell, Montana, lasted only three years
before he returned to the writer's life in New York. During those years
he traveled 25,000 miles in his van, driving to Texas and back at least
twice and wandering throughout the ten states and the 1.5 million
square miles that make up the Plains region just east of the Rocky
Mountains and the Continental Divide. It is the region that geogra-
phers say begins at the hundredth meridian, at the limits of twenty-
inch annual rainfall. Yet it is a region with boundaries that are difficult
to define.

Like a latter-day hippie in the westering tradition of the mountain
man, the cowboy, the prospector, the homesteader, the outlaw, the
rancher, the trucker, the Okie, and other types who have contributed
to images of the old West and the new, Frazier hit the road, hoping to
make himself part of the West that is, spiritually and mythically, en-
demic to the American experience. Like the settlers' wagons of old,
Frazier's van transported him across the Plains, into the landscapes
and mindscapes of the continuing processes of American history.

Frazier organized the chronicle of his personal journey as it inter-
sected with the larger historical, cultural, and geographical dimensions
of the Plains in a loosely thematic sequence of chapters dealing with
rivers, heroic native Americans, ruins, flora and fauna, hitchhikers,

soldiers, settlers, citizens, songs, weather, badmen and lawmen, towns, and explorers. As with all history of place, much is revealed in the naming of rivers, landforms, and landmarks. All of the fifty or sixty rivers coursing the Plains have two or three names and claims of "ownership"—native American, Spanish, and English. The explorations of Coronado and others in the mid-16th century, of Lewis and Clark in the early 19th century, and of subsequent immigrants from Europe are reflected in the names given rivers and the settlements that grew up around them.

The Missouri River served as the main watercourse and locale for settlement, first for Indians and later for white traders, including John Jacob Astor's American Fur Company, which in 1828 established Fort Union as a major trading post at the convergence of the Yellowstone and Missouri rivers. Thousands of buffalo robes and beaver skins were traded for staples and luxuries, until the economics of supply and demand shifted and the post was abandoned in 1867.

Others who had passed that way previously include Lewis and Clark in 1805, dispensing whiskey and fiddle music to celebrate their arrival at the wide Missouri; John James Audubon in 1843, studying and sketching birds; and artists Karl Bodmer and Rudolph Friedrich Kurz, in search of mid-century aboriginal beauty. During his visits to Fort Union after it was declared a National Historic Site in 1967, Frazier became friends with a Mandan-Hidatsa Indian, Gerard Baker, a national park ranger. Baker informed Frazier about many aspects of river history, including the 1,600 Mandan who died in the 1837 smallpox epidemic, carried up the river by the American Fur Company's steamboat, the *St. Peter's*. With Baker, Frazier learned how to take a sweat bath and throw an ax.

A second native American "guide" for Frazier was the Sioux hitch-hiker Jim Yellow Earring. He offered to take Frazier to the site of Sitting Bull's cabin on the Standing Rock Indian Reservation in South Dakota, where Sitting Bull had been sent in 1883. It was at his camp that the Ghost Dancers gathered in 1889 and invoked the end of white dominance and the return of the buffalo. Following Yellow Earring's directions, Frazier finally reached the site of Sitting Bull's cabin to discover a small plaque, high grass, and a rattlesnake.

To attempt to understand the Great Plains is to attempt to understand the tribes of Plains Indians and their conflicts with the encroachments of Anglo-American society and culture. Frazier discusses barter systems; buffalo hunting; tipi assembly and use; diet; medicine and child-rearing practices; the primacy of the horse; buffalo rifles; the invention of repeating arms; and the customs and mores of Cheyenne,

Crow, Cree, Blackfeet, Assiniboin, Kiowa, Arikara, Comanche, and other Plains Indians.

Before the white men came, there were 70 million buffalo on the Plains. With the coming of the railroads and advancing white settlement, including the use of barbed wire and the establishment of cattle ranching, the buffalo were soon all but obliterated. The Homestead Act of 1862 and attendant deep plowing, the great blizzard and winter of 1886-1887, the drought of the 1930s, and the strip mining of the 1970s and 1980s have wrought further havoc on the ecology of the Plains. The wild and woolly, shoot-'em-up, gunfighter-versus-lawman image of Dodge City during cattle drive days; the Lincoln County boy bandit and killer from out of New Mexico's frontier days, Billy the Kid; the notorious bank robbers Bonnie Parker and Clyde Barrow— all have perpetuated the badlands mythology of the Plains. The rapist Rick Read, who in 1932 became the last man lynched in Kansas, casts a more modern pall on Plains violence.

Frazier's two biggest Plains culture heroes, individuals he views as positive mythic forces, are, oddly enough, Lawrence Welk and Crazy Horse—the former enshrined through the marvels of television, the latter the subject of sculptor Korczak Ziolkowski, who "decided to make the largest statue in the world: Crazy Horse, on horseback, with his left arm outstretched and pointing." On a less grand but still heroic level are Frazier's rancher friend and old college buddy, George Scott, and the octogenarian museum curator and small-town historian Kathleen Claar of Oberlin, Kansas. Another hero is Frazier's eccentric New York Indian friend, Le War Lance, proud grandson to Crazy Horse, a flesh-and-blood link to the Plains' tragic-heroic past.

Good wishes for residual and future restoration of the utopian promise of the Great Plains are best represented for Frazier by the town of Nicodemus, Kansas, founded by black homesteaders in 1877. This spot, inhabited by fifty joyous Plains people, is less a ruin than a beacon of hope. Frazier serendipitously pulls into town during the annual Founders' Day celebration and is immediately accepted and welcomed as a celebrant of the spirit of sanguine goodwill and democratic freedom symbolized by the great spaces and vistas, the open miles and blue skies of the Great Plains—the idealized object of reverence for Frazier and other travelers.

The overriding tone of Frazier's *Great Plains* is elegiac, bordering in places, almost in spite of itself, on the apocalyptic. The frontier was declared closed by the U.S. Census Bureau in 1890, a date made all the more significant by Frederick Jackson Turner's assertion that much of American history could be judged in light of the opening and the closing of the "waves" of recurrent settlement and civilization advancing over savagery and toward the promise and progress of westering.

Frazier underscores Turner's beliefs in the significance of the frontier and its "ending," yet he undercuts Turner's Anglo-European assumptions about progress and white civilization and superiority. Epochs die; cultures die; animals and vegetation disappear; whole human civilizations change and vanish. Frazier, like so many before him, wanted to see and name and preserve what he could of the Great Plains, and he does so with sorrow and joy, humor and compassion, great sense and great feeling. His chapters on the American Indian and his anecdotes on his friendships with Gerard Baker and Jim Yellow Earring explore a different relationship between "paleface and redskin," portraying the native American as knowledgeable friend.

Frazier is one among many who have felt the urge to record in stone and on parchment that they passed this way: "Paso por aquí," were the words inscribed by Juan de Oñate at El Morro, just past the great staked plains of New Mexico. From the numerous prehistoric ages and their tracings; from the accountings and stories of early native American inhabitants; from the diaries and logs of European discoverers and explorers; from the westering journals of American explorers and settlers; from the historical hypotheses of social scientists such as Turner and Walter Prescott Webb—from all these times and in all these forms, the Great Plains have endured as a sublime stage for the vast geological and biographical drama of life and death, the mutability of endings leading to new beginnings.

Frazier's most ominous statistic, however, and the one that evokes less rage (as in the case of strip mining) than outright fear and trembling is the following. Of America's 2,750 land-based nuclear warheads, over 1,850 rest on Minuteman and MX missiles, housed ready for deployment in the Great Plains. Will the forces of nature ultimately stand any chance against the forces of humankind? If there should be a next great war, will there be a Great Plains—or another, more deadly and diabolical version of a final great American Desert?

Robert F. Gish

HAROLD MACMILLAN: VOLUME I, 1894–1956

Author: Alistair Horne (1925–   )
Publisher: Viking Press (New York). 537 pp. $24.95
Type of work: Biography
Time: 1894–1956
Locale: England

The first volume of the life of Harold Macmillan, illuminating his development as schoolboy, soldier, publisher, politician, and ultimately prime minister of England

> Principal personages:
> HAROLD MACMILLAN, the British statesman, intense, unflappable, loyal
> HELEN "NELLIE" MACMILLAN, his dogmatic, dominant, ambitious mother
> WINSTON CHURCHILL, the British statesman, his mentor and colleague
> ANTHONY EDEN, a colleague, brilliant but weak and feminine in Macmillan's opinion

Harold Macmillan's biographer, Alistair Horne, describes him in the preface to this first volume of his biography as a paradox: "the emotional romantic and stern pragmatist were but two facets of the same highly complex personality." This astute observation provides the reader with a lodestar to follow throughout this detailed and complex book.

Harold Macmillan was born February 10, 1894, into the prominent publishing family established by his grandfather, who had risen from a humble background as a Scottish crofter to wealth and importance. His grandfather's legacy placed high value on education while his stern, austere upbringing and strong religious convictions, passed on to his son, would be very much a part of young Harold's early life. By Macmillan's own reckoning, his American-born mother, Nellie, was the greatest influence on his life. She was to dominate his life until her death by her loyalty and intense ambitions for him. His father, Maurice, a taciturn man, was responsible for Macmillan's reticence in expressing himself on personal issues. He would remain, in his own words, "buttoned up."

Macmillan's inability to open up or to form easy friendships stemmed in part from shyness, which he never fully conquered. As a politician he labored long over his speeches. His shyness was accompanied by a tendency toward despondency. Neither of these qualities helped him as a student at Eton. After a short time, partly due to ill health, his mother brought him home and engaged a tutor, Ronnie

Knox. Knox's influence was to last a lifetime, although the relationship was marred by Knox's attempt to proselytize Macmillan on behalf of the Catholic faith.

Whatever else Macmillan's tutelage by Knox did, it prepared him well academically for Oxford. At Balliol College he excelled, gaining a First-Class distinction at the end of two years and forming his first real friendships. Perhaps the lasting lesson, one appropriate for a budding political figure, was learned from his philosophy professor: "If you work hard and diligently you should be able to detect when a man is talking rot."

When World War I broke out, Macmillan was commissioned into a training battalion but soon transferred, through his mother's influence, into the prestigious Grenadier Guards. Macmillan's wartime experiences were both traumatic and far-reaching. He received several wounds, which left one hand and hip permanently affected. Perhaps more profound was the experience of a newfound camaraderie with men of the working class. Many of his Oxford circle were killed, giving Macmillan a sense of obligation to pay his debt to life.

After the war, Macmillan found himself unable to settle into the family publishing business. Once again his mother used her influence to have him appointed as aide-de-camp to the governor general of Canada, the duke of Devonshire, whose daughter Dorothy would become his wife. Dorothy would prove a great political asset to her future husband with her lack of snobbery and her cheerfulness to counter his melancholy. Dorothy and Harold were married in 1920 and had one son and three daughters. Not too far into the marriage, Dorothy began an affair with Robert Boothby, a political colleague of her husband's, which continued until her death, although the Macmillan marriage remained intact.

While Macmillan worked at the publishing business off and on, it was obvious that his heart lay in the political arena. In 1924 he came in on a Conservative landslide, winning a seat in Parliament from a tough working-class district, Stockton-on-Tees. The thirty-year-old Macmillan had begun a new life.

During the next several years, Macmillan struggled with his shyness and his rather ponderous style. He demonstrated a genuine concern about the high unemployment rate in his district. When chided that his speeches sounded almost socialist, he responded, "Housing is not a question of Conservatism or Socialism. It is a question of humanity."

Churchill was so impressed with the young M.P.'s (member of Parliament's) lucid statements on derating (a means of relieving industry's heavy rate of taxation) that a strong link was forged between them that would never be broken and would, in a sense, make Macmillan's political life.

The loss of Macmillan's Stockton seat in 1929 and increasing despondency over his marriage proved to be both a curse and a blessing. It was a period of terrible self-doubt and loneliness, but it forged his character into one of survival with grace and courage. This period of his own depression coincided with national depression. Macmillan put his considerable scholarship and clear-thinking ability into writing tracts and pamphlets, all to be summed up in his far-reaching 1938 book, *The Middle Way*.

During that period his thinking seemed to lean to the left, although he remained more interested in plans and solutions than in labels. While Macmillan had his detractors, he nonetheless gained a reputation for courage, unflappability, and gentleness in the expressions of his beliefs. In his fifth election in twelve years, he won his seat by a large majority.

Macmillan and Churchill were to have many occasions in which they fell in and out with each other. They first fell out over India, with Macmillan clearly coming down on the side of nationalism, whose winds were blowing around the world. With Churchill out of office, it was the threat of World War II that brought them together again, Churchill very much "the old warlord," and Macmillan catapulted into a new interest in foreign affairs.

World War II saw many ups and downs for Macmillan's career. One of the highlights was his appointment by Churchill as minister resident at Allied Force Headquarters in Algiers, which enabled him to achieve cabinet rank yet allowed him to retain his House seat. Macmillan proved himself to be a superb diplomat working with the Americans under the leadership of General Dwight Eisenhower, gaining opportunities to meet world leaders such as Franklin D. Roosevelt and Charles de Gaulle. His reputation for unflappability made Macmillan valuable in his role as advisor both in dealing with the French and in establishing terms for the Italian armistice. Later he proved equally valuable in dealing with the warring factions in Greece and the new problems created by Soviet policy.

Macmillan's postwar efforts lay principally in his old interest, the area of housing. He was transferred from the Foreign Office to become chancellor of the exchequer. As successful as were his housing efforts, his involvement in the Suez crisis was to have far-reaching effects. Anthony Eden, by then prime minister, and Macmillan were at odds over Britain's Suez policy. But Macmillan, who depended upon his wartime experience with Eisenhower to guide his policy views, seriously misjudged the U.S. interest toward Suez and the Middle East. The rift that developed between the two countries would not heal for some time, during which Britain's fall from world-power status was an added burden.

With the collapse of the government's Suez policy and Eden's illness (which had severely worsened), Macmillan began to mend fences. Eden had left the government on physician's orders to rest, leaving Rab Butler, as deputy prime minister, and Macmillan holding the reins. Macmillan did not appear to have coveted the position of prime minister. However, when it became obvious that Eden's health would force his resignation, Macmillan was the overwhelming choice to succeed him. Macmillan demonstrated such adroitness in extricating himself from the disastrous Suez policy that his friend Butler had virtually no chance.

Macmillan's political astuteness and graceful handling of almost impossible problems, coupled with his personal loyalty and integrity, led him, at the close of this first volume of his official biography, to the brink of fulfillment of his mother's ambitious dream for him, the role of prime minister.

This account, packed as it is not only with Macmillan's life as a man, but also with world-shattering events, is a tribute to the biographer's art in that the reader does not get lost in the sheer weight of detail. Alistair Horne's powerful writing skill clearly illuminates the character of this most astute, complicated, even mysterious political leader. Horne's account is objective and displays a real understanding of the paradox that lay beneath the surface of his subject. At once emotional yet supremely pragmatic, scholarly, calm, and kindly, his character is skillfully developed and woven throughout the narrative. It would be difficult if not impossible to find any real weakness in this highly readable biography, with the possible exception of the absence of a chronology, the addition of which would be an asset to the reader in following and understanding the events in this most eventful life.

Elizabeth Bouvier Spencer

HAROLD MACMILLAN: VOLUME II, 1957–1986

Author: Alistair Horne (1925–   )
Publisher: Viking Press (New York). 741 pp. $27.50
Type of work: Biography
Time: 1957–1986
Locale: Great Britain

The second volume of the life of Harold Macmillan, one of the most influential of Britain's prime ministers, which explores both his personal and political fortunes

> Principal personages:
> HAROLD MACMILLAN, prime minister of Great Britain
> DOROTHY MACMILLAN, wife of the prime minister
> DWIGHT D. EISENHOWER, president of the United States
> JOHN F. KENNEDY, president of the United States

Volume II of Alistair Horne's official biography of Harold Macmillan begins with a bang by listing the myriad decisions facing him as he began his administration as Britain's prime minister in 1957. The country was deeply in debt in the aftermath of World War II and Suez; the economy was experiencing a slowdown; rifts had developed with its allies, especially the United States due to Suez policy; and British morale was low because of the nation's fall from first rank among the powers of the world. Many doubted Macmillan's ability to form a government strong enough to stay in power six weeks. But here Macmillan's skill in reading people became amply evident in his cabinet appointments. With a penchant for foreign affairs, he chose his old colleague Selwyn Lloyd as foreign secretary, thereby ensuring that for all intents and purposes he himself would stay in control. He exhibited uncommonly good sense in balancing both wings of the Tory party in his selections, balancing also his own nature of the aesthete versus the warrior in his selections.

During his early period in office, Macmillan had the support and good will of the British people and found his queen to be well-informed and receptive to his ideas. His wife, Dorothy, had been an asset throughout his political career because of her naturalness and friendliness. She was to become an even greater comfort to him as his time in office lengthened. During his first televised address, Macmillan, far from shrinking from unpleasant facts, immediately tackled the twin problems of defeatism and U.S. relations.

Relations with the United States required delicate handling and tact. In spite of their wartime alliance and personal friendship, Eisenhower and Macmillan had differed markedly in their policies during the Suez crisis. Macmillan did not want to approach his old friend hat in hand, but neither did he want to provide any excuse to prolong ill feelings. Their first meeting after Macmillan became prime minister was successful, and good rapport was established. However, good relations with the United States increased tensions with Germany, led by Konrad Adenauer, and France. Macmillan's goal was to see Britain become part of the European Common Market, but continued problems with Adenauer, Guy Mollet (his French counterpart), and, later, de Gaulle plagued him throughout his administration.

Elsewhere, Cyprus and the Middle East continued to heat up, with the United States and Britain often taking slightly different policy positions. Macmillan began to view Khrushchev as more dangerous than Stalin as Soviet involvement in Syria increased. With the world becoming a more precarious place due to the proliferation of nuclear weapons, Macmillan faced his own inner crisis as the warrior in him fought the intellectual. He believed that defense costs could be cut and chose an ideal man, Duncan Sandys, to fight the military bureaucracy. Meanwhile, he pushed the United States to rescind the McMahon Act of 1946, which prohibited the U.S. government from sharing nuclear know-how with an ally. Finally a joint declaration was issued in which the act was rescinded in exchange for Britain's agreement not to press for admission of Communist China to the UN.

In 1958, Macmillan and Lloyd successfully intervened at the request of the king of Jordan with an airborne operation against the Syrian threat. Anglo-American dealings in the Middle East, however, increased Macmillan's belief that U.S. policy there was far from clear. With Britain generally condemning partition except as a last resort for Cyprus, negotiations with the United States and Turkey resulted in the island becoming a republic with its own flag, a Greek president, and a Turkish vice-president, while the United Kingdom retained its key bases. It was, for the time, an enlightened policy in which everyone gained something and gave up something.

The biggest thorn in the prime minister's side was de Gaulle. It was through Macmillan's support of him against Roosevelt and Churchill in World War II (both disliked de Gaulle intensely) that the old general was able to take the helm of government in Paris. De Gaulle's personal vanity, however, and his contempt of Anglo-Saxons continually undermined the cooperation necessary to create a strong Europe against the increasing Soviet threat.

One of the major contributions Macmillan made in 1958–1959 was to undertake a mission to the Soviet Union to meet with Khrushchev. The two men "agreed to disagree" on the question of Berlin, but at least the channels of communication were kept open, helping to defuse a dangerous situation.

In 1959 the situation in Africa worsened, and Macmillan made a six-week trip himself. His "winds of change" attitude proved him to be a friend of African independence. In South Africa he delivered a courageous speech criticizing apartheid, the finest of his career.

Eventually, Macmillan's strong world leadership, built upon a position of strength at home, brought about a summit meeting between Western leaders and Khrushchev. But the tragic U-2 incident, coming just before the summit meeting, ensured its failure. This failure was a low point in his life, and it marked the beginning of a series of bad years, with stagflation at an all-time high and continued trouble in Africa and with his old bête noire, de Gaulle, all of which made Macmillan ill. Despite his defeats and disappointments, he was elected chancellor of Oxford, a joy that would console him for the rest of his life.

Certainly one of the other few joys that would come to him over the next few years of increasing pressures at home and abroad was his relationship with the new U.S. president, John F. Kennedy. The two men formed a lasting personal and political alliance, for they had much in common. A fortunate adjunct to their relationship was the felicitous choice of David Ormsby-Gore as Britain's ambassador to the United States and of David Bruce as his counterpart to Great Britain. Ormsby-Gore was a friend of Kennedy's and a relative by marriage, while David Bruce was sensitive and intelligent.

In 1962, weary from his many diplomatic journeys and unwell, Macmillan felt that he needed to stay at home and work on worsening domestic problems. In one of the few insensitive and little-understood decisions of his political life, he sacked Selwyn Lloyd and several other ministers in a shake-up that became known as the "Night of Long Knives." His personal popularity dropped from a high of 79 percent in 1960 to 36 percent in July 1962.

Elsewhere, the burdens of empire were keenly felt as South Africa, rather than make any concessions to its black majority, withdrew from the Commonwealth. The queen, ever ready to sacrifice her personal considerations for her country, made a state visit to Ghana at an extremely sensitive time in that country's history. Meanwhile, the Congo, again involving threats of a Soviet base in the heart of Africa, called for UN action and provoked one of the few sharp exchanges between Kennedy and Macmillan.

Macmillan was to prove himself invaluable to the young American president, however, through his availability during the 1962 Cuban missile crisis. What could have been a disaster of worldwide proportions was averted by sensitive but firm handling, due in no small part to Macmillan's wise counsel.

The 1963 Profumo scandal made 1962, as bad as it was for Macmillan, look even worse. Never far from the surface, Macmillan's hurt and resentment over his wife's longtime affair with Robert Boothby, coupled with his somewhat puritanical nature, caused him to delay action on the scandal until it erupted. The ensuing political unrest almost caused the government to fall. There was clearly some lapse on the part of his advisors, but nonetheless Macmillan received an unprecedented number of letters of support. In the midst of this latest outbreak of trouble, however, Macmillan received word that the long-sought Test Ban Treaty had passed the U.S. Senate. This news was especially heartening in view of Macmillan's long-established stance in favor of a halt in the nuclear arms race.

Cumulative stress finally brought a breakdown in Macmillan's health. His doctors diagnosed his prostate disease severe enough to require immediate surgery. Uncertainty over his health brought about his decision to resign. The queen visited her loyal P.M. in the hospital and was much moved as she accepted his resignation and written blueprints of how to proceed with the government.

Macmillan lived some twenty years after his fateful decision but with few consolations. His beloved Dorothy died, as did their daughter Sarah and son Maurice. Also devastating was the steady loss of his eyesight. After several times refusing an earldom, at the age of ninety, Macmillan finally accepted the title and was named earl of Stockton, appropriate in view of its early associations. He died in 1986, having outlived most of his ministers and with the distinction of having been one of Britain's most successful and popular prime ministers.

Without doubt, Alistair Horne has created a masterpiece of biography. The writing itself is of the highest order, lending great power to the telling of such a long and influential life. Macmillan is an exceedingly complex subject embodying within himself many opposites—a study in point and counterpoint. His ability to grow in office was itself unprecedented, as demonstrated in part by his metamorphosis from a shy, poorly turned-out politician to a confident, almost dapper statesman. Horne reveals Macmillan the man in his moments of glory and disappointment and makes him altogether real—so much so that it would be difficult for any reader not to shed a tear for the passing of such a great man from a world so sadly lacking in real leaders.

Elizabeth Bouvier Spencer

HARP

Author: John Gregory Dunne (1932–   )
Publisher: Simon & Schuster (New York). 235 pp. $18.95
Type of work: Memoirs
Time: The present and recent past
Locale: New York; Los Angeles; Hartford, Connecticut; Ireland; Germany

Writer John Gregory Dunne, confronted with serious cardiac problems, reflects upon his Irish-American heritage, his family, and his growth as a writer

> Principal personages:
> JOHN GREGORY DUNNE, the writer
> JOAN DIDION, a writer and the author's wife
> AUNT HARRIET, the last surviving family member of Dunne's parents' generation

The opening sequence of *Harp* plunges the reader into an intimate, wrenching moment in writer John Gregory Dunne's life. The phone rings at 4:30 in the morning, and when he answers, hastily thinking of all the family disasters it could portend, he learns that it is the cruelest, least expected loss: the suicide of his youngest brother, Stephen. "It is an imposition on the reader to write that paragraph," he says at the end of the passage, "but there are those of us for whom words have no meaning until they are down on paper." In this work Dunne puts his own life down on paper, from the catastrophic to the banal, not to record it or flaunt it, but simply to give it meaning and existence on his own terms.

Dunne's immediate acknowledgment that he has placed the reader in the center of another person's pain without warning or consent serves as a statement of intent, enabling the reader to understand the access the writer creates to his private life. Prompted by the development of cardiac problems that threaten to destroy his health and perhaps kill him, the writer searches his past and his heritage for some of the elements that mark his character, his writing, and his response to this crisis.

Dunne and his siblings are third-generation Irish-Catholic immigrants and the first generation whose lives are not dominated by their background. Although he has left his grandparents' Hartford, Connecticut, ghetto behind, Dunne recognizes the deep and unbreakable ties binding him to the Irish immigrant families of a century ago: "I am a harp, that is my history, Irish and Catholic, from steerage to suburbia in three generations." His grandfather, Poppa, had worked his way from meat clerk to bank president, moving out of scruffy Frog

Hollow and returning to his native land only on the occasion of his fiftieth birthday, alone. His two daughters, Dunne's mother and the spinster everyone called "Aunt Harriet," lived in his shadow. Aunt Harriet entered a convent after her mother died to avoid devoting her life to running Poppa's household, but when she found the religious life even more stifling that that of a well-to-do spinster, she returned to her father's house, tending to him until his death. When Dunne's own father died suddenly two days after Dunne's fourteenth birthday, Aunt Harriet once again set an independent life aside and came to live with her sister's family, becoming "a surrogate father" and watching the children grow away from the rigid ethnic codes so important in her own life.

Dunne's childhood in West Hartford, the "ne plus ultra of the immigrant Hartford Irish dream," instilled in the successful surgeon's son an acute and bitter awareness of the barrier between the Irish and the "Yanks," and he spent much of his youth and his time at Princeton attempting to leave his immigrant origins behind. His pronouncement at the end of college that he wanted to write provoked a violent reaction from his mother and Aunt Harriet, "as if I had said I had gone soft for an altar boy"; they offered business school instead. Accepted at Stanford, desperately wishing he were Episcopalian, Dunne rejected his family's plans and impulsively joined the army. He spent the next two years as a clerk in a field artillery battalion in postwar Germany.

Dunne's memories of these times weave in and out of a narrative that has as its often absent center the cardiac crisis the writer faces now, as he writes of it. A cursory medical examination by his life-insurance company turned up an irregularity that sent him to his doctor for a thorough examination that turned up the "glitch" that eventually landed Dunne on the operating table to undergo angioplasty for a severely occluded artery. The series of tests, doctors, and hospital rooms marking this progression provided Dunne with a wealth of material, a fact that he recognizes with irony. In writing about the medical developments and the difficult emotions they arouse, Dunne returns often to stories of his family, to vignettes of his adult life, scenes overheard and jotted down in his notebook, all the rich and simple details threatened by his uncooperative arteries.

After the angioplasty, Dunne and his wife moved from Los Angeles, their home for twenty-four years, to New York. Talking about the abrupt move in an intermittent self-interview he dubs "Internal Affairs Investigation," he points out that the life-or-death melodrama of undergoing the surgery left an anticlimactic depression in his life, which this sudden burst of activity was partially designed to erase. The move itself proved a rather melodramatic affair, complete with a nine-ton dumpster full of old papers and mementos, grim advice from New York friends who insisted "You don't understand, it's different in New York," and a blue Volvo from New Jersey crushed by a "jumper" falling from the roof of the St. Moritz Hotel.

When all of this excitement failed to restore Dunne's equilibrium, he took off in search of history, in the form of visits to Germany, where he first began to shed his immigrant persona, and Ireland, where the seeds of that persona had been planted a century and a half earlier. Dunne arrived in Wertheim, West Germany, in a somewhat sentimental mood. It was in his two years there, he reflects, that he grew to understand the scruffy world inhabited by "have-nots," people, like the enlisted men of his company, whose horizons stop well below the ambitious expanses of the writer's upwardly mobile childhood. His experiences there provided much of the inspiration for his output as a writer, and he returned to Germany with hopes of creating a further opportunity for inspiration. What he discovered is that there was no new inspiration to be found there, that his youthful experiences represented all this army base had to offer him, that this voyage of inspiration can disintegrate, at a moment's thought, into a fifty-year-old's indulgence of his memory, nothing more.

The trip to Ireland proved the more difficult journey. Dunne wanted to get an Irish passport, and he needed therefore to find his grandfather's birth records to establish his right to citizenship. Armed only with flattering Hartford obituaries of dubious accuracy, he set off for the parish listed therein as Poppa's birthplace. An Irish passport would have facilitated his European travels, but Dunne admits that there were less easily articulated reasons for obtaining this proof and proclamation of his ancestry; among them, that the document would force him to confront the years of rejection of his immigrant background and to acknowledge the influence it had had on his life and work. Whatever his motivation, no Irish passport was to be had, for he could uncover no trace of birth, baptism, or marriage records pertaining to Dominick Francis Burns in the parish of Strokestown.

Elizabeth Burns, a cousin of Aunt Harriet's whom Dunne consulted on his return from Ireland, offered the solution to the puzzle of the absent Strokestown Burns records: Poppa's parents, William O'Beirne and Elizabeth O'Beirne O'Beirne, emigrated to Hartford from Tubberpatrick, near Strokestown, with six children. Poppa and his brother were left with relatives in Strokestown, following their parents two years later. Burns's blunt observations about her generation gave added context to Aunt Harriet's difficult passage to death at ninety-nine, accompanied by the memories and accounts of the immigrant life that Dunne finally began to see as the necessary antecedent to his own.

His sister Ginny died of cancer a few months later. In the wake of these deaths, Dunne found his own looming once again as a collapse in the park led to new tests and the scheduling of open-heart surgery. The day before it was to be performed, however, it was canceled. Dunne's immense relief was tinged with an undeniable resentment that such a spectacular opportunity for material, the perfect ending to his book, had been at the last minute snatched from him. It was the inevitable reaction of the writer that Dunne's life and history have produced, and he accepts it with humor and grace.

John Gregory Dunne's *Harp* gives the reader an exhilarating taste of the workings of a writer's mind. The episodic format of the narrative, focusing now on Poppa's Hartford, now on a restaurant in Malaysia, now on a hospital bed in California, moves with the spontaneously structured rhythms of thought, observation, and memory. From the opening passage, Dunne has made quite clear how he intends to proceed in this endeavor; there are to be no subjects avoided, nothing left out or rewritten to soothe or entertain the reader. This is a writer's book, for and about the author, and any rewriting, manipulation, and censorship that take place do so to fulfill his own purposes: "a writer's life is his only real capital, his and his alone to invest, and to imagine, and to reimagine . . . ."

Harp is not, therefore, an accurate, objective memoir of Dunne's life, but rather a creation of history and emotion and fiction. There are many moments in the narrative in which the truth value, like that of Poppa's obituaries, is dubious, but, like the obituaries, each of these moments has an independent validity that has little to do with objective fact. The heart of the narrative is Dunne's voice, not the truths or half-truths or fictions it relates. This is a storyteller's voice, a glib Irish voice that glides and caresses and seduces and stings. The sudden shifts in tone and subject that mark the narrative's progress through the layers of memory and crisis succeed in engaging the reader because this voice is so utterly charming. Funny, apologetic, self-conscious to a fault, Dunne's voice fills *Harp* with a vibrant presence. Dunne himself may have been disappointed when his dangerous heart surgery was canceled, but *Harp*'s readers cannot help but rejoice that this voice, strong and entrancing, seems destined to tell many stories still.

Nancy Seybold

THE HEART OF THE COUNTRY

Author: Fay Weldon (1933–   )
Publisher: Viking Press (New York). 201 pp. $17.95
Type of work: Novel
Time: The recent past
Locale: Eddon Gurney, a distant suburb of London

*Natalie Harris's plight after she is deserted by her husband is related by
her friend Sonia who has been committed to an insane asylum*

> *Principal characters:*
> NATALIE HARRIS, a single woman who learns to enjoy life after
>   her husband leaves her
> HARRY HARRIS, Natalie's husband and owner of the bankrupt
>   Harrix computer firm
> BEN and ALICE, the Harrises' children, aged twelve and eleven
> ARTHUR WANDLE, an antique dealer with whom Natalie had
>   been having an affair before her husband left her
> JANE WANDLE, Arthur's wife, who breaks antique pots in re-
>   venge for his affairs
> ANGUS FIELD, an auctioneer who supports Natalie in return
>   for sex
> JEAN FIELD, Angus's wife, who belittles him
> BERNARD, an employee of Arthur and Angus, aware of their
>   dishonesties
> FLORA, Natalie's maid and Bernard's girlfriend, killed in a fire
>   set by an arsonist
> SONIA, narrator of the novel, who is in an insane asylum for
>   setting the fire that killed Flora

Beautiful Natalie Harris is totally surprised when she learns one day
that her husband, Harry, has abandoned her and their two children to
run off to Spain with his secretary, Marion Hopfoot, the queen of the
1978 Eddon Gurney carnival. An observer could be excused for believing that Natalie and Harry enjoyed a blissful suburban life with an
elegant modern house, Volvo station wagon for her and Cortina sports
car for him, an Alsatian named Jax, and children attending an expensive private school. In fact, Harry had been looting his failing computer company, taking out loans on the promise of nonexistent orders,
and leaving unpaid bills in his wake. Natalie finds herself in debt wherever she turns, and with no way to earn a living. Her parents have
died, and Natalie has never worked, depending on Harry's faithfulness
for her future.

Natalie is unprepared for life as a single mother and makes many
mistakes in the first weeks after Harry has left. Out of embarrassment
and the unrealistic hope that Harry will return with an explanation for
his absence, Natalie delays in applying for welfare benefits, thereby

losing several weeks of income. More costly is her trust in Arthur Wandle, the antique dealer with whom she had been having an affair before Harry left her, and Angus Field, an auctioneer. Both men tell her that the government will sell her house to collect the back taxes Harry owed, and that she cannot hope to collect much after her debts are paid. In fact, Angus sells Natalie's house to Arthur at half its true value. When Arthur later resells the house, he splits the profit with Angus. Angus and Arthur continually look for opportunities to profit from the misfortune or ignorance of others. Arthur combs the town's garbage dumps looking for antiques thrown away by people unaware of their value. Arthur and Angus both are childless and married to women who belittle their successes; neither wife works nor cares for her house, and each is usually unresponsive to her husband's sexual desires. Unlike Harry Harris, however, Arthur and Angus have not deserted their wives. Instead, they hunt for women with whom to have affairs. When Natalie loses interest in Arthur after Harry has left her, Arthur agrees to allow Angus to pursue her. At first, Angus's advances are rebuffed by Natalie, who declares, "I want my body for myself, thank you, for the time being."

At first, Natalie avoids the company of men and turns for advice and friendship to Sonia, the narrator of the novel. Sonia also is a single mother, whose husband left her when he found her in *flagrante delicto*. Since then, Sonia has become an expert on the welfare system and a shrewd appraiser of men. All men, in Sonia's view, hate women. They blame women for broken marriages, even though men are even more unfaithful than women. Both her husband and Harry Harris had more numerous affairs than did Sonia or Natalie. Yet women, in Sonia's opinion, have little choice but to put up with whatever men offer them. Citing apt statistics and feminist arguments, Sonia points out that all but the few women with professional careers of their own become worse off after divorce, while their ex-husbands improve their financial conditions. Sonia's sardonic and, at times, bitter attitude toward men increasingly colors her narration of Natalie's situation and thoughts. Sonia also presumes to imagine the feelings of Jane Wandle and Jean Field at their husbands' philanderings and their own inabilities to divorce due to a lack of career or other resources.

After Natalie's house and belongings are sold, she is placed by the welfare office in a hostel. The first night there, Natalie sees the fear and horror in her children's eyes and understands for the first time that she must struggle for her children's well-being. That night she moves them to live with Sonia. Ben and Alice become less snotty, more sensitive in Sonia's view, as they live with her and her own three children. Natalie sees Sonia as a friend, yet rejects her feminist theories and her lesbian advances. After three months, Natalie decides she wants to escape welfare and takes a job as a "gofer" at a quarry. She earns no more from working after paying taxes than she received from welfare, yet Natalie prefers to avoid the hassles of applying for supplemental benefits and the humiliations of having nasty and self-righteous welfare workers pry into her private life. At the quarry, Natalie's nice clothes are covered with dust, and she fears she eventually will get emphysema. At the end of her second week at work, Natalie is walking home in the rain after missing the last bus, when Angus Field offers her a ride home. Once seated in his car, Natalie hears out Angus's offer to put her and her children in a luxury flat he owns and pay her a salary if she becomes his mistress. To Sonia's horror, Natalie accepts the offer, moving out of Sonia's apartment the next day. The night that Natalie consummates her relationship with Angus, Harry returns to Eddon Gurney to announce that he wants his children to live with him in Spain. The children prefer a life with their wealthy father to the precarious existence with a mother dependent upon a lover's whim for her income and their home. With few tears shed, Alice and Ben join their father.

Natalie is happy with Angus, enjoying her capacity to give him pleasure and make him feel loved and sexually desirable. Only occasionally does she appear bothered by her status as a virtual prostitute. To pay her, Angus gives Natalie a job building a float for the annual Eddon Gurney carnival. Also working on the float are Flora and Bernard, a young couple living in a trailer next to the town dump where Arthur goes to find antiques. Bernard claims the dump antiques are his own, selling them to Arthur for a finder's fee. Bernard is aware of Arthur's affairs. To keep Bernard quiet, Arthur has given him a job selling banned toxic chemicals to local farmers from a temporary warehouse. Arthur also hired Flora, for whom he has sexual desires, to work on the carnival float, which is intended to advertise the contributions made by Angus and Arthur to the Eddon Gurney community. As the day of the carnival approaches, Sonia and her friend Roz also are hired to help build the float. Jane Wandle shows up to help, too. Once the women are all together, they discuss their resentments toward men in general and toward Angus and Arthur in particular. The women decide to make the float a true expression of the carnival spirit, a satiric expression of the nastiness and dishonesty of Angus and Arthur's personal and business affairs.

Angus is enraged at the float and ends his relationship with Natalie. Sonia, to express further anger at men, sets the float on fire. Charged with arson and the murder of Flora, who was killed in the fire, Sonia is committed to an asylum for the insane. Writing a book turns out to be Sonia's therapy. Through describing the forces that brought her to an act of violence against two men—Arthur and Angus—whom she barely knew, and which resulted in the death of a woman, Sonia is forced to imagine and re-create the lives of Natalie, Flora, Jane, and Jean. After the arson, Arthur ages rapidly and loses his appeal to women, so Jane becomes less jealous and happier with him. Jean becomes more tolerant of Angus, and their marriage improves. Natalie moves into the trailer with Bernard, finding a carefree life and sexual pleasure. Sonia's therapy is a success. Her psychiatrist releases her from the asylum and offers to marry her. Sonia declines, deciding "she must get on with changing the world, rescuing the country. There is no time left for frivolity."

Fay Weldon, speaking through her narrator, Sonia, displays a biting wit in *The Heart of the Country*. The pretensions and foibles of the rich, and those aspiring to become rich, are exposed in all their silly details. Cars, clothes, and homes are described to reveal facets of each character. While the novel is set in suburban England, in the era of Margaret Thatcher, it is a tale of the transformation of rural life and honest values by forces of greed and winds of fashion at play in the heart of many countries in the late 20th century.

The Heart of the Country is presented as a morality play. Sonia believes that each act by every person has an effect. She sees her task as trying "to decide exactly who to blame for what, and why . . . " It is enough "to drive a sane woman mad," and does drive Sonia insane. Yet, Sonia finds moral patterns in characters' actions. Bad deeds lead to unhappiness by those who commit them, as when Natalie drives by Sonia on a rainy day, splattering mud on Sonia's three children, and later that same day Natalie is deserted by her husband. Or when the owners of a luxury food store buy Natalie's dog for a generous price, they are rewarded by prosperity. Sonia finds moral order in random events. Her shrill feminism and anger toward men come from her identification of a continuing array of evil acts by men against the women they profess to love but in fact hate. Yet, Sonia in her narration empathizes with all people. Even as she ridicules their strivings and exposes their misdeeds, Sonia expresses the emotions that give motive to the moral as well as immoral acts of men, including Angus and Arthur. All the characters in *The Heart of the Country* engage the reader's sympathy. One wishes them all happiness and hopes they will practice the moral actions Sonia sees as the requisite to good fortune.

Richard Lachmann

HENCE

Author: Brad Leithauser (1953–   )
Publisher: Alfred A. Knopf (New York). 320 pp. $18.95
Type of work: Novel
Time: 1993
Locale: Boston and Cambridge, Massachusetts; Victoria, Indiana

A man-versus-machine chess tournament raises unsettling questions about life in the 21st century due to the growing presence of mechanical intelligences

> *Principal characters:*
> GARNER BRIGGS, a thirty-four-year-old law professor
> TIMOTHY "TIM" BRIGGS, Garner's brother, a twenty-one-year-old junior chess professional
> DORIS BRIGGS, a widow and mother of three: Garner, Nettie, and Timothy
> IMRE SZENDREI, Timothy's chess trainer
> VICTORIA "VICKY" T. SCHMIDT, an employee at the Boston branch of Congam International
> OLIVER CONANT, the chief programmer of ANNDY, a computer chess program
> LINDA FACCIONE, Timothy's fiancee and high-school sweetheart
> JACK WESTMAN, a representative of Congam International

Garner Briggs, a regimented law professor in his thirties, introduces his rigid behavior—and the narration of the novel *Hence*—with the explanation that by nature he is "uneasy in a city." Yet for twelve years he has lived and worked in Boston. Although he occasionally wonders why he remains in a city whose technological rhythms are in an unsettling way "in his blood" and seem to regulate his life, such fleeting introspections are no match for the mechanical forces that hold him transfixed. Whether humans and machines are equally matched is the thematic question the novel explores by way of a chess competition between Garner's younger brother, Timothy, and ANNDY, the world's highest-ranked computer chess program.

Garner learns of Tim's chess plans through his mother, Doris, an imposing, garrulous, sixty-two-year-old widow who is often an agitation to her children. She presents the news that Tim will compete in a chess tournament against a computer as evidence that Garner has lost touch with the family.

Garner calls Tim to learn more details, yet provides no emotional support for his brother. Garner ends the conversation having learned the cold, hard facts: Tim has been wooed by Congam International, the maker of the world's fastest computers, to play chess against its chess program, ANNDY, designed at the Massachusetts Institute of

Technology (MIT) and able to scan 365,000 chess positions per second.

Through flashbacks, Garner offers insights into his family's history in the small town of Victoria, Indiana. He reveals that Tim's identical twin, Tommy, died at age six after he fell off a slide. Although the boy suffered what appeared to be a minor contusion, the same night he died in his sleep. According to Garner, Tim claims to have little memory of his twin, a lapse that may indicate a serious underlying hurt.

Garner reveals that his late father, Boyce Briggs, hungered for a namesake but was thwarted by Doris, who named all the children. Doris also insisted on treating the twins as a matching set. She gave them similar names, dressed them identically—even on Halloween—and went to the extreme of having a mole on Tim's cheek removed.

Boyce, by contrast, remained removed from his family and society. Each day he isolated himself in his office at home and divided his time between a coin collection and journals that he filled with transcribed news clippings. After Boyce's death, Garner inherited his staggering accumulation of papers and coins, which Garner found "oppressive" in the methodical mental consistency they displayed. Garner fears that this same consistency will emerge in his own life.

Years later, unemotionally and, yes, methodically, Garner helps Tim prepare for the big tournament against ANNDY and accompanies him to the Totaplex Hotel, where as a guest of Congam's, Tim revels in financial freedom for the first time. Imre Szendrei, Tim's chess trainer, soon arrives at the hotel. Although Imre's appearance is peculiar, he is a comforting presence to Tim. Imre offers him discipline and the nudging reach of a potent imagination. Tim senses in his mentor an unquestionable benevolence and like-minded ambitions and drives. In turn, Imre sees in Tim untapped potential.

On the eve of the tournament, Tim meets Jack Westman, a representative of Congam, to review their contract. Jack has an affected manner, and his conversation is contrived. He is the impersonal corporation personified. However, the arrival of Congam employee Vicky Schmidt, for whom Tim feels immediate attraction, eases the meeting, for she adds authenticity. Vicky serves as the public relations liaison for both Tim and Congam, but her instinctive allegiance is clearly skewed toward Tim—man—as opposed to Congam—corporate machine.

Before the tournament, Garner and Tim visit the MIT campus, where they meet graduate student Oliver Conant, the chief programmer of ANNDY. Oliver leads them to the auditorium, where the competition ultimately occurs, to see ANNDY, the acronym for

"Androgynous Androidal Answer" or "A Nice New Dandy Yardstick for the Mind."

The following day, the tournament finally begins. To Tim's great humiliation, he is quickly defeated by ANNDY in the first match. Impulsively, before television cameras, Tim furiously stalks off the stage. Imre, ever the skilled technical and emotional coach, bolsters Tim's confidence and renews his winning spirit. Imre's standard advice to chess players is to concentrate on the opponent's mind and not the board. Here, he tells Tim, "You must play the machine and not the board."

The games now proceed uneventfully and evenly matched. As Tim discovers weaknesses in the machine, he becomes more comfortable and outspoken with the press, remarking to a *Washington Post* reporter that he will "beat ANNDY or die trying." This strikes the fancy of the press, which sensationalizes the notion of man against machine and dubs Tim a modern-day John Henry, alluding to the laborer who in the 1870s claimed he could dig a hole faster than a steam drill.

As Tim's public presence becomes more pronounced, so does his fascination with other public figures, particularly a twelve-year-old Japanese boy, Ma-chan, whose guardian prevented him from hearing any post-Mozart music. Ma-chan is hailed by the press as a musical miracle who can compose classical music that many mistake for Mozart's. Another prominent public figure who holds Tim spellbound is the Reverend Rabbitt, a maniacal but mesmerizing evangelist who lashes his palms and finally his throat during televised sermons. Tim's ambiguity toward both the creative (Ma-chan) and the destructive (Reverend Rabbitt) heralds his own radical actions to come.

As the tournament nears an end with Tim in the lead, Westman proposes a dinner foursome with Vicky and her friend Marian. Westman's selfish motives soon become clear as he flirts openly with Vicky, who rebuffs his sexual overtures with outright insults. However, Tim is clearly out of his social element and does not fully understand their conversation. Rather, he "experiences an old, powerful feeling of exclusion whose roots go deep as childhood, as distant as Victoria, Indiana."

Following dinner, the group decides to return to Tim's hotel room for some much-needed coffee. However, upon arriving at the Totaplex, Westman engineers a transparent excuse to take Marian for a walk. Vicky is both concerned for her friend and furious at Westman. She confides in Tim that good, innocent men such as himself are rare. Again, Tim is slow to perceive her amorous feelings even though she kisses him gently on the cheek. As Tim struggles to interpret her move, his eyes focus on his chessboard. He grabs a chess piece—the potent king—as though it could generate the strength that he lacks to reach out to Vicky as he desires. As Tim slowly advances toward her, he opens his fist for one last look at the conquering king and to his horror realizes that he holds a bishop, the symbol of his impotency with Vicky.

The next day, on the last game of the tournament, Tim cannot be found and remains missing for several days as Vicky arranges an adjournment of the contest. Garner receives a phone call from Linda Faccione, Tim's high-school sweetheart, left behind in Victoria many years ago. She informs Garner that Tim is with her and implores Garner to come "home." Upon arriving, Garner learns that Tim and Linda are to be married, but first Tim plans to finish the tournament. As the brothers take a walk, they discuss the future and see sights representative of their past loves and tragedies.

In the conclusion, Tim appears as the one conquering king. His success is not due to his ability finally to foil the machine. Rather, his history lies in his humanness, his assimilation of childhood emotions into a hopeful life with his beloved Linda. For Tim, that marks progress.

One need not understand chess in order to be absorbed in Brad Leithauser's *Hence*. Characterization is sharp and at times even uncomfortably familiar. A shift in point of view from first person to third in the fifth chapter adds purposeful inconsistency to the character of the apparent speaker, Garner. Since he abhorred his father's machine-like consistency, it is plausible that Garner has chosen to be a blatantly unpredictable narrator. The identity of the narrator is intended to be a mystery, for Leithauser's novel has two title pages, forming the structure of a book within a book. The first is *Hence: A Novel by Brad Leithauser* and the second, *Hence: A Meditation in Voices by Garner Briggs*.

Leithauser's symbolism is at times needlessly obvious, for the reader really recognizes the challenge: how to preserve one's individuality in a rapidly changing world whose pace is stepped up by technological progress. However, the value of Leithauser's point, and the way he blends the past with the present to dramatize progress, is handled masterfully. Indeed, whether humankind is an equal match for its own mechanical creations raises pertinent yet unsettling questions about life in the 21st century. In reading *Hence*, the reader cannot help but wonder whether his or her own interpretations of progress may be focused on too small a board.

Karin A. Nobile

A HISTORY OF THE WORLD IN 10½ CHAPTERS

Author: Julian Barnes (1946–   )
Publisher: Alfred A. Knopf (New York). 307 pp. $18.95
Type of work: Novel
Time: Noah's time to the present
Locale: The world, especially the seas; Mount Ararat; the moon; and heaven

A collection of stories and essays fashioned together as a postmodern novel that draws from humankind's real and imagined history an examination of the ideas of love, truth, and freedom

> *Principal character:*
> NOAH, the captain of the ark and, in this revisionist account, a drunk who was mean, graceless, and incompetent

A History of the World in 10½ Chapters is not a conventional novel at all, but rather a collection of stories, fables, and essays loosely held together with recurring themes, images, and ironies. Postmodernist in conception with its rejection of a traditional story line (each chapter presents different characters and situations) and its conspicuous use of structural invention, Julian Barnes's work is, nonetheless, straightforward, enjoyable reading. His gentle, ironic tone is the major unifying element of the narrative. This irony points to the presence of the author throughout the text as he changes styles and structures to bring forth his ideas. Barnes makes extensive use of comedy in these ten and a half chapters, which are largely concerned with transforming journeys frequently occurring at sea.

The first chapter, "The Stowaway," is a revisionist account of Noah's ark told by a woodworm. This stowaway reports that the traditional version of Noah's journey is wrong. Noah was "a puffed up patriarch who spent half his day grovelling to his God and the other half taking it out on [the animals]." A drunk and a poor sailor, Noah was the pick of a very bad bunch. The animals to him were little more than a floating cafeteria. The woodworm calls to question humankind's ancestry, since all are descended from Noah and "aren't too good with the truth . . . ignoring the bad things makes it easier for [humans] to carry on. But [they] end up believing that bad things never happen."

In the next chapter, "The Visitors," educator and television personality Franklin Hughes is forced to prove himself when his Adriatic lecture cruise is interrupted by Arab terrorists. The intellectual question of at what point altruism is overcome by self-interest in a life-preserving situation confronts him in a real-life situation. Unfortunately, he fails his test.

"The Wars of Religion" presents a mock manuscript of a 16th-century religious trial based on legal procedures and actual cases. The woodworms return to be tried for having "offended God by attacking his House." These "malefactors" have so eaten the bishop's throne that when he leans on the arm it breaks, causing the bishop to strike his head on the floor. He is "cast down into the darkness of imbecility" by these *bestioles*. They also have eaten away the closing words of this manuscript.

While the bishop's transforming journey is a straight line from throne to floor, Kath Ferris, in "The Survivor," makes a circular trip. Leaving a world of marital and nuclear disasters behind, she sails off with her cats. Concerned with survival, she comes to realize that "everything *is* connected, even the parts we don't like." The only way to survive is to face the truth and avoid fabulation ("you keep a few true facts and spin a new story round them").

"Shipwreck," the next chapter, is part factual account, part art history as Barnes explores Géricault's famous painting *Scene of Shipwreck*. Using an 1818 translation, Barnes describes the wreck of the ship *Medusa* and the grim struggle for survival amid the fighting, the thirst, and the cannibalism aboard the aimless raft. Then he turns to an exploration of the artist's motives and methods. Referring to the color plate of the painting included in this chapter, Barnes speculates on Géricault's steps as he turns history into art. The reader becomes one with the sufferers on the raft as they violently strain "for the speck of the rescuing vessel." There is no response, "just as there is no response to most human feelings. . . . We are all lost at sea, washed between hope and despair, hailing something that may never come to rescue us. Catastrophe has become art; but this is no reducing process. It is freeing, enlarging, explaining."

In 1839, several years after viewing *Scene of Shipwreck* in Dublin, Amanda Fergusson climbs Mount Ararat, believed to be the landing place of Noah's ark. This chapter, "The Mountain," deals with Amanda's mission to "intercede for the soul of [her] father." It is on this holy mountain that she wishes to find the just and merciful God and to purge her father's sins of disbelief. She falls down the mountain and is severely injured. Her traveling companion, wondering if Amanda did not cause the fall herself, has her taken to rest in a cave. Placed so that she can see the moon through the opening of the cave, Amanda prepares to be taken unto God. She dies during the night, leaving her companion to ponder upon what Amanda had maintained: "that there were two explanations of everything, that each required the exercise of faith, and that we had been given free will [to] choose between them."

"Three Simple Stories" presents the book in miniature, three sepa-rate stories. In the first, a male survivor of the *Titanic* is hired as a consultant for a movie based on that event. Barnes here again is ques-tioning humankind's "gene pool." "The heroes . . . went down nobly with the ship; whereas the cowards, the panickers, the deceivers found reasons for skulking in a lifeboat." In the second story, Jonah in the whale is compared with a more recent episode of a sailor who was swallowed by a whale and survived, presumably. Barnes uses these two events to question the basis of myth. Rather than referring back to humanity's collective memories, Barnes suggests that myth refers forward so that "myth will become reality, however sceptical we might be." In the last of the "three simple stories," the liner *St. Louis*, with some 900 Jewish refugees, embarks from Hamburg a few months before the start of World War II. The refugees wander the Atlantic for forty days and forty nights while politicians in potential host countries vacillate about asking them in. Finally, they return to Europe where several countries agree to take a quota of Jews. The Jews' chances for survival depend on the country to which they had been assigned.

"Upstream!" is a story told entirely in letters, postcards, and tele-grams from Charlie, an actor on location in the Venezuelan jungle, to Pippa, his lover, who has found out that he has been unfaithful. He describes to her the events that take place as they shoot the movie of two Jesuit missionaries' first contact with Indians. When his costar is drowned in a raft accident caused by the Indians, he becomes obsessed with the Indians' motives. Charlie believes that they are not primitives but advanced members of a "post-acting civilization." He feels that there may be some connection for the Indians between the actual incident and its reenactment. Perhaps, he muses, this movie reenact-ment is a renewal of a myth the Indians have held for 500 years.

"Parenthesis" presents the unorganized, stream-of-consciousness thoughts of a man lying awake beside his sleeping wife. It is an essay on the nature of love. "If we don't [believe in love]," he concludes, "then we merely surrender to the history of the world and to someone else's truth." Love, like free will and objective truth, defies the history of the world.

"Project Ararat" is the story of astronaut Spike Tiggler, who hears God's voice while kicking a football on the surface of the moon. "Find Noah's Ark," he hears God tell him, and his life is changed. He spends the next year studying the Bible; then he raises funds for Project Ar-arat. On the mountain, in the late 1970s, he finds the two caves Amanda Fergusson had found in 1839. In one of the caves, Spike finds a skeleton he believes to be Noah's. Scientific analysis reveals the bones to be only 150 years old and almost certainly a woman's. Undaunted by this evidence, Spike begins raising funds for the second Project Ararat.

"The Dream" finds a nameless narrator awakening to find himself in heaven. His food is perfect, his clothes comfortable; sex and golf are great. He meets famous people from Patsy Cline to Noah to Adolf Hitler. Heaven is "a continuation of life . . . but better." It turns out to be just what each individual wishes it to be. Hell is small, more like a theme park. People stay on for as long as they want the perfection, then they die off into nothingness. The chapter, and the book, ends with the narrator saying: "I dreamt that I woke up. It's the oldest dream of all, and I've just had it."

A History of the World in 10½ Chapters is a book about transforming journeys. Some journeys have happy conclusions; others are disasters. The narrative line goes back and forth—bobbing like a raft at sea. Each chapter brings new characters, new situations, and a different type of narrative. These are not spoofs, as the novel's title may lead the reader to believe. While some chapters are stronger than others, Julian Barnes unifies these disparate elements through control of tone and the stringing together of recurrences. Barnes points to the irony and humor of even the grimmest situations and treats his characters, even the more foolish ones, with a gentle, humane irony. Noah, the ark, woodworms, rafts, survival or death at sea, and the Flood are but a few of the many recurring ideas and objects that intertwine these pieces. Amanda Fergusson dies looking at the moon from Mount Ararat, and, nearly 150 years later, Spike Tiggler comes from the moon to find her remains. History is repeating itself over and over.

Internationally acclaimed novelist Julian Barnes has created a work that is thought provoking while being both entertaining and comic. His main concern is with ideas—love, objective truth, free will. They are, like the speck of a rescue ship to Géricault's raft, or Noah's ark, or heaven, or God, almost impossible to obtain. But each individual must continue to believe in them or surrender to the history of the world.

John Sokolnicki

HONORABLE JUSTICE: THE LIFE OF OLIVER WENDELL HOLMES

Author: Sheldon M. Novick
Publisher: Little, Brown and Company (Boston). 522 pp. $24.95
Type of work: Biography
Time: Mid-19th and 20th centuries
Locale: Boston; Washington, D.C.; Europe

*An intelligently written biography of Oliver Wendell Holmes placed within
the historical, social, and cultural perspectives of his time*

> *Principal personages:*
> OLIVER WENDELL HOLMES, a hardworking, ambitious, pas-
> sionate, and intellectual man who became a U.S. Supreme
> Court justice
> FANNY DIXWELL HOLMES, his wife

Sheldon Novick begins *Honorable Justice*, his biography of Oliver
Wendell Holmes, with a lengthy preface citing the reasons why previously there has been no full biography of Holmes. Authorized biogra-
phers either died before they could complete their work or gave up in
the face of inordinate difficulties, one of which was the sheer mass of
primary source material in the form of Holmes's letters, diaries, and
writings. Another difficulty was how to portray a man of Holmes's
complexity in both his personal and working life.

Holmes was born into a mid-19th-century, upper-class Boston family. Through his famous father, also known as "The Autocrat of the
Breakfast-Table" from his pieces by that name in the *Atlantic
Monthly*, Holmes was early introduced into Boston Brahmin society,
becoming closely associated with such well-known figures as William
and Henry James, Ralph Waldo Emerson, and Henry Cabot Lodge.
Holmes's father was a doctor who gave up his practice when Holmes
was a boy in order to pursue the more profitable career of lecturing
and writing. The doctor and young Wendell, who talked incessantly,
soon became verbal rivals, with Wendell gradually learning to hold his
own against his father's verbal assaults and to make logical, cogent
arguments.

Wendell's mother, although she indulged him as her favorite, also
taught him a strong sense of duty and encouraged him to accomplish
something every day. These characteristics developed at his parents'
knees were to be evident throughout his long career.

In 1857, Wendell entered Harvard. Already a prodigious reader, he
began to read more widely in the areas of poetry and philosophy and
to develop an interest in art. During this period two events occurred

that were to mark his life forever. The first was a pattern of visiting in the home of his old schoolmaster, where he met Fanny Dixwell, the young woman who much later would become his wife. The other was his battle experience during the Civil War. As this Boston-bred gentleman was himself seriously wounded several times and watched countless men die horrible, painful deaths, he developed a hardness about death that he would carry throughout his life: ". . . he had seen too much death to linger over lost friends or friendships." Even though he had enlisted, he seemed throughout his life embittered about mothers who send their sons off to war.

In 1864, Holmes entered Harvard Law School. While there he was profoundly influenced by the work of Henry Sumner Maine, whose book *Ancient Law* provided a much-needed contrast to the dry and more generally accepted thought of Jeremy Bentham. Holmes began to explore his own developing ideas about the nature of the law in his articles in the *American Law Review*. His early skirmishes with his father had bred in him an intelligent literary style. It was during this period that Holmes began not only to clarify his thoughts for himself but also to plant seeds of a simple yet revolutionary thought—that law did not have to depend upon political theory, but upon the decisions of the courts, that law could be a science. Holmes was to bring all these ideas together, refine them, and publish them in his book *The Common Law*, still in print after more than a hundred years.

After his marriage to Fanny, who was in poor health and, except for brief respites, was to remain so for the more than fifty years of their marriage, Holmes immersed himself in work. He joined a Boston law firm and wrote essays for the *American Law Review* as well as a revision of *Kent's Commentaries*. He later became editor of the *Law Review*.

Once this frenzied work period was over, Holmes traveled many times to Europe, most often without Fanny, who had become almost a recluse. A man who had always loved women, Holmes formed over his lifetime several long-lasting relationships well demonstrating his passionate nature, and while in Europe he made many well-connected friends who often supported his rather unusual ideas when his own countrymen seemed confused by them.

As Holmes moved forward in his career, in a manner that sometimes appeared agonizingly slow to him, through the Massachusetts Supreme Court to being its chief justice and then on to the U.S. Supreme Court, he remained dedicated to the pursuit of the answer to what was for him the essential question, What is law? The range of his opinions was vast, and his ability to handle heavy caseloads was extraordinary. Holmes's complexities are to be seen in his seemingly disparate opinions; he favored tolerance and fairness and yet failed to uphold the voting rights of Southern blacks. He often appeared to be a loner absorbed in his scholarly pursuits, yet he was capable of long-lasting, rich friendships.

In *Honorable Justice*, Novick has succeeded triumphantly in bringing order out of the chaos of material on Oliver Wendell Holmes, kindling endless speculation on and interest in what made him America's best-known and possibly greatest judge. Although the author presents a balanced portrait of Holmes's family life, education, war experiences, friendships, and career, the reader might wish for a greater understanding of the raison d'être behind many of Holmes's ideas. A bit more fleshing out of his internal motivations would have been welcome. The first several chapters seem to be more reportorial in nature, whereas later chapters explore Holmes's character more fully, allowing him to speak through his letters and diaries. Especially moving were Holmes's letters home during the Civil War. His relationship with his wife, although not discussed in an illuminating way, provides further insight into Holmes's character. In spite of his friendships, both casual and serious, with other women, he remained both loyal to and appreciative of Fanny. Novick has turned a shadowy figure of almost mythic proportions into a believable human being.

Elizabeth Bouvier Spencer

HOW WAR CAME: THE IMMEDIATE ORIGINS OF THE SECOND WORLD WAR, 1938–1939

Author: Donald Cameron Watt
Publisher: Pantheon Books (New York). 736 pp. $29.95
Type of work: History
Time: 1938–1939
Locale: Europe; the Soviet Union; Japan; China

A vividly detailed account of the diplomatic encounters and miscalculations that set the stage for World War II

Principal personages:
ADOLF HITLER, the Nazi chancellor of Germany
JOACHIM VON RIBBENTROP, the German foreign minister
JOZEF STALIN, the first secretary of the Soviet Union
VYACHESLAV MOLOTOV, the Soviet foreign minister
NEVILLE CHAMBERLAIN, the prime minister of Britain
NEVILE HENDERSON, the British ambassador in Berlin
EDOUARD DALADIER, the prime minister of France
GEORGES BONNET, the French foreign minister
BENITO MUSSOLINI, the Fascist premier of Italy
GALEAZZO CIANO DI CORTELLAZO, the Italian foreign minister
JÓZEF BECK, the Polish foreign minister

A wary reader would question the need for another book exploring the origins of World War II. Nevertheless, D. C. Watt, professor of international history at the University of London, has produced an important new work. Twenty years in the making, it is a labor of love and the capstone of a distinguished career. Combing the archives in seventeen countries, plumbing such diverse materials as private notebooks and official memoranda, it is a relentless piece of research. Within this volume Watt reexamines some popular conceptions about the fatal months preceding the war and reintroduces the role of personality into historical writing.

Some modern historians would insist that nothing can be learned from the historical process, that it is all a matter of interpretation; history is a flowing economic or social dynamic, from which scholars may pluck the facts to fashion their own particular ideas. Watt challenges this popular notion by showing that individuals can shape, often tragically, the course of world affairs. People's health, background, education, refinement, and emotions dictate their reactions to explosive, fast-moving events. And before the current technology and media boom, government leaders relied on the ability of their staff members to interpret and relay information.

In the anxious months covered in this work, leadership based its reactions on the reports of ambassadors and ministers, frequently with frighteningly naive or misguided views. Each primary actor, secondary character, or marginal player deluged his respective foreign offices with reports. Vague, prejudiced, or conflicting information made understanding difficult and concrete positions impossible. This unclear data, in fact, allowed the respective sides to misjudge and underestimate the other fellow's resolve and commitment. From this overwhelmingly confused diplomatic scene emerges Watt's major theme.

After the Munich settlement, Hitler and his foreign minister, Joachim von Ribbentrop, planned to launch a major European land war. It would be a lightning attack somewhere in Eastern Europe, probably in Poland or the Baltic states. This required the isolation of the region through direct annexation or by creating economic dependency in the bordering Central and Eastern European nations. Italy would have to contain France and patrol the southern flank along the Mediterranean. Because its leadership was so ready to appease, Britain would present no military problem. Once accomplished, Hitler would be free to unleash his racial theories on cowed Jews, Slavs, and other unfortunate minorities.

The key to this plan turned on German understanding of the Italian and British "minds." Mussolini's rise to and subsequent use of unbridled power was Hitler's model. Yet while Hitler had a ruthless, single-minded sincerity, Mussolini was a grasping opportunist. After his unremarkable attempt to control southeastern Europe by invading Albania proved fruitless, Mussolini's influence waned. Hitler rightly relegated him to the junior partner. European democracies viewed Mussolini's military force as inconsequential. He then attempted to realign with the Allies, or at least as a neutral. However, twenty years as a brawling, rough bully made other nations doubt Il Duce's new-found moderation.

Hitler's opinion of British willingness to sacrifice all of Eastern Europe to avoid a direct military confrontation proved totally incorrect. He completely misread three facets of viable democratic politics: public opinion, consensus decision-making, and minority reports. The average British citizen did not readily accept the British government's vacillating policies toward Germany. If the government continued to ignore public opinion it could find itself replaced. Decisions were not debated in private; British politics enjoyed a reasonably open forum. Each government ministry had its own agenda. Efforts to unite them behind a common goal was a slow, deliberate process. Yet personal accommodation did not translate into national policy. Because an individual ambassador gave in to Hitler's whims, this should not have been generalized as an English character trait.

However, the laborious process of developing the English resolve produced mixed signals. To the small nations of Eastern Europe, Hitler appeared invincible and England appeared distant. German actions were cold and flimsy and smacked of imperial condescension. Some countries, such as Bulgaria, were manned by weaklings and were swallowed into the German sphere of influence. Others, such as the Turkish regime, were controlled by the proud and stubborn who believed in the righteousness of their actions and survived. Certain individuals, such as the Slovak president, were honorable persons who treated Nazis with toleration and were broken for their efforts.

Two key nations, France and the Soviet Union, were watching these skirmishes with increased concern, and each was truly out to protect its interests. France was committed, despite any provocation, to avoid war with Germany, at all costs. French strength had been tested severely in World War I, and French honor had been affronted by Hitler. Now, French integrity would be compromised by the deceit and trickery employed by the foreign ministry to cloud its intentions. French ambassadors would lie about backing treaty obligations, and ministers would use any tactic to avoid diplomatic confrontation. France would be pulled into the fray as an unwilling ally and collaborator.

The Soviet Union was fitfully drawing itself from the evil era of industrialization and the Great Terror. Society was still frozen under the icy paranoia of Jozef Stalin. It was a land without the equipment, leadership, or willpower to commit to a land war. The Bolshevik ideology was still too strong to allow a complete alliance with either democracy or fascism. But Stalin was a very astute politician and a pragmatic, if devious, man. For the price of noninvolvement, to allow the Soviet Union time to recoup, he would make a pact with either side. Because Germany appeared powerful, he chose Hitler. This would prove to be Hitler's undoing and would become a pivotal event in 20th-century Russian history.

At this point the stage was set; each country's leadership had its preconceived notions firmly in place. Individuals were still trying personal diplomacy to win last-minute concessions, but each nation's leaders were now committed. Hitler made his move in Danzig and on the Polish border. He felt that history was on his side, and he did not care how other countries would respond. Surprised by the British response, Hitler was reduced to an infantile rage. He unleashed the "dogs of war" that would engulf the world.

Donald Cameron Watt has produced a fresh, lucid, rich account of the events immediately preceding World War II. His exhaustive research of thousands of European documents is given engaging voice in the prose of *How War Came*, a diplomatic history that presents confusing events clearly and chronologically. Watt's writing is precise, sharp, and focused. He clearly states his particular topic and addresses all the personalities and events that shaped its outcome. For the general reader who must organize the events, names, and locales, this structure is exceedingly beneficial.

But Watt, who is British, maintains a wry humor and a need to instruct. In the midst of a particularly complex explanation he will construct a beautifully timed aside to lighten the reader's burden. While outlining a certain individual's response, he will defend or attack the person in very specific terms. Watt has performed an invaluable service in this history. The personages who inhabit these pages emerge as interesting human beings. In a few phrases Watt paints an accurate, lively portrait of each figure. The reader can begin to experience how and why events developed in the manner they did. The human condition remains the same: people see and hear what they want, and they react according to individual self-interest.

Edward B. Rowe

IF THE RIVER WAS WHISKEY

Author: T. Coraghessan Boyle (1948–)
Publisher: Viking Press (New York). 224 pp. $17.95
Type of work: Short stories
Time: The present
Locale: Primarily the United States, particularly California

Sixteen stories focusing, usually satirically, on bizarre and extreme forms of behavior in modern life

T. Coraghessan Boyle once again proves himself a master of satire and absurdity in this most recent collection of short stories, all of which have been published previously in major literary magazines. Brought together in this way, they attest to the virtuosity of the author.

The opening line of "Modern Love," like most first lines in Boyle's stories, is wonderfully deadpan and understated, yet it effectively plunges the reader into the heart of the story. The narrator explains, "There was no exchange of body fluids on the first date, and that suited both of us just fine." He is deeply in love with Breda, whose pathological obsession with germs and disease dictates her approach to everything in life, including love. She refuses to make love unless each participant is clad in "a full-body condom." He agrees to undergo a battery of physical and mental tests that would make an astronaut quail and is finally rejected because he once sold shoes. He pleads with her, "Breda, please listen to me. We were so close." She answers, ". . . not that close."

The bleak epigraph to the collection, from Italo Calvino's *If on a Winter's Night a Traveler*, is an apt one for most of the stories in this collection: "You know that the best you can expect is to avoid the worst." In "Peace of Mind," Giselle Nyerges, a saleswoman for security systems, takes advantage of people who live their lives with this fatalistic sentiment as their motto. In hushed confidential tones she terrifies her clients with stories about the woman whose naked body was desecrated with a cigarette lighter and the "elderly lady and the overworked Mexican from the knife-sharpening service." The Hunsickers listen to her pitch in rapt attention and sleep well only when the "Armed Response" sign is planted in their front lawn. Flushed with success, Giselle hops into her Mercedes and brightly whistles on the way to her next client, Ellis Coles. He proves to be a madman who virtually holds her prisoner while he launches into a tirade about the individual's impotence in the face of a dangerous and degenerate society. Coles eventually releases her and goes on a shooting rampage that takes him by the Hunsicker home. The "Armed Response" sign, "like a red flag in front of a bull," draws him into the house, where he massacres the whole family.

Boyle is especially gleeful when aiming his barbs at those whose adrenalin pumps at the thought of making a sale or a deal. In "The Devil and Irv Cherniske," an updated version of the Faust legend, Irv sells his soul for riches and success to a devil dressed in a "Lacoste shirt, plaid slacks, and white Adidas." In "Hard Sell," Boyle indulges in full-scale hyperbole in creating a Hollywood image-maker who has been hired to sell the Ayatollah to the Western world. He is particularly skillful in creating the lingo for the manic self-important agent: ". . . about the beard. Tell him beards went out with Jim Morrison—and the bathrobe business is kinda kinky, and we can play to that if he wants, but wouldn't he feel more comfortable in a nice Italian knit?"

Eccentrics, madmen, and characters dominated by their obsessions pervade these pages. Zoltan in "The Human Fly" is single-minded in his passion to achieve fame at any cost. His death-defying feats border on the insane and ultimately prove fatal, but there is a certain integrity in his refusal to attempt less. His small-time agent suffers a few moral frissons as he watches Zoltan's deterioration, but is quite willing to embrace success after Zoltan's death when he sells his image for a Saturday-morning animated series. In "Me Cago en la Leche," Robert Jordan, grandson of Hemingway's character, is an angry young punk who travels to Nicaragua with hair gel and plastic explosives, seeking the ultimate thrill. He blows up a plane filled with Twinkies, Budweisers, and Cup of Soup, but is left behind by the "counter-counterrevolutionary" band to face the gunfire of the contras on his own.

The humor is at its blackest in "King Bee," in which a childless couple, the Mallows, adopt nine-year-old Anthony, a surreal nightmare of a child. He is obsessed by and identifies with bees because "they have no mercy." He greases his hair into spikes, dons a black T-shirt that says Megadeth, roasts the family dog in the oven, and attempts suicide with a utility knife. Anthony is institutionalized after he puts his "stinger" in a fifth-grade girl. The Mallows give up their jobs and relocate in an attempt to escape the barrage of death threats Anthony sends them. He shows up on their doorstep in hospital pajamas, six-feet tall and so obese that his eyes almost disappear, "sunk in their pockets of flesh." With him are 30,000 bees. The ending, in which Anthony spares the Mallows and submits himself to the wrath of the bees, is typically unsettling.

"Sorry Fugu" is the story of Albert, a young chef who has recently opened his own restaurant and is anxiously awaiting the visit of the city's foremost food critic, one Willa Frank, who is notorious for destroying restaurants with her scathing reviews. Her regular dining companion, "the Palate," dislikes everything he is served. Albert lures Willa into his kitchen where he feeds her the most exquisite delicacies that his culinary artistry can produce. He coaxes her gently from dish to dish, and Boyle makes it clear that this is an act of love for Albert, a seduction. Willa savors each bite in a kind of trance, and only toward the end of the meal does she admit to Albert that she brings the Palate along because she does not trust her own taste and is frightened by the risk involved in announcing that she likes something. "Sorry Fugu" is a thinly veiled attack on critics, but it is in no way vituperative. It is funny and brimming with some of the most marvelous descriptions of delectable dishes in literature.

"Drunk and in debt, on the run from a bad marriage, two DWI convictions, and the wheezy expiring gasps of his moribund mother," Davey McGahee hops a plane from New York to Ireland on impulse. At the opening of "The Miracle at Ballinspittle," he is in the midst of a crowd of believers, tourists, and the curious who have come to see the "snotgreen" image of the Virgin that reputedly moved its limbs one day. McGahee is shocked to hear his name called by the statue, who suddenly becomes a "hissing gargoyle," commanding him to look upon the sins of his life. There follows a litany of the sins committed by McGahee, each sin accompanied by visual aids. McGahee eventually disappears, leaving behind mountains of rotting food, oceans of alcohol, and a strange assortment of women from his fantasies (including Virginia Woolf and Emma Bovary). The tourism figures jump 672 percent in the aftermath of the miracle.

In "Sinking House," Muriel's husband, Monty, who in his final years "called her bonehead and dildo and cuffed her like a dog," has died, and Muriel turns on all of her faucets and sprinklers in order to drown out the sound of years of his drunken cursing and to wash away the contamination she feels surrounds her. Next door, twenty-three-year-old Meg Terwilliger begins to notice the water rising through her sunroom floor. Meg is absorbed by the minutiae of her daily life—her stretching exercises; picking up her daughter, Tiffany, from nursery school; dropping off her dog, Queenie, at the vet's. Meg and her husband try to reason with Muriel, but are forced to report the problem to the police who eventually take Muriel into custody. As she leaves, she sadly stares at Meg with a look that says, "this is what it comes to. Fifty years and this is what it comes to." Meg, clearly out of character, begins to muse about Muriel and the "wreckage of her life" and to speculate about her own life and future. In the end, Meg turns the sprinklers on, "just for a minute, to see what it felt like. She wouldn't leave them on long—it could threaten the whole foundation of her house. That much she understood."

In "Thawing Out," a young man, afraid of making a commitment to the woman he loves, leaves her to go to San Francisco for a vacation. He drifts aimlessly for six months and finally returns penniless, homeless, and unemployed, knowing only that all he wants is to be with her. She is a member of the Polar Bear Club, and a year earlier, after watching her plunge into the freezing water, he had ridiculed the practice as barbaric. Upon his return, he finds her once again at the water's edge. Wordlessly, he strips and takes the plunge with her to discover that the water is, as she had said, "warm as a bath."

The title story "If the River Was Whiskey," is similarly poignant, providing a glimpse of a family in dissolution, particularly a boy and his alcoholic unemployed father. They are on a vacation trying to heal old wounds and find some common ground on which to build anew, but it is sadly clear that the father's self-destructive impulses are relentlessly dragging them deeper into the maelstrom of despair.

Boyle is best known for his savage satirical attacks on the fads, foibles, and fantasies of men and women in contemporary life. He takes the reader's hidden fears and obsessions and inflates them to monstrous proportions until they provoke howls of laughter. At the same time, one is forced to shudder at the distortions while recognizing that human beings harbor the capacity for such extreme and bizarre behavior. The collection contains all of Boyle's favorite hobbyhorses including paranoia, greed and materialism, scatology, and violence.

In many of the stories, Boyle's prose is acid sharp and machine-gun fast, challenging the reader to keep up with it and not to flinch. But he can also lower the volume and slow the pace when he wants to explore the enigmas of human relationships. This is a rich and varied collection, displaying the ample range of Boyle's gifts.

Maria Brazill

INNUMERACY: MATHEMATICAL ILLITERACY AND ITS CONSEQUENCES

Author: John Allen Paulos
Publisher: Hill and Wang (New York). 135 pp. $16.95
Type of work: Science

Math professor John Allen Paulos's lucid and entertaining account of the mathematics illiteracy crisis in the United States

The word "innumeracy" has been in the dictionary for years, but its usage hereafter will likely be attributed to John Allen Paulos, who cogently brings it to light in *Innumeracy: Mathematical Illiteracy and Its Consequences*. Simply stated, innumeracy is the inability to deal with numbers and their functions. In discussing this counterpart of illiteracy, Paulos frequently uses anecdotes and quotations, including a weathercaster's announcement of "a 50 percent chance of rain for Saturday and a 50 percent chance for Sunday, [concluding] that there was therefore a 100 percent chance of rain that weekend." Paulos is not only flabbergasted by the forecaster's conclusion, but is dismayed that there is negligible indignation against such an innumerate statement. He further takes umbrage at the fact that while few educated people will admit to nonfamiliarity with such literary greats as Shakespeare or Goethe, most will readily admit that they have no knowledge of such mathematical greats as Euler or Laplace. Hence, innumeracy is presented here not as a symptom of the uneducated, but rather as the unfortunate condition of an entire society.

Paulos begins by challenging the public's comprehension of large numbers, which, as he convincingly reports, is actually incomprehension. Most people have little or no grasp of millions, billions, trillions, and so on. Paulos recalls a doctor describing a certain procedure as (1) having a one-in-a-million-risk factor, (2) being ninety-nine percent safe, and (3) usually going quite well. Another example of large-number folly appears on the package of the original Rubik's cube. It read that the cube could attain more than 3 billion states, which while not untrue is grossly understated; the number of possible states actually exceeds 4×10^{19} (the scientific notation for 4 followed by nineteen zero's). The "more than 3 billion" statement is comparable, Paulos says, to posting a sign at the Lincoln Tunnel that reads "New York, population more than 6."

If the understanding of large numbers is generally lacking, the concepts of probability and coincidence are even less well comprehended. Innumerates have a tendency to underestimate the frequency of coincidences; they often give inordinate significance to ordinary correspondences while overlooking legitimate evidence. For example, if 367 people gather, it is 100 percent certain that at least 2 of them share the same birthday. But to be only 50 percent certain, how many people must gather? Half of 367? No. The correct answer (for which Paulos gives a concise derivation) is 23 people. It is likely, however, that those 23 would marvel at the coincidence of a shared birthday rather than appreciate the mathematical principle that prevailed.

Paulos clearly points out the harmonious association he finds between innumeracy and pseudoscience. The careless reasoning that leads to a belief in pseudoscientific "evidence" can be traced back to the misapplication and misinterpretation of mathematical principles.

> Even such fundamental mathematical verities as . . . "1 and 1 are 2," can be misapplied: one cup of water plus one cup of popcorn are not equal to two cups of soggy popcorn. . . . If one's models . . . are no good, the conclusions that follow won't be either. . . . Any bit of nonsense can be computerized—astrology, biorhythms, the *I Ching*—but that doesn't make the nonsense any more valid.

Thriving among such nonsense is parapsychology, and Paulos has no compunction about labeling ESP proponent Uri Geller a charlatan, paranormalist S. G. Soal a practitioner of chicanery, parapsychology pioneer J. B. Rhine a deviser of faulty experiments, and self-described psychic Jeane Dixon a purveyor of fatuous predictions. Even renowned educator Horace Mann is disdainfully included as one who revered the practice of phrenology (the reading of bumps and contours on one's head) as "the guide to philosophy and the handmaiden of Christianity." Journalist and political leader Horace Greeley was another brilliant man who succumbed to the 19th-century preoccupation with phrenology; he advocated the phrenological testing of all railroad engineers.

The most pervasive pseudoscience today is astrology. For many it is a way of life, while for others it is no more than the amusement of a daily horoscope. Cumulatively, however, astrology is not amusing but distressing, because, as Paulos says, "if people believe astrologers and astrology, it's frightening to consider whom or what else they'll believe. It's especially so when, like President Reagan, they have immense power to act on these beliefs."

Paulos describes recent experiments involving 30 astrologers and 116 clients. For each client, the astrologer was given three anonymous personality profiles, one of which was the client's. Using client-supplied astrological data, the astrologer was to pick the proper profile. The astrologers were correct about one out of three times, which is no better than *anyone's* chance. Unfortunately, revealing such facts usually has little, if any, impact on believers.

What are the origins of a national innumeracy that afflicts even the educated? What promotes an essentially math-poor society? In Paulos's words, the reasons are "poor education, psychological blocks, and romantic misconceptions about . . . mathematics." He is critical of the conventional presentation of mathematics beginning in grade school. The dearth of imagination in math textbooks is a major educational deficit. And non-math-major teachers, especially those in the lower grades, are woefully undereducated in math. How does weak grade-school math translate into math at the graduate and research level? It translates poorly. In fact, in 1986-87, American universities awarded 739 doctorates in mathematics; of these, fewer than half were conferred upon U.S. citizens.

Paulos makes a strong case for acquiring a defensible knowledge of statistics. Indeed, the very lifeblood of Western socioeconomics is the collection and interpretation of statistical data. As an innumerate society, Americans are particularly vulnerable to the willful, as well as the unwitting, misuse of statistical analysis. A good example is the polling process. One should always ask of poll results, "What exactly do these results represent? Who or what were actually surveyed? What professional, cultural, or other relevant factors were either favored or ignored?" Such queries promote a healthy skepticism toward what is commonly manipulation of the blind acceptance of numerical data. As an example, it is much cited that one out of every eleven women will develop breast cancer, but when the source of this statistic is clarified by Paulos, the resulting analysis, though still worthy of attention, is far more reasonable and far less terrifying:

> [The statistic of one in eleven] applies only to an imaginary sample of women all of whom live to age eighty-five. . . . At age forty, approximately one woman in a thousand develops breast cancer. . . .

It is important, also, to question the outcome of a mail-in questionnaire. The respondents of such a survey are a self-selected sample, which nearly always effects biased results. For this very reason, the use of self-selected studies is valued highly in advertising—it is a technically legitimate method of convincing the purchasing public of just about anything.

Paulos concludes by pointing out the dichotomy of a society that is critically dependent on math and science and yet fosters indifference to its own innumeracy. He is angered at a media-bred obsession with a hostage on a jet, while the environmental deterioration of the planet receives relatively little public passion. "The discrepancies between our pretensions and reality are usually quite extensive," Paulos writes, but his "desire to arouse a sense of numerical proportion and an appreciation for the irreducibly probabilistic nature of life—this, rather than anger, was the primary motivation for the book.''

Mathematics is not a particularly popular subject in the English-speaking world. To write a book about it, specifically directed to the American public, would seem futile, at best. To find that book on best-seller lists throughout North America for weeks on end would seem unimaginable, at least. But the book exists. *Innumeracy* is John Allen Paulos's latest and great contribution to the cause of Western numeracy.

The present state of innumeracy deserves his vituperation, but Paulos never berates his readers. He comes across as a patient and benevolent parent—wishing to inspire, eager to teach, quick to amuse, and ever vigilant against the guises of ignorance that ensnare the uninformed. Even his assaults on the pseudosciences, for which he apparently has only contempt, are good-natured and restrained. The restraint works—his message comes through loud and clear, and it is far more palatable than what could have been overindulgent acerbity.

Numerates and innumerates alike will appreciate the humor that characterizes the book. Explaining the multiplication principle, Paulos creates the example of taking a group photo of eight Western leaders. His question is, In how many possible poses would President Reagan be standing next to Prime Minister Thatcher? This scenario already is more entertaining than the typical high-school problem of arranging blue and red socks in a drawer. The real Paulos touch, however, comes when he says that to answer the question one should first "assume that Reagan and Thatcher are placed in a large burlap bag"—a suggestion having little to do with the math, but nonetheless a valid problem-solving allusion worth thinking about.

Most of what Paulos says is worth thinking about. It really is time that Americans overcame their mathematical inadequacies and invested some serious interest in the proliferation of numeracy among schoolchildren. One of the best ways to promote a more positive math environment in the schools is to correct negative math attitudes at home. John Allen Paulos's *Innumeracy* is a good place to start.

Christine Lindberg Stevens

IN OUR IMAGE: AMERICA'S EMPIRE IN THE PHILIPPINES

Author: Stanley Karnow (1925–   )
Publisher: Random House (New York). 494 pp. $24.95
Type of work: History
Time: 10th–20th centuries
Locale: The Philippines and the United States

The story of the Philippines from antiquity to the present, focusing on U.S.-Philippine relations since 1898 when the Pacific archipelago became a U.S. possession following the Spanish-American War

> Principal personages:
> EMILIO AGUINALDO Y FAMY, a 19th-century Filipino national-
>   ist
> CORAZON AQUINO, president of the Philippines since 1986
> DOUGLAS MACARTHUR, the American most admired by Filipi-
>   nos
> FERDINAND MARCOS, president of the Philippines, 1965–1986
> SERGIO OSMEÑA, president of the Philippines, 1944–1946
> MANUEL LUIS QUEZON Y MOLINA, president of the Philip-
>   pines, 1935–1944

There are places American media moguls consider "off the news map" because too few Americans understand or care about developments there. Such a place is the Republic of the Philippines—aside from periodic reference to the sensitive political issue of U.S. bases, the Subic Bay navy yard, and the Clark airfield. Easily sensationalized events are an exception, of course, as when Benigno "Ninoy" Aquino was gunned down at the Manila airport on his return from the United States in 1983 or when his widow, Corazon "Cory" Aquino, success-fully rallied "people power" to depose the corrupt dictator Ferdinand Marcos in 1986. Even so, the American public seemed to be less interested in the political significance of the events than in the minutiae of the assassination, the metamorphosis of a housewife to president, or the mind-boggling shoe collection of Marcos's wife, Imelda.

This is ironic in light of the close historical bond between the two countries since 1898, when the 7,000 or so islands making up the ar-chipelago became the first (and only) colony of the United States. Stanley Karnow, the author of this book, was himself unprepared as a newly arrived foreign correspondent to find people speaking American English and very knowledgeable about the United States—almost as if they were "some kind of lost American tribe that had somehow become detached from the U.S. mainland and floated across the Pa-cific." *In Our Image: America's Empire in the Philippines* is, then, one American's efforts to go beyond the headlines to the historical conjuncture.

Karnow devotes two chapters to the story of the Philippines before American colonial rule, beginning with the trade ties established by the Chinese in the 10th century. The "discovery" of the islands, as reported in history books, came in 1521 when Ferdinand Magellan made landfall, strode ashore with the royal Spanish standard, and planted a wooden cross. Karnow found fragments of this cross, real or bogus, displayed in a shabby pavilion on a noisy street in downtown Cebu, the large city standing today where Magellan landed.

For over three centuries thereafter, the Philippines (named for Philip II, king of Spain) remained under Spanish rule. The heritage from this period included administrative unification, economic growth, establishment of the Catholic faith, the beginning of an educational system, and a long tradition of corruption and exploitation by Spanish officials and missionaries. The wealthy Filipino families who wield the real political power in the Philippines today can all trace their rise to the graft-ridden land-grant system of Spanish rule. By the end of the 19th century, however, the Filipino people were rebelling and got their first national hero and martyr when José Rizal was accused of fomenting insurrection and executed by the Spanish in 1896.

Meanwhile, Spain was experiencing trouble in its Cuban colony, and Americans, in a mingling of anticolonial fervor and economic interests, began pressing Spain to free Cuba. Tensions were high when an explosion sank the U.S. cruiser *Maine* in Havana in 1898, precipitating the Spanish-American War. Among the provisions of the treaty ending that war was Spain's relinquishing the Philippines to the United States. Thus did the United States acquire a colonial "empire" in Asia.

Without a policy for this eventuality, William McKinley, then U.S. president, floundered while the public debated the morality of U.S. governance of the Philippines and the army moved to establish law and order in the "protectorate." There were, however, Spanish holdouts and nationalists to contend with—the Filipinos wanted independence, not just a change of colonial regimes—and what Karnow dubs "America's forgotten war" erupted in 1899. This brutal American-Filipino conflict, with atrocities on both sides, dragged on for three years, ending only after the capture of the "president of the Philippines," Emilio Aguinaldo, by a daring ruse.

The period from July 4, 1902, when the warfare was declared officially over and U.S. laws were imposed, to July 4, 1946, when the Philippines were granted full independence, became one long experiment by an idealistic America in fostering democracy overseas, and many colorful personalities punctuate the history of these years. Karnow is particularly good at creating vignettes of historical figures. William Howard Taft, the first civilian governor and source of the expression "little brown brothers," was a jovial fat man with a terrible temper. Manuel Luis Quezon, first president of the Philippines (1935–44), was adept at captivating women and crowds; his arrival in a town in khakis and pith helmet, triumphal palm and bamboo arches overhead, would draw people to listen for hours to his histrionic political speeches. His successor as president, Sergio Osmeña, was almost his opposite—a somewhat plodding but very competent politician who handled opponents with subtle humor rather than confrontation. When one irate foe yelled, "I want you to know that when I get angry, I send everybody to hell—my wife, my children, everybody," Osmeña smiled, "That is terrible, but I never intervene in family affairs."

The overpowering personality of Gen. Douglas MacArthur seemed to divide people into adulators or scoffers. Karnow appears to belong to the latter. MacArthur was a superhero to Filipinos, but Karnow saw a bundle of paradoxes—a soldier who showed signs of cowardice; a macho figure almost pathologically submissive to his pushy mother, "Pinky"; a moralizer who contrived shabby schemes to advance his overweening ambitions. Karnow is critical of many of MacArthur's military decisions regarding the defense of the Philippines as the Japanese approached and even takes some of the mystique out of the most famous image of MacArthur's role, the general wading ashore on his return with the victorious U.S. forces. MacArthur had ordered a boat for himself and his party, but the harried navy beachmaster, too busy with more urgent matters, barked at the messenger, "Let 'em walk." Cameramen caught his scowl (interpreted as determination) and afterward, realizing the symbolic value of the shot, reenacted the performance for another camera crew.

Yet his battle for Bataan and the notorious Bataan Death March, when Americans and Filipinos by the tens of thousands died side by side, are indelibly inscribed in Filipino memory, the ultimate proof of the special U.S.-Philippine bond. And with independence in 1946, the Philippines began a new era as a "democracy."

The fledgling Filipino government faced awesome problems, however, from reconstruction after the war to a rising Marxist opposition, and the parallels between Filipino democracy and American democracy kept fading. Then in 1972, Ferdinand Marcos, who had been president since 1965, declared martial law and assumed dictatorial powers.

Karnow got to know personally both Marcos and Corazon Aquino, who won Marcos's ouster in an election by promising to restore democracy. Marcos's fall was due far less, however, to a Filipino clamor for democracy than to "the sheer weight of his flagrant mismanagement and venality." Marcos confided to Karnow (before his death in 1989 in Hawaiian exile) that calling the election was "the biggest mistake I ever made."

"Cory" Aquino, in her first three years in office, has had some successes (promulgating a new constitution and holding legislative elections) but has had to suffer through five coup attempts and faces recurrent insurgencies and economic chaos. Karnow apparently has his fingers crossed for her.

Stanley Karnow asked himself three questions. "What propelled the American s into the Philippines? What did they do there? And what has been the legacy of their rule?" *In Our Image: America's Empire in the Philippines* answers these questions in a brilliant narrative history that has the pace and pull of a novel. To achieve this "fresh, kinetic quality," which was his intent, Karnow added to his credentials as political scientist the writing skills acquired in more than thirty years as a distinguished foreign correspondent in Asia. From Magellan to MacArthur to Marcos, the heroes and villains Karnow portrays are indisputably human and fallible.

Enhancing the value of this meticulously researched history are a detailed chronology of events, a list with biographical sketches of the principal players in Philippine history, and extensive bibliographic essays by chapter on the sources. The bibliographic essays are also, in effect, a full and expert guide to further reading.

So masterful a retelling of how and why the United States became a colonial ruler in Asia and of the love-hate interaction between Filipinos and Americans ever since is hard to fault. Some readers, however, may wish the author had drawn on his long familiarity with U.S.-Philippine relations to express more of his personal views. Karnow says this might have raised the specter of revisionism, and, in any case, his overriding feeling was "humility in the face of an enormously complicated subject." Diffidence of this kind is a rare virtue. *In Our Image* will pass the test of time.

Adrienne Suddard

IN TRANSIT: TWENTY STORIES

Author: Mavis Gallant (1922–   )
Publisher: Random House (New York). 229 pp. $17.95
Type of work: Short stories
Time: The 1950s and 1960s
Locale: Primarily cities and towns throughout Europe

A collection of short stories whose characters both reflect and defy the environments in which they exist

Many of the principal characters of *In Transit*'s twenty stories are English (or, at least, English speaking), but by choice or circumstance they are visiting or residing on the Continent—nearly always under conditions less than favorable. While this may not be so for all the principals, one common quality prevails: they are believably real, commanding the attention, and often the empathy, of the reader.

In a Spanish coastal community, young Laurie attends "The Circus" with his mother, who is unamused, and his father, who is ignoring them in favor of any and all strangers within earshot. Laurie observes that, as usual, it is "more important to [his father] to be loved by foreign peasants and fishermen than by his own family." The distance between Laurie's parents clearly is a hateful one. When it is intimated that his mother could conceivably leave her husband and her children, Laurie is suddenly ill. Up until now, he has wrestled with two unpleasant ideas: he and his mother would leave his father or he and his mother would stay. "He had never supposed she could go away alone."

On the morning of her fifty-first birthday (April 1), the narrator of "April Fish" receives a present from her three young adopted sons: a green Venetian-glass fish, a gift she deems as dull and tasteless as the boys themselves. She *is* impressed with the present from her brother —an original letter written by Sigmund Freud—but when she learns that she will be unable to adopt a Vietnamese girl, everything else is meaningless.

The terminally ill Mrs. Glover is resigned to death, "without a word of complaint," but there is "A Question of Disposal" where two things are concerned: her cherished house in London and her bachelor son, the thirty-four-year-old Digby. She accompanies Digby and Janet, his fiancée of seven years, on what she alone knows to be her final holiday: a trip to the place in Spain where Digby and Janet first met and became engaged. Janet is Mrs. Glover's only hope that both her house and her son will be looked after. The trip, however, plants the first real seeds of doubt in Janet's mind. Perhaps she may not marry Digby, after all.

Stella, raised in the English country, is unhappy living "In Italy" with husband Henry and their baby boy. Stella is ten months younger than her stepdaughter, with whom she has a strained, somewhat competitive relationship. Henry, in his late fifties, torments Stella with his boasting chatter about wills and money, all of which he happily spends on himself, his intention being that there be nothing left for any heirs.

Bea had a son, Roy, when "Malcolm and Bea" met in Canada. Bea was pregnant with Malcolm's daughter when they were married. Now in France, soon to be moving, they are a family detached from one another, save for Bea's love of baby Ruth. Malcolm's tacit discontent, Bea's caustic bite, Roy's autistic qualities—each is the others' vexation. Talk of separating is a waft of salvation, but staying together is just the way things are.

Billy Apostolesco dislikes leaving Canada for any reason, but it is like "The End of the World" to have to be in France waiting for his father to die. Billy's father had deserted his wife and three children when Billy was a young boy. Now an adult, Billy has been called to the dying man's bedside in a pitiful French hospital. Although Billy— compassionate, hurt, forgiving, angry—expects otherwise, there is not a hint of fatherly regret, not even a whit of gratitude for an abandoned son's presence.

Years ago, Amabel's best friend, Catherine Plummer, died from spinal meningitis. When Amabel invites herself to spend "New Year's Eve" in Moscow with Colonel and Mrs. Plummer, she is seeking the comfort of parental-type love. What she instead encounters is the emotional emptiness of two separately distant strangers.

Oliver had been "An Emergency Case" in a Geneva hospital following the car accident that claimed the lives of his parents. The perceptions of this small child as to what happened, what is happening, and what will happen are quite contrary to the raw facts and virtually unnoticed by the well-meaning adults who have been supervising his care. The result is a particularly poignant and touching piece of prose.

Gitta's lover once called her "The Captive Niece" of Aunt Freda. The late, alcoholic Aunt Freda had raised Gitta, and theirs had been a mutually dependent relationship. Now, Gitta is a would-be actress living in a Paris hotel. Her lover has just moved in, having left his wife and children in England. For lovers, they are barely loving. Their discourse carries more of an edge of distrust and sadness than of contentment and passion.

Olivia's "Good Deed" was no doubt inadvertent. She is far too manipulative to have truly cared about Hugo and Wendy, the marriage of whom she practically arranged single-handedly. Olivia, described by her late husband as "made of marble," is left to age in the French Riviera alone, indeed like a cold, white stone.

At age forty, Guy has never enjoyed secure employment, but he believes in the "Better Times" he has promised Susan, his eighteen-year-old bride. Out of necessity, they are wintering in the South of France in the wretchedly cold house of Susan's Aunt Val. It is a tenure so distressing to Susan as to nearly crush her, but in the end, Guy's untiring optimism wins back her confidence . . . at least for now.

"The Wedding Ring" belongs to Jane's mother. When it disappears in the tall Vermont grass, young Jane, who sees through the quasi-innocent presence of a male houseguest and her mother's flair for the dramatic, questions just how accidental the loss of the ring was.

"Vacances Pax" is the name of Stuart Fenwick's vacation colony, the attraction of which is the notion of "one Europe": each bungalow flies a different flag, welcoming guests from throughout Europe to take holiday together, there in the South of France. Among the present group of visitors is Valerie, a tall fat girl with whom Fenwick is fairly smitten. The infatuation is unrequited, yet Fenwick thoughtfully prepares for the traditional Midsummer Night's bonfire, the embers of which are jumped over by engaged couples. He gathers sweet-smelling herbs for his fire, musing that "Valerie might be induced to leap over the ashes. . . . The thought of great Valerie leaping cheered him."

In "The Statues Taken Down," two New York youths visit their estranged English father in Paris. While young Hal is planted in a movie house watching a vampire festival, Dorothy sits in the park poring through her father's poetry, grappling with the clues to his past and fascinated, yet perplexed, by the symbolic references to her mother.

The English widow Mrs. Parsters has lived "By the Sea," on the south coast of Spain, for twenty years. She lords an air of superiority over all with whom she communes, which includes the tourists on the beach. Presently, the Tuttlegens of Germany and Mrs. Owens of the United States are being favored by her company. Mrs. Parsters's no-siness and bossiness are somewhat abrasive and almost comical, but her perceptions are not all wrong.

In "The Hunter's Waking Thoughts," Colin accepts an invitation to his lover's family estate outside Paris. He assumed that he would share a bed with Nathalie, but while she is enjoying the comforts of the main house, his room is one of many in a lodge for visiting hunters. As if it is not bad enough that Colin has to endure the offensive presence of these pseudosportsmen, the hunter in the room next to his is Nathalie's husband.

In another story set in the French countryside, "Careless Talk," the only things that neighbors Mary and Iris have in common are their native English language and "their condition in a world they believed intended for men." That seems enough to cement a friendship . . . ultimately, perhaps it is not.

The narrator of "When We Were Nearly Young" looks back nine years, recalling the time she lived in Madrid. One of a foursome of close friends, she was the only foreigner and nonrelation. The group's interdependence was based largely on the bond of chronic poverty, and their "friendships were nourished with talk of money [they] expected to have, and what [they] intended to do when it came." When the narrator's money actually did come, the unity of the four crumbled, irretrievably.

Madame Gisèle is all out of "Questions and Answers" for Amalia, who annoys the card-reading mystic with her repetitive stream of ponderings, all of which center on an elderly friend, Marie. The setting is Paris. The characters are Romanian. The dialogue is some of Gallant's best.

In the title story, newlyweds Philippe and Claire Perrigny are "In Transit," traveling through Scandinavia on their honeymoon. Affected by the "permanent, flowing quarrel" of an elderly American couple in an airport, momentarily captivated by a young woman in a park, and frequently reminded of his ex-wife, Philippe privately reflects on the precarious threads of a marital relationship.

If the twenty stories in *In Transit* are characteristic of Mavis Gallant's other works, it is not surprising that this is her ninth collection of short stories. She gives short-story readers what they want: the evocation of much image with the expense of little verbiage.

One of Gallant's gifts is her ability to create graphic portrayals in mere words or sentences, not paragraphs or pages: "Peggy was too tall, too thin, her teeth were too large and white. Slumped in the doorway, she looked like a cynical horse." But it is not enough to economize on the prose that fashions the picture. To the reader's gratification, Gallant's stories go further to evoke something more— all those elusive human perceptions from within and without; the tastes and smells of pleasure and discomfort; the ache of sadness; the tiring, private grasp on personal survival.

Christine Lindberg Stevens

ÌSARÀ: A VOYAGE AROUND "ESSAY"

Author: Wole Soyinka (1934–   )
Publisher: Random House (New York). 262 pp. $18.95
Type of work: Memoirs
Time: 1930s to the early 1940s
Locale: Ìsarà and other Nigerian cities

*Akinyode Soditan, principal of a Nigerian school, moves beyond the secu-
rity of his profession to become involved in politics and business, culminating
in a successful effort to crown a new ruler of his home city, Ìsarà*

Principal characters:
>   AKINYODE SODITAN, a Nigerian school principal
>   SIPE EFUAPE, his best friend and a successful businessman
>   PA JOSIAH SODITAN, Akinyode's father
>   MARIAM, Akinyode's mother
>   REVEREND BEESTON, the British principal of St. Simeon's, the
>   school Akinyode attended as a youth
>   RAY GUNNAR, a Trinidadian in London who fraudulently
>   makes money from African students
>   AKINSANYA, Akinyode's choice to become the next Odemo
>   (king) of Ìsarà
>   ERINLE, rival candidate to become Odemo

Wole Soyinka, the Nobel Prize-winning Nigerian author, was in
exile when his father, known as "Essay," died. Several years later,
Soyinka was allowed to return to Nigeria. At his father's home he
opened a tin box containing correspondence between Essay and his
friends and colleagues. As Soyinka explains in an "Author's Note,"
he decided "not to continue with real names . . . to eliminate any
pretense to factual accuracy in this attempted reconstruction of [his
father's and fellow teachers'] times, thoughts, and feelings." *Ìsarà*,
then, is a fictionalized memoir, evoking the life of a Nigerian teacher
during the years before and during World War II, a period when modern Nigerian national identity was set in relation to British colonial
influence and in anticipation of the coming independence of Nigeria.
    Every year, Akinyode Soditan (the fictionalized persona of Soyin-
ka's father) returned to his home city, Ìsarà, for a reunion with his
parents and the other "ex-Ilés," the men and women who had been
forced to leave Ìsarà for other cities in Nigeria or for Britain in order
to advance their careers and make their fortunes. Soditan had first left
Ìsarà as a child to attend St. Simeon's, a church boarding school established to train Africans to become teachers or to enter the native civil
service. Reverend Beeston, the British principal of the school, wanted
Africans to advance, but not too far. The reverend's attitude and that
of the other British teachers toward their African students was ex-

pressed in the term they used for their students—"Simeans," a cross between the name of the school and simians. One student organized a committee to protest the name. The reverend promised not to call students "Simeans," but then expelled the organizers of the protest.

Akinyode enjoyed school, later becoming a principal himself. He was active in the union of Nigerian teachers, lecturing and writing for African education journals. Akinyode was a sensation at a teachers' conference when he advocated, as African teachers' first duty, replacing "a colonial mind with a cultivated mind." Akinyode occupied an ambiguous and precarious position, educated by colonial teachers and eager to instill British knowledge and mores in his students, yet concerned with building the dignity of African teachers and students. Akinyode was active in demanding pay raises for African teachers and in replacing British principals and teachers with Africans. Yet, he was the quintessential British schoolmaster in his frequent flogging of unruly students. He opposed the efforts of some Nigerians to sabotage the war effort against Hitler. Akinyode believed that Nigerian loyalty to the Allied cause would hasten Nigerian independence after the end of World War II. At the same time, Akinyode applauded the effort of "Activity," the scoutmaster who attempted to raise a brigade to fight in Ethiopia against Mussolini but was thwarted by the British colonial governor.

Throughout the war years, Akinyode and his family and friends tried to anticipate the effects of the fighting on their personal and national aspirations. Akinyode repeatedly rejected the offers from his best friend, Sipe Efuape, to join him in business. Sipe was a civil servant who used his position to find profitable deals and who established a series of profitable enterprises. Akinyode was convinced, however, that the flux of the war years would bankrupt any African business, although Sipe steadily became wealthier, profiting from the misfortunes of rival African and British businessmen. In contrast to Sipe, Akinyode's wife and mother usually lost money through their involvement in women's credit unions and trading companies.

Sipe's one intervention in the world of intellect and culture was inspired by Ray Gunnar, a Trinidadian of Indian origin who settled in London and became a janitor in a boarding house for African students who were attending or attempting to enter British universities. Ray Gunnar noted that Africans often spent money to take correspondence courses or to buy worthless credentials in hopes of being admitted to legitimate British universities. Ray Gunnar studied the advertisements, imitated them, and soon received a steady stream of applications to his post office box for the "Ray Gunnar Inter Correspondence School." To expand his business, Gunnar opened a drama school, promising scholarships to students willing to pay a large fee to apply to the school. Sipe read the advertisement, mourned his inability to abandon his businesses in Lagos, and decided to establish his own drama troupe in the Nigerian capital.

Sipe's dramatic ambitions ended in failure; however, he later used his dramatic interests to stage the crowning of Akinsanya as the Odemo (king) of Ìsarà. The last chapters of Ìsarà recount the struggle between Akinsanya and Erinle for the crown of Ìsarà. Sipe and Akinyode were the principal backers of Akinsanya. Just when the two friends were sure that they had lined up all the support they needed, Olisa, the regent, put forward Erinle as a rival. Olisa broke Ìsarà custom, which prescribed a democratic vote at a mass meeting as the way to choose the Odemo, by killing one supporter of Akinsanya. Erinle's violent allies drew inspiration from Hitler and saw themselves as fighters against colonial rule. Their position was ironic, since Akinyode believed that the British would be the main opponents to Akinsanya's assumption of the Ìsarà crown. Akinyode and Sipe forced Akinsanya, a fiery speaker against colonial rule, to promise not to speak out on colonial politics until he had won British approval for his election and been safely installed as Odemo.

Erinle's final victim was Goriola, nicknamed the gorilla for his vigorous enforcement of sanitary laws in his position as a civil-service inspector. When Goriola arrived at a house to write a citation, Erinle's men believed that he was a spy and attacked him. The violence against a civil servant shocked many people in Ìsarà, swinging popular sentiment once again behind Akinsanya. Thus, fear of provoking British anger allowed the true anti-British candidate, Akinsanya, to become Odemo.

Once Akinsanya's appointment as Odemo was assured, Akinyode celebrated his position of influence and respect. No longer just a cautious school principal, he had become a canny political leader among his people in Ìsarà and with his fellow African educators throughout Nigeria. Akinyode, while still cautious in business and in his personal life (unlike his father and Sipe, he was faithful to his wife), was daring in politics. He pushed to the limits the anticolonial action possible under the double constraints of British rule and the dangers of World War II. Akinyode's pride was expressed when he received a visit from Wade Cudeback, a prominent British educator with whom he had corresponded and whose letters filled the tin box Wole Soyinka found after his father's death. Akinyode greeted the Britisher as an equal, welcoming him to his home of Ìsarà.

Wole Soyinka conveys the ambitions and emotions of the men of his father's generation. Limited by colonial rule and handicapped by the inadequate educations they received from their British teachers, Akinyode Soditan and his friends nevertheless found their own paths to understanding the colonial situation and to plan ways of escaping subordination on both a personal and a national level. Soyinka's pride in his father is conveyed on several levels in *Ìsarà*. Akinyode Soditan, as fleshed by Soyinka, is an eloquent and profound speaker, able to meld the language and wisdom of traditional Nigeria with a largely self-taught command of European literature and philosophy. Akinyode's sense of justice and truth is presented in various incidents, as he struggles to get what is due to him and other teachers from the British, and as he describes his vision of African community. Akinyode is aware that he is part of the last generation to live under colonialism and that he has an obligation to educate his children and his students for lives as rulers of their own destiny. Akinyode expresses that sense in his writings and teachings, and in his struggle to make the selection of the Odemo of Ìsarà an example of revived Nigerian democracy and autonomy.

Ìsarà also gives readers the flavor of life in Nigeria during the 1930s and early 1940s. The very language of Soyinka's writing combines English and native expressions (carefully translated in footnotes) and shows how each character's actions are guided by a varying mix of British and Nigerian beliefs and customs. Women emerge as the most tradition-bound; businessmen such as Sipe are Nigerian only in their desire to become rich instead and in spite of the British. Yet, even the materialistic Sipe is swayed by the teacher Akinyode's efforts to move his people to take pride in being Nigerian. That pride is found through the exercise of native rights and by the creation of a new way of life borrowed from the British only when European ways could be used to assert the coming Nigerian independence. *Ìsarà* is by turns comic and tragic, yet always a beautiful and moving tribute to "Essay" and the other fathers of Wole Soyinka and his generation of independent Nigerians.

Richard Lachmann

JOHN DOLLAR

Author: Marianne Wiggins (1947–   )
Publisher: Harper and Row (New York). 214 pp. $17.95
Type of work: Novel
Time: 1917; the present
Locale: Rangoon, Burma; St. Ives, Cornwall; "The Island of Our Outlawed Dreams," the Andamans

The compelling narrative of a shipwreck that causes British colonial schoolgirls to revert to savagery

> *Principal characters:*
> CHARLOTTE LEWES, a British schoolteacher
> JOHN DOLLAR, a sailor, Charlotte's lover
> NORRIS "NOLLY" PETHERBRIDGE, one of Charlotte's students, daughter of the Reverend Petherbridge
> AMANDA SUTCLIFFE, another of Charlotte's students
> SLOAN AND SYBIL OGILVY, twins, also Charlotte's students
> RUBY "OOPI" FRASER, the youngest of the students
> SHAUNA FRASER, Ruby's older sister, a student
> GABRIELLA "GABY" ORTIZ, a Portuguese girl, a student
> JANE NAPIER, the daughter of Colonel Napier, also one of the students
> MENAKA "MONKEY" LAWRENCE, a half-Indian, half-British girl, Charlotte's student and lifetime companion

It is doubtful that the Cornish town of St. Ives ever beheld a spectacle to equal that of the aged Indian woman who comes into town with the dead body of her far older companion, Charlotte Lewes. The Indian, Menaka, runs afoul of British bureaucracy in the matter of gaining the deceased entrance to the local cemetery, lacking proof that Charlotte was Church of England. In the end she is compelled to bury the dead woman herself, under cover of darkness. As she labors on alone, she recalls another burial, and before that a double murder, but who was buried and who was left for the sharks is revealed in a flashback that forms the body of the book.

The story begins in 1917 with Charlotte, newly widowed in the Great War. To escape her feelings of despair and self-pity, she takes a job as a teacher in Rangoon, Burma. On the passage out she first encounters the self-satisfied, exploitative aspects of the British Empire.

In Rangoon, Charlotte teaches only the daughters of British colonials. Menaka is one. Her father has returned to England, leaving her and her Indian mother behind. Her name is corrupted to "Monica," but the other girls call her "Monkey," and treat her with disdain. Even Gaby Ortiz is more socially acceptable; she may have Portuguese blood, but at least she counts as "white."

Charlotte falls in love with the East. Unlike her fellow expatriates, she does not devote herself to trying to recreate a little England in Burma, nor does she mention her homeland with the reverence due Paradise. She adapts to her new home gladly and revels in the alien beauty surrounding her. She also tries to come to terms with her enforced celibacy.

One night, while visiting a lovely site called the Inle Lake, Charlotte spies a pod of freshwater dolphins, reputed to be blind. On an impulse she swims with them. Only when their midnight swim is done does she realize that the sailor John Dollar has been watching her, fascinated. The two of them begin a passionate love affair.

All goes well until the occasion of the king's birthday arises. The English of Rangoon are searching for a spectacular gift to send their sovereign. John Dollar mentions the fact that many of the Andaman Islands have changed since a survey of 1888. It is decided to rename one such island—called originally by Marco Polo "The Island of Our Outlawed Dreams"—in honor of His Majesty.

The colonials mount an expedition to the island that can best be described as a combination school outing, formal dinner, and hunting and fishing party. Three boats are used for a full complement of native servants, the leading citizens and their wives and children, and the boys' and girls' teachers. On the day of the expedition, Shauna Fraser menstruates for the first time and is forced to stay home, but her little sister Ruby, called "Oopi," is allowed to go.

Although their destination is an uninhabited island in the middle of a tropical sea, the British bring with them every conceivable trapping of civilization, necessary or not. Through the labors of their native servants—whose true names are conveniently forgotten so that their employers may refer to them as the days of the week, *d'apres* Robinson Crusoe's man Friday—the colonials enjoy a banquet complete with Royal Worcester fine bone china, Irish leaded crystal, silverware, sherry, gin, live pigs to be slaughtered and eaten on the spot, and a vast array of other delicacies and comforts.

The banquet as a symbol of civilization at its most refined is interrupted by an influx of turtles to the beach. They have come ashore to lay eggs, but some atavistic urge causes many of the children and adults to attack and massacre the innocent animals. The mood is further upset by the discovery of a hermit crab that has adopted a skull as its home. One of the party recognizes it as human.

The next day, most of the adults leave for a day of hunting on another island. The boys stay on one of the remaining boats with their teacher, the girls on another. John and Charlotte make love aboard his boat, spied upon by the girls. In the morning, there is something disturbing about the silence reigning over the boys' boat. The whole atmosphere seems oppressive. John fears the worst and goes over to check. He discovers the quarters below awash with blood and no sign of survivors or corpses. While en route back to the remaining boat to warn the girls, he and the rest are caught up in a tidal wave caused by a seaquake.

The girls regain consciousness on the beach. No adults are to be found. They are not even aware of how long they have lain unconscious. They attempt to sort matters out and take charge of themselves while awaiting the rescue they are certain will come. Nolly Petherbridge, daughter of the Reverend Petherbridge, soon establishes herself as one of the leaders. Oopi is too young for leadership. Amanda Sutcliffe starts out in a leading role, but soon sinks into a silent, self-absorbed depression when beach-debris evidence leads the girls to conclude that all of the ships were destroyed and no one has survived to rescue them. Gaby shows more initiative, suggesting that they use one of her beloved kites as a signaling device. The twins, Sloan and Sybil Ogilvy, have always been so close that they regard themselves as a single person. One has sustained a broken leg, meaning that the other must carry her everywhere, uniting them now in body as well as spirit. Jane Napier does not really care what becomes of herself. Since her brother's death in the war and her mother's suicide, she feels superfluous and unloved. Monkey feels great affection for her, but the gulf of race and social conventions prevents her from approaching Jane. As for Monkey herself, she is automatically assigned the role of laborer.

On an expedition to the other side of the island, Gaby and Monkey make a momentous discovery: John Dollar is alive. He is paralyzed, but the girls manage to bring him back to their beachhead, where they do him as much harm as good trying to patch him up with a salvaged medical kit. Nolly soon assumes her father's religious leadership role, converting the care of John into a kind of idolatry. For his part, John is desperate to get the girls off the beach, up to the safety of the headland. Only he knows the full significance of the boys' disappearance.

The girls obey him without question, and just in time. Shortly after their move, several native canoes reach the beach. The fathers of the girls have been captured. The girls watch, despite John's imploring them to close their eyes, as the child-sized natives kill, roast, and eat their fathers before paddling away. The cannibalism episode is a turning point for all. Oddly enough, it is this event that brings Amanda out of her depression. The natives have left behind live fire. In her place, John turns silent. Under Nolly's unwitting direction, he receives a daily overdose of quinine that may eventually kill him, while the girls take none. Oopi dies of malaria. Monkey discovers a freshwater pool on one of her expeditions to find food to tempt Jane to eat, but on her return is told that Jane has finally died of self-starvation. Sloan and Sybil are smothered in quicksand.

Gaby becomes suspicious of Nolly and Amanda, who have taken to mysterious, solitary sessions at night with John. She confides her doubts to Monkey, and while the other two are away they pull back the sheet covering John's legs. To their horror they discover that Nolly and Amanda have been eating him alive, by degrees.

Surprised by the guilty pair, who are armed, Gaby and Monkey flee into the jungle. Gaby is treed and forced to leap to her death when Nolly and Amanda set the tree afire. Monkey runs to the inland pool, where she discovers Charlotte, still alive. Charlotte was temporarily blinded in the accident, but is fine now. Monkey tells her that John is still alive, but cannot make Charlotte understand the horror that has befallen him. They see smoke from the headland. Monkey knows this means that Nolly and Amanda have finished off John, but she walks on with Charlotte, who thinks it is a rescue signal. Here the book ends.

The reader who cannot recall the beginning of the book, which describes what Charlotte and Monkey did to Nolly and Amanda, must return to it. Even those who remember are left feeling somewhat unsatisfied, not knowing how Charlotte and Monkey were ultimately rescued from the island. Although this may irritate, it serves to underline effectively the true horrors that have taken place, not distracting from them by tying up loose ends of the story.

Although *John Dollar* seems to be a repetition of *Lord of the Flies*, with a female cast, it is more. Marianne Wiggins has a keen eye and ear for satirizing British imperialist society, as well as using the girls' improvised worship of John as the means to comment on organized religion. It is unfortunate that certain touches lack subtlety: the temporary blindness that keeps Charlotte from the others is too convenient; John Dollar's name itself leads one to think of heavy-handed puns on "Dollar-worship." Despite this, the scenic descriptions are entrancing, the passions real.

Esther M. Friesner

THE JOY LUCK CLUB

Author: Amy Tan (1952–   )
Publisher: G. P. Putnam's Sons (New York). 288 pp. $18.95
Type of work: Novel
Time: The present
Locale: San Francisco

The stories of four mothers born in China and four daughters born in America who gradually recognize that a love stronger than cultural differences binds a mother to her daughter

Principal characters:
   SUYUAN WOO, AN-MEI HSU, LINDO JONG, and YING-YING ST. CLAIR, four Chinese-born mothers
   JING-MEI WOO, ROSE HSU JORDAN, WAVERLY JONG, and LENA ST. CLAIR, their four American-born daughters

What is called "the generation gap" is as old as human history and probably bedeviled our preliterate ancestors in their caves, too. Today, however, as people move more freely around the globe, there can be another level of perplexity, a generation gap compounded by a culture gap. Amy Tan uses fictional characters to describe how the awesome cultural gulf between East and West complicated mother-daughter communication for four Chinese-American families in San Francisco.

This is a novel without a plot, in the usual sense anyway, but with aspects of a Chinese puzzle. There are four mothers and four daughters, four divisions of the book, and four stories in each division. Thus the stories total sixteen, the square of four, which is considered to be, among other things, of feminine gender in ancient Chinese numerology.

Less obscure is the literary rhythm of the four sets of stories. In the first set are the mothers' tales of their lives in old China (the daughter of one who has just died speaks for her mother), and in the second the daughters recall attitudes toward their mothers as children growing up in America. The third, aptly titled "American Translation," tells of the daughters' quandaries where American and Chinese ways seemed to clash. The fourth set portrays the transcendence of mother love over differing cultures, a simple truth the daughters eventually grasp.

The Joy Luck Club came into being in San Francisco as a group of four Chinese immigrant women assembled to play mah-jongg (somewhat like an American bridge club), the hope for "luck" being their principal "joy" in their new and alien surroundings. The mah-jongg sessions were also the occasion for exchanging stories, jokes, and gossip, as well as for bragging about their children. Suyuan Woo, who had organized the club after fleeing China before the Communist take-over in 1949, had always wanted her daughter Jing-mei to be a dazzling success—maybe as a child star like Shirley Temple or a concert pianist —and worked hard to make this happen. But Jing-mei became an ad-agency copywriter, married and divorced an American, and regularly downplayed her Chinese parentage. Jing-mei as a child had imagined the Joy Luck Club to be "a shameful Chinese custom, like the secret gathering of the Ku Klux Klan or the tom-tom dances of TV Indians preparing for war." And then there was the story of her mother's journey on foot, told over and over, from Kweilin to the wartime capital of Chungking far to the northwest to escape the advancing Japanese. Along the way, her mother had had to abandon her precious possessions as too heavy to carry and, in one version, finally her two infant daughters slung over her shoulders. But the end of the story kept changing, and Jing-mei dismissed her mother's saga as another Chinese fairy tale.

Another Joy Luck Club mother, An-mei Hsu, had watched her mother suffer from the rigid mores regarding the place of women in old China and ultimately commit suicide. While mourning the prema-ture death of her husband, a scholar, her mother had been cruelly tricked into the bed of a wealthy merchant and raped. The only path open to her after this "loss of face" was to become his concubine. Young An-mei spent much of her childhood in the merchant's luxuri-ous house and saw the vicious intriguing the concubines engaged in to survive. An-mei learned from the experience how to "shout" for jus-tice. Her daughter, Rose Hsu Jordan, had like her mother married a doctor, an American dermatologist, but the marriage was breaking up mainly because Rose, herself a free-lance production assistant for graphic artists, was too dependent, too willing to let others make de-cisions and take responsibility. Possibly the accidental drowning of her brother Bing at age four had something to do with this. Rose remembered being told to watch her little brother during a family beach outing. Afterward everyone tried to accept some "responsibil-ity"—her father for suggesting the outing, her mother for distracting her attention at a crucial moment. But Rose also remembered the eerie time at the beach the following day with her mother. At first her mother appealed to God in consonance with her membership in the First Chinese Baptist Church in San Francisco. When the futility of these prayers became evident, her mother said, "An ancestor of ours once stole water from a sacred well. Now the water is trying to steal back. We must sweeten the temper of the Coiling Dragon who lives in the sea. And then we must make him loosen his coils from Bing by giving him another treasure he can hide." With that her mother threw a blue sapphire ring, a family heirloom, far out into the water.

To her daughter, Lindo Jong was someone who always saw black where there was white, devastatingly critical of everything, such as her boyfriends. But Lindo Jong knew the misery of a bad marriage. Betrothed at age two, Lindo Jong was left behind at age twelve with the family of her future husband when a flood forced her parents to move away from their native Taiyuan. For four years, Lindo worked as a servant in her future home, the traditional preparation for marriage, gradually sinking into complete submissiveness. Her marriage at age sixteen was a disaster from the first night, when her husband, terrified of females, made her sleep on a sofa. As time passed without a pregnancy, her husband lied to his mother that Lindo refused to sleep in his bed. Bound by her promise to her parents to be a good wife and thereby honor the family, the young bride had to devise some creditable escape, which she did by feigning a dream in which the ancestors threatened three terrible "signs" (ingeniously plausible) unless the mismatch were ended. The money her mother-in-law gave her to get rid of her got her to America where her future children could enjoy "the best combination: American circumstances and Chinese character." Alas, her daughter "followed [Lindo's] Chinese ways only until she learned how to walk out the door by herself." Her daughter Waverly became a national chess champion as a child, her picture in *Life* magazine, but gave up playing because her mother was hovering over her and taking all the credit. Their standoff continued under various guises through Waverly's first marriage and seemed to Waverly to be a barrier to acceptance of her prospective second husband, an easygoing American tax attorney. There is a very amusing account of his first dinner with the family, his obliviousness to Chinese customs obvious from start to finish. But then Waverly, listening to her mother tell of their illustrious ancestors in Taiyuan, confused "Taiyuan" with "Taiwan."

The fourth mother, Ying-ying St. Clair, felt invisible to her daughter Lena, as a lifeless old lady with yellowing eyes, because, "I rubbed out my face over the years washing away my pain, the same way carvings on stone are worn down by water." Born to wealth, widow of a prosperous American clothing manufacturer, Ying-ying saw emptiness in the materialistic life of her daughter and son-in-law, partners in a successful architectural firm. Recalling the "tiger spirit" of her youth in China, Ying-ying decided to provoke the tiger spirit in her daughter—passing her spirit to Lena "is the way a mother loves her daughter"—and began by letting a vase in the guest room crash to the floor.

Three of the mother-daughter stories are left in flux, but in a poignant final chapter, Jing-mei Woo fulfills her mother's secret wish: at the Joy Luck Club, after her mother's death, Jing-mei was told that those two infants abandoned on the way to Chungking had been found living in Shanghai, and travel money from her mother's mah-jongg "winnings" was pressed into her hand. Her father finally shared with her the full story of the tragic journey and her mother's agony over the years. Once in China, everything about her mother came rushing back in her memory, and Jing-mei met her half sisters—"her same eyes, her same mouth"—with tears rolling down her face.

The stunning success of this first novel by an unknown author is both hard and easy to explain. How does one explain best-seller status for a string of stories full of overlapping narratives by eight women so indistinctly characterized as to seem at times interchangeable? Where are the bizarre plot twists or the exciting confrontations and the surprising denouement? Maxine Hong Kingston has won much acclaim for Chinese-American novels where East meets West on a battlefield strewn with American prejudices and Chinese inscrutability.

The Joy Luck Club is different. With astounding skill, Amy Tan writes a story of love surmounting cultural barriers. Moreover, her characters are ordinary people living ordinary lives, grappling with complex emotions hidden in their hearts. The subliminal articulation of their hopes and fears in their "stories" told to one another has the suggestive power of poetry. Thus the struggle of these Chinese mothers and their American daughters to understand their bonds holds lessons for mothers and daughters everywhere. The popularity of a book so enlightening about the Chinese immigrant experience in America, so moving as a story of mother love, and so beautifully written is quite easy to explain.

Adrienne Suddard

KEEP THE CHANGE

Author: Thomas McGuane (1939–)
Publisher: Houghton Mifflin (Boston). 230 pp. $18.95
Type of work: Novel
Time: The early 1980s
Locale: Montana; New York City; Florida

A young man seeks his inheritance but instead finds his true identity

Principal characters:
JOE STARLING, a thirty-year-old artist
JOE STARLING, Sr., Joe's father
LUREEN STARLING, Joe's aunt
SMITTY STARLING, Joe's uncle
MR. OVERSTREET, the Starlings' neighbor
ELLEN OVERSTREET, Overstreet's daughter
BILLY KELTON, Joe's childhood friend, later enemy
IVAN SLATER, Joe's best friend
ASTRID, Joe's girlfriend

At age ten, Joe Starling is mesmerized by a huge painting of white hills that his banker and rancher father takes him to see at an old, dilapidated mansion on which the bank has foreclosed. The image will haunt him into adulthood.

An only child growing up on a Montana ranch, Joe is named after his father, a brusque, gregarious, decisive go-getter whom Joe idolizes. Joe Starling, Sr., however, does not much like or understand his son and has difficulty showing affection. Joe's mother demonstrates more sensitivity and wants her son to be well educated to enable him to improve himself. Joe's extended family includes his father's ne'er-do-well brother, Smitty, and schoolteacher sister, Lureen.

A second event from adolescence that has a lingering effect on Joe is a fight, at age thirteen, with his best friend, Billy Kelton. Joe's father witnesses the fight, encouraging Billy to beat up his son, to teach Joe that even a "best friend" should not be trusted. The boys are enemies from then on, and Joe is left feeling both the sting of his father's betrayal and a profound sense of loneliness.

At a Kentucky military academy, Joe makes friends with Ivan Slater. Joe's father is transferred to Minneapolis, but he keeps the ranch, leasing it to his shrewd neighbor, Mr. Overstreet. Mr. Starling lets Joe know that one day the ranch will be his (a prospect about which Joe feels ambivalent) and expresses the desire that Joe will keep the ranch out of Overstreet's hands. The summer Joe is seventeen he works at the ranch under Overstreet's overseer and has his first sexual encounter with Overstreet's daughter, Ellen, who is dating Billy Kelton.

After high school, Joe attends Yale University, majoring in art. Upon graduation he moves to New York City and becomes a successful painter. His father, ill and alcoholic, declares bankruptcy. He has the foresight, however, to sign the ranch over to Lureen in time to save it, hoping someday to pass it on to his son. When her brother dies suddenly, while driving to bankruptcy court, Lureen keeps the ranch, as she says, for Joe. Smitty, however, begins to think of the ranch as his own. Joe's mother dies a year later.

After a couple of years in New York, Joe inexplicably loses the ability to paint. He moves to Florida, where he meets Astrid, a beautiful, vivacious Cuban. They live together happily for three years. Joe illustrates operators' manuals for the sometimes preposterous inventions that his old friend Ivan Slater markets and also receives payments for the lease of the ranch.

When the lease money stops coming in and the bills pile up, his relationship with Astrid begins to deteriorate. Joe steals her pink convertible one spring day and heads for Montana. There he finds Lureen the same, although now retired, and Smitty more eccentric than ever and drinking heavily. The two live together and fantasize about going to Hawaii. The ranch, no longer leased, is run down. Lureen tells Joe that if she could find somebody to run it for her, she would buy the cattle. Joe volunteers for the job and assembles a motley herd of yearlings. Slowly the ranch is rehabilitated.

Early in his stay Ellen phones him. She is now married to Billy, although currently they are separated. After exchanging pleasantries, Ellen asks Joe if he would like to meet his daughter. Astonished, Joe answers, "Yes." Ellen tells him that Billy does not know the truth about Clara. Joe has a brief, passionate affair with Ellen, but she refuses to discuss his meeting Clara any further.

Although Joe has not been in touch with either Astrid or Ivan, he decides to meet Ivan in New York. After saving him from choking on a piece of steak, Joe tells his friend that he will no longer be working for him. Ivan responds curtly that Joe is not to worry about it, as he is quite replaceable. Their friendship appears over.

Soon Joe hears from Astrid. After a few nasty letters back and forth, she appears on his doorstep. Joe finds that he is as in love with Astrid as he ever was, but, for understandable reasons, their relationship is strained. Nevertheless, she moves in.

Aunt Lureen phones Joe to tell him that Uncle Smitty has been trucking shrimp up from Louisiana. One load went bad, and Smitty is having difficulty collecting his $30,000 claim from the insurance company. The problem is that Smitty buried the spoiled shrimp, and they decomposed before the adjuster arrived to investigate. Lureen naively asks Joe if he thinks there should be any shells left, as the adjuster said. Joe realizes that the ranch was used as collateral to finance the shrimp fiasco as well as the cattle and that there will be little money left from the sale of the cattle in the fall. After talking with a lawyer from the insurance company, Joe urges Lureen and Smitty to settle up with them, or Smitty will face fraud charges.

In the meantime, Astrid is hospitalized with stress-induced colitis. Joe misses her terribly. When she is discharged, she makes a real effort to adapt to life in Montana, and she and Joe resume sexual relations.

At Lureen's request, Joe visits his aunt and notices a pile of tropical-style clothing in the kitchen. Lureen says that she has something for him and hands Joe a file folder. Even before he opens it, Joe realizes that it contains the deed to the ranch and that Smitty and Lureen are going to Hawaii with the money from the upcoming sale of the cattle. He also realizes that the ranch is bankrupt. Nevertheless he feels a strange elation at possession of the deed because of all it symbolizes for him.

Joe's curiosity about Clara persists, and he decides he must have a glimpse of her. He hides in a grove of trees near the Kelton house until Billy comes out with Clara. To his astonishment Joe recognizes that she is clearly Billy's child and also that she is retarded. His old hatred of Billy dissolves into compassion.

After further discussion with the insurance company, fraud charges against Smitty are dropped, and at the court hearing he is merely reprimanded by the judge. Autumn comes, and the cattle are sold, the money deposited in Lureen's account. In the meantime, Astrid has decided that Montana is definitely not the place for her, after having made every effort to adapt. That same night Ivan arrives at the ranch to take her away. Tired and irritable, yet too proud to admit the predicament he is in, Joe lashes out against his friends. Before leaving, Astrid expresses the hope that someday Joe will realize that Montana is not the place for him, either. Joe cries himself to sleep.

Recovering from his despondency, Joe drives out to the old mansion to see the painting of the white hills that so inspired him as a child. He finds it as he remembered it, but when he climbs up onto the huge mantel to get a closer look, he sees that there is really no painting there at all—just the pattern of the white plaster wall inside the frame. After the initial shock has passed, Joe understands the message that his father intended the "painting" to convey to him: will and imagination can bring life out of nothingness; it is all in the way one looks at things.

Joe returns to town to share his discovery with Ellen. She and Billy are now back together. Joe asks her why she lied to him about Clara, and she says that it was her father's idea to gain a claim of sorts to the

Starling ranch. Not understanding Joe's excitement about the picture, Ellen thinks she is being kidnapped and yells, "Help!" out the window. A high-speed chase ensues with the townspeople, including Billy, following Joe's truck. Joe finally stops and is confronted by Ellen's husband, who dismisses everyone else. This time Billy does not want to fight with Joe. The two men talk. Joe confides to Billy that he will soon lose the ranch because he knows by now that he is not the sort of man to stay and fight for it. Billy confides that Overstreet has always made him feel as if he came to the marriage empty-handed and that it would mean everything to him to possess the Starling property that his father-in-law has always coveted. That night Joe dines with Lureen, who has been left behind by Smitty, now in Hawaii. Joe warns her to be ready for Smitty's return when the money runs out.

The ranch is sold to Billy, and, fortunately, Joe is able to see beyond the irony of the situation to the appropriateness of someone rooted to the area getting the ranch. He is also happy that his father's wish that the ranch be kept away from Overstreet has been fulfilled. Joe has lost his inheritance but has discovered himself in the process. He phones Astrid and they agree to start over.

Keep the Change deals with perennial themes: lust for land, responsibility for inheritance, the meaning of "home," and the conflict between fidelity to one's true identity and living up to others' expectations. The story unfolds in unexpected twists and turns, as does life itself. The reader follows Joe on his quest for self-awareness, concerned about what will happen next to the novel's rather ingenuous hero. Joe is likable, hardworking, resourceful, resilient, forgiving, and generous; sometimes, however, the reader has difficulty understanding his thoughts and feelings and must infer them exclusively from Joe's actions. Humor, too, takes the reader by surprise, as in the descriptions of Ivan's inventions or Joe's meeting with a lawyer. Ultimately, a pattern emerges, and there is a satisfying rightness in the various characters' fates, not in terms of strict materialistic justice, but in their finding their appropriate roles in life.

Leslie M. French

LATECOMERS

Author: Anita Brookner (1938–   )
Publisher: Pantheon Books (New York). 248 pp. $16.95
Type of work: Novel
Time: The late 1930s to the present
Locale: Primarily London

The tale of Hartmann and Fibich, whose close, fraternal friendship endures from childhood, despite the many differences in their personalities and out-looks, and the people who figure in the shaping of their lives

> *Principal characters:*
> HARTMANN, an optimist and voluptuary
> FIBICH, a gentle but gloomy businessman
> YVETTE, Hartmann's decorative, self-centered, yet thoughtful wife
> CHRISTINE, Fibich's kind wife, who struggles to free herself from her disheartening youth
> AUNT MARIE, Hartmann and Fibich's well-meaning but scatterbrained caretaker during their youth
> MARIANNE, Hartmann and Yvette's daughter, meek and retiring, who escapes from life into a marriage of convenience
> TOTO, Fibich and Christine's son, a troubling, almost larger-than-life dynamo, an actor

Hartmann and Fibich (both named Thomas, so everyone—even their wives—calls them by their surnames) are inseparable friends in Anita Brookner's novel *Latecomers*. "They had been together since childhood and could no more think of living apart than they could of divorcing their wives, although their temperaments were diametrically opposed and they rarely thought alike on any matter." Hartmann is five years older than Fibich, but they are connected by similar childhood experiences. Both are Jews whose parents sent them to England from pre-World War II Germany. They never saw their parents again. They met as schoolboys in a dreary English boarding school during the war, where their friendship was the only saving grace in an otherwise intolerable situation; in later years, they came under the casual stewardship of Hartmann's Aunt Marie, whom Fibich also came to regard as a true relative. And they eventually set up business together using funds put aside for them by their parents. If their childhood experiences were a compelling tie, the business sealed the bond: "The day they had both installed themselves in their first little office in the Farringdon Road had been one of deep emotion for them both. Nothing, perhaps, would ever affect them so again, apart from the birth, health, and destiny of their children."

The two men, printers by trade, started out in the greeting-card business, which made them a comfortable if unexciting living for about twenty years. Then Hartmann—in the sort of inspired vision that is his particular forte, as compared to Fibich's methodical but necessary ability to contend with never-ending business details—hit upon a fitting diversification: photo-copying machines. This enterprise, although hardly exciting, has made them very well-off indeed.

It is, appropriately enough, Hartmann who is more able to enjoy these material rewards. Fibich moves through life timidly, fearful of letting himself revel in the fruits of his accomplishments. Hartmann, however—as suits someone with his name—is a considerate, generous hedonist. He is robust in his pleasures. He delights in comfort, luxuriating in a radiantly warm and well-furnished house, immaculately tailored clothes, fine cuisine. Hartmann's voluptuous enjoyment of the good life is in part innate, in part a reaction to the dreariness of his wartime adolescence, about which he has no desire to brood. "Everything amused him now, all prospects were viewed with indulgence. He was a sophisticated man, sophisticated enough to know that fond recollection of the past was mere sentimentality. . . ." Hartmann does not know how he achieved it, but he does recognize that he has been fortunate in managing to let the past go. As he likes to remind himself, he has "come through." Introspection and analysis are not activities that grip his attention.

Even his wife, Yvette, is well suited to Hartmann's life plan. She is decorative, supremely self-absorbed and self-confident, well aware of the fine figure she cuts. Her "peculiar attraction was based not on looks so much as on various forms of self-advertisement." Yvette, like Hartmann, had a disturbing childhood whose memories she prefers to bury (she does not always succeed—she sometimes wears an expression of "blankness or loss"), but she maintains perennial serenity and an inviting home environment for Hartmann. She is an amusement, an appropriate mate for a man who prefers concentrating on the more pleasant aspects of life.

Christine, Fibich's wife, is as different from Yvette as Fibich is from Hartmann. She has managed to recover somewhat from a lonely, emotionally abusive girlhood, but she will always suffer from a certain isolation. Christine is well aware that this characteristic presents problems, for herself and for her relationships. She would like to emulate Yvette's extravagant self-confidence, for instance, but ultimately she is able only to settle for a long-overdue acceptance of her own strengths—a calmness, a subdued attractiveness, a generosity and gentleness of spirit.

It is ironic, considering that the couples are fairly well matched (albeit not extravagantly in love), that their children are so different from them. The temperaments of Marianne Hartmann and Toto Fibich are more like those of the other couple than of their own parents. In her excessive gentleness and timidity, Marianne is more like Fibich and Christine. The Fibiches' son, Toto, however, is tumultuous and almost frighteningly aggressive.

It is understandable that the Fibiches invariably feel more comfortable with the obedient and bland Marianne; they observe Toto with bewilderment, wondering (guiltily) how they could have produced such a disturbing child. The Hartmanns, for their part, are more able to revel in Toto's self-centered presence and are concerned about their daughter's lack of personality and spirit. In adulthood, Marianne (a compliant, lackluster wife and mother) and Toto (an intriguing actor) become even more like their parents' alter egos. Only Toto is able to "come through," in his own way, capitalizing on the best characteristics of his parents' sensitivity and the Hartmanns' delight in life's pleasures.

It is Fibich who emerges as the central figure in *Latecomers*. Hartmann is a relaxing and reassuring presence; Fibich, however, is unsettling. His anxiety radiates from the pages. The reader feels it in his insomnia and touchy digestion as well as in his ambiguous relationship with Christine. The nature of Fibich's feelings toward his wife is something of a mystery. He probably loves her as much as he is capable of loving any woman, yet while he is kind to her, he is relentlessly distant. Christine did not marry Fibich for romantic love—"it was yearning, longing, a desire to compensate for all the loveless years"—but she does try to create a true home. Fibich's inability to take advantage of that potential for security and love is a loss for them both. Christine's inability to break through her own demons is a further tragedy.

Fibich, even with Hartmann's prodding and Christine's desire for warmth, will never be able to achieve the human potential for joy and fulfillment. He is anxious and withdrawn; he cannot enjoy his family, his home, his thriving business. He is weighed down by his childhood. At the urging of his analyst, Fibich wants to return to Berlin to trace his beginnings, but he is afraid to do so. ("Hartmann's solution to this problem had been breathtaking in its simplicity: get rid of the analyst.")

It is not until late in life that Fibich dares to visit Germany. It is a trip that fails to resolve absolutely his conflicts with the past, but Fibich—the latecomer—does approach a gentle and melancholy understanding of himself and his loved ones. Sadly, this belated appreciation comes at a time when, author Brookner intimates, Fibich's life is coming to an end.

Anita Brookner's cool, measured writing style is at its peak in *Latecomers*. Control and subdued subject matter, which are well suited to her relation of the story of Hartmann and Fibich, are the hallmarks of her fiction. While *Latecomers* is not as assured and compelling as her best-known novel, *Hotel du Lac*, Brookner has fashioned a book that is nonetheless appealing for its low-keyed approach to an analysis of everyday life. Her characters are average people—if *anyone* is indeed average—whose stories illustrate the many different roads available in any given circumstance.

Some people—like Fibich, and to a lesser extent Christine and Marianne and perhaps even Toto—feel the weight of their personal histories strongly. Others are able to shake off the burden and enjoy the many small and large pleasures that make up life. None of Brookner's characters manages to achieve the ideal human balance of realistic introspection and joyous celebration of life's offerings, but this failure brings the reader to the conclusion that everyone has that capacity—even those who are latecomers.

Lisa M. Clyde

THE LIFE OF GRAHAM GREENE, VOLUME I: 1904–1939

Author: Norman Sherry (1925–   )
Publisher: Viking Press (New York). 783 pp. $29.95
Type of work: Biography
Time: 1904–1939
Locale: England; West Africa; Mexico

A sweeping, detailed biography of novelist Graham Greene with sources well balanced among letters, literary works, and interviews with Greene and others

> *Principal personages:*
> (HENRY) GRAHAM GREENE, one of the great novelists of the 20th century
> CHARLES HENRY GREENE, his father
> MARION GREENE, his mother
> HUGH GREENE, the brother with whom Graham had the closest relationship
> VIVIEN DAYRELL-BROWNING, Graham's wife

Henry Graham Greene was born in 1904 in Berkhamsted, England, one of six children of Charles and Marion Greene. The long line of the Greene family was a distinguished one, but one against which Graham would later rebel and one that provided him with much material for his writings.

His was a sensitive nature. In this first volume, Greene is described as a loner and secretive in the extreme. Many of the terrors and fears he felt as a child he kept to himself, but much later he would transfer them to his fictional writings. In the preface, biographer Norman Sherry quotes John Keats: "A man's life of any worth is a continuous allegory and very few eyes can see the mystery." Therein lies the key to Graham Greene the man. Mysteries abound. There was a certain predisposition to secretiveness as part of a shy, inward nature, illustrated by an event early in his childhood. When he first discovered he could read, instead of sharing his excitement with his family, he hid in a far corner of the attic and read to himself.

This tendency toward secretiveness was further developed as a defense against the unspeakable experiences he underwent at the Berkhamsted School, of which his father was headmaster. That unfortunate fact made his fellow students think he was a spy. His lack of athletic ability and his wont to hide out and read poetry further set him off from his peers. He not only experienced isolation but was often the victim of cruel jokes and torments.

As terrible as these tortures he had to endure were, they provided him with a theme common to many of his works: the "betrayed one." "The Judas figure, a powerful character in some of Greene's finest novels, could well have been derived from Wheeler," one of his three primary tormentors. Greene was driven to many suicide attempts both during his school years and for a time thereafter. He appeared to struggle philosophically throughout his life over the attractiveness of "the escape" on the one hand and the mortal sin of suicide on the other.

One of the mysteries that was so much a part of Greene's life was his ambivalent attitude toward sex. His early encounters came in a state of revulsion engendered by his father's extreme measures against homosexuality in his capacity as headmaster. When Greene first encountered mild pornographic pictures, he was disgusted, even fearful of the feelings they aroused.

His first love was Gwen Howell, his sister's governess, who awakened in him real passion. As a student at Oxford he had a number of encounters with prostitutes, probably somewhat out of a sense of curiosity. This obsession, in one form or another, seems to have haunted him throughout his life.

In 1925, bored with Oxford life, he met his future wife, Vivien Dayrell-Browning. He was to court her with passionate, revealing letters for two years, amid her reluctance, before she finally agreed to become his wife.

Vital to Greene's development as both man and writer was his conversion, during the long period of his courtship of Vivien, to Catholicism. During his pursuit of her, when she tried to end the relationship, refused his proposals, and insisted upon a celibate marriage, he began to feel that his atheism in the face of her ardent Catholicism was the great stumbling block. He decided to get instruction and become a Catholic out of a sort of desperate boredom as well as a desire to comply with the faith of the woman he so frantically wanted to marry.

Far from being an empty duty, Catholicism subsequently became central to Graham Greene's understanding of life. He seemed, all his life, to be "hounded by God," in a "notion that God has a special commitment for each of us, though we may not know what the mission is." (The reader is given the feeling that, well into his eighties, Greene is still wrestling with his mission.)

Greene's beginnings as a writer emerged out of his prolific reading. His first published stories appeared in the *Berkhamstedian*. He later edited the *Oxford Outlook* and while still a student submitted a volume of poetry and prose to the publisher Blackwell. In 1923 he began work on his first novel. True to his need for secrecy, he told only one friend about his book. The novel was rejected, and for the next year or so

Greene was engrossed with finding a job, hoping especially to work for *The Times*. He eventually landed a position with the *Nottingham Journal*, left there, and tried *The Times* again, this time with more success.

In 1929 his first successful novel, *The Man Within*, was published, and for a time he and Vivien were happy, although when the very beauty and purity he so admired in his wife became too much for the highly sexed Graham, he began his sexual wanderings. (However, Vivien's purity was not so great as to prevent them from having a daughter, Lucy, and a son, Francis.)

The strength of *The Man Within* led Greene to resign his position with *The Times*, and he and Vivien moved to Chipping Campden so that he could devote himself full time to writing. But his first novel proved to be a false start. As Greene struggled with other unsuccessful novels, the money began to run out.

Stamboul Train was to prove the turning point in Greene's writing career. From then on he pursued a lifelong passion for direct observation and experience in the making of his novels. He abandoned romanticism for a closely-observed realism. Everything was grist for his mill: all was part of life, and all life could be used—his early childhood, his family relationships, and, most of all, his journeys.

Greene's journey through Liberia with his cousin Barbara was the first of many he made to little-known places in search of inspiration and perhaps his mission. It was a hazardous journey, one that may have harkened back to his old days of suicide attempts. He was an ardent admirer of the works of Joseph Conrad, and there are many parallels to be found between Greene's Liberian journey and Conrad's motives in writing *Heart of Darkness*, one of which certainly was to make money by writing a travel book.

By the time Greene planned his trip to Mexico, he had published many novels and short stories. But it was *The Lawless Roads* and *The Power and the Glory*, both written out of his Mexico experience, that established his reputation as one of the finest novelists of the century.

Greene's religious beliefs included belief in an unstable universe. Presenting to God a picture of this universe, to Greene, can come only through the eyes of one person at any one time. In this view he differs markedly from Lawrence Durrell, whose central characters are only finally (if ever) revealed through the eyes of many observers. Greene needed to experience the human condition at all levels, leading the reader to wonder at his motives in many of his actions. Greene's genius lay not only in presenting an authentic atmosphere and a sense of place, but also in creating strong, believable characters who inhabit that place. *The Power and the Glory*, considered his finest novel, is a remarkable work in that it brings together Greene's powers of observation, research skills, and sheer writing genius.

It is tempting in such a long work as this to get lost in detail, and it does happen here. A chronology at the beginning would have been helpful in wading through such an eventful life as Greene's. But Sherry is to be highly commended for a thoroughly professional job of research. To biographically examine as intensely shy and secretive a subject as Greene presents a task difficult enough, not to mention the prodigious amount of material that was available.

Sherry deals extremely well with all the mysteries that surround Graham Greene. He never gets into psychological hot water, but he deals with what he knows, not what he might conjecture. The mystery of Vivien is a prime example of this. She came into Greene's life when things were at their blackest for him. He had undergone dreadful school experiences, attempted suicide, wandered purposelessly at Oxford, and undergone psychoanalysis. Vivien's stable character and the extreme love and passion she generated in him appeared, at least for a time, to focus his energies. What lay behind this all-consuming need for Vivien and his later loss of interest deepens for the reader a realization of the complexities of Greene and a respect for the skill of the biographer. It does appear, however, that so much detail, even to minutiae, such as what Greene ate for breakfast at school, tends to benumb the reader to the crucial events in his life. As absorbing as Greene's life is, the reader must persevere in order to absorb the whole of the book.

Elizabeth Bouvier Spencer

A LITTLE STRANGER

Author: Candia McWilliam (1955–   )
Publisher: Doubleday and Company (Garden City, N.Y.). 181 pp. $15.95
Type of work: Novel
Time: The present
Locale: England

A woman becomes so indolent during her pregnancy that she cannot see that the family nanny has been plotting to replace her in the life of both her husband and her son

> Principal characters:
> DAISY, a young English wife and mother, of comfortable means
> JOHN, Daisy's four-year-old son
> MARGARET PRIDE, John's scheming, wicked nanny
> SOLOMON, Daisy's husband and John's father

The English love stories about the family nanny. A good nanny story is a most beloved reading experience. Candia McWilliam's jaunty novelette *A Little Stranger* follows in the frolicsome tradition of nanny books. But it becomes a modern day parable when the heroine, Daisy, discovers, almost too late, that beneath superficial appearances are dark, insidious forces.

When Daisy hires a nanny to take charge of the upbringing of her four-year-old son, John, she believes that she has made the perfect choice in Margaret Pride, who from all appearances seems the perfect nanny to set aright the country manor in the lush English land. Margaret is short, pretty for a nanny, prefers to be neat, and when she arrives has trouble keeping her figure. Daisy says, "She had the round wrists and belted midriff of one who has trouble shifting the puppy fat which makes young women appear middle-aged before time."

At first, there is only one thing about Margaret that Daisy does not like: her scent. "It was a smell of blossom and powder, not pungent but very strong." Although Daisy does not know it, this objectionable scent is a hint of Margaret's dark secrets, and her horrific treacheries.

When Margaret comes to live in the house with the family, everything seems perfect. Daisy's husband, Solomon, is pleased. Her young son, John, seems to love his nanny. Margaret herself is hardworking and efficient, a buzz of domestic activity, good at thinking ahead and planning things so that events will not catch her off guard.

To Daisy, "Margaret was as orderly as she had claimed to be. . . . Nothing was out of place, nothing missing. It was surely in such a rational and ordered state that John's spirit would grow confident and free, untroubled by chaos."

With her son needing nothing she could give him, relieved of petty domestic burdens, with her husband frequently far from home either hunting or tending to business affairs in busy London, Daisy becomes inspired with an insouciant romantic outlook on her most perfect, well-ordered life. Out in the garden one evening, she tells herself, "Perhaps I could make solid the expressed desire of my husband and Margaret by conceiving a child. There I would be, with my children, the keystone of the family monument."

Like a modern-day Dr. Pangloss, Daisy believes that she has the best of all possible worlds—natural, orderly, provident. So she lets Margaret take charge of all aspects of her life and prepares to give birth to a second child.

In her pregnancy, Daisy, who is part Dutch, grows fatter at the waist, eats and eats, and tends her beloved tulip garden. During this period, Daisy notes that Margaret, too, is changing shape and is beginning to win her struggle against food. In her slimmer state, Margaret has also taken to wearing pretty black dresses and shoes with high heels.

One day Margaret complains to Daisy about some of the other servants who have come into her room and cleaned it while she was away. She is insulted by the hint that she does not keep it nice. Daisy, puzzled by this infantile outburst, has always thought Margaret's room was exceptionally tidy. Although she has noticed "her room was still heavily scented with that peculiarly sweet perfume. It overlay all other airs in the room."

Daisy decides that Margaret is being "oddly artificial" and has been dressing for effect. She also notices that Margaret has begun to nick away at the corners of her mouth where "dense little cuckoo-spits of froth had formed. These were whiter than her teeth, and she nicked them away, one, two, as though it were a regular, unconsidered, aspect of hygienic maintenance."

Daisy begins to grow slightly aware that something is amiss when she receives a letter addressed to her about which she knows nothing. Her thoughts on reading this letter are, "But who could they have confused me with? Who could possibly be interested in pretending to be me?" Despite this warning that she is the victim of a mysterious conspiracy, Daisy dismisses the letter as junk mail, and only later learns the depth of Margaret's secret, and treachery.

Margaret's secret is that she is adept at deception. She is able to make the surface of things run smoothly and efficiently. Underneath this well-ordered state, however, Margaret is warlike and of a strong and destructive nature. She is a lover of war movies and, as though by instinct, attacks Daisy, whom she perceives as weak.

All during her stay in Daisy's household, she has been secretly plotting an invasion of sorts and has been coveting the affections of not only Daisy's son but her husband Solomon, whom Daisy describes as "so handsome, so milord, so very dressed, such a man as I had dreamed of." Margaret, too, dreams of such a man and by an unnatural, superhuman force of will, and by secretly vomiting into a suitcase hidden in her sweetly smelling room and by strong diet pills, she has transformed herself from a dowdy nanny into a fetchingly handsome woman with a handspan waist.

She has even drawn Daisy's son John into her conspiracy to replace his mother by molding his character into that of a baby prince—godlike, intolerant, cutely knowing, contrived, and made of brass. To keep her secrets, she has also threatened the child by telling him that his mother would beat him if he should tell of her secret lover who comes at night into the nursery room, or of her familiar routine of vomiting into a suitcase, which he has seen and thought was part of the grown-up woman's toilette.

This fantastic conspiracy is revealed to Daisy by hints at first from the family doctor, who is aware but duty bound not to tell of Margaret's bulimia, and eventually by Margaret herself, while ironically reading the book *Patience Rewarded* to Daisy, who is bedridden after a fall on the stairs. Daisy's eyes begin to open to the truth about Margaret:

> Then, as though in alarm, she continued speaking, maybe to ensure my silence. She appeared terrified at the mention of the doctor. She smelt, suddenly, of acetone. The sockets of her arms were circled with sour cloth. Her lips showed white gums. I knew then that I was struggling for the life of my child. "I can't see those nannies any more. They say it's your doing he loves me. He loves me. And so does the child you call your son. He loves *me*."

Margaret is, of course, sick, not only of body but also of mind. She does nothing while Daisy goes into labor. She wants her to die. Her perverted mind believes that she will win the husband, the house, the big cars by this triumph over Daisy.

Her erotic fantasies of romancing the husband come to an abrupt end when Solomon, warned by neighbors that something is not right at his home, rushes in, cursing the nanny as a bitch for smashing up the car, and saves Daisy, not from the pain she is experiencing, but from the vituperative, obsessive voice of Margaret, which tells Daisy that if she had any sense of what is proper, she would die.

Daisy says, "She had already started taking my name; it was only a little way from taking my life. The longer I was unhelped, the better it would be. She hoped that the baby would live, and she and Solomon would bring it up as their own."

Daisy almost does acquiesce to Margaret's insane desire, but the thing that saves her is the little stranger inside her belly, kicking to be alive. This struggle for life makes her realize that she, too, had been mad, and that now she was fighting sane. After Margaret is taken away, Daisy tells herself, "I should have smelt her illness. . . . To me, she looked simply rather enviably slim, because I knew I was unenviably fat."

Candia McWilliam has written an entertaining story that explores the world of the superficial and finds beneath its glossy surface terrible, murderous monsters in the form of a nanny. The book itself is much like the story McWilliam tells, in that it seems too superficial and easy to dismiss as a trifle. There is almost no tension or conflict in this story. The ending, although not surprising to the reader, is anticlimactic. Not until the reader reflects on the many mysterious hints and subtle suggestions that are buried in the story does he or she find that there is much going on worthy of serious consideration. Because of its jigsaw-puzzle clues, and its curious references to Nietzsche's *Ecce Homo* and his other basic writings, this novelette may be too subtle for its own good. On reflection, however, there is much more substance than first appears. And much of what is at work is deadly serious human business.

John E. Stevenson

LORD BYRON'S DOCTOR

Author: Paul West (1930–   )
Publisher: Doubleday and Company (Garden City, N.Y.). 277 pp. $19.95
Type of work: Novel
Time: 1816–1817
Locale: Europe

A novel that re-creates the exploits of the Romantic poet Lord Byron during a period of less than a year as seen from the highly imaginative perspective of Dr. J. W. Polidori, Lord Byron's doctor and traveling companion

Principal characters:
GEORGE NOEL GORDON, Lord Byron, poet and roué
DR. J. W. POLIDORI, Lord Byron's young doctor
PERCY BYSSHE SHELLEY, poet and friend of Lord Byron
MARY SHELLEY, author and Percy's wife
CLAIRE CLAIRMONT, Lord Byron's mistress, Mary's half-sister

George Noel Gordon, Lord Byron, the prolific poet and dissolute playboy, found himself exiled from England by scandalous rumors of incest with his half-sister, Augusta. Lord Byron planned a journey to Europe to meet with his friends the Percy Bysshe Shelleys in Geneva, Switzerland, and from there on to a final destination in Italy. Byron hired on a personal physician, Dr. J. W. Polidori, to accompany him. Byron was a man who adored having inferiors around him, fawning and bowing, but who felt much intimidated by equals or superiors. He was a bawdy, lusty type who used people around him as stepping stones to achieving whatever he desired.

Polidori was a 20-year-old Italian Scotsman, the son of an Italian living in London. He was a recent graduate from the University of Edinburgh, where he was the youngest student to receive a medical degree. A very impressionable young man, Polidori, or Polly as he was called by Byron, was in awe of those with titles and power, the perfect foil for Byron. Young Polly began his second education at the sometimes abusive feet of one of the most infamous rakes of his times. Byron's sexual escapades were legendary, and Polly became his devoted protégé. He was further encouraged to hang on Byron's every word as he had been offered 500 pounds by Byron's publisher to chronicle Byron's daily deeds and misdeeds.

Polly began his tenure as Lord Byron's doctor in April of 1816, the two of them traveling in an immense custom-made carriage, complete with bed and dining space. The fact that Byron slid out of London without paying the 500 pounds due on the carriage spiced up the journey even more for Byron. Off they went with a primary destination of Geneva, there to meet up with the Shelleys.

Their travels took them through Ostend, Bruges, Ghent, Antwerp, and Brussels; Byron often "relieved" himself by bedding various and sundry "ladies," and regaled Polly with minute details of each of his conquests. Polly found Byron's tastes decidedly too indiscriminate and was saving himself for a girl from Italy, land of his father. However, Byron, at age twenty-eight, was less interested in taste and culture than he was in living life to the fullest, and he looked for the extremes, both good and bad.

As they made their way toward Geneva, Polly and Byron established the basis of their relationship, with Byron taunting Polly whenever he was in a mood, using his wit with some venom. Polly, however, forgave Byron his "pets," because poor Byron was wifeless (wife Anne sent him away for committing some unmentionable crime against her), he was deformed (clubfooted), and he was a virtual exile.

In his primary role as caretaker of Byron, Polly was often requested to examine Byron's genitals and discovered that Byron experienced pain in his testicles after having sex. After some careful questioning, it was Polly's private opinion that Byron's childhood nurse, May Gray, had sexually abused him. Polly also treated Byron's clubfoot, as best he could, for the damage had been done in early childhood, and there was no remedy. Another duty as physician was to help Byron keep his weight in check. Thinness was a concern and a constant battle for Byron.

Byron and Polly reached Geneva and rented the Villa Diodati, which afforded them a magnificent view of the lake. The Shelleys (poet Percy Bysshe and his young wife Mary) and Mary's half-sister, Claire Clairmont (Lord Byron's London mistress), arrived very soon after, and all five set up housekeeping. But fast upon the Shelleys' arrival, Polly became an outcast, replaced by Shelley as Byron's companion. Polly, in his jealousy, soon discounted Shelley as a histrionic windbag, but he did develop a crush on Mary and was charmed by her "Gothick" ways. He found Claire a bit too forward and aggressive, although he was impressed by her stoicism and strength.

When Byron and Shelley would go off on their sojourns to surrounding areas, Polly was left out, and he began spending much time in town. By using his "friendship" with Byron as his entrée, Polly soon ingratiated himself with the leading local English families, who also used his services as a physician. Included in his social rounds was a visit to the local brothel, and there Polly would rendezvous with Gaby Saxonnex. This particular entanglement ultimately caused Polly great distress. He foolishly began to romanticize her, only painfully to discover her true mercenary nature: Polly found himself joining in a ménage à trois with Gaby and his friend Rossi. Polly was filled with self-disgust by this tryst, and then with dismay: Gaby had given him gonorrhea. Polly turned to his medicine bag to drown his sorrow in opium.

As the summer lengthened, the company at Villa Diodati settled in. Everyone was writing: Lord Byron worked on *Darkness*; Shelley toyed with the *Hymn to Intellectual Beauty*; Mary had begun developing *Frankenstein*; Claire copied Byron's poems; and Polly had started his story, *The Vampyre: A Tale* (somewhat loosely modeled on several characters in Polly's life, in particular Lord Byron). Many times, Polly engaged in abstract discussions with Mary about *Frankenstein*. In fact, he proposed to her the use of lightning as the animator of the being created from parts.

Polly, now the house doctor, discovered that Claire was pregnant with Byron's child. He also discovered that Byron had contracted venereal disease. But still, Polly was just the hired hand and even found himself excluded from the group's use of nicknames for one another (Mary called Lord Byron "Albe," and Byron called Shelley "Shiloh"). Polly and Byron began to bicker frequently. Polly was binging more and more frequently on opium and brandy, and would fantasize about Byron's bowing in obeisance to him. Finally, their arguments escalated, and after a particularly vicious verbal fight, Byron resolved to discharge Polly.

Polly confronted Byron with his knowledge of the rumor that Byron was planning to banish him. To soften the blow, Byron admitted that if Polly stayed with him, he would end up seducing him. Polly was devastated, nevertheless; Byron was, after all, his idol. Byron was firm, however, and Polly prepared to take his leave of the company at Villa Diodati and in town.

During one of his last examinations of her, Polly, who had been lusting after the pregnant Claire, made love to her. Byron had grown bored with her and had become verbally and physically abusive, so Polly and Claire, both rejected by Byron, had grown ever closer. Polly dreamed of a life with her, but she was not interested, since she still pined for Byron and would leave as planned with the Shelleys. They were to return to England while Byron continued on his journey toward Italy.

The sad day of parting came on September 16. The Shelleys had already departed. Byron had recalled a past retainer to accompany him on to Italy. Polly, too, headed toward Italy, but in a much reduced style, for he was nearly penniless.

It was a lonely, disturbing journey through the Alps for Polly. One day, a couple of weeks later, quite by chance, Polly met up with Byron and his new entourage and, in a weak moment, begged Byron to take him back—but to no avail. Byron snubbed him again.

Upon his arrival in Milan, Polly, with the help of several letters of introduction from his friends in Geneva, started to rebuild his life. He even would socialize with Byron on occasion. Then, just as he felt at home (he was, after all, in the land of his father), Polly had a row with a high-ranking Austrian officer at the opera and was summarily ordered out of Italy.

Polly returned to London and to his father's begrudging support. As soon as possible, Polly traveled to Bath to see Claire, still living with the Shelleys and awaiting the birth of her child. Although she had not given up on Byron, Polly began a liaison with her, hoping against hope that he might replace Byron in her affections. It was not to be.

Success continued to elude Polly, and he still was turning to his opium for solace. The relationship with Claire slowly unraveled; she was completely preoccupied with her new daughter, Allegra. Polly went from mishap to mishap until, finally, he learned that Byron had written a letter to a mutual friend in which he claimed to dislike Polly and even to have contempt for him.

Polly was completely undone by Byron's disloyalty and indifference. After making careful plans, he prepared a strong poison and killed himself. To Polly, it seemed the only way that he could find relief from his vast disappointment in himself.

Paul West has written a novel, *Lord Byron's Doctor*, that offers an astounding mixture of literary components: part memoirs; part biography; part social criticism; even part travel; and, without a doubt, part humor. West, a prolific writer himself, exposes the rarely shown side of the brilliant poet George Noel Gordon, Lord Byron, the man that was the rake, the roué, the debaucher. West reveals Byron's dark side by juxtaposing it with the fresh, innocent, almost virginal young Dr. Polidori. The novel, which is West's re-creation of the actual diary of Dr. J. W. Polidori, written about his journeys with Lord Byron in 1816, captures, in the vernacular of the day, the social mores of Europe in the early 1800s. The novel is thought provoking and evocative, one the reader will not be able to put down.

Constance Clyde

LOVE LIFE

Author: Bobbie Ann Mason (1940–   )
Publisher: Harper and Row (New York). 241 pp. $17.95
Type of work: Short stories
Time: The present
Locale: Western Kentucky

Fifteen tales of love and loss among ordinary people, set in western Kentucky

Love Life, Bobbie Ann Mason's first collection since the critically acclaimed *Shiloh and Other Stories*, opens with the title story, the tale of a retired schoolteacher named Opal. Opal spends her days alone, daydreaming, watching rock-music videos, and sipping peppermint cordials. Restless, she longs for a life of travel and excitement. Her much-traveled niece Jenny, on the other hand, is attempting to settle down; the man who claims to love her, Randy, is an unimaginative real-estate salesman who cannot understand Jenny's reluctance to commit herself to married life. Aunt and niece find each other somewhat aloof and curious, and each is reluctant to share her innermost secrets. Jenny, for instance, admires her aunt's quilts, but is allowed to see only the ones Opal calls "crazy quilts." Finally, giving in to what she regards as her niece's nosiness, Aunt Opal relents and shows Jenny her burial quilt. This quilt, which comprises sewn-together tombstone shapes, represents Opal's family tree. Impulsively, she gives it to Jenny, thus creating a bridge of intimacy that allows the two women to share a wealth of hitherto hidden thoughts and emotions.

"Midnight Magic" tells the story of Steve, a perpetually adolescent hot-rodder who cannot understand the strange new kinds of lives that have caught up with his once-carefree friends. To Steve, responsibility consists primarily of getting up, working at the mattress factory, maintaining his jacked-up sports car, and doing his laundry. Drunk on weekends and apparently without ambition, Steve cannot understand the ominous turn his best friend's marriage has taken; typically, he forgets to meet Doran and his wife, Nancy, at the airport and has to hurry to get there. On the way he sees, on the side of the road, what appears to be a dead body. He reports it from a phone booth off the highway, the moment finding him uncertain and afraid.

"Hunktown" is the story of a couple, Joann and Cody, whose marriage is rocked by Cody's suddenly resurgent desire to become a country singer. Unemployed, he has been living off Joann, spending his weekends in Nashville cutting the record he hopes will propel him to the big time. As he spends more and more time away, Joann is eventually faced with the choice of either staying with her good job and home or following her husband's dream.

In "Marita," a young girl's unwanted pregnancy forces both her and her mother to reexamine each other's needs and destinies. Told in a split narrative, each perspective is carefully detailed.

"The Secret of the Pyramids" is about grief and a woman's struggle to transcend the death of a prominent businessman with whom she has had an illicit affair. A seemingly inconsequential tale—the story of how an Illinois town got its name—becomes the focal point of a series of poignant memories.

In "Piano Fingers," a drugstore clerk, Dean, romanticizes his life by imagining himself as the star of a new television detective series entitled "Ballinger." Ballinger is glamorous and helpful and is a defender of the poor and the innocent. In reality, however, Dean cannot transcend either his ordinary life or his domineering wife; in defiance of both he treats his daughter, who has been told by her instructor that she has "piano fingers," to an expensive instrument. For one perfect moment, he is indeed Ballinger.

"Bumblebees" is the story of Barbara and Ruth, two women who, against considerable odds, have bought and renovated a dilapidated farmhouse. Ruth, recovering from the shock of losing her husband and daughter in an automobile accident, is terrified of the bees that occupy the house's attic. Barbara's daughter, Allison, is home from college and less tolerant of Ruth's eccentric ways than is her mother. A critical understanding is reached among all when a flood isolates them from the rest of the community, forcing them to confront both their fears and themselves.

"Big Bertha Stories" are Donald's strange tales of a machine he uses in his work as a strip-miner. A troubled Vietnam veteran, Donald alternately amuses and frightens his wife and son with odd, romanticized flights of fancy concerning Big Bertha. It is eventually Jeannette's task to separate the real man from the fictional one, a process that, first, must include her own redemption.

"State Champions" chronicles the unlikely rise to fame of the 1952 Cuba Cubs, their surprising success serving as a backdrop to the narrator's coming-of-age experiences in the seventh grade. It is a time of innocence, of unlimited expectations, and of impossible heroes—all of which are eventually tempered by the realities of daily life and death.

Mickey, of "Private Lies," trapped in an unfulfilling marriage, dreams of finding the daughter he and his first wife, Donna, gave up for adoption eighteen years before. To that end, he resumes a relationship with Donna, whom he now finds strange and fascinating. Together they fly to Florida, the site of their original honeymoon, and only at this time are they able to make right everything except the one, long regretted action that has haunted their lives.

"Coyotes" is about two people on the edge of discovering each other's real self. Cobb thinks he has found the perfect woman to marry in Lynnette; it somehow does not matter that their habits, life-styles, and occupations are totally dissimilar. The turning point—the point at which they can either move forward or walk away—occurs during a coyote hunt near Cobb's brother's house. As in so many of these stories, the reader is left to wonder, and imagine, the eventual outcome.

"Airwaves" is about a woman named Jane who is learning to live alone now that her boyfriend, Coy, has moved out. She believes, sometimes at least, that she loves Coy, but she is not really sure; like most men she knows, he fulfills only some of her needs. Living alone, collecting unemployment benefits, Jane resumes her relationship with her father, who is an aged heavy drinker and a chronic complainer. It is through him that she eventually discovers some hidden truth about herself; by the time Coy is ready to move back in with her, she has made plans to join the army. Lonely as she is, she decides that "the sounds of warfare would be like the sounds of rock and roll, hard-driving and satisfying."

In "Sorghum," a bright young woman, trapped in a devastating marriage, suddenly takes up with an electronics-store owner she meets at a sorghum plant. He is from Memphis, has a good deal of money, and is eager to introduce her to his wealthy friends in the city. Lying to her husband, who does not care what she does, Liz accompanies Ed to a dinner party. Intimidated by the other guests' fancy clothes and the furnishings of the house, Liz instantly feels out of place. Retreating to the spacious, marbled bathroom, she dips a toe into the hot tub, not sure if the unbearably hot water is "a punishment, or an acquired taste that would turn delicious when she was used to it."

"Memphis" is also about choices. In this story, Beverly, the mother of two children, is forced to decide whether or not she will rejoin her estranged husband and move to Columbia, South Carolina. The thought of her children moving so far away terrifies her, but then so does the prospect of losing her newly found, and hard earned, independence. Accompanying her friend Jolene on a weekend fling in Memphis, she is still unable to make a choice. Her ex-husband tells her, "You're so full of wants you don't know what you want." She reasons that times have changed, that she does not have to live the kind of life her parents did, but, eventually, it is her own inability to make a decision that decides her fate.

Sam, the main character in "Wish," is eighty-four years old and lives with his sister Damson. Every Sunday, after church, they drive out into the country to visit their other sister, Hortense, and her husband, Cecil. Sam's life is filled with routines and nostalgia, and Damson is beginning to worry that he is finally getting old. "No, I ain't old," he tells her. "Old is in your head." Later, alone in his room, Sam relives the circumstances of his wife's death, going on to remember his first, and most cherished, love, Nettie, and how he had unbuttoned her dress, the one with "self-covered buttons, hard like seed corn."

With *Love Life*, her sixth book, Bobbie Ann Mason continues to delve deeply into the hearts and lives of ordinary Kentucky people. In this collection the reader finds schoolteachers, store owners, factory workers, clerks, and singers. All are bound together by a common search for love. Most do not have it, cannot find it, or allow it to slip through their fingers unrecognized. More than anything else, Mason's stories are a reminder that human tragedy is often measured in degrees, in the slow passage of time, or in the seemingly contented routines used to mark lives. Like other contemporary writers of what is sometimes called minimalist fiction—most notably the late Raymond Carver and Donald Barthelme—Mason employs a variety of voices and perspectives to illustrate her themes. In virtually every story, the resolution is left unknown, as if to allow the reader to stand in the shoes of each main character. Love stories all, these tales are, ultimately, about people's ability to adapt to changing lives, expectations, and disappointments. Set in and around both the rural and urban Kentucky, *Love Life* rings throughout with charm and authenticity.

David Alvarez

LOVE'S EXECUTIONER AND OTHER TALES OF PSYCHOTHERAPY

Author: Irvin D. Yalom (1931–)
Publisher: Basic Books (New York). 270 pp. $19.95
Type of work: Essays
Time: The present
Locale: The San Francisco Bay area

A psychotherapist describes the techniques he used to enable ten patients to confront their "existence pain" and thereby find meaning in lives governed by fears of death and doubts about their value to others

> *Principal personages:*
> IRVIN D. YALOM, a psychotherapist struggling to impart meaning to his patients' lives
> THELMA, a patient who is in love with her former therapist
> CARLOS, a patient who is dying of cancer
> SAUL, a patient who fears that three unopened letters contain accusations that will end his career
> MARGE, a patient who was abused as a child by her father
> BETTY, an overweight patient with a compulsive eating disorder
> MARVIN, a patient with marital problems

Irvin Yalom, a psychotherapist and professor of psychiatry at Stanford University, has developed a new method of "existential psychotherapy," which consists of confronting the universal, inevitable, and often disturbing realities of human existence. The prologue to *Love's Executioner* describes his theory of individual psychology and the role of psychotherapy in alleviating neuroses. The following ten essays each present a case study that together reveal Yalom's methods of helping patients who often do their best to prevent treatment of their anxieties.

Yalom believes that anxiety emerges from four givens of existence: inevitable death, the responsibility each person has for the course of his or her life, the ultimate aloneness of life, and the absence of obvious meaning to life. In the face of such fearsome realities, people find fortitude, not in a philosophy of meaning, but in a life of meaningful action. Yalom's existential psychotherapy aims at allowing individuals to find bases for action and to overcome paralyzing anxieties. Yalom treats his patients through a combination of individual and group therapy.

Thelma came to Dr. Yalom after twenty years of unsuccessful treatment with numerous other psychotherapists. One doctor, Matthew, had seduced her and then after a three-week affair abandoned her, refusing any further contact. For the next eight years, Thelma had alternated between fantasies of resuming her affair with Matthew and deep depressions when she realized he wanted nothing to do with her. Thelma's husband, Harry, was often away and offered her little emotional support.

Dr. Yalom believed that he needed to destroy her illusions about Matthew. Yalom considered Matthew to be a disgrace to the profession of psychotherapy, a man who seduced patients to affirm his own damaged sexual self. After months of unsuccessful therapy, Yalom decided that the only solution was to arrange a three-way session with Thelma, Matthew, and himself. At the session, Yalom learned that Matthew had had a nervous breakdown just before he seduced Thelma. His remorse over violating the therapist-patient relationship had led Matthew to abandon psychology and become the manager of a fundamentalist Christian health center.

A session with Dr. Yalom and Matthew served to destroy Thelma's illusions about Matthew and about the importance of their affair in both their lives. Thelma was bitter at Yalom for leaving her without her most cherished fantasy of a future life with Matthew. Yalom feared that his effort at forcing Thelma to face reality had misfired. When Thelma was interviewed six months later, however, other researchers found her less depressed and no longer suicidal. Although Thelma had abandoned therapy with Dr. Yalom after that session, she had gone ahead on her own to reconstruct her life in acknowledgment of her separation from Matthew.

Carlos was dying of cancer. His main regret was that chemotherapy caused him to lose his hair, making him unattractive to women he hoped to seduce. His one emotional focus was his son and daughter, who lived with their mother in South America. Carlos's cruel attitude toward women was revealed in group therapy when he showed no concern for two women in the group who recounted their experiences as rape victims. In a private session with Dr. Yalom, Carlos said he would like to rape women if he could get away with it. Dr. Yalom used Carlos's love for his daughter to make him realize that women were as vulnerable as he. Carlos built a system of morality on his growing empathy for others. He founded a group for other terminal cancer patients. Eventually, Carlos brought his children to stay with him, teaching them how to face the inevitability of their deaths through the courage with which he faced his own.

Saul had finished therapy with Dr. Yalom three years before returning to him with a new fear. Saul received three letters from the Stockholm Institute and refused to open them, certain that they contained denunciations from Dr. K, a world-famous scientist with whom Saul had collaborated on an article. Saul had been an orphan, brought up by an aunt who had never loved him. He looked to Dr. K, among others, as a father figure from whom he desired approval but feared rejection. Dr. Yalom was unable to convince Saul to open and read the letters. Saul's fear of their contents caused him a psychosomatic paralysis. Yalom feared Saul was slipping into psychosis and would need to be hospitalized. Saul was saved by a phone call from a friend who informed him that Dr. K had died. Saul calculated that the letters had been sent after K's death. Suddenly relieved, Saul opened the letters and found that they were notices of K's death sent to all former visitors to the Institute, and a letter from K's widow in which she enclosed a partially written letter by K to Saul, expressing admiration for Saul's work. That single validation allowed Saul to escape from his depression.

Marge was a fearful, subdued person. As a child she had been sexually abused by her father. One day in therapy, Marge's place was taken by a second personality, a vibrant seductive woman. Dr. Yalom had been bored by Marge, but he enjoyed and was attracted to her double. Yet, he realized that if he were to show preference for Marge's second personality, she would not progress. Instead, he refused to allow Marge to give way to her double in therapy. Over time, Marge was strengthened by Dr. Yalom's preference for her original personality and was emboldened to kill off her double by integrating the most attractive aspects of her second personality.

Betty, a twenty-seven-year-old woman weighing 250 pounds, proved to be a personal challenge for Yalom. He initially did not want to treat her, because fat people disgusted him. He found nothing appealing in her personality, either. Before working with her successfully, he had to identify and overcome his own negative associations and his feelings of boredom with their relationship. He helped her to see her feelings of emptiness, and he encouraged her to join the group therapy sessions, where she was helped by Carlos. Betty's own father had died of cancer, and she became fat as a defense against her fear that she would get cancer, become thin, and die. Carlos's courage in facing death allowed Betty to overcome her own fear of death. She enrolled in a liquid-diet weight-reduction program. As she lost weight, Betty relived and confronted the childhood traumas she had endured as she had gained weight. Eventually, she was able to socialize and date, and Dr. Yalom found her an engaging and attractive person.

The final essay presents Marvin, who came to Dr. Yalom because he had horrible migraine headaches whenever he failed to consummate sexual relations with his wife. Marvin was distant from his emotions, yet he was able to express his fears in dreams he refused to understand. Over time, Marvin confronted the ways in which he had narrowed his emotional life and acknowledged the resulting intensity of his fear of dying unfulfilled. Marvin was unusual in the effort he made to translate the lessons of psychotherapy into changes in his everyday life and in his relationship with his wife. He told her every detail of his sessions, provoking her to confront her fears of socializing and of leaving the house. Like Carlos, Marvin learned that the morbid fear of death can be overcome if one makes the attempt to express emotions through the actions of connecting with others. As Marvin deepened his relationship with his wife and helped her address her phobias, he became more confident of his own worth and sure of her love for him.

The ten essays of *Love's Executioner* are compelling reading. Even the shortest pieces make the reader empathize with each patient and his or her fears and desires. The case studies provide a demonstration of Dr. Yalom's contention that each person fears death and isolation and seeks meaning in life through full relationships with others. Yalom is able to highlight the core of each patient's fear and show how the source of each neurosis is hidden from both patient and therapist by the logic each person constructs to justify and explain a stunted emotional life.

Irvin Yalom emerges as a full person, as well, in these narratives. *Love's Executioner* is unusual in its depiction of the therapist's own uncertainties and fears. Yalom discusses the phenomenon of countertransference, in which the therapist's own desires and neuroses are projected onto a patient, thereby disrupting therapy. Yalom reveals his own efforts, at times unsuccessful, to view his patients objectively. He often compares a patient's fears with his own, showing that each person suffers from existence anxieties in some form. Yalom also presents his thought processes as he tries to understand a patient's psyche and to devise an appropriate therapy. He explains how he must adjust his treatment in the light of new evidence revealed through analysis. He discusses how his failures in treatment provide him with important lessons, which can sometimes be used to help that patient and at times are valuable when facing other patients at later times. Yalom's humility and his sympathy for even the most difficult patients animate each essay. Through his example, Irvin Yalom demonstrates the essential humanism in the theory and practice of psychotherapy.

Lyn Miller-Lachmann

THE MAMBO KINGS PLAY SONGS OF LOVE

Author: Oscar Hijuelos (1951–   )
Publisher: Farrar, Straus and Giroux (New York). 407 pp. $18.95
Type of work: Novel
Time: 1940s–1980
Locale: Cuba and New York City

An aging Cuban-born musician recalls the heyday of his group, the Mambo Kings, when they appeared with Desi Arnaz on the I Love Lucy *show, and the events that led to the waning of his musical career*

> *Principal characters:*
> CESAR CASTILLO, a Cuban-born mambo singer
> NESTOR CASTILLO, Cesar's younger brother, trumpet player for the Mambo Kings
> DELORES FUENTES, Nestor's wife
> EUGENIO CASTILLO, Nestor's son
> VANNA VANE, Cesar's principal girlfriend in the heyday of the Mambo Kings
> BERNARDITO MANDELBAUM, one of Cesar's closest friends
> DESI ARNAZ, the famous Cuban-born producer

In the summer of 1980 the aging mambo musician Cesar Castillo checks into the Hotel Splendour in Harlem in order to drink himself to death. In the hours before he dies, he remembers the years during which he and his brother Nestor performed as the Mambo Kings and appeared on the *I Love Lucy* show. He remembers as well the tragedy that took his brother's life and proved to be the turning point in his own. Passing through his mind are the many people he and Nestor encountered along the way—in their Cuban village of Las Piñas; in Santiago de Cuba; in Havana; and in New York City, where they moved to make it big at the time of the mambo boom.

Cesar and Nestor Castillo were the two youngest sons of a farm family in rural Oriente Province, in Cuba. Eight years older than Nestor, Cesar was the rebel of the family. He remembers his father (who is still alive at the time of Cesar's death) as someone who beat him constantly and showed little affection or approval. As soon as he could, Cesar left home to live on his own in Santiago de Cuba, the largest nearby city. He met the orchestra director Julian Garcia and married his daughter. Garcia's orchestra proved to be a productive apprenticeship for Cesar, but the marriage ended because Cesar abused his wife and had affairs with other women. Soon after moving to Havana, they were divorced.

In temperament, Nestor was the opposite of his rebellious, boister-ous older brother. The baby of the family, he suffered several near-fatal bouts of illness. He became his mother's favorite and developed into a reserved, brooding, emotionally fragile young man who had nightmares of his childhood struggles with death and premonitions that he would die young. Influenced by the brother he always admired, Nestor joined Cesar in Havana. The two worked in a restaurant by day and tried to make it in a very competitive music business. One night, Nestor met a young woman who had just fought with her lover. Her name was María, and the twenty-two-year-old Nestor fell in love with her. For several months they had an intense affair; then María returned to her former lover. Nestor was shattered. With María he had been happy; he would never know such joy again. He began to write —and often rewrite—a song entitled "Beautiful María of My Soul."

In January 1949, Cesar and Nestor moved to New York. They settled in Harlem, and a cousin helped them find day jobs. They met other musicians from Cuba and Puerto Rico and formed the Mambo Kings. Cesar sang for the group; Nestor played the trumpet. This was the golden age of the mambo, and the brothers played clubs all over New York and New Jersey. They recorded a number of single records and three albums, and their songs were rerecorded by other musicians. Although they did not attain the kind of success that allowed them to quit their day jobs or to enjoy the luxurious standard of living of the most famous popular musicians, they played without regrets or resentments, for the sheer joy of creating music. The music scene brought them many friends, including Bernardito Mandelbaum, a Jew from Brooklyn whose love of the mambo made him an honorary member of the Latin music community. Shortly after arriving in New York, Nestor began to date Delores Fuentes, a young Cuban-born woman. Delores had been very attached to her father, who had died recently and who, like Nestor, had been an unhappy and brooding man. Delores and Nestor married in 1950.

Whereas Nestor remained faithful to Delores (although he still pined for his lost María), Cesar had affairs with numerous women. His favorite was the large, blonde, elegant Vanna Vane. For struggling mambo musicians like Cesar, "to be seen with a woman like Vanna was prestigious as a passport, a high-school diploma, a full-time job, a record contract, a 1951 DeSoto." In 1955 the Mambo Kings were playing in a club in Harlem when Desi Arnaz appeared. He heard them play "Beautiful María of My Soul" and wanted to meet them. After the concert, Desi and Lucille Ball went to Nestor and Delores's apartment (where Cesar also lived) and talked until three in the morning. Desi wanted to give his fellow Cubans their big break, and he invited them out to California to appear on *I Love Lucy* as Ricky Ricardo's two Cuban cousins who played "Beautiful María of My Soul" on the show. Cesar loved their trip to California. Nestor missed his family in New York. He was almost too nervous to perform on *I Love Lucy*, and when Cesar found him a prostitute, he was sick with guilt.

Back in New York, Cesar used the money he made from his appearance to buy a new DeSoto. The Mambo Kings were at the height of their popularity, but their success would last only one year. In January 1957, as they were driving back from a gig in New Jersey—Nestor behind the wheel and Cesar and Vanna Vane having sex, drunk, in the back seat—the car skidded on a patch of ice and hit a tree. Nestor died almost instantly.

For Cesar, Nestor's death was a turning point. He had not only lost his closest friend and musical partner; it was almost as if Nestor's melancholy character had been transferred to Cesar. Cesar began to carry around the inspirational book Nestor had bought to try to enliven his spirits and maintain a more positive attitude. Shortly after Nestor's death, Cesar returned to Las Piñas to visit his family. His father was more hostile than ever, and the country itself was changing, with the rise of Castro's guerrilla movement. Back in New York, his relationships with the rest of the band members deteriorated. He refused to accept another trumpet player to replace his brother, and he drank heavily before and during the concerts. He was asked to leave the Mambo Kings. He joined the merchant marine for two years and then returned to his old apartment building, where Delores and the two children, Eugenio and Leticia, still lived.

Cesar took a job as the building's custodian. He remained close to many of his old friends, particularly Bernardito Mandelbaum, who was a graphic artist in New York. He also became a surrogate father to Nestor's children and guided Eugenio through a stormy childhood and adolescence. Occasionally, someone would come to him to propose a revival concert, and he did continue to perform occasionally. At one point in the 1960s, an entrepreneur with underworld ties approached him to open a nightclub in Harlem. Although initially suspicious, Cesar agreed. A new wave of Cubans, including two of his brothers, was coming to New York to escape Castro's rule, and Cesar wanted to help them with employment opportunities and community contacts. Unfortunately, the club was losing money. Mambo had gone out of fashion, and the club's only patrons were old men and embittered exiles. The sleazy entrepreneur bought Cesar out and turned the club into a center for drug dealing.

As he passed through middle age, Cesar's health declined rapidly. Always somewhat overweight, he became obese. Excessive drinking led to ulcers and liver failure. His voice was ruined, and he no longer performed. Two years before checking into the Hotel Splendour, he ended up in the hospital with liver disease and internal bleeding. For a few months he followed his special diet but again lapsed into his old habits. Looking at the world outside his building, he could not believe how it had been transformed. Not only had musical tastes changed, leaving him behind, the city itself had become menacing and violent. He took refuge in his apartment, with its shelves of Mambo Kings artifacts and 78-rpm records from the 1940s and 1950s. Occasionally, he would stumble drunkenly into a shelf, destroying some of the fragile 78s, and then he would have to scour the used record stores to replace them. He remained attractive to women, but even then, he knew his interest and potency had faded.

Cesar has chosen to die in the Hotel Splendour because of his many nights there with Vanna Vane, symbol of his long-gone success. He checks into the hotel after saying farewell to all his friends one by one. The most difficult is Eugenio, now a moody young man working in a bookstore in Greenwich Village; he does not even tell Eugenio he is planning to die. And he does die, the morning after his night of drinking and remembering, while listening to his brother's famous song, a copy of the lyrics that he had written out himself lying next to him.

The greatest strength of *The Mambo Kings Play Songs of Love* lies in its characters and the relationships among them. Cesar and Nestor are presented as full human beings, fundamentally different in temperament but so close that when Nestor is killed, Cesar takes on aspects of his personality. When Cesar himself is dying, he writes out his brother's song; at that point, his identification with the lonely, melancholy Nestor is complete. Rounding out the story are other characters who care about Cesar and try to keep him alive, not because he was once famous but because they love him.

Oscar Hijuelos shows in vivid detail his knowledge of and affection for the Cuban-American community in New York and the music scene there. Musicians are portrayed from the inside, as people trying to earn a living and to express themselves through an art form that for a time binds the community together. When mambo goes out of style, when Cesar and his friends are old men unable to come to terms with the changes going on all around them, the reader feels their isolation and pain. Hijuelos's ear is unerring—his language is of the mambo, and his mood is nostalgic for a bygone era. This is a profoundly moving work, a tribute to a cultural past and to the people who created it.

Lyn Miller-Lachmann

METAPHOR & MEMORY: ESSAYS

Author: Cynthia Ozick (1928–   )
Publisher: Alfred A. Knopf (New York). 283 pp. $19.95
Type of work: Essays

Thirty essays, including several book reviews, that discuss aspects of language and literature

The first essay in *Metaphor & Memory* begins with a review of Ozick's first impressions of *Enemies of Promise*. Her lack of early success caused her to interpret Cyril Connolly's book as a discussion of failure. In rereading the book years later for review, she discovered it to be about "groans of success" and very poorly crafted as well.

Ozick uses the word "humanities" to refer to a single force, the force of "culture." In "Crocodiled Moats in the Kingdom of Letters," she bemoans the splintering of the humanities into schools, camps, genres, factions. Literature "is really about something," namely people. If it does not hold together, how will an individual gain self-knowledge? "A Short Note on 'Chekhovian' " defines the essence of fine craft: "meticulous humanity . . . solidity and precision." Of Chekhov, Ozick observes "he teaches us us."

In "The Function of the Small Press" Ozick observes that the formerly independent, spirited, and idealistic small publisher seems to have lost its "unifying agenda." Nevertheless, it still manages to "keep the new talents warm."

"The Question of Our Speech" addresses the roots of one of the largest issues of today. Ozick believes that the loss of the habit of reading, and reading true literature in the schools, is responsible for poor speech and communication skills.

The artist, from Leonardo da Vinci to all others, may be a "Bad Character." A painting is a fiction like a novel. But sometimes the fiction is the master of the artist. Perhaps the model for the Mona Lisa was not a woman, but she "comes to life . . . with our connivance."

In the essay "Of Basilisks and Barometzes," Ozick plays with the reader's connivance. She writes of books that were never written because such books are "reliably superior to words actually on a page."

"A Translator's Monologue" is similar in that Ozick presents some rules that are important and useful in translating poetry, but above all considers these rules to be false. To translate a poem, the translator must believe that the translated version of the poem already exists, he must simply find it. The translator must become the poet. And the translation of the poem is not a separate thing, but the same thing. These are false propositions, but necessary.

"Emerging Dreiser" is a review of a biography of Theodore Dreiser. Biography may have two reasons for being. One is to chronicle, the other is to illuminate a character. In order to illuminate through a biography, the biographer must "become" his subject. Is this a false proposition?

In "The Apprentice's Pillar," Ozick asks again, what is truth and what is fiction? Did the "art" of biography cause the death of the novel, or the other way around? Even though novels do not tell stories any more, one enjoys biography for "the trustworthy satisfactions of a still-coherent form, the ancient name of which is Story."

"The Muse, Postmodern and Homeless" describes the "no-man's land . . . where anything goes" caused by the loss of a "center." Modernism saw, or said, that values no longer held outside of the self. "Story" began to be lost. Postmodernism has lost even the self-center that characterized modernism.

Italo Calvino's tales of *Under the Jaguar Sun* are partly a return from the modernist antistory literature to the "idea of myth." But, "by driving story right down to its biological root . . . he nearly annihilates metaphor."

In contrast, J. M. Coetzee's novel *Life & Times of Michael K* is presented in "The Sister Melons of J. M. Coetzee" as a beautifully crafted metaphor. Its only flaw is the too explicit repetition of the "message" at the end.

"George Steiner's Either/Or" is a reply to an essay that tries to understand how the artist works. Steiner's thesis is that American art is not "indigenously American." The democratic society does not honor high culture, and without honor art does not flourish. But Ozick points out a contradiction in his essay since he also insists that isolation is necessary for art to thrive. The question of why writers do or do not write is left for discussion in other essays.

In "On Permission to Write," Ozick builds a case for the artist's need for isolation by describing the isolation and prolific productions of a young man who has sometimes written to her. Yet, isolation is not enough, because "he wants to be paid attention to." Some writers are sufficient unto themselves, only needing from others that they be read. Other writers try to be a part of society, to be good citizens. Is this a conflict for art?

In "A Word on Life and Art," Ozick seems to answer the question. "Life is that which . . . interrupts."

"Henry James's Unborn Child" is an unfinished story about a couple who ask an artist to paint a portrait for them of the child they have not been able to have. Ozick studies the relation between this theme and Henry James's childlessness and the unresolved ambiguity of his sexuality. Did he fail to complete this story because he could not give himself "permission to write" on a theme too close to himself?

In "What Drives Saul Bellow," Ozick finds that the telling of the tales is so full of "Bellowness" that they must be known as his. She also dismisses the identification of fictional characters with living models by noting that "the life on the page resists the dust of flesh."

In another review, Ozick concludes, "Any reporter can make literature into subject matter. Ah, but to make subject matter into literature!" "O Spilling Rapture! O Happy Stoup!" is full of references to magical tales, but how is the magic achieved?

Ozick describes herself as "pinched perfectionist." She builds a metaphor with "The Seam of the Snail" to contrast herself to her mother's lavishness. She wonders how her writing can, in its narrowness, represent her mother.

Two short essays, "North" and "The Shock of Teapots," hint at the source of Story, the magic and the lavishness. A visit to the North brings an unexpected and overwhelming feeling of recognition for and belonging to a place where the author had never been. Other travels present similar feelings, as when a familiar object, such as a teapot, is encountered in a new place. Traveling allows one to see and discover "the marvelous globe of the human eye."

"Primo Levi's Suicide Note" is about the possible meaning that may be found in the final work of an Italian Jewish chemist who was liberated from Auschwitz in 1945. She also compares Primo Levi with other "survivors" to try to understand why "the victim who has escaped being murdered will sometimes contrive to finish the job." The answer may be that "death is under the governance of hell, and it is in the nature of hell to go on and on."

"Sholem Aleichem's Revolution" is about the man who invented respectability for Yiddish storytelling. Because of the Jewish respect for learning and the language of learning, Hebrew, Yiddish was generally disparaged, but Sholem Aleichem discovered a long and worthy tradition behind this vernacular.

"S. Y. Agnon and the First Religion" is a review of Agnon's *Edo and Enam*. The story is about an ancient religion that is translated and transported into Hebrew and Jerusalem. Ozick surrounds this review with reminders of the need for and the pitfalls of translation in a more prosaic world.

When Europe allowed Jews to become citizens, it also expected them to "de-Judaize themselves." By joining with the majority culture, Jewish culture has "narrowed and darkened." "Bialik's Hint" explores this problem for Jewish writers, and concludes that a fusion of Jewish culture with the majority culture must be inevitable.

"Ruth" is a review of that book of the Bible. The Book of Ruth is short, but "to talk of it takes much longer." In Ruth, "the extraordinary is found here, and here, and here."

Imagination and inspiration are the deeper side of "Metaphor & Memory," the final essay of the book. Inspiration, Ozick feels, is "ad hoc and has no history" while metaphor "transforms the strange into the familiar" and "interprets . . . memory." Through metaphor, one can imagine what one has not known.

Metaphor & Memory begins with a warning that these essays cannot be taken as tenets for interpreting the author's intents. Each essay is separate and has something different to say, yet they seem to speak often of the same questions and themes. Language and its many aspects form the basis of the unifying agenda.

Cynthia Ozick admits that "nothing matters to me so much as a comely and muscular sentence," and these essays are full of such sentences. But more than just the sentences are well-crafted; Ozick deals in imagery and form at all levels in her writing, and much of it needs more than one reading to be fully appreciated.

Janelle Stevenson

MODERN IRELAND: 1600–1972

Author: R. F. Foster (1949–)
Publisher: Penguin Books (New York). 688 pp. $35.00
Type of work: History
Time: 1600–1972
Locale: Ireland

A social, political, and economic history of Ireland from the end of the Elizabethan wars in 1600 to "Bloody Sunday," 1972

> *Principal personages:*
> HUGH O'NEILL, the leader of the last great Gaelic counterattack against the Tudor reconquest in 1600
> THOMAS WENTWORTH, Lord Deputy of Ireland, who encouraged Irish loyalty to Charles I and was eventually beheaded in 1641
> OLIVER CROMWELL, the civil and military governor of Ireland, who left an indelible imprint on Irish history through a series of bloody raids and massacres
> THEOBALD WOLFE TONE, a frustrated imperialist and the acknowledged founder of Irish nationalism in the late 1700s
> ROBERT EMMET, the leader of the United Irishmen, a revolutionary, and an orator, who led the Dublin uprising in 1802 and was hanged in 1803
> DANIEL O'CONNELL, the greatest leader of Catholic Ireland, who caused the crisis that led to Catholic emancipation
> CHARLES STEWART PARNELL, a campaigner for land tenure and political reform, who became a national hero and founder of the political system "Parnellism"
> EAMON DE VALERA, the president of Sinn Féin and the first Dáil Éireann, who supported and fought for a thirty-two-county Gaelic republic

R. F. Foster's masterful one-volume history *Modern Ireland: 1600–1972* begins with Hugh O'Neill's heroic, although unsuccessful, resistance to the Tudor reconquest in 1600. True, Ireland had technically been a lordship of the English Crown since the 12th-century conquest and, in 1541, Henry VIII went so far as to declare himself "King of Ireland." Nevertheless, the beginning of the 17th century saw a new commitment on the part of England to impose effective and total rule. As would continue to be the case for the next four centuries, England's attempt to superimpose itself upon an "ancient identity, alien and bizarre," would be characterized by strife, confusion, and violence. The main reason for this was that Ireland in 1600, as later, was characterized by fragmentation: "varieties of people, defining their 'Irishness' differently, many of whom denied the legitimacy of the official state apparatus and lived indifferently outside its writ."

In 1600, Ireland was an overwhelmingly agricultural society, its people subsisting primarily on milk and meat. To Englanders they were a dirty, lazy, dishonest people whose laws were unethical and inequitable. Nevertheless, to many, the foreign nature of Irish society was appealing, as was the climate and landscape, and the early part of the 17th century saw an increased Anglicization; by the 1620s the Old English, or "English of Irish birth," were firmly entrenched. Catholic and clannish, they nonetheless represented an ideological schism, torn between Gaelic tradition and New English values. The New English—Protestant and possessed with a superior attitude—settled their plantations in and around Ulster. Whether this pattern of English settlement was to be seen as a policy of Anglicization or colonization mattered little; the aim was to establish a Protestant stronghold, loyal to the Crown, in Ireland. The subjugation and ill treatment of the Irish tenant farmers by English landlords resulted in the Ulster rebellion of 1641. A coalition of Old English, Irish gentry, and the dispossessed resulted in the rise of Confederate Ireland, a resistance that was at least formally defused with a peace treaty seven years later.

The subsequent rise of Oliver Cromwell held drastic implications for Ireland; commissioned in 1649 "to enforce the control of Parliament and ensure the progress of the new Protestant land settlement," he—in just nine months—cut a bloody swath through the country, justifying his actions as "a godly retribution upon the 'barbarous wretches' who had contrived the rebellion of 1641."

The last half of the century, a period known as Restoration Ireland, saw a rapid development of the arts and literature as well as clashes over religion and the increased use of English as the principal language. An increased standard of living, accompanied by a rise in population, led to the beginnings of the Ascendancy class. This class, or elite, was composed of Anglicized Irish, mostly Protestant, and they represented what many historians have since regarded as a golden age. Landed, professional, and educated, the Ascendancy class dominated law, politics, and "society." A civic culture, this Irish aristocracy constructed the great buildings of Dublin and the modern urban layout in general.

In the 18th century, Ireland became more urbanized and more polarized religiously. Ulster benefited from the industrial revolution in Britain and, accordingly, prospered. Correspondingly, the establishment of the potato as a staple crop contributed to the fortunes of rural society.

The reverberations set off by the American Revolution heightened the call in Ireland for parliamentary independence, giving rise to such movements as Volunteerism and Patriotism. "Patriots" were mostly transplanted Englishmen, and their interests were on behalf of colonial nationalists, which excluded three-quarters of the Irish population. Groups such as the United Irishmen and revolutionaries such as Theobald Wolfe Tone began, by the 1780s, to radicalize and promote Catholic demands. By 1793 parliamentary franchise, as well as certain civil and military rights, had been won. Nevertheless, continued violence led to the imposition of martial law in 1795 and, soon thereafter, some of the most concentrated episodes of violence in Irish history. By the beginning of the 19th century, leaders on both sides of the conflict were calling for a constitutional union between Ireland and England. In 1801, after strenuous debate, the Act of Union took effect.

By 1828, the great Catholic leader Daniel O'Connell was calling for a repeal of the Union. Agrarian violence escalated in the 1830s, with the correspondent rise of various secret societies. By the 1840s the foundation of Irish nationalism was almost exclusively Catholic, whereas Unionist adherents were primarily Protestant.

The Great Potato Famine of 1845–49 changed the essential nature of Irish society forever. The rapid succession of blights hit the farmers, the small farmers particularly, hardest; industrialized Ulster was affected least. Population patterns were altered virtually overnight. In the early 1840s the population stood at 8,200,000; by 1851 there were 2,225,000 fewer people. Disease, starvation, and emigration were the key factors. Altogether, it is estimated that the famine accounted for at least 775,000 deaths, and possibly as many as 1,500,000.

From the famine rose the beginnings of true modernization. Language, education, and industry saw great advances, although postfamine years saw a continuation of political violence. The postfamine years were also marked by an increase in emigration, the United States and Britain being the primary destinations. Indeed, the years after the famine saw the establishment of themes—land, politics, and nationalism—that would dominate Irish life and politics until the 20th century.

Irish history during the 1880s and 1890s revolved around the mercurial figure of Charles Stewart Parnell. An advocate of land tenure reform, he mobilized Irish society through the careful cultivation of nationalists and agrarians. As a mass movement for tenant defense, Parnellism—as the man's position quickly came to be called—fed off agrarian outrage and encouraged a polarization of attitudes. His calls, and those of others, for home rule were complicated by the existence of Ulster and its loyalty to Britain. By the 20th century, Irish politics had become dangerously radicalized, the new nationalism that was Parnell's legacy creating the conditions that resulted in the Easter Rising of 1916.

The insurrection of 1916, brief and bloody as it was, led to the election of Eamon de Valera and the eventual emergence of Ireland as an independent republic. The Anglo-Irish war, instigated by the extremist elements of the Volunteer movement, raged until 1921, resulting in the creation in the south of the Irish Free State, a twenty-six-county dominion within the British Empire, while Ulster (Northern Ireland) remained part of the United Kingdom. The civil war of 1922–1923 further hardened divisive positions. The Free State of the 1920s and 1930s remained resolutely anti-British and anti-Ulster. The Free State became fully independent in 1937, and during World War II it remained neutral. Ulster's position was distinctly pro-British. The Free State (the Republic of Ireland) and Northern Ireland were further divided with the Republic of Ireland Act in 1949, which, with the severing of the republic's ties to the Commonwealth, dashed any hopes for an end to Partition. Modernization, the issue of church in government, and a drifting away of the Irish government from the British model characterized the Ireland of the 1950s and 1960s. In conclusion, 1972—a year in which Ireland was accepted into the EEC (European Economic Community), the Stormont parliament and government in Northern Ireland were suspended, and a provisional cease-fire ended the outbreak of violence in Derry—must be seen as the year "when many old moulds were broken with apparent decisiveness."

With *Modern Ireland: 1600–1972*, R. F. Foster does much to demystify and enlighten that turbulent, and often confusing, subject called Irish history. Interpretive and accessible, it considers an astonishing array of issues: plantation society, colonization, emigration, Ascendancy culture, nationalism, and Partition are all explored in detail, as is Ireland's complex and violent relationship with Britain. In utilizing a vast array of sources and inspirations, Foster does much to explode traditional myths and misconceptions, particularly those regarding the potato famine and emigration patterns. Likewise, the complex and sometimes contradictory Irish social patterns are examined, as well as their contributions to the violent nature of Ireland's heritage. The portrait that emerges is one of a continuously evolving nation, the conflicts and divisions of which remain to be resolved.

Bertie Sweet

THE MOST BEAUTIFUL HOUSE IN THE WORLD

Author: Witold Rybczynski (1943–)
Publisher: Viking Press (New York). 211 pp. $18.95
Type of work: History
Time: The recent past
Locale: Countryside south of Montreal

An architect argues that the design of a boat shed recapitulates the history of architecture, stressing the abiding value of appropriateness

Witold Rybczynski was a junior professor of architecture at Montreal's McGill University when he decided to take up sailing. He needed the relaxation, but he could not afford to buy a boat. So he bought building plans for a boat and read a book by Joshua Slocum, the first solo circumnavigator of the globe, who also made his own craft. But in order to build a boat, Rybczynski had to have a shed in which to build it. He could not buy one, so he would make it himself.

The story of *The Most Beautiful House in the World* follows Rybczynski as he buys land and builds his shed, then renovates it as a home. But the narrative is interrupted so often, at such length, that the interruptions themselves form the meat of the book. These interruptions show how a single process of design embodies the entire history of an art.

The first digression starts when Rybczynski contemplates building a boat shed. The task recalls a memory from his student days. In a famous introductory work, the textbook author proposed this distinction: "A bicycle shed is a building; Lincoln Cathedral is a piece of architecture." Rybczynski remembers scribbling "Why?" in the margin.

Years later, he has the answer. It is a matter of history. The Lincoln Cathedral is part of the history of architecture and sheds are not, so sheds are not considered architecture at all. Rybczynski remarks that history is necessarily a matter of what remains from the past. Since modern architects, looking to the past for models, have found only the massive structures that have survived—the imposing creations of princes and kings—the whole view of the art has been skewed toward such monumental works.

Rybczynski points out that of course the questions of design so elegantly solved in the great cathedral structures are also required by the simpler needs of common shelter. Naturally, he will treat his boat shed as architecture, a piece of considered design. The rest of *The Most Beautiful House in the World* shows how the author's shed embodies his whole understanding of his art.

The first thing to do is find a site for the structure. It must be within commuting distance of his university, so he draws a fifty-mile radius on a map, centering on Montreal. He and his wife find that land north, east, and west of the city is either too expensive or too remote. They drive south to look for land. They find an abandoned apple orchard, beautifully sited on high flat ground sheltered by hills.

Rybczynski later learns that the location satisfies the strictures of *feng-shui*, the Chinese art of geomancy. In another interruption of his story, Rybczynski explains this traditional art by which the ancient Chinese situated buildings and even entire communities. The art is still followed in Hong Kong, where a *feng-shui* practitioner is consulted on the design of even the enormous glass boxes of modern office buildings.

The clashes in Hong Kong between *feng-shui* masters and the celebrated Western architects hired to design office buildings introduce a theme of the book, a critique of Modernism. The Western architects are among the most elegantly trained exponents of the International School, heirs of the Modernist tradition. The way traditional geomancers correct their design is the first instance in a stream of examples the author offers, of severe Modernist building plans later modified by context, by the place the building is put, by the buildings that surround it, by the needs and expectations of its users. Throughout the book, Rybczynski raises example after example to show that Modernism itself relied on the specific needs and social contexts of different patrons and sites. The strength of Rybczynski's criticism of Modernism is that it is hardly an attack at all. According to Rybczynski, an architect need not rebel against the past, as did the Modern movement. One need not even rebel against the recent past of the Modernist masters. One must simply consider the needs and context, physical and cultural, of the proposed building.

Now that he has chosen the site, Rybczynski tells how he designed his shed. First he must explain, however, what an architect is, and how he or she works. This leads to a digression into the history of toys, especially building blocks. Architecture, he then explains, is mostly a matter of playing with toy houses. Few architects can actually build a house, but every one can make ingenious models to play with on his desk. They also draw houses in playful ways, from different perspectives, or "cutting" the three-dimensional structure along different planes: cross section, facade, and bird's-eye. These "sections" turn the house design into a board game for the architect to manipulate for hours on his desk.

At this point in *The Most Beautiful House in the World*, the author abandons himself to the spirit of play. The story of his building project no longer alternates in an orderly way with ruminations on history. The remaining chapters mix digression unceasingly into the narrative. Rybczynski explains every movement of his thought during the process of making what came to be his home. He compares the play of design to the useful whimsy of fine cooking, and the structure of a house to the digestive system. He discusses the way that Frank Lloyd Wright's buildings fit into their landscapes, and shows that Ludwig Mies van der Rohe's glass boxes fit into their own contexts. He provides a history of books about architecture, starting with Vitruvius, Alberti, and Palladio. He discusses all the rituals that surround beginnings, from handshakes to weddings to the founding of Montreal. He talks about all the local examples of Canadian sheds that he considered for his design, and their ancestors in the American colonies and in ancient England. He talks about all the famous architects, from Inigo Jones to Thomas Jefferson, who designed barns. He tells about his childhood stamp collection. He warns against the perils of architectural drawings, how they seem exact but are in fact tricky illusions. At the Académie des Beaux Arts the students make museum-quality drawings of buildings that are never made, while such great architects as Alberti and Le Corbusier often worked from crude sketches. He praises his good friend the architect Vikram Bhatt, who nudged him to build and lent a hand. He walks the reader through the laborious process of building without power tools. When he decided to retrofit his shed as a home, he acquired his wife as a client, and so he talks about the difficulties of working for a customer. This leads to the question of how people adapt to a building that may have been designed without their needs in mind, such as the Pentagon and the Georges Pompidou Center. He discusses functions that buildings serve beside shelter, like the mnemonic system of the ancients, where buildings served as aids to memory, and the orientation of ancient Hindu and Roman communities to reflect the order of the universe. Rybczynski points out that while communities are no longer designed this way, ultimately most buildings are symbols reflecting the human body, with its axiality, frontal symmetry, head, and arms. Similarly, he points out that contemporary architects who pretend to follow the teachings of semiology, the study of signs, are in fact refusing to use the systems of sign that people actually use in daily life. He defuses the struggle between design for form and design for function by pointing out that people expect both to be at work. They treat a building as if it has a form that designates its functions, whether or not that function played a part in the design process: if a door looks as if it is on the front of the building, people will try to enter that way.

Rybczynski's wild miscellany of observations on his craft follow one another smoothly in the course of his narrative. The final chapter, titled the same as the book, brings a tighter focus. He discusses the houses that three writers—Mark Twain, Sir Walter Scott, and Robert Louis Stevenson—built for themselves, and how each reflected the style and career of each author. Rybczynski moves on to George Bernard Shaw's writing shed, and the watercolors of Carl and Karin Larsson, professional artists whose most popular work depicts the interior of their jerry-built cottage. Finally, he shows how a Mexican clerk, over the period of years, uses scavenged materials to build his family a lovely home on some waste land. Rybczynski concludes, "The most beautiful house in the world is the one that you build for yourself."

Witold Rybczynski is one of the world's authorities on appropriate technology for housing in the Third World. He has spent decades building test walls out of rammed earth, old bottles, and ground-up industrial ash, in a search for affordable materials that will really meet the needs of the world's homeless. Two of his previous books, *Taming the Tiger* and *Paper Heroes*, take to task those in the appropriate technology movement who have exported their own longing for simplicity to the Third World, where it is often not appropriate at all. *The Most Beautiful House in the World* does not mention this part of Rybczynski's career, but it carries forward his central concern for appropriateness and uses it to create a coherent system from all the jumble of his interests in the history of architecture. *The Most Beautiful House in the World* is a moving and original introduction to the art that most shapes daily life.

Dan Duffy

MOTHER COUNTRY

Author: Marilynne Robinson (1944–   )
Publisher: Farrar, Straus and Giroux (New York). 261 pp. $18.95
Type of work: Social criticism
Time: The 20th century
Locale: England

Largely overlooked in the East-West nuclear arms race, Britain is a major environmental polluter due to wastes from its Sellafield nuclear plant, government-run for profit despite hazards to public health and working-class welfare

Mother Country is an unusual book, consisting of elements of the polemical tract, the in-depth monograph, history, journalistic reportage, and political analysis, yet fitting neatly into none of these categories. In essence it is an extended essay on a single industrial plant, the Sellafield nuclear reprocessing plant in Great Britain, and the effect of its operations on the environment and public health. But in describing Sellafield, the author deals extensively with British social history in an unusual way. Hers is an angry book—angry because so much heedless damage has been inflicted upon the environment, and consequently upon the lives of the British working classes, in the name of profit, and because the rest of the world by its silence has given tacit consent to such action. Like Rachel Carson's *Silent Spring*, which unmasked in an earlier period the chemical mistreatment of the American environment in the name of agricultural profit, this book lays bare the "conspiracy of silence" that has preserved Britain's image, particularly for Americans, as a society with similar values and a parallel commitment to environmental protection, thus allowing the British government to carry out policies that are the reverse of that commitment.

The book's organization, like its theme, is unusual, consisting of an introduction and two parts, separately labeled. Other than these breaks, the writing is seamless in character, as the author develops her theme. The introduction, while somewhat more polemical than the rest, presents a view of British governmental policy and environmental practice that is quite different from the one usually held by outsiders and especially dear to Americans, the heirs in many respects to British civilization. As Robinson points out, there is a great irony in the locating of the Sellafield plant in Cumbria on the Irish Sea, this being an area associated with the natural world of Beatrix Potter and William Wordsworth that for most people is synonymous with British literature. Yet the plant routinely fouls this natural world by dumping nuclear wastes into nearby rivers and the Irish Sea, daily releasing significant quantities of plutonium and other toxins into the environment.

When Cumbrian sheep were tested and found to be radioactive, the cause was said to be the nuclear accident at Chernobyl in the Soviet Union, yet Sellafield "is so productive of contamination that there is no reason to look elsewhere." The fact that food sources—in an area where food production forms the basis for the economy—have never been tested systematically is characteristic of British welfare-state policy, which always favors industrial profit over public health.

That an institution such as Sellafield is allowed not only to continue its operations but also to turn a handsome profit from the reprocessing of the nuclear wastes of other countries and making plutonium available to buyers regardless of political affiliation raises the question of whether Britain is indeed the home of a virtuous and public-spirited society. Yet most Americans persist in this view. To them, to go to the "Mother Country" is to go "where profit is no god, to a nonviolent society, a community of goodwill and mutual obligation." The result of this myopic vision, as the author notes, is not only continued contamination of Britain's social and natural environment but the very real possibility of further global deterioration, at a time when the Earth can ill afford such a condition.

In part one, the author shifts focus from the singular to the collective, from one nuclear plant to the body of British social history and institutions that have made such a plant possible. The emphasis on profit and the exploitation of the "working classes" to attain that profit have a long history. Exploitation as a *raison d'être* of British economic life dates back to the Poor Laws of Edward III of 1349. These laws were built on the principle that the minority (the ruling class) has a right to the labor of the working majority, "with no obligation to acknowledge its value." The Poor Laws, refined over the centuries, have excluded basic personal and legal rights from workers on a permanent basis, an exclusion confirmed in 19th-century English capitalism-industrialism and more recently in the welfare state set up by William Beveridge in the 1940s. But many centuries ago, when the commons (unowned public land) was enclosed, the English agricultural laborer lost the right to his own labor, gained by grazing his animals or growing his food there. Since then the working class became—as it still is—an object of charity, forever circumscribed and lacking access to national wealth or well-being. The differences between British and American labor in this area of economic life is clear.

The author spares few writers and social thinkers in her attack on the injustices of the British social system. She takes dead aim at such respected figures as Daniel Defoe, Henry Fielding, Jeremy Bentham,

John Stuart Mill, Herbert Spencer, and Thomas Carlyle, among others. In her view, they have failed because, by criticizing members of the system rather than the system itself, they have contributed to its perpetuation. Thus Carlyle, who is traditionally considered the major advocate of change in the social structure to benefit the "working poor," emerges as defender of the system, insisting that laissez-faire would ruin them by replacing natural limits by an undisciplined freedom. What is needed, according to Carlyle, is more effective leadership by those who are "naturally superior."

Robinson has a devastating critique of those "naturally superior" ones, the upper-class English gentry. The game they like to play at country-house gatherings, she writes, is Philanthropy: "The rules of this game are very simple. One must justify things as they are by attacking things as they are." One after another, they decry the sufferings of the poor, with wit and moralizing, not as a virtuous concern but as an evil to be avoided. The very term "working class" has a special meaning in Britain. From the Poor Laws through Darwinism, Fabian socialism, and now the welfare state, the working class has subsidized the profits of the British industrial system without ever having a breath of fresh air or a taste of clean water.

In part two, the author returns to her "singular" subject, Sellafield, and its role in Britain's nuclear policy. Her first statement is a masterpiece, setting the problem in terms no one can fail to understand: "[While] I know very little about plutonium, . . . I know better than to pour it into the environment." There is a double irony in this policy, in that the British Official Secrets Act limits dissemination of damaging information, yet government publications, when read with care, document the appalling effect of nuclear waste not only on the natural environment but also on human beings. The author also assures her readers that the great bulk of her sources consists of newspaper articles. Yet despite this wide publicizing of environmental damage from Sellafield and a vote in the European Parliament in 1986 to close it down, the plant grows and grows, with ever more facilities being built "at great expense (to the Germans and Japanese), to make it capable of extracting uranium and plutonium from new kinds of nuclear wastes."

In her conclusions, Robinson returns to the "why" theme—why Britain, so often seen to be the most civilized of societies, has for thirty years or more pursued a nuclear policy destructive to her own people and their environment, and potentially to the entire world. One reason lies in the British national interest, the drive to remain a world power. Commercial profit is another; this small island nation, through resolving the costly problem of creating nuclear energy for other nations in its role as "universal dustman," assures a handsome return on a modest investment. A third reason lies in America's inability to measure the "Mother Country" by standards of morality and ethical behavior applied elsewhere in the world. The author's hope, and it is a slim one, is that "there is a real world, that is really dying, and we had better . . . make ourselves rational and morally autonomous adults, [able] to recognize the grosser forms of evil . . . and confront them."

The strengths of *Mother Country* by Marilynne Robinson lie in the writing, in the impassioned language with which the author addresses an unpopular topic. Her points are mostly well made and couched in rational, sober explanations. A map, statistics tables, and a few graphically chosen photographs would have strengthened the book, as would an index.

There is perhaps unduly harsh treatment of environmental groups such as Greenpeace, which should not be blamed for perhaps overlooking Irish Sea contamination in its efforts to call attention to the diversity of worldwide problems. But these are mere cavils compared with the overpowering urgency of the topic. Robinson is to be commended for her boldness, and one hopes for the widest possible circulation of her book.

William Spencer

MY SECRET HISTORY

Author: Paul Theroux (1941–)
Publisher: G. P. Putnam's Sons (New York). 511 pp. $21.95
Type of work: Novel
Time: 1956–1984
Locale: Boston; London; Nyasaland; Uganda

Andrew Parent, writer and traveler, chronicles his life from age fifteen to his mid-forties and explains his secret reality

> Principal characters:
> ANDREW (ANDRE) PARENT, the narrator, a writer and traveler
> JENNY, his wife
> JACK, his son
> FATHER FURTY, a priest who befriends Andy
> TINA SPECTOR, Andy's first girlfriend
> LEILA MAMALUJIAN, a wealthy friend of Andrew's
> LUCY, one of his girlfriends
> EDEN, his American mistress
> MR. MAHADEVA, an Indian friend

Andrew Parent saved his own life during the summer when he was fifteen, or so he believes. Better than having money, which he has not, Andrew has already discovered the secret of his own happiness: secrecy. Events of this summer embolden his hidden nature to assert itself. The visible Andrew is a dutiful son and busy altar boy at St. Raphael's in Boston, where he assimilates the pastor's constant teaching of man's sinfulness. It is the familiar message of his parents, whose dearest wish is that God might call him to be a priest. Awareness of his own sins and curiosity make Dante's *Inferno* logical reading material. Andrew's secret self is preoccupied with lustful thoughts of Tina Spector, whom he takes to the sandpits to watch his target shooting. Chicky De Palma, a much bolder altar boy, fuels Andrew's secret self with tales of his own sexual exploits, offered as they prepare for mass. Tina's allure is greatly enhanced when Andy learns that she is half Jewish and therefore already damned. When Father Furty arrives at St. Ray's, he befriends Andy. His genuine acceptance of Andy leads Andy to see happy possibilities in himself and the priesthood. When Father Furty becomes ill and dies, Andy experiences his first sense of loss. Father Furty's funeral is the third funeral at which he serves, so he is entitled to serve at a wedding. Instead, Andy runs off to lose his virginity with Tina Spector, in defiance of church, parents, and his own public persona.

At nineteen, Andrew becomes Andre, an angry young man, secretly wallowing in vitriolic ill will toward the wealthy. Reading Baudelaire suits his mood. A lifeguard job at the Maldwyn Country Club lasts only two weeks because Andy breaks the rules against reading and talking to club members, while poorly concealing his resentment of their leisure. Before he leaves, a lonely, attractive, middle-aged woman, Leila Mamalujian, lends Andy *The Henry Miller Reader* and invites him to lunch. For the rest of the summer, Andy is one of three lifeguards at a pool where the pay is better, the hours are shorter, and discreet reading is allowed. Here he meets Lucy, a quiet blonde girl who works at a bookstore and goes to Boston University. From the beginning, their friendship is primarily sexual. Mrs. Mamalujian makes several expensive and futile efforts to seduce Andre. Throughout the summer they see each other. She buys him gifts and meals while he enjoys her company and, more important, the secrecy. His pleasure with both women is heightened by their unawareness of each other. Besides earning money, Andre's goal this summer is to dine on whale steak. Twice he does, and both times his enjoyment is spoiled. At one dinner, Mrs. Mamalujian elects to tell him that she is leaving her husband, and at the other, Lucy cannot conceal her vegetarian's revulsion at the meal. The summer ends after a frantic attempt to find an abortionist for Lucy with money borrowed from Mrs. Mamalujian.

Other people's expectations daunt Andre. He wants to go "anywhere out of this world," and he does. By age twenty-three he is a Peace Corps volunteer in Nyasaland, where he is headmaster at a school run, until recently, by the British. Andre is replacing Mr. Likoni, who left to join the new government as Nyasaland becomes Malawi. Andre is a popular headmaster at Chamba Secondary, performing his duties and handling discipline with some leniency. Purposefully, he avoids assigning homework due Fridays so that teachers have no weekend papers to grade. His own weekends are spent at the Beautiful Bamboo Bar, selecting girls to make love to, usually three per weekend. To Andre the situation is ideal; he enjoys unlimited, guilt-free sex without compunction. The only other American is another Peace Corps volunteer, Ward Rockwell, an odd young man who is genuinely eager to build the best latrine ever. Andre's idyll ends when the new government takes over and the school's atmosphere becomes political. Worse yet, the Bamboo girls start charging for their love. By now Andre is ready to move on and start writing about his experiences as a way to free himself from them.

Andy's next home is Kampala, Uganda, where he teaches adult education. His travels to Ghana, Nigeria, and England supply material for articles, while his adventures with women satisfy his desire for concealment. His most frequent girlfriend is Rashida, an African girl. Meeting Jennifer is a turning point in Andy's life. She is English, independent by nature, and eager to begin teaching. Andy falls in love with her and, lonely when she leaves, pursues her to Nairobi. When she becomes pregnant, they marry. Andy is delighted with his new life and stunned by Jenny's discontent without a job. After a mob of Africans overwhelms them in their car, Andy decides that it is time to leave Africa.

Andre and Jenny make a home in London with their son, Jack. Jenny works, and with the security of a home, Andy feels comfortable traveling to India, Japan, and Vietnam for long periods gathering material for books. The tone of Jenny's voice coming to him on a phone in Siberia, alarms Andy and sends him home. Sensing that Jenny has been unfaithful, Andy plays detective while professing to write his book. He schemes and searches even after she admits to seeing someone. In the meantime, Jenny and Andy live together, by turns at peace or quarreling. Andy harasses Jenny until she tells him the man's name. In a ridiculous confrontation at a house party, Andy barges in, terrifies the guests, forces his rival to eat the note he wrote to Jenny, and shoots him with a water pistol. Jenny is infuriated. Andy is finding a sense of liberation, however, in transforming his travels into a book, and he slowly regains his equanimity. After the book is completed, Andy and Jenny reconcile and plan a trip to the United States.

Some years pass. At age forty-three, Andy is a successful author with two of everything. He has a home in London with Jenny and Jack and a home in Cape Cod. He also has a girlfriend, Eden, who makes herself available when he is in the states. After three weeks in Cape Cod, he and Eden leave for India, where Andy intends to compare impressions with a visit some years earlier. At age thirty-four, Eden is a beautiful, energetic, sensual woman. As a traveler, Eden suffers the discomforts and inconveniences valiantly; her natural vitality restores her when the bad food or heat gets her down. She is a dutiful sightseer and a naive shopper. Her passion at unexpected times and places adds zest to Andy's trip. Crying in the shower and occasional rueful comments reveal Eden's discontent with their relationship, but Andy never suggests that it will change.

After their trip, Eden returns to the United States and Andy to London. Jenny is happy to see him, although she must readjust to his presence. Andy performs little chores around the house, as he had in Cape Cod. Later he bicycles to Jack's school to see his son. At fifteen, Jack is self-conscious and reserved in his affection. He is happy to see Andy but independent, as his upbringing has made him. Andy takes a second trip to India, this time with Jenny, a sharp contrast to Eden. She is far more independent and self-assured, caring more for practicality than style in her appearance, taking discomfort in stride, and choosing sights to see with decisiveness. Unlike Eden, Jenny believes that only insecure people need to surround themselves with acquisitions. Nearing the end of the trip, Andy takes Jenny to meet his friend Mahadeva, a poor man who had once made a suit for Andy and refused payment for it. He wants to show that the misery of poverty and premature aging has not dimmed the vital spirit of this man and his family. Having taken Eden there previously, Andy might have anticipated what followed. Mahadeva's daughter mentions that "other auntie" who did not eat so much as Jenny. Andy's secret is out, but not so much a secret as he believed, for Jenny claims to have known for years. Andy cannot assess her feelings from her reflective mood and enigmatic comments. She speaks of life being an illusion and of the need for letting go. Before they leave India, Jenny tells him he will have to choose. Andy replies that he knows what to do.

My Secret History is a thoroughly engrossing, imaginative, humorous novel from first page to last. Theroux fills his story with an enormous variety of characters, each one an individual bearing cultural idiosyncrasies. The result is fascinating cultural portraits of Malawi, Uganda, India, and England, each framed by specific time and circumstance. Theroux finely balances the life of his main character on a rich, and potentially overwhelming, foundation.

Andrew Parent is a complex, likable, irritating man. As he grows older and reflects on the double life he chooses to lead, he begins to understand that both lives are incomplete. His deepest secret self is the writer, bearing a literary self-license to be a parasite. His reality is the writer alone, observing, composing, manipulating others while sacrificing intimacy. At a time early in his marriage, Andrew reads a Chekhov story about a man with a double life. The feeling of sadness that Andrew experiences may be an acceptance of the necessity for such duplicity, or it may be regret that he is not unique. It never occurs to him that it is the human condition—not his, not the writer's—to have a secret self, nor does he allow others the indulgence of their desires that he takes for himself. He resembles a foreign country that one wants to visit but not live in. In the end, when he claims to be "pretty sure" he knows what to do, the reader feels less confident than he that a man of such complex imagination can move in one direction. That direction remains his secret.

E. P. Tischer

NICE WORK

Author: David Lodge (1935–   )
Publisher: Viking Press (New York). 277 pp. $18.95
Type of work: Novel
Time: 1986
Locale: Rummidge (Birmingham), England, and environs

A mordantly funny critique of British industrialism with its emphasis on utility and facts, and how, through emotion and imagination, two people learn to better their lives

> *Principal characters:*
> VICTOR "VIC" WILCOX, a conservative, aggressive industrial
>   manager
> ROBYN PENROSE, a left-leaning, feminist lecturer of English
>   literature
> MARJORIE WILCOX, Victor's wife
> CHARLES, Robyn's not-so-true lover and literary confidant
> BASIL PENROSE, Robyn's acquisitive brother

Victor Wilcox, managing director of J. Pringle & Sons, lives in his five-bedroom, four-bath neo-Georgian home about two miles from the center of Rummidge, a gray industrial city in the gray Midlands section of England. His home life is far from ideal. His three listless teenage children are not living up to his expectations, and his plump, Valium-popping wife, Marjorie, barely interests him at all anymore. He regards his marriage as a mistake he must live with and his family as a source of irritation. His life is one of routine and sameness typified by the six business suits he "wears in daily rotation." His only escape is his twenty-four minute drive to work, when he can feel totally in control and bask in the "effortless superiority" of his Jaguar V12. Here he can listen to his cassettes of Jennifer Rush, Carly Simon, and other female vocalists "moaning and whispering of women's love" as he drives through the area known as the Dark Country. This section of the Midlands received its name from "the pall of smoke . . . and the film of coal dust and soot that covered it, in the heyday of the Industrial Revolution." The area has since changed from a coal to a "metal bashing" industrial base. Many of its inhabitants, drawn to England in the boom years of the 1950s and 1960s from India, Pakistan, and the Caribbean, are now bearing the brunt of the country's high unemployment. Vic hardly notices this world or these people as he floats by. He is barely in his office when Stuart Baxter, his division's chairman at Midland Amalgamated, is on the phone telling him that Pringle's business is down again this month.

Somewhere near the middle of Vic's daily commute is the University of Rummidge, where Robyn Penrose holds a temporary post as lecturer in English literature. Beginning the second year of her three-year term, Robyn has little hope of staying on, since the university is suffering under the deep budget cuts of the Thatcher administration. To solidify her position or, at least, to make herself more attractive to a prospective employer, Robyn is writing a book about the 19th-century industrial novel in England. Her approach is leftist and feminist. One of the things she is trying to prove in the book is that the self is merely a feature of capitalism and does not really exist. Neither, she holds, does love exist. There is only language and biology.

She has had a relationship with a man named Charles since they were undergraduates together several years previously. As a student, Robyn took part in student politics, advocating progressive causes, while Charles led a more subdued, private life. He pursued a more conventional literary direction that landed him a permanent teaching position. Since his job is in Suffolk, they live separately, spending only weekends with each other. Their relationship has become more of mind than of body, yet they do keep coming back to one another.

Vic and Robyn are brought together by the Industry Year Shadow Scheme, wherein a university representative follows an industry manager in order to gain a more complete understanding of the work. There is an immediate suspicion between these two opposites. Vic is outraged at having to put up with this trendy leftist feminist and acts rudely toward her. Robyn is put off by his constant insistence of "Who pays?" She is appalled by the dirt, noise, and mindless repetitive work. She had not expected anything "so like the satanic mills of the early Industrial Revolution." Vic's disdain for the workers, his adherence to money as the basis of judgment, and his strong belief in English capitalism all become topics for debate. He explains that his goal is a fully computerized, twenty-four-hour-a-day, machine-manned, "lightless" factory that will relieve men of menial tasks. She sees, however, that this will make workmen redundant and challenges him to spend "more money preparing people for creative leisure." The workers do not like these jobs anyway; they are just conditioned to work. All jobs should be like hers: "nice work" because it is meaningful and rewarding. At a meeting that afternoon, Robyn learns that they are going to pressure a worker, Danny Ram, out of his job. She leaves the meeting to search out Danny and to warn him of the plot. Vic is at her house the next morning telling her that she must come to the foundry because her intervention has caused a walkout.

Basil, her brother, drops in on Robyn and Charles. He is eager to show off his BMW, his clothing, and his new girlfriend—all the rewards of being a merchant banker in London. His girlfriend, Debbie, is a well-dressed, well-paid foreign-exchange dealer but, Robyn observes, of a decidedly lower-class background. She does not notice, however, that Charles has been paying close attention to their guests.

As the Shadow Program progresses, Vic and Robyn gradually begin to gain respect for one another, although both refuse to admit it even to themselves. Indeed, Vic is becoming so enamored that he invites Robyn to Sunday dinner with his family. Marjorie senses that something may be up and barely speaks to Robyn.

Robyn receives a call from Basil informing her that his Debbie is now seeing her Charles. Consequently, when Victor asks Robyn to accompany him on a business trip to Frankfurt, she is glad for the diversion. Once there, Robyn's knowledge of German helps Vic bargain for a needed piece of machinery. They celebrate in their posh hotel's pool, sauna, and nightclub, ending up in bed together. Vic confesses that he has been in love with her for weeks and is now prepared to divorce Marjorie. Robyn denies that there is such a thing as love and sneaks off the next morning, returning home alone. Once he is home, Vic begins to act peculiarly as though he is inhabiting a dream world. He begins to read books Robyn has told him about and writes several letters to her that go unanswered.

Robyn spends Easter vacation with her parents, where she finishes her book. When she returns she finds a letter from Charles in which he tells her he is "going to become a merchant banker," and has taken up with Debbie. Vic's behavior has so worried Marjorie that she begins exercising and joins Weight Watchers. Vic invents a second phase to the Shadow Scheme so that he can sit in on Robyn's classes. Over the weeks, he tries to force his affection on her but gets nowhere. He does, however, begin to acquire a taste for literature, Tennyson in particular. In one of their conversations he challenges her: "If you don't believe in love, why do you take such care over your students [or] Danny Ram?"

Their affair ends when both receive important telephone calls. Stuart Baxter phones Vic to tell him that Pringle has been sold to its competitor and he is out of a job. Robyn's call is from critic Morris Zapp, who tells her that he has sold the American rights to her book. He also offers her a lectureship in the states, a position much more stable and promising than the one she presently holds.

Vic is happily surprised at how supportive Marjorie can be when he tells her about his job. He finds that he is over his infatuation and is now seeing things in his wife that he had not noticed for years. They decide to start a family business. The major part of their funding comes from Robyn, who has just received a huge inheritance from her eccentric uncle. Robyn's department chairman comes up with a plan he believes has a good chance of keeping her on at Rummidge University. He will try to redirect some funds. Although the future is not guaranteed, she decides to stay on.

In *Nice Work*, David Lodge updates the 19th-century condition-of-England novel. The main concern of the principal characters is work and the nature of their jobs. The novel is thought provoking, but it is also quite funny. Although he explores Vic's and Robyn's characters deeply, Lodge maintains enough distance to stand back and judge them. Although both Vic and Robyn turn out well in the end, both have enough flaws to appear less than heroic. Vic is oblivious to many personal things occurring around him, such as his children's behavior or his secretary's affair. Robyn is an expert on the industrial novel but had never been in a factory. The minor characters provide much of the humor. Vic's secretary, Shirley, likes to show off pin-up pictures of her daughter and hints that she might pose for the company calendar.

Much of the humor comes from the dialogue, which Lodge handles quite well. The descriptive prose also is full of understated comic asides. But the overall feeling of the novel comes from its realism. The reader is pulled into the narrative, never doubting the reality of the characters or the setting, and experiences the dirt and grime of Rummidge as well as the motivations of Vic and Robyn. Lodge also exhibits a firm knowledge of both the academic and industrial worlds. *Nice Work* is a tale of England in the 1980s that, apart from a few colloquialisms, is perfectly applicable to American society, and accessible to its readers.

John Sokolnicki

NIXON: THE TRIUMPH OF A POLITICIAN 1962–1972

Author: Stephen E. Ambrose (1936–)
Publisher: Simon and Schuster (New York). 736 pp. $24.95
Type of work: Biography
Time: 1962–1972
Locale: Washington, D.C.; New York City

The second volume of a biography of Richard Nixon, covering the years of his return to politics and his election as president in 1968 and 1972

> *Principal personages:*
> RICHARD MILHOUS NIXON, the 37th president of the United States
> PAT NIXON, his loyal wife
> JULIE NIXON EISENHOWER, their younger daughter
> TRICIA NIXON COX, their older daughter
> HENRY KISSINGER, the national security advisor, appointed by Nixon
> SPIRO AGNEW, Nixon's vice-president
> JOHN MITCHELL, the attorney general and later head of Nixon's reelection campaign

The American public and media were mistaken in November 1962 if they believed Richard Nixon's announcement that he was leaving politics. Despite losing the 1960 presidential election to John Kennedy and the 1962 California gubernatorial election to Pat Brown, Nixon had a number of unique political assets. He had experience in both the House and Senate, as well as eight years as U.S. vice-president; he was the logical spokesman for the Republican party; and he still had considerable support in business, finance, and politics. In the spring of 1963, appearing on Jack Paar's television program, Nixon announced his intention to speak out on current issues. The Nixon family moved to New York City, where Nixon joined the law firm of Mudge, Stern, Baldwin, and Todd. Nixon now had an income, an expense account, opportunity for travel, and an influential social circle. Nixon used a family vacation to Europe as an opportunity to meet with European leaders and hold press conferences. During the first year after his "last" press conference, Nixon held nearly fifty press conferences, gave interviews, and wrote magazine articles. He criticized President Kennedy for the decision to sell wheat to the Soviet Union, his lack of support for President Diem of South Vietnam and possible complicity in his assassination, and problems in NATO. Clearly, Nixon never left politics.

With the assassination of Kennedy, the turmoil of the civil rights movement, and increasing U.S. involvement in Vietnam, Nixon used

1964 to express his views on President Johnson's policies. Although not an active candidate for the GOP nomination, Nixon was not averse to breaking a deadlock between Nelson Rockefeller and Barry Goldwater, should one develop. However, the California primary gave Goldwater the nomination before the convention. After introducing Goldwater at the convention, Nixon campaigned for Republican candidates. Goldwater's defeat and heavy Republican losses created an opportunity for Nixon to rebuild his leadership position.

In 1965 and 1966, Nixon established a campaign position for 1968. Maurice Stans gathered financial backers, research staff, and writers. At every opportunity, Nixon demanded an escalation of the war in Vietnam, specifically urging bombing of military targets and mining the harbor at Haiphong, and denounced the antiwar movement on college campuses. A master of contradiction, he also championed academic freedom and urged Democrats not to criticize Johnson for the conduct of the war. Nixon campaigned for selected candidates, helping Republicans regain forty-seven House seats and three Senate seats. In 1967, Nixon traveled extensively to Europe, Russia, the Far East, Latin America, and Africa. In an effort to overcome his reputation for deviousness, he talked frequently to reporters. His broad factual knowledge and sensitivity to middle-class fears made his speeches quite successful. Nixon spoke out in favor of welfare reform, against school busing for desegregation, and against growing lawlessness. By the end of 1967, Nixon had far more support than his competitors, Governors George Romney and Ronald Reagan.

As in other campaigns, Nixon had one basic campaign speech, a general, middle-ground approach with room enough to attack left or right extremists. His call for new leadership was perfectly timed, for the Soviets were now conceded to be a nuclear equal and the Vietcong had launched an enormous offensive. The press found Nixon less accessible when he started using televised question-and-answer sessions with citizen panelists. Both Johnson and Nixon realized that escalation of the war had not worked; a negotiated settlement, rather than a military victory, became the goal. Johnson announced not only a deescalation but his decision not to run for reelection. Hinting at his own plan for peace, Nixon had large primary victories in New Hampshire and Oregon and won the nomination at the convention with a long-sought endorsement from Dwight Eisenhower. Despite considerable opposition, Spiro Agnew was Nixon's choice as running mate. As he prepared to face the Democrats, Nixon was in a far stronger position than in 1960 because he had in mind a new foreign policy based on détente and domestic issues requiring change rather than a record to defend. Unfortunately, his closest staff members were men whose names became household words a few years later—John Mitchell, H. R. Haldeman, and John Ehrlichman.

In the debacle that was the 1968 Democratic Convention, Hubert Humphrey was nominated, leaving "doves" with no presidential candidate. Nixon's strategy was to attract all the fearful and discontented, a large constituency in 1968. Nixon promised voters to stop inflation, support Israel, end the draft, and "end the war on an honorable basis." He said little about foreign policy, George Wallace, the Republican party, or Spiro Agnew.

The peace talks in Paris were apparently bogged down over who should take part in the negotiations, with the greatest stumbling block being South Vietnam's General Thieu. A possible bombing halt, with its suggestion of peace at hand, was enough of a threat that Nixon secretly discouraged Thieu's participation in the talks. In reality, no American politician was willing to admit that the war was already lost. In the election, Nixon won less than one percent more of the popular vote than Humphrey, and the Democrats still had a majority in House and Senate.

The primary quality Nixon sought in selecting staff and cabinet members was personal loyalty. His appointments divided power, created competition, and aggravated antagonisms. Nixon was the only unifying element in his administration. One of the first and most influential appointments was Henry Kissinger as national security advisor. Although different in most ways, "they were born conspirators." A daily "News Summary," of twenty to fifty pages, gave Nixon a detailed, if slanted, report on what was being said about his administration and world news. Nixon's reactions and instructions to staff, often written in response to this summary, reveal an obsession with his image; a concern for public perception overshadowed concern for accomplishments. Nixon's primary foreign policy goals were to end the Vietnam War in some acceptable manner, to link participation in the SALT talks with outstanding political problems, and to establish contact with China. On the domestic side, problems of inflation and student unrest would be mitigated by ending the war, cutting defense spending, and limiting the draft.

By 1972 the war was still not over. Ground troops were slowly withdrawn as Vietnamization was phased in. Bombings in Laos, Cambodia, and Hanoi and the mining of Haiphong harbor were intended to speed negotiations, yet on campuses there were strikes and demonstrations, including deaths at Kent State University. The Gulf of Tonkin Resolution was repealed as Congress tried to exert more influence over the war. Public and secret negotiations continued, with Kissinger in constant motion. "The phased, slow-motion retreat was the worst mistake of his Presidency."

In the spring of 1971, Nixon's secret diplomacy led to a Soviet agreement to limit antiballistic missiles, preparatory to further arms-control negotiations. Nixon visited China in February 1972, and some trade agreements were reached. Although George McGovern ran as the peace candidate in 1972, the public expressed confidence in the negotiations. These highly popular achievements, together with Nixon's measures to control inflation, led to his reelection with 60.7 percent of the popular vote.

The burglary of the Democratic National Committee offices in the Watergate complex took place in June 1972, but its connection to the White House went undiscovered until October. The well-organized group behind it, the previous burglary of a psychiatrist's office, the existence of bugging devices and tapes, and above all, the attitude of hostility toward perceived enemies remained to be disclosed in the future. Perhaps that is why Nixon used the word "melancholy" to describe his mood following his reelection.

As he did with the first volume of the Nixon biography, Ambrose has written a remarkably informative and fascinating book. The complexities of Nixon are matched by those of the ten years covered in this book. Ambrose does justice not only to Nixon and other public figures but also to the issues of the times and the feelings of the American people. He is not a dispassionate biographer, but his feelings enhance the telling of the story without distortion. To those who lived through these years, many of the names and roles are familiar, with the exception that Charles Colson's influence appears greater than expected. Ambrose significantly dims Henry Kissinger's starring role as statesman and portrays him as a self-serving politician. In the background, and ever supportive, are Pat, Julie, and Tricia.

Richard Nixon may forever elude understanding. How one man could have a wise and prescient view of the United States' relations with other nations and, at the same time, enormous distrust and contempt for the American public and those around him defies comprehension. Ambrose, without access to court-locked material and without reliance on books by Nixon's inner circle, lets Nixon's words document his actions and attitudes. If there is fault in Nixon himself, there is, likewise, little to commend in his manner of conducting the nation's business during these years.

E. P. Tischer

OLDEST LIVING CONFEDERATE WIDOW TELLS ALL

Author: Allan Gurganus
Publisher: Alfred A. Knopf (New York). 718 pp. $21.95
Type of work: Novel
Time: 1861–1984
Locale: The southeastern United States

Lucy Marsden, widow of the last surviving Civil War veteran, spins tales and memories spanning more than a century

Principal characters:
  Lucy Marsden, the long-suffering wife and widow of Will Marsden
  Captain Will Marsden, The U.S. Civil War's last surviving soldier
  Castalia, a former slave to the Marsdens and Lucy's best friend
  Ned Smythe, young Will's best childhood friend whose death haunts the Marsdens throughout their lives
  Lacy Marsden, the Captain's vain and wealthy mother whose estate and life are forever ruined by Sherman's march to the sea

Lucy Marsden's long and event-filled tale begins from the Lane's End nursing home where, at age ninety-nine, she is living out her last days, as full of spunk and opinions as ever. Having outlived all nine of her children, she is left with nothing save her memories, most of which revolve around the life of her husband, Captain Will Marsden.

Willie Marsden was only thirteen years old when he left home with his best friend, Ned Smythe, "holding hands like girls that age would," to fight for the Confederacy in 1862. The events of Will's three years in the war would dominate the remainder of his long life, the same tales he told and retold countless times eventually becoming as familiar, and painful, as Lucy's own memories. Dispensed in a rambling narrative, generously interspersed with her own thoughts and digressions, these tales gradually reveal the sad, haunted, and ultimately tragic life that was Willie Marsden's. Although on the losing side, the Captain took pride in the fact that he had outlived the winning side and everyone else as well.

In his first taste of action, young Willie confronts a Yankee soldier charging directly into his hiding place. "Hey," he yells, "This spot is mine. . . . go away, or else." But the Yankee soldier keeps coming and Will is forced to shoot him. Horrified, he drags the mortally wounded Yankee into his foxhole, sees that he is just a boy like himself. This boy, Simon Utt, begs Will with his dying breath to take and return his gold watch to his family back North. Will agrees and, for the rest of the war and many years after, guards the watch as his most treasured possession. Many years later, having corresponded with the bereaved Utt family, Will journeys at last to Simon's New England home. There, while being celebrated as a hero and samaritan, he reveals, and unburdens himself of, the truth.

In another story, Lucy repeats the tale of how, after being shot in the knee, young Will nearly loses his leg to a saw-happy doctor. He, and his leg, are saved by a kindly veteran tailor, Sal Smith, who will one day make his fortune inventing waterproof garments. It is with Sal that Will watches General Lee make his sad way to Appomattox Court House to surrender the Southern cause.

Still, of all the stories the Captain relates, the saddest and most profoundly transforming is the story of how his beloved friend Ned is shot down from a sycamore tree by enemy gunfire. The incident, and Will's helplessness, torment him the rest of his life. Nearly fifty years later, having kept Ned's tintype and bugle the whole time, having visited Ned's bereaved mother every Thursday since the war ended, and having named his first son after him, Captain Marsden, Lucy, and their nine children revisit the site of Ned's death. The Captain, as he is known throughout his adult life, climbs the fateful tree, so much taller now, and surveys the scene himself. Over the next two months his hair and beard turn white.

After Appomattox, the war over, Will walks the entire distance to his home in Falls, North Carolina, only to find his mother's grand estate burned to the ground by General Sherman. His mother, formerly known as one of the richest and most beautiful women in the South, has been horribly scarred by the flames and abandoned by her suddenly free slaves. Over the years to come, the Captain says almost nothing about his experiences during the war, letting the others do all the talking. It is only as he is nearing fifty that he suddenly acquires the storytelling itch, at which point he ceases to look forward, his energies instead devoted entirely to re-creating the past.

The Captain is fifty-one years old when Lucy, fifteen, sees him marching, in full uniform, in a veterans' parade. She is entranced by his celebrity, presence, and darkly handsome face. Before long she is rushed into marriage, a state for which she is distinctly unprepared. While the Captain is away at work, Lucy, still a child, is forced to share a house with Marsden's former slave and current housekeeper, Castalia. Proud, huge, and enormously intimidating, Castalia is openly scornful of Lucy and her inexperience. Lucy, meanwhile, afraid at first, slowly begins to learn the history behind this imposing woman who so thoroughly runs her husband's life while practicing voodoo in the hall closet and raising minks. Castalia's history is revealed through a series of long and sometimes fantastic recollections of her abduction as a three-year-old girl in Africa, her torturous journey to America in a slave ship, and her years of devoted service to Lady Marsden before the war. She is also revealed as one of Will's early lovers and as a companion to Will's father as well. As the years pass, Lucy and Castalia become fast friends, the homemade coat she has fashioned from her pet minks growing as steadily as her ever-increasing girth.

By the time Lucy is twenty-seven, she has borne the Captain nine children. As these children grow they, like herself, are constantly subjected to the Captain's treasure trove of war stories. The Captain, meanwhile, growing ever more obsessed with the past, squanders much of the family's hard-earned money on all manner of antique firearms, storing them under the bed. Lucy is more often than not left at home while her husband travels from country to country, attending various war anniversaries and gatherings. By now, he has taken to wearing his full-dress uniform almost everywhere he goes. He has also become more violent, bashing Lucy whenever the mood strikes him.

For a long time there were other veterans who remembered the Captain's rank and role in the war, but as they slowly but surely passed the age of lucidity and died, there were fewer survivors to dispute the Captain's version of events in "the Great War Betwixt the States." The Captain, who has kept close track of who yet survives, is numbered among the very last. Now a true celebrity, he is photographed and interviewed constantly, while Lucy's role is reduced to being little more than the Captain's tour guide. She tolerates, and even enjoys, most of it but is never able to forgive her husband for the hunting accident that cost her son Ned his eyesight. It is after that tragedy that she burns the Captain's guns and tries to leave him. It is only her children and Castalia that prevent her from doing so. Still, things are never the same as the Captain grows irrevocably distracted by the past, the war, and the lives she never knew becoming more real than what she has seen with her own eyes.

A stroke reduces the Captain to a mental and physical invalid, and Lucy's days are filled with meeting his many needs. People still come to see him, to take his picture, but the Captain—although still able to rattle off his more famous stories—is beyond anything having to do with the real world. Finally, he asks Lucy to take him back once again to the place where Ned Smythe was killed. She does, after considerable difficulty, and it is there, while sitting beneath the same tree in which Ned was killed, that the Captain tries to strangle her. She breaks free and survives, but she is deeply wounded in body and spirit. Still she remains devoted to him, even as he grows increasingly incoherent and helpless, until the day when, having destroyed Castalia's precious mink coat, he gets Lucy in his grasp once again and she is forced to bludgeon him to death with his empty sword scabbard. The war, at long last, is over.

Oldest Living Confederate Widow Tells All is Allan Gurganus's first novel and the result of nearly ten years' work. Authentic in tone, as rambling and nongrammatical as Lucy's own voice, it presents the gritty, sometimes comic, legends of the Civil War in the language of its time. Lucy is not shy about naming names, reweaving facts, or adding her own, often cutting, opinions of a man and a world obsessed with war. Through Captain Marsden's tales the reader learns not only of the great events and personalities that shaped the War between the States, but some of the sideshows as well, both real and imagined. Small-town family life and scandals, eccentric characters, and brutal images of combat are all depicted in Lucy's blunt, unflinching terms. She describes, from a highly personalized point of view, what it might have been like to have been a slave, to have ruled over them, and to have lost everything except one's own dignity. In a life whose ties and memories stretch from Fort Sumter to the *Challenger* disaster, the great transformations that have overtaken American life are detailed. Throughout it all, Lucy is often weary: "Sleep will, if nothing else does, save us . . . . Times, this long life seems the insomnia that's keeping me from what I most dearly deserve."

Most of all, Lucy's story is about the joys of survival. Very late in life, flying over the Southeast in a plane, Lucy notices how the landscape below is streaked with a bright, zigzagged path of green. She is surprised, and somehow gratified, to learn that the green is the living scar—the dead trees grown back even brighter—of Sherman's terrible march to the sea. "Colors *are* the deeds and sufferings of light," she concludes. "The fact is fair. People recover. Ain't it something, what folks can spring back from?"

David Alvarez

ON THE GOLDEN PORCH

Author: Tatyana Tolstaya (1951–   )
Publisher: Alfred A. Knopf (New York). 198 pp. $17.95
Type of work: Short stories
Time: The present
Locale: The Soviet Union

A collection of tales of ordinary life in the Soviet Union in which cruel realities are given a dreamlike quality

Tatyana Tolstaya's remarkable collection opens with "Loves Me, Loves Me Not," a wistful, dreamy remembrance of childhood with the nanny Maryvanna. The children in Maryvanna's charge think her silly and oppressive and resent her stuffy tales of the past. Intertwined with these recollections are the narrator's bittersweet memories: mysterious trips to the market with her father; hot baths after cold days in the dark Russian winter; and the haunting, scarcely remembered images of the earlier Nanny Grusha. Slowly, vague images and events start to take shape as the children realize that their nanny, the despised Maryvanna, is leaving them at last. Winter, they discover, is gone, the long summer of their youth ready to begin.

Simeonov, the lonely, balding translator in "Okkervil River," spends his time curing processed cheeses and listening to an old, cracked record of his favorite singer, Vera Vasilevna. He is deeply in love with her and imagines that the words on her recordings are meant exclusively for him. While hiding from his plain and oppressive lover, Tamara, he imagines clandestine meetings with the eternally youthful Vera, who he knows is surely dead by now; "Where are you now, Vera Vasilevna," he wonders aloud. "And which rain—Parisian light blue or Chinese yellow—drizzles over your grave, and whose soil chills your white bones?" Simeonov is amazed when he discovers that she is, indeed, still alive. He imagines her as "a half-blind, impoverished, . . . stick-legged old woman" and resolves to find her, to reveal the depths of his long-suffering soul. However, after journeying to the far end of the city and locating her shabby apartment, he is astonished, and somehow dismayed, to be greeted by a large and hearty woman— Vera herself—in the midst of a riotous birthday celebration. Simeonov is disappointed at her proud and crusty vitality, so far removed from his imaginings, and even more so by her choice of friends and suitors. Vera persuades him to let her use his bathtub, smoke his cigarettes, eat his food while he tells himself that the real Vera Vasilevna died long ago. He is suddenly happy to be reunited with the unglamorous Tamara, his romance lost and his own, ordinary life renewed.

"Sweet Shura" is the story of Alexandra Ernestovna, an old woman in shabby clothes whose one vanity is her wonderful hat, atop which snowballs, lilies of the valley, cherries, and barberries recall the four seasons. She has been married three times: first to a famous lawyer; then to a famous physician; and, finally, to a thin whining man who died unremembered. It was Ivan Nikolayevich, however, whom she met in the Crimea long ago, who has always owned her heart. He had begged her to leave her husband and run away to the south with him. Why hadn't she gone? She had bought a ticket, packed her bags, and sat by a window until it was too late. "Maybe if you learn the magic word . . . if you guess it; if you sit down and think hard, . . . there has to be a door, a crack, an unnoticed crooked way back there to that day." He is yet waiting for her, she is certain, pacing the dusty platform, agitated; in death, young and slim, Sweet Shura floats "to the lost platform . . . and dissolves in the hot midday sun."

The title story, "On the Golden Porch," is a surreal mosaic of a child's splintered vision of the world of adults. Uncle Pasha, small, meek, an old man—he is fifty—is married to Mother but secretly adores Veronika Vikentievna and her bed with the glass legs. Years pass like the seasons, and the once magical possessions of her uncle grow tacky and cheap. He dies, is left unburied, while his favorite clock, "the golden Lady of Time, drinking bottoms up from the goblet of life, will strike a final midnight on the table for Uncle Pasha."

"Hunting the Woolly Mammoth" is about Zoya and her determined attempts to ensnare her lover, Vladimir, into marriage. She is beautiful but no longer young, while he is boring, predictable, and thoroughly unlikable. Still, if she is married to him she can enjoy her perfect right, as his legal wife, not to share in his outdoor activities or other dull pursuits; instead, she can sit in front of the television, smoke, and drink to her heart's content, and maybe flirt with one of the surgeons she had once coveted. But first, she must subdue the beast. Very carefully did she set her traps, dig her pits, and bind her nooses; dishonest, cheating methods are these, she knows, but these are the rules of the game, the hunt. "I aim . . . let loose the arrow: *Whrrrrrrr!* and he's a goner. And I drag the carcass home."

Vassily Mikhailovich in "The Circle" is sixty years old, and the blood creaks in his veins. In his long, dull life of being married he has learned such secrets as "the grievously brief lifespan of sour cream" and the way to clean Arctic-fox fur (with farina grains heated in a dry skillet). He longs to reinvent his life, to become a medieval alchemist, the daughter of a millionaire, or even a widow's beloved cat. It is only the image of Isolde, his imaginary lover, that gives his life meaning. But his trip around the world, his circle, is ending and, finally, even the treasured image of Isolde proves unfaithful, and it is then that he "gratefully accepts from gentle hands his well-earned cup of hemlock."

In "A Clean Sheet," Ignatiev is a troubled man. His child, Valerik, is ill, and his careworn wife has quit her job to tend their son. Ignatiev is profoundly depressed, his life miserable. One night, while meeting a friend after work, he learns of a wonderful operation that can restore one's vitality and make that person an overnight success. This friend introduces Ignatiev to an acquaintance who has had the operation; where once this man was poor and sad, he is now a powerful leader of industry: "A gold pen in his pocket, and look at the pens in the granite slab on his desk. Look at the desk calendars. And a fine cognac behind the square panes of his cupboard—well, well!" Ignatiev is not sure, however, if he should have the operation; finally, scared, he submits himself to the doctor, has the procedure done, and emerges happy, heartless, and determined to rid himself and his life of such burdens as a sickly child and a careworn wife. He is a new man.

"Fire and Dust" is the strange and eerie tale of Rimma's slow dissolution into old age. Her story begins on a hopeful note, her life full of wonderful dreams for the future, and she is the envy of her friends. Inexorably, however, her dreams begin to erode as odd and sometimes wearisome people begin to populate the house in which she lives. One of these, the visitor Svetlana, who is known to all as Pipka, is beautiful save for her black, rotten teeth, and she is perpetually brimming with fantastic adventures and unlikely happenings. In the end, however, Pipka disappears, and the dreams that were Rimma's become as dust, the fire that made them long extinguished.

"Date with a Bird" captures the fleeting light of a Russian summer and a young boy's romance with an imaginary lover, Tamila, who "smoked thin cigarettes in a long . . . holder with jangling copper rings, drank something from small shot glasses, . . . and laughed as if she were crying." The young boy, Petra, decides that he will marry her one day, but it is the death of his grandfather—a victim of the Siren Bird—that convinces him at last that no one can escape one's fate.

"A person lived—a person died." So is summed up the long-forgotten life of "Sonya." A dull, stupid woman, Sonya is the victim of a cruel joke by her friend Ada, who portrays herself as a distant, secret admirer. The correspondence that begins continues, often passionately, for many years. It is only during the war that the letters cease and the secret is revealed, perhaps, to the foolish Sonya. The final fate of either party is never revealed, although the reader is invited to imagine.

Fastidious, articulate, and a brilliant entertainer, Filin is "The Fakir." A collector of odd and beautiful things, the teller of improbable tales, Filin charms his rough, ordinary guests with his knowledge of all things splendid and opulent. It is only Gayla who pierces his intricate cover, revealing him to be as secretly poor and desperate for companionship as everyone else.

"Peters" is a soft, homely boy, raised by his grandmother and unable to understand his difficulty in making friends. Well-mannered and impeccably behaved, Peters finds himself a loner. The reader follows his life into his sad old age as he fails time and again to make friends or find a satisfying romance. In the end, wanting nothing, Peters smiles gratefully as life "running past, indifferent, ungrateful, treacherous, mocking, meaningless, alien—marvelous, marvelous, marvelous."

Tatyana Tolstaya, the great-grandniece of Leo Tolstoy and the granddaughter of Alexei Tolstoy, graduated from Leningrad University in 1974, and was in 1988 the writer-in-residence at The University of Richmond. Her stories are tales of people who live on the very margins of existence, their generally unsatisfying situations eased by colorful dreams and impossible mirages. Throughout, her characters are as children in their innocence, their mental wanderings, and their great need to be clothed in warm layers of love. There is a beauty to be discovered in even the severest of predicaments, and time enough always to sleep a little longer, to weave a more perfect dream. The raw materials of such wonderful, imagined lives are invariably found in the often mundane rituals of waking life. At a glance, or over a lifetime, harsh realities are transformed, made colorful, or rendered meaningless as, always, the dream proves larger than reality.

David Alvarez

ORDINARY LOVE & GOOD WILL

Author: Jane Smiley (1949–   )
Publisher: Alfred A. Knopf (New York). 197 pp. $17.95
Type of work: Two novellas
Time: The present
Locale: The United States

A detailed exploration of two disparate marriages, one already ended in bitterness and another about to be irrevocably transformed

> *Principal characters:*
> RACHEL KINSELLA, a fifty-two-year-old mother of five, who presides over an uneasy reunion of her offspring
> MICHAEL KINSELLA, her son, just returned from teaching in India
> JOE KINSELLA, Michael's twin brother, who is desperately trying to reestablish the closeness he and Michael enjoyed as youngsters
> ELLEN KINSELLA, Rachel's daughter, whose own chilling tale of childhood neglect sheds new light on her mother's life and marriage
> BOB MILLER, a Vietnam veteran who lives with his family in an almost entirely self-sufficient environment
> LIZ MILLER, Bob's wife, who has discovered God
> TOMMY MILLER, the Millers' troubled youngster
> LYDIA HARRIS, the mathematics teacher whose house Tommy destroys

Ordinary Love, the first of Jane Smiley's two remarkable novellas, is centered on the return from India of Rachel Kinsella's son Michael. He has been gone two years, teaching mathematics in an impoverished community, and has returned a sick, emaciated shadow of his former self. His transformation is made all the more striking by the comparison with his twin brother, Joe. Rachel's family, which consists of five grown children, gathers at her old, big house, eager for tales of Michael's adventures and filled with concern for his diminished appearance. Michael is fatigued and evasive, preferring not to talk about the things and places he has seen. As he says, "Actually, I have more thoughts about America now than about India. . . . People who've been there for years still talk about it. Nobody gets any closer to understanding it."

Joe tries almost desperately to reestablish the closeness he and his brother once shared as youngsters, but he is disappointed at how little they have left in common. "There's nothing there. We don't think alike anymore. I am on my own now." Rachel finally tells Joe, who is in his mid-twenties, "There's something to be said for being by yourself."

Rachel knows quite well just what solitude is all about. When the twins were only five, twenty years before, she had an affair with a neighbor. Her husband, Pat, a gifted medical researcher, was appalled when she told him, and it was then that she lost her family. She kept the house, however, and over the years, as raising five children took its toll on Pat, Rachel gradually regained custody of the youngsters again. Still, the circumstances behind the broken marriage had always been concealed; even now, with her entire family grown and close at hand, she is reluctant to reveal the inner feelings and disappointments that caused her to destroy what appeared to be a perfect marriage.

Finally, it is her daughter Ellen who provokes the truth. Ensnared in a difficult marriage herself, she remarks to Rachel, "I don't have time for another man." Her mother grins knowingly, and the expression is noticed by Ellen. Finally, after much pressure, Rachel tells her what was on her mind: "My experience is that you make room for anything you want, if you want it enough. Even an inconvenient man." It is not long after this that Rachel finally pours out the entire story for the whole family. Her unexpected candor is matched by Ellen, who reveals a disturbing episode of neglect and abandonment by her father in England. Rachel is forced to recognize that there were consequences, sometimes terrible ones, for her long-ago, irresponsible actions.

Completing the cycle of revelation is Michael's story of a bitterly broken engagement in India. In light of this, his actions and attitudes seem more understandable. He and Joe reach a significant, if uneasy, truce once Michael reveals his plans to accept a teaching job in Korea. As for Rachel, she is left with the knowledge that she has left her children with the two cruelest gifts she had to give: "the experience of perfect family happiness, and the certain knowledge that it could not last."

Good Will is the story of the Miller family and their carefully designed life of self-sufficiency on their small farm in rural Pennsylvania. Here, the Millers grow their own food, build their own furniture, and make their own clothes; ever resourceful, Bob Miller has, over the years, accumulated a treasure trove of castoff tools and implements. Until the birth of their son, Tommy, their income averaged around $150 per year; now, with property taxes and a growing child, they make do on about $350. From their hideaway in the hills they can look down upon the nearest civilization, the tiny town of Moreton.

And yet, for all their self-reliance, there are still things that connect the Millers to the rest of the world. The most important of these is their son, Tommy. The Millers reluctantly allowed him to attend kindergarten so as to alleviate his isolation; since then he has attended school regularly, traveling by bus, although the Millers feel that they are near to making a decision regarding home education. A seemingly perfect little boy, Tommy is bright, good with animals, and well adapted to life without television, electricity, and telephones. It is therefore a great surprise to the Millers when Tommy's teacher sends a note home detailing the child's willful destruction of a young black girl's toys. Angry and distraught, Bob Miller takes great pains to journey to Tommy's school, where he learns of other behavioral problems. Determined that his son should learn the consequences of his actions, Bob, at great expense for the Miller family, pays for the toys and makes Tommy earn their worth through farm chores.

Liz Miller, meanwhile, is attending the "Bright Light Fellowship" church, a pentacostal sect of which Bob is extremely distrustful. He is astonished that his wife, a college graduate, could fit in so easily with the poor, rural worshipers who make up the congregation. He is even more amazed, and disturbed, when, without warning, she announces to him that she has been saved. Bob, hardly a religious man himself, feels the beginnings of a rift widening between himself and his wife of twelve years.

Problems continue for Tommy as once more he harasses his new classmate, Annabel. This time, an unexpected visit by Annabel's mother, Lydia Harris, proves that he has destroyed the girl's coat with a scissors. At first, Liz does not want to believe it. Bob, however, knows it is true; he also knows there is no way he can afford to replace the coat. As repayment, he goes to work repairing Lydia Harris's house in Moreton. Working together, the two form a tentative bond. Bob learns that she is a mathematics professor, teaching at the nearby university. She assures him that he has handled the situation with Tommy correctly and that there will likely be no more problems. This seems to be the case as Lydia Harris, unannounced, brings her daughter Annabel to the farm to go ice skating with Tommy. To Bob's surprise, there seems to be no hostility between the children; they play and tease as any other children would. Bob, however much he is attracted to Lydia, finds her child to be arrogant and spoiled. "I'm glad she's not our kid," he concludes.

When Liz suddenly stops going to church Bob is concerned. He knows something is wrong but does not know how to approach the subject. He is suddenly confounded by the distance that has arisen between them. Forcing the issue, he learns that Liz has had to make a choice. "There wasn't room in my life for two of you. . . . You and

God.'' They are brought together again by the sudden and unexpected death of their horse's foal, but this sad event proves only to be an omen of a greater disaster to come.

The Millers' idyllic existence is transformed forever when, for reasons they will never understand, Tommy sets fire to and destroys the Harris house in Moreton. In the bitterness and confusion that follows, Tommy is placed with a counselor, as are both parents, and the family is forced to move back into town. Bob gets a job working construction, while Liz takes a job as a clerk in the university bookstore. They buy a car, a television, and three clocks. Liz, although attuned to her new life, weeps when she thinks of the past. Bob does not. He is a fractured man with a fragmented life; the wishes he once harbored have all been fulfilled. Now, in the aftermath, he realizes that ''though wishes express power or desire, their purpose is to reveal ignorance: the more fulfilled wishes, the more realized ignorance.''

With *Ordinary Love* and *Good Will*, Jane Smiley continues the high standard of fiction writing that has, over a span of six books, earned her a National Book Critics Circle Award nomination and the praise of author/critic James Atlas, who has said of her: ''no writer of the generation now in its thirties has written more movingly about what it feels like to become one's parents.'' The two stories presented here are strikingly different from each other in tone and style. In *Ordinary Love*, the tale is told from an older woman's perspective, which is one of both experience and regret. Through a subtle and often disarming narration, Rachel chronicles the consequences of the selfish act that both destroyed her marriage and had profound implications for her children's development.

By contrast, the idyllic, self-created world of Bob Miller in *Good Will* is told in a man's voice. Large, consuming, and sensitive nearly to a fault, Bob's presence—in the story itself and in style—completely overshadows the intentionally mysterious personalities of his wife and young son. It is Bob's tragedy, just as it was his world that he created. Likewise, the consequences of his self-made life-style weigh heaviest on his own shoulders. In the end, these two novellas raise more questions than they answer, not the least of which is how parents balance their own aspirations with those of their offspring.

Bertie Sweet

OURS: A RUSSIAN FAMILY ALBUM

Author: Sergei Dovlatov (1941–)
Publisher: Weidenfeld and Nicolson (New York). 135 pp. $15.95
Type of work: Memoirs
Time: The early 1900s to the present
Locale: Primarily the Soviet Union

Russian émigré Sergei Dovlatov profiles four generations of his family with humor and affection

Principal personages:
> SERGEI DOVLATOV, a writer, the chronicler of his family's recent history
> ISAAK, his paternal grandfather
> DONAT AND LEOPOLD, Isaak's sons
> STEPAN, Sergei's maternal grandfather
> NORA, MARA, and ROMAN, Stepan's children
> ARON, Mara's husband
> BORIS, Mara's son
> LENA, Sergei's wife
> KATYA AND KOLYA, Sergei and Lena's children

In *Ours*, Sergei Dovlatov chronicles the four most recent generations of his Russian family. Each touching, satirical, loving, and irreverent chapter focuses on a particular relative and is as much a portrait of modern Soviet history as it is of Dovlatov's kin.

Isaak was Dovlatov's paternal grandfather. When a wineshop opened next door to his delicatessen, Isaak and the vintner became friends, having long discussions at each other's place of business. "In a year's time they had drunk up everything in the wineshop and eaten the delicatessen out of business." Isaak was an enormous man—nearly seven feet tall—with an appetite to match. He always ate a full meal before dining out, but it never made a difference. As a soldier, his size had won him an assignment on the front line. ("If a horse gave out . . . Grandpa would drag the cannon through the swamp.") Many years later, he was nearly the ruination of an American export firm. It seems Isaak volunteered to try out its "Magic Bed" during a public demonstration: "Soon the hall was littered with the wreckage of wonder beds." Much to Isaak's disappointment, his son Leopold settled in Belgium. A friend of Leopold's once made a visit to Isaak's home. Not much later, the innocent Isaak was arrested as a Belgian spy and shot.

The author's maternal grandfather was Stepan, a handsome man "known for his harsh temperament." True to his obstinate self, Stepan, on one notable occasion, defied everyone, including God, by planting himself in his study while all others fled the city of Tiflis, where an earthquake was predicted to occur. Occur it did, and all that remained of Stepan's house was a pile of debris. Amid the ruin sat Stepan, dozing in an armchair.

Stepan's son, Roman, was quite the *kinto* (in short, a hell-raiser). At age fourteen, his *kinto* wit got him into some memorable trouble. The occasion was the seventh anniversary of the Georgian Soviet Socialist Republic. His sister Aniela, addressing a capacity crowd, began, "It has already been seven years." As though frozen in time, poor Aniela repeated those six words—not once, but twice. Suddenly, Roman's loud voice penetrated the utter silence: "It's already been seven years and no one's married Aniela!" Aniela disappeared in tears, and Roman was held in a police station for twenty-four hours.

Uncle Leopold, Isaak's youngest, was a born finagler. As a teenager, he once scammed a storeowner out of a large sum of money using a bogus Stradivarius, a phony red moustache, and a convincing bit of dual-role acting. Leopold turned expatriate as a young man, settling in Brussels, where he became a successful lumber dealer.

Aunt Mara was an editor. Among the books she worked on were those of Tynianov and Zoshchenko. Dovlatov admires such credentials, yet underlying his respect for Aunt Mara is an undisguised disregard for editors, as a rule: "If a writer is good, it would seem an editor is not needed. If the writer is bad, no editor can save him." His philosophy notwithstanding, Dovlatov is proud of the high esteem in which Mara was held in her field. Most of the books in her library had "personal inscriptions from the authors, often touching and tender ones." It is with sad resignation that he recalls the selling of this fine library upon her death—the inscriptions were torn out to ensure a speedy, "less awkward" sale.

Dovlatov was very attached to Mara's husband, Uncle Aron. The two men argued incessantly. "Uncle railed against rock music, the defector Baryshnikov, and General Andrei Vlasov. [Dovlatov] took stands against socialized medicine, 'Swan Lake', and Feliks Dzerzhinski." Toward the end of Aron's life, the bantering continued from his sickbed; it was not without its moments of private confession and concession. "A small portrait of Solzhenitsyn hung near the head of his bed. He took it down whenever guests came."

Mara's sister Nora is Dovlatov's mother. Her biography is an essay of praise for a self-sacrificing single parent whose life in the Soviet Union was marked by sharpness of insight, endurance of hardship, and a lifelong hatred of Stalin. She was a proficient copy editor, and her unfaltering support for her son's writing career, even when it landed him in prison, will always remain with Dovlatov as an emblem of their inseparability. (Nora emigrated to the United States with him in 1978.)

Dovlatov's father, Donat, divorced Nora when their son was eight. The theater was both his career and life. Indeed, the theatricality of the stage comprised, and even perverted, his perception of life in general, a perception that deified Stalin and extolled the Communist party —even though his father, Isaak, had been executed and his own livelihood had been jeopardized more than a few times. In fact, when his son, in 1978, suggested he accompany him to the West, the unemployed Donat was shocked. "Whoever heard of such a thing—leaving the stage in the last act? Three minutes before the final curtain and the applause?" (Donat emigrated in 1979.)

Cousin Boris is Mara's son. The events of his life unfolded in a bizarre incongruity. By Soviet standards, he was the exemplary youth —top student, soccer player, good son. One day at school, however, Boris climbed onto a window sill, "skillfully calculated his trajectory," and urinated on the school director from head to foot. As an adult, Boris's indiscretions were of a more serious nature, and before long, he had established an inexplicable pattern of wavering from model citizen to convicted criminal. But the essence of Boris and the influence he wielded remained constant. In or out of prison, he was brilliant, affable, respected, and never too far from getting exactly what he wanted. Much to the author's regret, Boris said no to joining the Dovlatov emigration.

One Dovlatov that did make the move to the West was Glasha, an "irresistible" fox terrier the author describes as "a born nonconformist," for whom emigration was inevitable. Years before, in Russia, Glasha spent several months away from her family, in the custody of Dovlatov's friend Bobrov, a game warden who convinced Dovlatov of Glasha's need to be in an environment conducive to her instincts. When Bobrov reneged on his agreement to return the dog in two months' time, Dovlatov and another friend made the arduous, icy trek to Bobrov's remote residence. (The account of this "outing," including a cast of characters from the KGB, is truly comedic.)

The courtship of Dovlatov and Lena was far from one of convention, and even further from anything that could be construed as romantic. Essentially, Lena appeared one morning on Dovlatov's couch, following an all-night party. The ever calm, never emotional Lena just kept returning every evening to Dovlatov's apartment, preparing meals and sleeping on the couch. This surreal relationship baffled Dovlatov to no end, and he never did get an explanation of her presence or intentions, but they married, anyway. Dovlatov knew very little about his wife, except that she was unperturbable to the point of driving him mad. "Anything that could ruffle her serenity took [him] by surprise." One big surprise was her radical decision to leave the Soviet Union with their daughter, Katya. In fact, Lena and Katya were settled in New York some time before Dovlatov himself seriously considered emigration. (The Dovlatovs were formally divorced in Russia; today they live as a married couple in New York.)

Dovlatov's story of Katya is about a girl whose childhood is not remembered well by her father. He does recollect the agonizing days when a very sick little Katya was hospitalized, when even her mother was forbidden visitation. Dovlatov shares some poignant early memories of his bright and precious daughter, but much of the characterization of Katya is marked by a father's perception that he has always been and will continue to be in many ways disappointing and in most ways "only Papa."

Dovlatov concludes his family album with a word about his infant son, born in New York City:

> His name, in Russian, is Nikolai; we call him Kolya. Someday he . . . will have his own history, but it will be . . . of another, American family. With Kolya, this book is done. I hope it is clear to everyone that it has been his story.

Sergei Dovlatov's *Ours* is best described by its subtitle: *A Russian Family Album*. The reader who opens this unimposing little book finds a collection of verbal portraits, so vivid and articulate as to rewrite an old adage—perhaps "one chapter is worth a thousand pictures." Unlike the tedium often associated with the reluctant perusal of another's family album, reading *Ours* is a welcome passage into the lives of persons who immediately ignite attentive interest. Their biographer, Dovlatov, is a brilliant wit and a gifted writer. His humor hangs on every phrase—and on every thought behind every phrase. Much of what he writes carries a message that there is nothing so sweet that it does not have a cutting edge, nothing so tragic that it does not find its way back to the risible condition known as life.

Ours is a delightful piece of literature, to be read and treasured by those who have parents, or children, or uncles, or cousins; by those who came to America from the Soviet Union, or from other faraway places; by those who have never been in America; by those who have known no home but America. In brief, *Ours* is everyone's.

Christine Lindberg Stevens

PAUL ROBESON

Author: Martin Bauml Duberman (1930–   )
Publisher: Alfred A. Knopf (New York). 804 pp. $24.95
Type of work: Biography
Time: 1898–1976
Locale: The United States and abroad

The life and times of the actor-singer Paul Robeson, perhaps the most passionate advocate of racial equality in his time

Principal personages:
> PAUL ROBESON, athlete, entertainer, and ardent defender of oppressed people everywhere
> ESLANDA "ESSIE" GOODE ROBESON, Paul's articulate and energetic wife
> PAUL ROBESON, JR., the Robesons' only child

There is perhaps no more original, remarkable, and—ultimately—misunderstood public figure in recent U.S. history than Paul Robeson. A distinguished athlete, a scholar, an actor, and a singer, he was also one of the most vocal and controversial civil rights advocates of his era. Discredited, disavowed, and continually harassed by those determined to undermine his credibility, he eventually was forced into a life of obscurity, his pioneering deeds and heroic courage all but forgotten by both his successors and the world at large.

Born in Princeton, New Jersey, in 1898, the son of a former slave, Robeson was determined from the start to transcend the considerable racial barriers faced by black Americans in the years prior to World War I. As an undergraduate at Rutgers, he won honors and fame as an All-American athlete, orator, and Phi Beta Kappa scholar. In 1921, while a student at Columbia Law School, Robeson married the energetic and intellectually gifted Essie Goode. It was Essie who encouraged Paul to develop his acting and singing talents once it became obvious that racial inequity would impede his progress in the legal profession. Meeting critical acclaim for his first professional role, in *Taboo*, Robeson went on to star with Eugene O'Neill's Provincetown Players in *All God's Chillun Got Wings* and *Emperor Jones*. At the same time, he began to gain recognition as a talented singer of spirituals, and his rapid rise as both an actor and singer resulted in an invitation to perform in England.

After the racially charged atmosphere of the United States, the Robesons were relieved to encounter a more tolerant reception in Europe. While there they met and began associations with the continent's leading entertainment and political figures. His political life still ahead of him, Robeson's entertainment accomplishments in the 1920s carried him steadily from one success to another, eventually culminating in his triumphant Broadway performance of *Othello*.

A multitude of plays, concerts, and even movie roles followed, the near universal acclaim of white critics being tempered by some in the black community who believed Robeson's roles to be demeaning to his race. Gradually at first, then with an ever-increasing zeal, Robeson began to seek artistic vehicles that would meaningfully reflect his African heritage and growing identification with Soviet culture and philosophy. In late 1934 the Robesons made their first visit to the Soviet Union, a stay that cemented Paul's lifelong admiration and support for the Communist system of government.

In 1938, Robeson's growing political interests prompted him to travel to Spain in order to witness firsthand the bloody revolution that was threatening to destroy that country. Inspired by the insurgent Republicans' courage in general and the heroism of a young black enlistee, Oliver Law, Robeson was deeply moved. He wanted earnestly to make a film about Law and the bravery he represented, but the project never got off the ground. From this point on, Robeson grew increasingly disenchanted with the motion-picture industry and its commitment to "mediocre entertainment."

By the 1940s, Paul Robeson's popularity had reached its peak. His stage work and concerts met with near-uniform applause, and his performance of "Ballad for Americans" in the Hollywood Bowl attracted the largest crowd ever to attend an event there. Still allying himself with the Communist party, as well as with the Communist-influenced National Negro Congress, Robeson spoke ardently of the need for Russian war relief; since the Soviet Union was now a wartime ally, such a stance was considered, by most, entirely respectable. J. Edgar Hoover of the FBI, however, was suspicious of Robeson's loyalties, thus beginning the pattern of surveillance and harassment that would follow him the rest of his life. Robeson continued to crisscross the country, tempering his attacks on Fascism with repeated reminders of the need to oppose repression of blacks at home. With his unanimous acclaim in *Othello*, Robeson's place as a giant in both the arts and humanities seemed assured.

In 1945, Robeson was awarded the prestigious Spingarn Medal by the National Association for the Advancement of Colored People (NAACP). In his acceptance speech, Robeson struck an overtly political note, denouncing renewed signs of hostility by the United States and Britain toward the Soviet Union. Voicing concern over the events following Franklin Roosevelt's death, he went on to point out what he perceived as a drift away from civil rights on the domestic scene and renewed colonialism in the international arena. "Full employment in Russia," he said, "is a fact, and not a myth, and discrimination is non-existent. The Soviet Union can't help it as a nation and a people if it is in the main stream of change."

Subsequent concert tours and acting engagements served only to increase Robeson's outrage at the wretched circumstances facing black Americans. His anger was compounded by Winston Churchill's speech warning against the Iron Curtain's expansionist policies. Campaigning vigorously for Henry Wallace and the Progressive party, Robeson's increasingly strident tone—combined with a growing fear and mistrust of Communism on the part of the American public—earned him considerable personal hostility, as well as the enmity of President Truman. The FBI, meanwhile, continued with its nearly frantic efforts to prove that Robeson was indeed a member of the Communist party (he had not been and never would be). In 1948, testifying before the Senate Judiciary Committee, Robeson neverthe-less refused to answer that question on constitutional grounds, using the forum instead to promote the ideals of the Progressive party. The subsequent disaster at the polls seemed to many to be a mandate for Truman to get tough with Communists, both at home and abroad, and with their sympathizers as well. The long and bitter process by which Paul Robeson would, inexorably, be transformed from a respected black American of unparalleled achievement into a national pariah had begun.

In 1949, Robeson vigorously defended accused Communist leaders on trial in New York, claiming, "I, too, am on trial." But it was his remarks in Paris that same year that drew the most vociferous re-sponse. An Associated Press dispatch misquoted Robeson, attributing to him the following words: "It is unthinkable that American Negroes would go to war on behalf of those who have oppressed us for gener-ations against a country [the Soviet Union] which in one generation has raised our people to the full dignity of mankind."

The firestorm that developed did much to ruin Robeson's career. While white editors and politicians castigated him for his lack of patri-otism and branded him a subversive, the black community was equally quick to distance itself from his alleged remarks. The ensuing backlash culminated in an extremely violent clash between citizens and concert goers in Peekskill, New York; nearly overnight, Robeson's audience disappeared. He continued to speak, but his forums grew increasingly limited. Concerts and speaking engagements were canceled, as was an interview on NBC television with Eleanor Roosevelt. Still, Robeson and his views remained popular abroad, his frequent visits to England and the continent serving to buoy both his spirits and his conviction.

However, after he protested Negro involvement in the Korean War, both his passport and his right to enter Canada or Mexico were revoked by the U.S. State Department.

The next eight years proved agonizing to Robeson. Vilified at home, he was not allowed to accept any awards or offers to speak and perform abroad. Inevitably, his health began to suffer, resulting in a severe bout with depression in 1957. From the sidelines, he continued to voice his opinions, but no one seemed to be listening. Ironically, his enforced inactivity coincided with a period of change for black Americans in general, a movement from which he felt increasingly estranged. Finally, responding to international pressures, the State Department restored Robeson's passport in 1958. Embarking on a final whirlwind of activity that culminated in the English presentation of *Othello*, Robeson visited the Soviet Union, Germany, Czechoslovakia, and even Australia. However, the last fifteen years of his life were marked by inactivity and seclusion, his unshakable depression and ill health reducing him to a mere shadow of the vital figure who had so long aroused such controversy. A brief flurry of appreciation and tributes marked his final years, but his fame and reputation would never be entirely restored. He died in 1976, his courage and accomplishments virtually unknown to a new generation of Americans.

With *Paul Robeson*, Martin Bauml Duberman succeeds in recounting both the accomplishments and the trials of one of America's most dynamic and controversial public figures. Utilizing an exhaustive collection of notes and sources, Duberman likewise examines Robeson's private life: his long and sometimes stormy marriage, his many adulterous affairs, and the multiplicity of his friends and enemies from all walks of life. Perhaps most challenging, however, is Duberman's careful and nearly complete exploration of Robeson's complex and sometimes contradictory political philosophy, a set of deeply felt beliefs that would do much to undermine this man's sincere efforts on behalf of racial and social equality. Finally, and with touching eloquence, Duberman—in his discussion of Robeson's final years—conveys the sad extent to which this remarkable man's achievements have been so largely forgotten.

David Alvarez

PEACEMAKING AMONG PRIMATES

Author: Frans de Waal (1948–   )
Publisher: Harvard University Press (Cambridge, Mass.). 294 pp. $29.95
Type of work: Social science
Time: The present
Locale: Arnhem Zoo, the Netherlands; Madison Primate Center, Madison Wisconsin; San Diego Zoo, San Diego, California

Primatologist Frans de Waal reports on his observations of the method employed by chimpanzees, rhesus monkeys, and other primates to restore peace after episodes of aggression

> *Principal personages:*
> FRANS DE WAAL, the author, a research scientist who studie primates
> NIKKIE, the alpha (head) male of the Arnhem chimpanzee col ony
> YEROEN, a male who supported Nikkie
> LUIT, Nikkie's challenger
> ORANGE, the dominant female rhesus monkey at the Madiso Primate Center

In this important study, Frans de Waal describes observations o primates both in the controlled environment of zoos and in the wild Violence among primates has been described from earlier observa tions, and the conclusion has been drawn that violence is normal fo all primates, including humans. However, de Waal notes that natura mechanisms exist among primates for conflict resolution so tha aggression can be kept under control and societies can continue tc function.

The first group de Waal discusses is the chimpanzee population a the zoo in Arnhem, the Netherlands. The chimpanzee colony wa dominated by a coalition of two adult males, Nikkie and Yeroen. Nik kie was the stronger of the two and could dominate Yeroen physically but Yeroen was older and more experienced. Either of them migh have been dominated by Luit, another male, but he was unable tc prevail against the coalition of Nikkie and Yeroen. Technically, Nikkie was head of the colony (demonstrated by the fact that all the othe members would exhibit submissive bowing and grunting before him) but he was heavily dependent on Yeroen. Since Nikkie and Luit woulc chase each other away from sexually attractive females, Yeroen ben efited by being able to enjoy the largest number of sexual contacts ir the community.

Generally Nikkie and Yeroen were in agreement. However, when ever they expressed antagonism, Luit would seize the opportunity tc perform intimidation displays, "hooting with his hair on end and hurling stones and branches in every direction." The only way to restore order would be for Nikkie and Yeroen to make peace. Nikkie would stretch out his hand to Yeroen. As soon as Yeroen accepted an embrace from Nikkie, Nikkie would approach Luit and perform a dominance display. Luit, realizing that the coalition had been reformed, would bow and grunt submissively before Nikkie.

Eventually, Nikkie started to allow Luit sexual access to the females. As the coalition broke down, researchers discovered evidence of a night fight involving the three males. Both Nikkie and Yeroen showed deep injuries, but Luit, who was almost untouched, emerged as the alpha male. The uneasy peace that followed this development was shattered when the researchers discovered the results of another night fight, in which Luit was fatally injured.

Despite this sobering evidence of violence, the incident was a rare exception in the life of the colony. After the death of Luit, the frequency and speed of reconciliations actually increased.

De Waal went to the Primate Center at Madison, Wisconsin, to study rhesus monkeys. Unlike chimpanzees, rhesus monkeys are organized in matrilineal hierarchies. Females stay with their mothers and derive their position from them. Adolescent females must assert their position by dominating lower-ranking females, which they do with the support of their own kin and, frequently, that of higher-ranking females. Rhesus monkeys are extremely aggressive, and fighting is common. Dominant monkeys are accorded a "fear grin" from lower-ranking monkeys.

Rhesus monkeys also have means of reconciling, however. When members of the same family—two sisters—quarreled, de Waal recorded their gradual approaches to their mother, Orange. Each of them began to groom Orange, and gradually they began to embrace and lip-smack toward each other. Males sometimes mount each other in turn to signify an end to their quarrel. Rhesus monkeys stare fixedly at each other during confrontations, so they do not make eye contact when reconciling. Often this makes their behavior appear almost accidental, as former adversaries sidle up to one another or brush against one another and then begin to groom.

Another group studied by de Waal and his colleagues was the stump-tailed monkeys. Among this group, reconciliation was often signaled by one monkey presenting his or her bottom to the other. An embrace known as "hold-bottom" follows, as the monkey clasps the bottom presented and the two monkeys sit together like this, sometimes with evidence of sexual arousal. Sexual activity is very common among stumptails, not only between males and females, but also between same-sex partners. Stumptails also use a ritual reprimand in which a subordinate presents a wrist or leg to another monkey; a mock-bite is administered. Injuries never result.

At the San Diego Zoo, de Waal studied the bonobo, a sophisticated small ape that was confused with the chimpanzee until 1929, when it was recognized as a separate species. Graceful, acrobatic, and fond of playing in water, bonobos even play games such as blindman's buff by covering their eyes with a banana leaf or holding their eyes shut with their fingers. Even more than the other primates studied, bonobos have an active sex life. Females are receptive seventy-five percent of the time, and sexual activity occurs between same-sex pairs as well as opposite-sex pairs. Because of their physiology, face-to-face matings are common. Females commonly engage in "GG-rubbing" (genito-genital rubbing) in a variety of positions.

Sex is linked very closely to food-sharing. Subordinates frequently beg food from dominates, and sexually attractive females sometimes take food from a male after mating. Sharing food occurs in family groups (a mother with her child, for example), and close female friends share, also.

Sometimes sex occurs in conjunction with feeding time, but no exchange of food follows. De Waal speculates that sex may be used among bonobos to resolve tensions over food. Another view is that sex at feeding time is merely an arousal phenomenon in which excitement over food translates into sexual arousal.

In order to study this question, de Waal and his associates studied bonobo behavior both before and after incidents of aggression and compared the behavior to baseline behavior, or behavior at times when aggression was not a factor. Before the outbreak of aggression, grooming behavior was far below the baseline behavior, and grooming remained low after aggressive outbreaks. However, embracing, friendly touching, and sexual contact increased markedly after incidents of aggression.

De Waal's final chapter discusses human beings. He laments the paucity of research into reconciliation in humans, ascribing it to the view that all aggression is harmful. Instead, he argues, it should be recognized that aggression is part of human society and will be as long as individuals are different from one another. However, he notes that many human relationships—marriage, for example—frequently have conflicts that are resolved, and that such conflict and resolution may be a sign of the strength in a relationship, since conflict would not be possible in this context if people did not feel secure in the other person's affection and willingness to forgive confrontations.

De Waal speculates that the human ability to use language may allow humans to handle reconciliation in a more sophisticated way than the primates do. For example, children exhibit a whole range of behaviors based on their ability to talk to each other, from cooperative propositions ("I'll be your friend") to object offering ("You can play with my doll if you give me some of your marshmallows") or from explicit apologies to symbolic offers ("I'm going to bring you my truck"). Adults may be more sophisticated in their use of these methods, but there is not a great deal of difference in the offer of flowers or a dinner to reconcile a marital argument, or even the offer of economic aid from one country to another.

De Waal notes in his conclusion that this book "has, I trust, demonstrated that appropriate countermeasures evolved along with aggressive behavior, and that both humans and other primates apply these measures with great skill." He makes his case convincingly, although the reader may feel that humans are actually lagging behind some of their primate relatives in peacemaking behavior.

What is most fascinating in this work is the degree of complexity and variation in the different societies de Waal discusses. He notes early in the book that the amount of information that has been collected on other primates is minute in comparison to the studies of biologists, social scientists, and psychologists on the human race, and that a great deal more may be discovered about how animals organize themselves and communicate with each other. Although much of what he presents is, as he notes, based upon thousands of hours of detailed observation and the compilation and comparison of the data, the information is presented in a way that any nonbiologist can easily comprehend. It is, moreover, an incredibly fascinating look at other societies.

Elizabeth J. Jewell

A PEACE TO END ALL PEACE: CREATING THE MODERN MIDDLE EAST 1914–1922

Author: David Fromkin (1932–   )
Publisher: Henry Holt and Company (New York). 635 pp. $39.95
Type of work: History
Time: 1914–1922
Locale: The Middle East

A detailed diplomatic and military history of World War I in the Middle East and its consequences, told primarily from the point of view of British foreign policy and the effect on the Ottoman Empire and the Arab clans

Principal personages:

WINSTON CHURCHILL, first lord of the Admiralty and first lord of the Exchequer, British civilian military planner in World war I

DAVID LLOYD GEORGE, British war minister and later prime minister, leader during "war socialism," and drafter of British postwar Mideast policy

LORD KITCHENER, a British hero, minister of the War Committee; a strong advocate of Arab dreams and demands in the Mideast

KING HUSSEIN, the Hashemite Arab clan leader of the Hejaz region of the Arabia peninsula; the protector of the Islamic "Holy Places"

FEISAL and ABDULLAH, the sons of King Hussein and postwar leaders of the new countries Iraq and Transjordan

DAVID BEN-GURION and VLADIMIR JABOTINSKY, Zionist leaders, representing, respectively, the positions of compromise and confrontation over the Palestinian mandate

MUSTAPHA KEMAL, a military leader and political heir to the young Turks, "founder of the modern, secular Turkish State"

During the 19th century, it was relatively easy for Britain to maintain world law and order through diplomatic and military means. The sudden growth of the industrial base led to a technological explosion that allowed England to produce a large army and navy. British hegemony resulted from aggression and then a benign neglect toward the conquered people.

The foreign service became the domain of the "time-servers." Content to administer local affairs from the comfort of their enclaves, foreign officers allowed "the natives" to remain in their traditional worlds. No meaningful interaction or understanding passed between the rulers and the ruled. What interested the ministers and their staffs was the grand scope of the "Great Game."

This was the term used by British imperial apologists to identify

English attempts to limit Russian expansion in the Middle East and India. Russian czars, locked in the cold, brutal world of Moscow, had for centuries longed for a warm-water trading port. For Russian "manifest destiny," the natural places to look were the British-ruled lands of Persia, Afghanistan, and India. In the smug arrogance of imperialism, British leaders, without knowing local conditions, would use native pawns to checkmate Russian encroachments. Throughout the 19th century this approach worked well. During the modern era, this blighted mentality, combined with 20th-century warfare, resulted in tragic consequences.

Other European nations and the United States had refined and improved on British manufacturing, production, and administrative methods. The various branches of the foreign service—Home Office, Cairo, and India—were advocating separate, private agendas. The seamless garment of British alliances, to prevent Russian expansion, were ripping apart. Yet British writing, notions, and administration of foreign affairs remained nestled in an exceeding, and often misguided, self-confidence. Nowhere was this more evident than in the attitude and war aims toward the remnants of the Ottoman Empire.

Like the Austrian and Chinese versions, this multinational corporate state, comprising various religions, languages, and cultures, was being dismantled slowly. Centuries-old political and social institutions, like the caliph and grand vizier, were losing their legitimacy to the forces of modernization. Young military leaders, known collectively as the "Young Turks," seized political power and were searching tentatively for European technology and expertise. This loosening of the age-old bonds revived the old clan vendettas, religious schisms, and land claims among the Arab tribes. To the English, this area, made up of the current alignment of Mideast states, appeared ripe for exploitation.

British civil servants, believing the concept of accepting the "white man's burden," slanted their memoranda on the Mideast situation accordingly. These young men could not conceive that the Arabs could govern themselves, and therefore they believed that the Arabs would willingly accept British guidance. They wanted to graft urban, middle-class Christian values onto nomadic, tribal, poor Islamic societies. The Arabic inability to accept Western norms consistently amazed them. A rudimentary understanding of Arab languages, history, and religion contributed to this outlook. Rather than learning these disciplines, British "Arab experts" relied on frauds, charlatans, liars, and eccentrics to formulate foreign policy. This would result in the overreaching, paternalistic view that they knew what was best for the Arab peoples.

As for the Arabs, the tribes were willing to loosen the oppressive political control of the Turks but did not want it replaced with infidels.

The key principle in their lives was the Islamic culture: its religious, moral, and social teachings and laws. For these people, religion permeated to the core of their existence. Be they members of the Wahhabi sect or the Sunni majority, Islam was the elemental force. Clan chieftains or religious leaders were concerned not with national identities, geopolitical boundaries, or industrialization, but with maintaining their traditional values. They had to accept British aid to do this. As a temporary measure, they would become Westernists.

These conflicting values had flowed along their separate courses, unaware of the other's presence. They would collide in the period 1914-1918, on the battlefields of the Eastern war. The British Home Office and War Ministry, buttressed by the glowing field reports, assumed that the war against the Turks would be brief. After the Ottomans were disposed of, the British would establish an Eastern flank and end the war against Germany. Military and political leaders, oblivious to the realities, were not prepared for Turkish resistance at the Dardanelles, the Gallipoli fiasco, and the Baghdad campaign.

Angered, puzzled, and finally frustrated, the British had to try to reassess their Mideast policy without compromising their basic principles. This involved short-term, poorly conceived appeasements to the various factions so that the war could be won. British leaders had no intention of honoring these agreements in the postwar world. The Arabs were promised regional autonomy, religious freedom, and financial aid. To the rising force of Zionism, a promise of the biblical Palestine was held out: there, without Arab interference, the Jewish farmers would be free to experiment with their agricultural innovations. The war allies—Greece, Russia, and France—were promised prized parts of the Anatolian peninsula and the Syrian mandate.

Once the war aims had been achieved, the principal participants did not conform to British wishes and accept their roles. From 1919 to 1920 sporadic and unrelated rebellions sprang up throughout the Arab world. Small skirmishes were fought among the Allies over the Ottoman spoils. War-weary England, numbed by the slaughter in Western Europe, would not permit more young men to enforce government promises. U.S. foreign policy, throwing off President Woodrow Wilson's idealism, was unwilling to police the region.

British meddling had created a social and political vacuum, one that Arab, Zionist, and foreign influences were unable to fill. Halfheartedly, Britain attempted to prop up this unworkable structure. Artificial states were established, nominally ruled by Arab leaders created by British foreign officers. Enough aid was granted to half-complete modernization projects. And England tried to fulfill its commitments, attempting to satisfy all participants, but pleasing none.

David Fromkin is an international attorney of considerable reputation. To this work he brings a lawyer's gift of gathering evidence, assessing detail, and discovering nuances in language. He has an ability to plow through administrative reports, separate the wheat from the chaff, and reach the kernel of truth.

In this case, writing like a lawyer proves to be a benefit. This massive work is laid out like a legal brief. Fromkin has a major premise that he is trying to defend, has assembled all pertinent information, challenges contrary opinions, and reaches a conclusion. In another circumstance this format could prove to be deadly reading, but for the general reader, unfamiliar with Mideast history, this style is necessary. It keeps the issues, actors, and locations in their proper and appropriate perspectives.

Fromkin's work would have been even more impressive if he had relied more on primary sources rather than secondary accounts. While it was not the intent, the focus of the book still flows from the imperialist point of view. This does not detract from a magisterial history. It was a daunting task, and Fromkin acquitted himself with verve. He increases the reader's understanding of the ongoing issues and directs sympathies to all participants. After reading his work, one can no longer pick up a contemporary news article and make a snap judgment on Mideast issues.

Edward B. Rowe

THE PEOPLE AND UNCOLLECTED STORIES

Author: Bernard Malamud (1914–1986)
Publisher: Farrar, Straus and Giroux (New York). 269 pp. $18.95
Type of work: Short stories and an unfinished novel
Time: 1870–1985
Locale: The United States

A Jewish immigrant joins a tribe of Indians, is elected chief, and strives to save his newfound people from destruction

> Principal characters:
> YOZIP, later renamed Jozip, a Jewish immigrant who becomes chief of "The People"
> ONE BLOSSOM, the old chief's daughter and Yozip's secret love
> INDIAN HEAD, Yozip's rival for leadership and the heart of One Blossom
> JOSEPH, the Christian name of the old chief who appoints Yozip his successor

Yozip Bloom, a wandering peddler from Zbrish, Russia, is making his slow way through the Pacific Northwest when he is accosted by two outlaws; in desperation, he abandons his pacifistic views and fights back, subduing his assailants. Among the witnesses of this event is an old, braided Indian and an equally old sheriff; seeing Yozip's bold action, the sheriff suddenly appoints him marshal. Yozip has no time to settle into his new duties, however, because he is promptly kidnapped by a band of Indians. He is brought to the Indians' village, where he is met by the tribe's chief—the same aged Indian he had seen in the town just days earlier. The chief explains that his is a peaceful people, and that the members of the tribe have lived peacefully in their valley for many years. Now, with gold having been discovered in the nearby hills, the white men interfere with their land, their animals, and their lives. The chief speaks of the papers he signed long ago, but the white men continue to do as they please. He pleads with Yozip to join their tribe, to learn their ways so that he might speak to the white men on their behalf. "The white men must respect our ways. He must live in peace with us and not kill Indians with bad thoughts and words that burn. You must say this to them with drops of blood in your mouth."

Yozip, more through accident than skill, manages to pass a rigorous initiation test, earning the grudging respect of his fellow braves. Pleased, the old chief sends Yozip east on a train to speak to the white men in Washington on behalf of the tribe. Yozip, clad as an Indian, eventually locates the Bureau of Indian Affairs but is ill-treated and ridiculed. Disconsolate, Yozip returns, only to find that the old chief,

Joseph, is on his deathbed. With his dying words the old chief names Yozip leader of the tribe of the People.

Renamed Jozip, in honor of the passed chief, the new leader of the People is full of self-doubt. Nevertheless, he does a good job and earns the respect and friendship of his greatest rival, Indian Head. Indian Head is engaged to One Blossom, the old chief's daughter, but she is secretly in love with Jozip. It is at this time that Jozip and the People are warned by soldiers that they will have to leave their valley. Jozip argues his tribe's cause as best he can but is warned that death and destruction will await those who resist. Some members, like Indian Head, want to stay and fight, but Jozip, a pacifist at heart, decides to lead the People on a journey north to Canada. The trek is slow and hazardous, and there is much grumbling amongst the People. Indian Head in particular is angry with One Blossom's suddenly overt affection for Jozip.

Such emotions are shoved aside when the soldiers catch up to the tribe and attack them. Still, the People fight valiantly, inflicting great losses under Jozip's leadership. In the end, the people lose fourteen of their own, including One Blossom. Disheartened, Jozip is determined to make peace with the soldiers, to try to talk reasonably with them. He approaches their fort with a white flag, is shot at, and captured. By the time he is released, he knows that he has done everything within his power to save the People, and that it is not enough. In the next battle, what few members of the tribe that survive are captured and placed aboard a train that will take them to their new reservation. The story of the People ends here, although the author's notes reveal that subsequent chapters hold forth the promise of Jozip's continuing struggles to defend and redeem the people he has taken as his own.

Of the sixteen stories that follow, ten were published in magazines from 1943 to 1985. The first, "Armistice," tells the story of an old Jewish grocer who has grown discouraged and frightened by the terrible events in Europe preceding World War II. As his fears grow, so too do the taunts of Gus, a deliverer of meats whose imagination is fired by the distant Nazi conquests. The eventual confrontation, and its result, reflect a microcosm of that time's rapidly hardening positions.

"Spring Rain" is the story of George Fisher and his disappointment in his daughter, Florence. George knows that the girl lacks his sensibilities and will never get the kind of man she is seeking. Her boyfriend, Paul, during a surprise visit while Florence is out, reveals as much himself. The two men go out for a long walk in the rain, their sudden friendship and understanding for each other immediately transcending Paul's lesser relationship with Florence.

"The Literary Life of Laban Goldman" is about an elderly Jew who spends his nights in school rather than with his wife. Despite her constant whining, he is determined to not miss an evening out. In class he reads a letter he has had published in the newspaper; triumphant, he escorts a younger classmate to a cafe for coffee. His wife and daughter discover him there, bury him with false accusations, and cause Laban to rue the life he has chosen.

"The Grocery Store" is set near the end of a pair of long and unhappy lives. Sam and Ida have watched their business slowly fail, and their spirits with it. Ida blames Sam for everything, but reconsiders when an accident with the gas radiator nearly takes him from her.

Manly pride in the face of financial ruin is the subject of both "The Place Is Different Now" and "An Apology." In the former, a down-and-out diabetic, possibly retarded, seeks a kindness he has never known, and in the latter, an abused peddler stands watch before a policeman's house until he has received what he considers a suitable apology.

In "Riding Pants," a butcher's son learns the harsh reality of his existence when he loses both his prized riding pants and his dreams of a world he will never know. Similar in tone is "A Confession of Murder," in which a son dreams of murdering his hated father. So convinced is he of his crime that he turns himself over to the police, the subsequent inquiry revealing the depths of his insanity.

"The Elevator" takes place in Italy, where a retired American must solve a conflict between his maid and an imperious landlady. The resulting hardening of positions, and eventual capitulation, reveal as much about the two cultures as about the warring participants.

In "An Exorcism," an older, moderately successful writer befriends a younger, struggling would-be author. Fogel is skeptical of the younger man's talent, but Gary is both earnest and respectful. Through a long and troubling correspondence, Fogel eventually begins to learn that he is being used; when a story that openly mocks him is published by Gary, he feels betrayed. Finally, in an attempt to prove his friendship, Gary visits Fogel and reads him a long, disturbing story. Fogel's final act says as much for his own creativity as it does for Gary's lack of the same.

"A Wig" chronicles a woman's heartbreak as she suddenly begins to lose her hair. Trapped in her own fears, she lashes out at her daughter who, at twenty-eight, refuses to think about marriage or her career. In the end, Ida's despair is tempered by the knowledge that her daughter's hair, and youth, are vanishing, too.

In "Zora's Noise," a cellist's second wife inexplicably begins to hear a strange, high-pitched sound; as the noise escalates, so does the woman's anger. Her husband and their neighbors hear nothing. Finally, to his surprise, the cellist both hears the noise and sees an apparition of his first wife.

The last two stories, "In Kew Gardens" and "Alma Redeemed," are examples of Malamud's interest in fictive biographies and represent his own need for a stylistic departure. The first is a journey into the imagination of Virginia Woolf, while the second is about Gustav Mahler's wife, Alma, and her ability to communicate with her former husband's ghost.

Bernard Malamud, author of such classics as *The Natural*, *The Assistant*, and *Dubin's Lives*, had completed sixteen of twenty projected chapters of a novel to be entitled *The People* upon his death in 1986; his notes reveal that he was nearing a conclusion, and it is indeed likely that a finished novel would have been able to join his other works in both stature and readability. As it is, *The People* is more than ably written, moving, and at times hilarious. There are sections that appear to be less finished than others, but these small imperfections in an otherwise fine tale should be seen as rare insight into a distinguished author's craft.

The sixteen stories that follow *The People* span forty years of Malamud's life and reveal, through their greatly varying styles and locales, evidence of the author's growth and development during a long career. Particularly interesting are the last two stories of the volume, "In Kew Gardens" and "Alma Redeemed." In these richly imaginative tales the reader can foresee Malamud's determination to continue the experimentation and daring that signaled the beginning of his career. Also of interest is "A Confession of Murder," a self-contained story that is actually the opening section of a discarded novella titled *The Man Nobody Could Lift*. Its themes, which revolve around the desparate, often impossible requirements of communication, would eventually find fruition in *God's Grace* (1982).

Bertie Sweet

POLAR STAR

Author: Martin Cruz Smith (1942–   )
Publisher: Random House (New York). 386 pp. $19.95
Type of work: Novel
Time: The present
Locale: The Bering Sea

When a murdered girl's body is brought up in the fishing nets of the Polar
Star, *a Soviet factory ship, a former senior investigator for homicide in Moscow, Arkady Renko, comes painfully back to life as a detective*

> Principal characters: ˙
> ARKADY RENKO, a former senior investigator of homicide for
>   the militia in Moscow
> ZINA PATIASHVILI, the murder victim
> KARP KOROBETZ, the ship's model worker, a brutal criminal
>   whom Arkady had sent to Siberia
> SUSAN HIGHTOWER, an American representative on board the
>   *Polar Star*
> ANTON HESS, the "fleet electrical engineer," in reality a naval
>   intelligence officer aboard the *Polar Star*

The *Polar Star* is a Soviet ship that, as part of a joint U.S.-Soviet
venture, processes the fish that U.S. trawlers catch. It carries a crew
of 300, including 50 women, and 4 American observers. When the
body of a woman from the ship, Zina Patiashvili, is brought up in one
of the nets, Arkady Renko, who works on the "slime line" processing
fish in the bowels of the ship, is asked to investigate. Thus Martin Cruz
Smith continues the story of Renko from his earlier novel *Gorky Park*,
in which Renko was introduced as a chief inspector of homicide in
Moscow. Throughout this novel, bits and pieces of the previous two
years of Renko's life are explained. After a terrifying stay in a psychiatric unit, Renko is rescued and heads for Siberia. He works as a night
watchman and in a slaughterhouse, moving every time he sees signs of
official interest in him. When the novel opens, he has been at sea for
ten months without setting foot on land.

Partly because of the presence of the Americans, but also because
they know they must present a report when the ship finally returns to
Vladivostok, the captain, Marchuk, and the ship's political officer,
Volovoi, ask Renko's help in investigating the death. Renko agrees to
spend one day asking questions. Accompanied by Slava Bukovsky,
the third mate, he sees the Americans on the *Polar Star*. Renko has
determined that Zina died on the night of a dance during which one of
the U.S. ships was tied alongside the *Polar Star*. He visits the *Eagle*
and speaks to Captain Morgan and three crew members, Coletti, Rid-

ley, and Mike. Renko's questions on the *Eagle* and later on the *Polar Star* reveal that Zina was promiscuous and that she was on deck, waving, every time the *Eagle* was transferring fish to the *Polar Star*.

Renko and Slava make their report to Marchuk, Volovoi, and Anton Hess, a man who is introduced to Renko as the fleet electrical engineer. Slava explains the death as a regrettable accident and recommends that any further investigation be left for the authorities in Vladivostok. When asked to sign the report, Renko refuses, explaining that Zina could not have fainted and then flipped over a railing that would have come up to her ribs, that her body did not show signs of drowning, and that both the bruises and the knife wound on her body occurred after death. Although Slava and Volovoi argue against it, the captain and Hess urge Renko to continue investigating. To their surprise, Renko refuses.

That night Renko realizes that the possibility of investigating has made him feel alive again. The next day he approaches Anton Hess for advice, intimating that an investigation might uncover things not related to the murder. Hess reassures Renko, telling him that Renko should seek him out if he has any doubts or concerns. Renko determines from their conversational cat-and-mouse game that Hess is a member of naval intelligence, not the KGB.

Renko searches Zina's cabin and asks one of her roommates, Natasha Chaikovskaya, to assist him in his investigation. A large woman with "nice eyes, as black as Stalin's but nice," she is at first suspicious but flattered. She agrees to help him.

Renko finds among Zina's things a collection of playing cards, all the queen of hearts. Zina's rock-music tapes contain taped conversations as well. Renko hears a man singing Russian thieves' songs; a younger Russian voice that talks about a warm, humidity-controlled place on the ship; and an American voice that Renko identifies as Mike, the man from the *Eagle*.

Renko looks for the place on the ship that was described on Zina's tape but is attacked by several men. A gasoline-soaked gag is placed in his mouth, a sack is pulled over his head, and he is thrust into the icy freezer section of the ship. Natasha hears him laughing—drunk on gasoline fumes—and rescues him.

Renko encounters the ship's trawlmaster, Karp Korobetz, and suddenly recognizes him as a man he sent to prison years before. Although Korobetz tells Renko he is reformed, he also tells him that a ship at sea is a dangerous place and that Renko should be careful.

The *Polar Star* goes into the Alaskan port of Dutch Harbor, the highlight of the trip for many of the Russians, who are eager to purchase American goods. Although Renko does not have the papers that would allow him to go ashore, Hess takes him along. Renko has a few drinks and accompanies Susan Hightower to her room. Looking out the window, he notices Mike, the man from the *Eagle*, walking away from town. Renko follows him. By the time Renko arrives at an abandoned artillery gun battery, he finds Mike dead. Volovoi and Korobetz come in and beat Renko. When Volovoi says that they will tear the ship apart to find something against Renko, Korobetz stabs Volovoi and in his fight with Renko sets the gun battery ablaze. Korobetz locks Renko in, but there is an escape hatch (Renko decides that it was used by Mike's killer), and Renko makes use of it.

Back on the *Polar Star*, which is heading for the Arctic ice, Zina's death has been declared a suicide based on a note that Slava found. Renko no longer has any official reason to investigate, but he discovers the secret compartment on the ship, which proves to be an intelligence station used by Hess. Hess explains that the *Polar Star* is towing a sonar cable that allows him to identify U.S. submarines.

After more questioning, Renko discovers that Zina's queen-of-hearts cards represented lovers—she would collect a queen from each lover. He also discovers that she was involved in a drug-smuggling operation run by Korobetz and the Americans on the *Eagle*.

The *Polar Star* slows to a stop because the sonar cable has become entangled on the ocean floor. The crew holds an impromptu dance, during which Renko leaves; trying to avoid Korobetz, he ends up spending the night with Susan Hightower. In the morning the ship is surrounded by ice, and radio contact with the *Eagle* has been lost.

Renko starts off across the ice toward the *Eagle*, using a compass for guidance. Although he hears someone behind him, he continues doggedly on, but before he reaches the other ship he looks back to see Korobetz closing in on him, carrying an ax. They board the *Eagle* unseen by the crew members. Renko suddenly realizes that Korobetz was the man singing on Zina's tape, the man she lived with before she joined the ship. Korobetz wants to kill Renko, but first he wants to find out who killed Zina.

Renko has figured out that Zina was killed aboard the *Eagle*, not the *Polar Star*, and hidden there before being thrown overboard. The marks on her body indicated the size and shape of the place she was hidden. Renko and Korobetz search the *Eagle* together for the spot. Renko finds an intelligence station and realizes that the station on the *Eagle* contains an acoustic transmitter rather than a receiver. "The outline of a wonderful joke was taking shape. . . . The disks were recordings, and all the submarines on them had been decommissioned or dismantled. Morgan and Hess were circling the Bering Sea, one spy sending false signals for another spy to collect in triumph."

In Ridley's cabin, Renko finds a pack of playing cards. Korobetz is distraught when he realizes that the queen of hearts is missing and that Ridley must have given it to Zina after sleeping with her (in fact, Renko has palmed the card). They find the storage locker where Zina's body had been hidden just as Ridley, Coletti, and Morgan appear. Ridley admits that Zina was on the *Eagle*. She wanted to defect to the Americans, but Ridley thought that the success of the drug-smuggling operation depended on everything else remaining normal. Morgan orders Ridley to let Renko go; Coletti shoots and wounds Morgan. Ridley stabs Renko with an ice pick, but Korobetz, enraged at the realization that Ridley killed Zina, sinks a grappling hook into Ridley and kills him. Morgan and Coletti agree to radio the *Polar Star* that Korobetz and Renko are on their way back.

The two set off over the ice, smoking and talking companionably, until they reach a hole in the ice, probably made by a polar bear attacking a seal coming up for air. Korobetz attacks Renko and manages to get his head into the icy water, but Renko rolls over and holds the ice pick at Korobetz's throat. They stop fighting, and Korobetz concludes that if he goes back to the *Polar Star* he will eventually be arrested for the smuggling scheme and sent back to a prison camp. He strips, revealing a body covered with tattoos, before diving headfirst into the water.

Renko makes it back to the ship. As they finally arrive in Russia, Marchuk tells Renko that "on the radio they're starting to refer to you as *Investigator* Renko, whatever that suggests." Renko answers, "It could mean anything"; in the sunrise, out of the haze, he finally sees the shores of home.

Martin Cruz Smith has written a gripping novel that is much more than the sum of its parts. The detective story is intricately plotted, and the reader is given insight into Renko's deductions. However, finding out who killed Zina is less gripping than following the story of Renko's psychological rebirth. The setting becomes almost another character in the novel, as the reader is vividly shown the dank hold of the ship, the cold sea waters covered with mist, and the white, featureless landscape of the ice. Characters, setting, plot, and dialogue all combine to create a novel that the reader races to finish, and yet, perversely, is sorry to see end.

Elizabeth J. Jewell

A PRAYER FOR OWEN MEANY

Author: John Irving (1942–   )
Publisher: William Morrow and Co. (New York). 543 pp. $19.95
Type of work: Novel
Time: 1950s–1980s
Locale: Gravesend, New Hampshire; Toronto

A contemporary parable about the nature of faith, fate, and miracles

> *Principal characters:*
> OWEN MEANY, a "chosen one," the diminutive son of a quarry
> owner
> JOHN WHEELWRIGHT, the narrator and Owen's best friend

John Irving's *A Prayer for Owen Meany*, in the finest tradition of New England literature, takes on major philosophical and political questions such as faith, predestination, and the Vietnam War, yet still captures the flavor of the New England landscape and the character of the region's people. Like Irving's previous novels, it is both humorous and tender. The author's first line sets the tone for the rest of the novel:

> I am doomed to remember a boy with a wrecked voice—not because of his
> voice, or because he was the smallest person I ever knew, or even because
> he was the instrument of my mother's death, but because he is the reason
> I believe in God; I am a Christian because of Owen Meany.

The book's narrator is John Wheelwright, the descendant of the founder of Gravesend, New Hampshire. He is the son of the alluring Tabitha Wheelwright and an unknown father; the circumstances of his conception remain a mystery.

The land around Gravesend had been purchased by the Rev. John Wheelwright from an Indian sagamore named Watahantowet, whose totem was an armless man. This totem is one of the many symbols in the narrative that prefigure Owen Meany's fate. Others include an armadillo, a dressmaker's dummy, and a statue of Mary Magdalene.

The reader's first view of Owen Meany, John Wheelwright's best friend, is as a ten- or eleven-year-old boy being passed around over the heads of his Sunday-school classmates. Owen has two readily distinguishing characteristics. One is his diminutive stature, and the second is an extremely high-pitched voice, a condition that will never change. Some, like John's grandmother, believe that his voice has been ruined by exposure to dust from the Meany granite quarry and monument shop. Owen Meany has two loves: baseball and John's mother. These two fatefully cross paths when Owen accidentally kills Tabitha Wheelwright when he hits a foul ball during a Little League baseball game. She had stopped for a moment on the sidelines to meet the eyes of someone in the stands. John and Owen believe that it must have been John's father.

Owen, devastated by the accident, gives John his prized collection of baseball cards. John's stepfather, Dan Needham, explains that this is only a gesture and that they cannot be kept. John in turn gives Owen his precious stuffed armadillo, which Owen returns minus its front claws. The armadillo has come to symbolize Owen; it is telling John that, "GOD HAS TAKEN YOUR MOTHER. MY HANDS WERE THE INSTRUMENT. GOD HAS TAKEN MY HANDS. I AM GOD'S INSTRUMENT." As the reader learns later, "Owen didn't believe in coincidences. Owen Meany believed that 'coincidence' was a stupid, shallow refuge sought by stupid, shallow people who were unable to accept the fact that their lives were shaped by a terrifying and awesome design." From his earliest childhood, Owen and his parents have believed that he is a "chosen one" specially selected to carry out the work of the Lord. His parents contend that he is the product of a virgin birth. This claim has led to their banishment from the Catholic Church.

After the death of John's mother, life goes on for the two boys. Gravesend is populated by a colorful assortment of New England characters whose portraits enliven the novel. Among the artfully etched characters are John's cousins from the North Country—Noah, Simon, and Hester. Noah is very physical, dull, and normal; he devotes his childhood to rough play and beating up his younger brother. Irving finds the essence of Simon's character in one sentence: "Simon loved to fall—he skied to crash." Hester is the neglected and abused younger sister in a male-centered household. She harbors vast amounts of sexual aggression and family animosity. She becomes promiscuous as a teenager, Owen Meany's girlfriend as a young woman, and eventually "Hester the Molester," the queen of hard rock. The family's pet is the unforgettable Firewater, the possessor of unbelievably bad breath.

What will become one of the most memorable periods of John and Owen's childhood is the Christmas that Owen plays the Christ Child in a Sunday-school pageant and the Ghost of the Future in Dickens's *A Christmas Carol*. He completely reinterprets both roles. Owen portrays the Christ Child as being born "miraculously," but this Christ also makes certain demands.

> Not only does he demand to be worshiped and adored—by peasants and royalty, by animals and his own parents—but he also banishes his mother and father from the house of prayer and song itself. I will never forget the inflamed color of his bare skin in the winter cold . . . a vision of the little

Lord Jesus as a born victim, born raw, born bandaged, born angry and accusing.

As Dickens's silent ghost, he terrifies the audience, but, in a fever, he also has a terrifying vision: he sees his own grave with the date of his death.

Despite the fact that Owen Meany now knows his fate, he has a relatively normal adolescence. Since he will no longer touch a baseball, his favorite physical activity is working on a routine in which Owen and John run down a basketball court, John picks up Owen and has him dunk the ball in under three seconds. Owen, who is very bright, also writes "The Voice" column for the Gravesend Academy newspaper and is an outstanding student. Since John is not a good student, Owen, whose tuition is being paid by John's grandmother, becomes his intellectual mentor. His chief concern is that John learn how to be a good reader and that he acquire faith. He makes it a point to remind John that, "JUST BECAUSE A BUNCH OF ATHEISTS ARE BETTER WRITERS THAN THE GUYS WHO WROTE THE BIBLE DOESN'T MAKE THEM *RIGHT*! (Owen's voice is rendered in capital letters throughout the book to indicate how grating and strange it is.)

By the time the boys are seniors at the academy, Owen knows three things: that his voice will not change, when he is going to die, and that he is God's instrument. What he is waiting to learn is why his voice will not change, what he is supposed to do, and when he is supposed to do it. Meanwhile, Owen becomes a thorn in the side of the academy's new headmaster and eventually is expelled. As his final act at the school he asks the rather cowardly Rev. Mr. Merrill to say a prayer for him in front of the whole student body, defying the headmaster. In his life's single act of courage, Merrill leads the prayer for Owen Meany.

Expelled shortly before graduation, Owen loses his scholarships. He applies for an ROTC scholarship to the University of New Hampshire because he needs the money and because he now has learned more about his fate. He has a dream in which he, as a first lieutenant, dies saving a group of Asian children. He now must prepare to meet his fate. Against the background of the expanding Vietnam War, he becomes an avid student of military science. He also is Hester's lover, a summer quarry worker, and John's mentor in matters of faith.

Since Owen believes that his fate awaits him in Vietnam, he applies for a combat branch of the army upon graduation, but much to his frustration, he is assigned to be a casualty assistance officer in Arizona. He escorts home the bodies of men killed in Vietnam. He helps John evade the draft by cutting off a section of his trigger finger with a diamond saw.

As the day approaches when he is fated to die, he is increasingly frustrated. He has learned some Vietnamese so he can help save the children and has kept himself in good shape, but he is not in Vietnam. He invites John to Arizona to help him understand why God's plan is not unfolding. He then tells John about his dream and the fact that John was in the dream but that he had talked him into cutting off his finger to avoid fate.

On the predestined day of his death, Owen and John go to the airport to escort the body of a man killed in Vietnam. As the body is unloaded, the plane also disgorges a group of Vietnamese orphans. When the grief-crazed brother of the dead soldier throws a grenade at Owen, John, and the children, Owen yells in Vietnamese for them to get down; they listen because his voice is high pitched like theirs. Then John and Owen learn why they spent hours learning to dunk a basketball in under three seconds: they succeed in getting the grenade up and away from the children. Only Owen is killed. His life has met its fated end.

After Owen's death, with clues that Owen left for him, John discovers that the Rev. Mr. Merrill is his father. Also with inspiration from Owen, John is able to use a trick to bring his father back his lost faith. John then leaves America and the curse of the Vietnam War behind and goes to Canada.

A Prayer for Owen Meany is a profoundly religious book. It explores the questions of faith, fate, and miracles in a contemporary setting and comes down on the side of Christianity and revealed religion. Irving's theology may, at times, be a bit idiosyncratic, but the strength of his faith comes through in this novel.

Owen Meany is an angel who helped to bring life and faith to those around him. Some of his last words were, "WHOSOEVER LIVETH AND BELIEVETH IN ME SHALL NEVER DIE." And at the very end, as he rose up to heaven, he let John know that, "YOU'RE GETTING SMALLER, BUT I CAN STILL SEE YOU!" Owen Meany was a profoundly modern angel—blessed but not sweet. In creating him, Irving drew both a memorable character and an example of living faith.

Even those for whom questions of faith are not particularly pertinent will find *A Prayer for Owen Meany* entertaining reading. Few modern authors populate their books with such a compelling cast of minor characters and such a wonderful assortment of humorous vignettes.

Christine Brendel Scriabine

THE PRICE OF EMPIRE

Author: J. William Fulbright (1905–   ) with Seth P. Tillman
Publisher: Pantheon Books (New York). 243 pp. $17.95
Type of work: Essays

A collection of commentaries on national affairs since World War II, the U.S. constitutional system, and foreign affairs

In the first essay, "The Cold War: The U.S. and the U.S.S.R.," Fulbright examines relations between the United States and the Soviet Union, proposing some improvements for the future. He argues that pervasive hostility toward the Soviets is not a U.S. reaction to communism, as he once believed, but rather an expression of aggressive competition toward a rival. The U.S. attitude toward other communist nations reveals no similar intensity of dislike. A contest for power is a dangerous self-indulgence in the nuclear age. Americans must change their thinking, as the world has changed. This means recognizing that the new weapons systems allow no winners in a contest. The United States must abandon both its claims to moral superiority and its denial of selfish motives. Such a condescending pose cannot help but be offensive and provocative to the Soviets.

Since World War II the "cold-war school" of thought, with its insistence that the United States and the Soviets are absolute enemies, has dominated foreign policy. Experience shows that no problem can be solved and no cooperation can be sustained if the fundamental expectation is treachery. Less consideration has been given to the "détente school" of thought, which says that Soviet behavior since Stalin has been more pragmatic and cooperative than Soviet rhetoric would suggest. Each time Soviet-American relations have shown signs of improvement, something unforeseen has happened to hamper détente. Nevertheless, progress has been made, most importantly the ABM (antiballistic missile) treaty of 1972.

Recent changes in Soviet leadership and U.S. policies offer promise for improved relations. Americans need not approve of the Soviet system to cooperate in keeping the two nations from the economic disaster of endless weapons systems. Each can compete constructively to improve the quality of life in both countries, and if democracy is the superior system, surely it will become apparent. A prerequisite to a peaceful future is an attitude of confidence that the two nations can coexist, negotiate disputes, and cooperate. It is a mutual obligation to the world.

One of the issues Fulbright would have liked to debate when he was a senator is the merits of the principle of separation of powers. In

"Our Constitutional and Political Impasse," Fulbright discusses the advantages he sees in the parliamentary system and the problems created in the U.S. system when one party has legislative control and the other executive control. When the executive is one party and the legislature the other, the result is debate without resolution, stalemate, and failure to assume responsibility on both sides. The close-knit elite who originally designed the Constitution has long since given way to a heterogeneous populace more concerned with individual rights than with political unity. Political action committees promoting special interests have gained the strength lost by the political parties. Without continuity in legislative leadership, there is little sense of a national interest upon which to build a foreign policy. Presidential agreements with other countries are in doubt until approved, or attempts are made to circumvent the need for legislative approval. The outcome is mutual disrespect between executive and legislature.

Under a parliamentary system, the country would be divided into districts whose elected representatives would then elect a leader. Such a system assures the election of an experienced leader, accountable to his or her peers and the public. It also mitigates the influence of special-interest groups and ends the practice of packaging presidential candidates for media. A leader who loses the confidence of the people can be easily replaced without disruption, and experienced representatives need not choose between keeping elected positions and making bids for leadership.

In "Vietnam Revisited" Fulbright looks back with some regrets at his role in the tragedy of Vietnam. Until the early 1960s, neither Fulbright nor anyone else in the Senate was particularly interested in or knowledgeable about the conflict in Vietnam or the U.S. role as advisers. In retrospect, Fulbright wishes that he had held hearings when President Johnson argued for the quick approval of the Gulf of Tonkin resolution in 1964. The inquiry of 1967 by the Senate Foreign Relations Committee revealed the misrepresentation underlying the Tonkin resolution. As Fulbright learned more, he argued privately with Johnson against escalation, and in 1965 he sent the president a memo, favoring a unified Vietnam under Ho Chi Minh over a weak democracy. When Fulbright made his criticism public, Johnson broke off relations. Throughout the rest of the war there was little Fulbright could do except to hold hearings where opposition could be voiced. Fulbright also came to believe that China was not trying to take over Southeast Asia. The U.S. experience in Vietnam should have demonstrated that U.S. values cannot be imposed on another society; the price of such vanity is too high.

In "Our Militarized Economy," Fulbright examines all the damaging repercussions of an economic policy that has given military spending top priority since World War II. For a politician even to question defense policies and budgets guarantees a charge that he is unpatriotic. In the public mind, and with the help of Defense Department public relations, military spending has become synonymous with security and survival. The United States has created weapons systems beyond the point of redundancy, to be in a position of strength to negotiate arms reduction with the Soviets, who have been doing the same thing. Only recently have both nations confronted the neglect of other areas of technology and domestic programs. Military and space programs have monopolized some of the finest minds as well as wielding enormous power over resources. Ordinary working people, contractors, and corporations all have a vested interest in maintaining weapons production, not only for the nation's defense but also for sale around the world. With an enormous federal debt and a poor competitive position in the technological marketplace, only decisive presidential action can prevent economic collapse and restore the world's respect.

A combination of idealism and self-interest has led the United States to intervene in the affairs of countries in and out of its declared sphere of influence in Latin America. "Intervention" discusses U.S. policies and actions in Lebanon in 1958, Cuba, the Dominican Republic, Nicaragua, Guatemala, and Iran. Fear of communism, as well as the mistaken belief that the Soviet Union was orchestrating every revolutionary movement, has been a major reason for intervening, but not the only one. Others include a failure to acknowledge the rights of other countries to shape their own affairs, a desire for economic control where there are U.S. investments, and an overestimation of its own power. The nation can protect its own citizens by removing them, rather than by using their safety as a pretext to send in troops. Interventions, both overt and covert, have gained little and cost much, and in many cases have been of dubious value to the countries involved. Foreign aid given through the United Nations and the World Bank is a way of giving assistance free of political interference.

In "The Middle East," Fulbright sees little hope of a general settlement to end the conflicts of the past decades. He supports the outline of a settlement put forth in the Security Council Resolution 242 of 1967. In such a settlement, Israel's right to exist is explicitly acknowledged, the Palestinians gain self-determination, all have equal access to the old city of Jerusalem, Israel withdraws to its 1967 borders, and the United Nations and great powers guarantee all these provisions. One major obstacle to settlement is Israel's intransigence regarding Palestine and its own borders. The other is Israel's control of U.S. policy on the Middle East through highly effective and well-financed lobbies. An objective analysis of all interests has been impossible. Possibly the improved relations between the United States and the Soviet Union can lead to an end of the impasse and the achievement of some agreement.

"Seeing the World as Others See It" is Fulbright's eloquent plea for empathy among the nations of the world. Despite humankind's long tradition of fighting and dying, all the while professing the noblest intentions, Fulbright sees a possibility for peace if Americans can develop enough imagination to perceive the world from standpoints other than their own. As a first step, this requires humanizing any discussion of armed conflict so that everyone is conscious that human lives, not statistical abstractions, are the issue. A working, vital United Nations, supported by all its members, can effectively keep the peace and negotiate differences. Fundamental changes in attitude among nations depend on leaders whose education includes some experience living in other countries. The Fulbright scholarship program was developed in the 1940s with this goal in mind. An understanding of another culture's history and experience can alleviate misunderstanding of its motives, fears, and ambitions. The future depends not on strategy and expertise but on leadership in compassion and tolerance.

The persuasive power of Fulbright's essays lies in his reasoned, thoughtful tone. Looking back at events and personalities, he never slips into good-old-days sentiment nor lapses into bitterness. His harshest words are for John Foster Dulles, whereas events have led him to increased respect for Dwight Eisenhower. His critical analysis of the past provides direction for the future. Perhaps his most disturbing observations are the frequent admissions that political realities so often prevent honest debate of issues. His cautious optimism for the future is not just wishful thinking. For every problem he discusses, he offers an approach or solution for leaders who have the courage to take it.

The common thread connecting Fulbright's assessment of the past and his proposals for a better future is his recognition that the nation's "childhood" is over. The future demands maturity, free from selfish bullying, name-calling, and blaming the other fellow. Fulbright's advice, a national change of attitude, is the antithesis of the politically popular quick-fix. Those in power in the United States ought to heed the words of this clear-thinking and articulate elder statesman.

E. P. Tischer

PROFESSOR ROMEO

Author: Anne Bernays (1930–)
Publisher: Weidenfeld and Nicholson (New York). 277 pp. $18.95
Type of work: Novel
Time: 1960s–1980s
Locale: Harvard University

A witty, caustic tale of a Harvard professor's sexual indiscretions with students and the subsequent penalties

> *Principal characters:*
> JACOB BARKER, a Harvard professor of psychology
> NANCY, Jacob's first wife
> GUY, Jacob's son
> SUSAN, Jacob's second wife
> ANITA ANDREWS, Jacob's girlfriend, later the Dean of Women's Affairs
> BENNIE, Jacob's closest friend
> OTTO VON STAMPLER, Jacob's mentor in graduate school
> DEAN FROMME, the Dean of Arts and Sciences at Harvard
> PATRICIA WEISSMAN, ELAINE FERRIER, KATHLEEN PETERS, three students who bring charges against Jacob

In the fall of 1985, Jacob Barker, known as Jake, receives notice from the Dean of Arts and Sciences at Harvard University that he must answer allegations of sexual harassment. Jake is forty-five, married, a professor in the psychology department, and author of a successful book. His conduct with female students, termed "inappropriate" and "unwelcome," will be the subject of a closed hearing, and suitable, although unspecified, penalties may be imposed. With good reason, Jake is distressed. His lively and varied sexual exploits originated in his days as a Harvard graduate student and have continued, with few lapses, for two decades.

Jake sits in his office contemplating his past. As a young man in the early 1960s, Jake could easily identify his assets. He was proud of his thick, sandy hair; his trim physique; and, above all, his irresistible blue eyes. Moreover, his attractive body was matched with a brilliant mind. In his first year of graduate school, he became the protégé of Professor Otto Von Stampler, a former disciple of Freud. Early on, Jake published in scholarly journals and became the youngest teaching assistant. Von Stampler was confident that Jake, if anyone, would be the one to identify the basic differences between the sexes. Jake was flattered when Von Stampler offered him lodging in his home in exchange for household chores but hastened to invent an excuse for declining. Such an arrangement would preclude his busy, indispensable sexual conquests of three or four different girls a week. Giving parties was Jake's response to the possible envy other graduate students might feel toward his charmed life.

Among Jake's girlfriends, Nancy Swan, a graduate student in anthropology, had an indefinable attraction beyond her beauty and intelligence. Jake thought he might be in love and want to marry Nancy, although his friend Bennie disparaged the notion that Jake could enjoy a lifetime with any one female. Jake gradually discarded his other girls in favor of Nancy. Bennie thought Jake equally foolish to marry Nancy when she became pregnant and would not consider abortion. Jake and Nancy had a small wedding in Von Stampler's garden and spent a rainy honeymoon in Cape Cod.

Despite their crowded apartment, a shortage of money, and Nancy's miscarriage, Jake was fairly content and wanted the marriage to succeed. Nancy worked intensely toward her doctorate degree, and Jake commiserated when she failed to get a fellowship. By 1968, Jake was a popular assistant professor, enjoying his teaching and the turmoil on campus as the students, with whom he sympathized, registered their protests by destruction. At home he resented Nancy's obsession with their baby son, Guy. He knew that their differences would divide them sooner or later. To salve his feelings of jealousy and neglect, he feigned an advisory interest in a freshman, Patty Weissman. Over coffee, he flattered her intelligence and persuaded her to go to a motel. He could not tell if her reluctance was coy or genuine, but his own passion was near impossible to revive after he saw her emaciated body.

It was ten more years before Nancy and Jake agreed to divorce. Guy, at ten, appeared to be the victim of their unhappiness; he was overweight, unable to make friends, and failing in school. Jake moved to his own apartment and countered the loneliness by eating out and seeing Anita Andrews, an assistant professor in the psychology department and one of two female professors. Her work on adult gender roles complemented Jake's research on developmental differences in intelligence in the sexes. Besides being intelligent and passionate, Anita was direct in speech, generous by nature, and less emotionally volatile than Nancy. Jake even considered abandoning student seductions.

Thanks to the retired Von Stampler's recommendation, Jake gained tenure and the rank of associate professor while many of his colleagues were let go. However, as he approached forty, he knew that his achievements did not match his early promise. Anita suggested that Jake write a book that she would help edit. More than simply editing his manuscript, Anita recast Jake's research conclusions from a feminist perspective. Jake did not object to this tone nor to the relegation of statistics to appendices, although he took a more objective view of laboratory findings. He hoped the book would give him the income to pay the increased bills for Guy's psychiatrist and special diet, with some left over for himself. With a literary agent, publisher, and editor, Jake completed his book, *Cleopatra's Nose.*

Jake was in the doldrums after he finished the book. He and Anita drifted apart as she made a successful effort to become Harvard's first Dean of Women's Affairs. Calling to congratulate her, Jake was disturbed by her fierce intention to discover and punish those guilty of sexual harassment. He knew she would not agree with his opinion that those professors who avoided sexual involvement with students did so from fear rather than moral integrity. She also misunderstood the mutuality of these sexual exchanges; there was neither force nor victim.

Jake's life was unsettling in other respects. Guy asked to change schools and confessed that he was gay. As he expected, Jake had no luck convincing Nancy to take Guy at his word. Two student affairs ended badly. Jake's seduction of Elaine Ferrier, a student who wanted advice and a recommendation for graduate school, was slow and deliberate. His fantasy died a sudden death at the sight of Elaine's abdominal scar of which he felt she should have warned him. Then Kathleen Peters not only spoiled their rendezvous with her ill-timed menstrual cycle, but informed Jake that on campus he was known as Professor Romeo.

In the meantime, Jake had several meetings with Susan Cheng, who was planning the promotional tour for his book. She was young, beautiful, and ambitious. Jake fell in love. They married, despite a twenty-year age difference and her mother's opposition. For a year, love and determination kept Jake at the proper distance from his students. They bought a house with book profits, and Susan became pregnant. He could even afford to have a student, Billy Forest, live in and help out. Jake was a fixture at Harvard when Dean Fromme's notice arrived, throwing him into turmoil.

At first, Jake cannot bring himself to confide in Susan. He does tell his friend Bennie, who is sympathetic but surprised by Jake's willingness to risk career and family so often and so foolishly. In a meeting with Fromme, Jake learns that Anita has affidavits from Patricia Weissman, Elaine Ferrier, and Kathleen Peters, charging an exchange of sex for grades. With unexpected aplomb, Jake flatly denies the accusations and receives Fromme's hearty support and advice to call a lawyer. Eventually he repeats the accusations and his denials to Susan. She wants to be supportive but becomes emotionally distant and preoccupied by her pregnancy. The therapist that she insists Jake see can do little because Jake has no desire to give up his sexual exploits. Still awaiting the hearing, Jake visits Guy, who has been injured in an accident that appears to have been a suicide attempt.

The hearing takes place in Dean Fromme's office. Anita Andrews is in charge, calling her witnesses for testimony that is predictable. Jake is not allowed to have a lawyer present, so he interrupts, questions, and denies as best he can. Most of the time, Susan sits dutifully by his side. Dean Fromme continues the pretense that he is in control of the process. A few days later, the outcome is announced and newspaper headlines proclaim Jake's dismissal. Susan stays until their daughter, Lily, is born and then leaves to stay with her mother. Jake tries to write but collapses in lethargy in his empty house, where Guy visits him and suggests a similarity in their positions as social outcasts. Unable or unwilling to change, as Guy advises, Jake thinks he will just "honor his true nature."

Jake Barker is the quintessential reprobate. Neither tragic nor pathetic, he is a small-souled figure barely worth despising. A moral void enables his seductions of students, diverting the passion and commitment that might have turned intellectual promise into achievement. He prefers the challenge and danger of seduction to the discipline of love, marriage, or career. Apparently competent in his research, he does not protect its integrity, preferring the financial rewards and recognition of marketable pop psychology. The cause of Jake's defective character remains as much a mystery at the novel's end as it is at the beginning, but charm and intelligence create a successful mask for half a lifetime. When his private sweat and tears subside and the guilty verdict is pronounced, the reader feels no sympathy, no satisfaction, and no curiosity about his future.

Because other characters are seen only from Barker's skewed perspective, the reader surmises, rather than feels, the emotional damage that Jake inflicts. It is a marvel that Guy never gives up searching for the paternal in Jake. Focusing on Jake's petulant disappointment, Bernays develops the seduction scenes humorously. One wonders why only these three come forward later with grievances. The opportunistic Anita, the puppet Dean Fromme, and the venerable, lascivious Von Stampler complete this caricature of academic life that makes the reader wince more often than laugh.

E. P. Tischer

THE REMAINS OF THE DAY

Author: Kazuo Ishiguro (1943–   )
Publisher: Alfred A. Knopf (New York). 245 pp. $18.95
Type of work: Novel
Time: 1920s-1956
Locale: England

> On a holiday motor trip through the countryside, an English butler remi-
> nisces about his life and work and finds himself questioning long-held values
> and beliefs

> Principal characters:
> STEVENS, the middle-aged butler of Darlington Hall
> LORD DARLINGTON, the late owner of Darlington Hall
> MISS KENTON, the former housekeeper of Darlington Hall
> MR. CARDINAL, a journalist, Lord Darlington's godson
> MR. FARRADAY, an American businessman, the new owner of
> Darlington Hall

Mr. Farraday, recent purchaser of the historic English estate Darlington Hall, believes that his staff should, occasionally, get out of the
house and see the world. At his suggestion, his butler, Stevens, the
narrator of this novel, reluctantly sets out on a six-day motor trip
through the West Country of England. Although eager to please his
new master, the old-fashioned British servant is disconcerted by the
American's jocular good humor and bantering style of conversation.
Repartee confuses Stevens, causing him to feel embarrassed and awkward. He remembers a time when visiting valets would gather before
the fire in the servants' quarters and analyze the fine points of master-
servant relations; but now, in the unlikely event that a guest were
accompanied by a valet, conversations would probably be about football and take place at the local pub.

At a rest stop outside the city of Salisbury, Stevens pauses to con-
template the understated splendor of the countryside. Comparing the
qualities of "Great" Britain to the qualities of a "great" butler, he
decides that both terrain and servant possess a fundamental restraint
and unshakableness. Unlike the dignity of a landscape, which is natural, "professional" dignity can be achieved only through years of self-
training and the diligent inhabiting of one's role.

Stevens plans to visit Mrs. Benn, formerly Miss Kenton, during his
journey. Thirty years ago, Stevens hired his own aging and ailing father as underbutler and Miss Kenton as housekeeper. Although Stevens has not seen her for twenty years, he hopes that the nostalgic
tone of her last letter—in which she mentions that she is separated
from her husband—indicates a desire to return to Darlington Hall.

Recalling with pleasure their professional relationship, Stevens puzzles over the curious unease that grew between them over the years.

He remembers one occasion especially, for it became a turning point in his acquisition of professional dignity. In 1923, during the weekend of an important international conference held at the Hall, he was in charge of serving the final banquet even as his own father lay dying upstairs. In hosting the conference, Lord Darlington's ostensible motive was to spread international goodwill and unity, but his real concern was to placate a German-hating French diplomat. Darlington wanted not only to bring peace to Europe but to rebuild a Germany devastated and disgraced by war. Much to Darlington's irritation, a cigar-smoking, boisterous American delegate privately alerted the Frenchman to the group's pacifist agenda. During the banquet, Stevens instructed Miss Kenton to nurse his father as he himself was preoccupied with matters of world import. As Stevens recalls, the evening was a triumph at which he played his role well. The French delegate ultimately rejected the arguments of the "greedy" American and pledged support for Darlington's cause. Rather than abandon his post in the dining room, Stevens asked Miss Kenton to close the eyes of his dead father. After the successful dinner, a guest informed Stevens that he had tears on his face. Surprised, the butler supposed that he was merely tired.

Stevens continues his motor trip, stopping at villages along the way and practicing his bantering skills with some success. He thinks back on the German ambassador who, although a Nazi, was a true gentleman and a frequent visitor to the Hall. Darlington instructed Stevens to "let go" the Hall's two Jewish maids in deference to his guest's "comforts." A year later, after severing his ties with the anti-Semitic Blackshirts, Darlington asked Stevens to see what he could do to relocate the women and make amends. On learning of Darlington's change of heart, Miss Kenton was shocked to discover that Stevens had always disapproved of the firing but never believed it proper to express his opinions. She confessed to moral cowardice in never having carried out her own threatened resignation.

Midway in his journey, Stevens runs out of petrol near Devon, where he is offered lodging by a pleasant local couple. Alone in his room, he reflects on the time that Miss Kenton discovered him in the privacy of his pantry reading a romance novel. He was shocked that she had intruded on him and then dared to question his reading material (chosen only for its rich and illuminating dialogue) at a time when he was clearly divested of his "role." Soon after that episode, Miss Kenton cooled to him and withdrew. In time she announced that she was keeping company with a gentleman friend from town. Recognizing that she was devoting more time to her new interests, Stevens suggested that they discontinue their evening ritual of meeting over cocoa in her parlor to discuss the events of the day. She objected strongly, but he insisted. Distressed by this particular memory, he consults Miss Kenton's letter once again. He wonders if he is mistaken in thinking that she wishes to return to the Hall.

His hospitable hosts invite neighbors to the house who engage in heated discussions about local concerns. It reminds Stevens of the time Lord Darlington called on him to answer pointed political questions posed by guests. Having no knowledge of current matters of state, Stevens admitted ignorance and was excused. Later, apologizing for having embarrassed Stevens, Darlington made his point: ordinary citizens cannot understand the complexities of modern government. Stevens agreed. He believed that his duty was to find someone whose political wisdom he trusted and give that person absolute loyalty.

When Stevens arrives at his destination, where he is to meet Miss Kenton, he recollects another incident. One evening, Mr. Cardinal, Darlington's godson and an outspoken young journalist, visited the house seeking information on a meeting to take place that night among Darlington, the German ambassador, and the prime minister to accept an invitation to visit Herr Hitler and establish diplomatic links. Stevens remembers that shortly after this incident he passed Miss Kenton's room and heard her crying softly—although she had only recently announced her engagement to her gentleman friend. He remembers feeling strangely downcast as he passed her door and continued with his duties.

His journey's end finds Stevens sitting on a pier at dusk, idly observing strangers as they stroll and banter. He relives his visit with Miss Kenton two days earlier. Although she admitted to an occasional longing for the life she "might" have lived—perhaps with Mr. Stevens—she told him she loved her husband and separated from him periodically but only temporarily, always returning and behaving sensibly. Stevens told her that soon after Darlington lost a libel suit against a newspaper he became an invalid, declining rapidly.

Striking up a conversation with a stranger, Stevens confesses that his old standards of professional excellence are hard to achieve with his new employer. He wonders how much "dignity" can be achieved by a life spent trusting to another's wisdom only, a life where one's mistakes are not even one's own. The stranger encourages him to look to the evening—the remains of the day—which is often the best part. Stevens thinks that perhaps he will work to improve his banter and pleasantly surprise Mr. Farraday.

Born in Nagasaki and reared in England, Kazuo Ishiguro is the winner of England's prestigious Booker Prize for this, his third novel. *The Remains of the Day* is a finely crafted narrative detailing the seemingly random recollections of an aging English butler as he motors through the countryside. The voice of Stevens--restrained, formal, and exquisitely polite—engages the reader with its childlike candor and heartbreaking simplicity.

This charming novel tells the story of a man who has always believed vigorously in duty and in observing one's station in life. By denying his own individuality he could hope to attain a kind of perfection in service. But when his own true nature can no longer be denied, and as old ideals cease to have meaning, perfection becomes harder to achieve. His own tears confuse him, and he has no language with which to acknowledge his feelings toward others or theirs toward him. By listening to the quiet voice within and allowing himself to find satisfaction in his less-than-perfect service for his less-than-perfect employer, Stevens will most surely find a new kind of peace in the years left to him.

While conjuring up a "perfect butler" from a vanished time of grand and gracious living, Ishiguro subtly hints at the quiet dehumanization of those whose labor made that world possible. Gentle and bittersweet, this deceptively simple tale surprises the careful reader with its depths of psychological and political implication.

Wendy DuBois

THE ROAD FROM COORAIN

Author: Jill Ker Conway
Publisher: Alfred A. Knopf (New York). 238 pp. $18.95
Type of work: Autobiography
Time: The mid-1930s to the early 1960s
Locale: Primarily Australia

Historian Jill Ker Conway, who during her adulthood has served in many distinguished academic and administrative posts in the United States, chronicles her early childhood and coming of age in Australia

Principal personages:
JILL KER CONWAY, historian and college administrator
MRS. KER, Jill's mother
MR. KER, Jill's father
BOB KER, the oldest child of the Ker family, six years older than Jill
BARRY KER, the second child of the Ker family, four years older than Jill

> On the plains, the horizon is always with us and there is no retreating from it. Its blankness travels with our every step and waits for us at every point of the compass. Because we have very few reference points on the spare earth, we seem to creep over it, one tiny point of consciousness between the empty earth and the overarching sky.

This excerpt is part of Jill Ker Conway's penetrating description of the western plains of New South Wales, a region and way of life that form a persistent subtext in her autobiography, *The Road from Coorain*. The words convey the sense of the overwhelming nature of the Australian bush as well as a person's relatively small place in the world. It implies that to make a difference, one must determine one's own goals and work at achieving them bit by bit.

In several ways, the passage is also appropriate as a metaphor for Jill's life. As portrayed in *The Road from Coorain*, Jill Ker has few—but, nevertheless, very powerful—"reference points" in a looming social and emotional landscape. The most important are her parents, her brothers, and Australia itself. As she nears adulthood, Jill's own will becomes another reference point, or guideline. Meanwhile, Jill must find her own "consciousness," that is, define her own self-image, in order to fulfill what she considers to be her potential, despite burdensome cultural and familial pressures and obstacles.

The birthplace and early childhood home for Jill is Coorain (an Aboriginal word meaning "windy place"): 18,000 acres of grassland in the Australian bush. Here "the primal force of the sun shapes the environment. . . . Painters find it hard to capture the shimmer of that warm red earth dancing in the brilliant light, and to record at the same time the subtle greens and greys of the plants and trees." Owning such a property had been Jill's father's dream for years. In 1929, taking advantage of an Australian program for "soldier settlers," he and his wife decided to try raising sheep.

Mr. Ker was a Roman Catholic, orphaned young, with "a mercurial temperament, and a wicked sense of humor that won men and women friends with ease." Mrs. Ker, antagonistic toward organized religion, was a "natural beauty" who had "boundless physical and intellectual energy. She was a 'new woman,' a professional trained nurse, used to independence and responsibility," very unusual for a young woman living in the Australia of the 1920s. Although very different from each other in background and beliefs, the couple shared a crucial bond: the drive to excel. Their tireless efforts sustained Coorain through years of drought, until they were able to luxuriate in a subsequent period of more benevolent weather and prosperity.

The Kers had, at first, two children—Bob and Barry. It was to her dismay that a few years after Barry's birth, Mrs. Ker learned that she was pregnant again. Due to benign uterine growths, her gynecologist warned her to have an abortion and a hysterectomy. In characteristic rebellion, Mrs. Ker refused. Jill Ker Conway reflects:

> Her decision certainly placed her in some danger. . . . If her gynecologist's predictions were fulfilled, help would be minimal and very slow in coming. . . . In later years, it was a tale she was fond of telling me. She did not seem to understand that I was troubled to know that on the one hand I had been unwanted, and on the other brought into the world at considerable hazard to my mother.

Despite a periodically ambiguous and troubling relationship with her mother, Jill's childhood in the bush was idyllic. The members of the family were united by their common commitment to Coorain. Mr. and Mrs. Ker were devoted, loving, and harmonious; the children were close to one another, to their parents, and to their environment. They survived the great drought of the 1930s through sheer will; the rains that came in 1939 allowed them to consolidate their gains in their homestead.

It was the drought of the early 1940s—against the backdrop of the war in the Pacific—that proved the turning point. "The unfolding of a drought of these dimensions has a slow and inexorable quality. The weather perpetually holds out hope. Storm clouds gather. Thunder rolls by. But nothing happens." Mr. Ker, watching his animals weaken and die and his land be ravaged by dust storms, began a long, painful decline. He now became silent and introspective. Jill remembers:

> One troublesome aspect of the frustration of my parents' dreams was the

extent to which they transferred their ambitions to the children. My brothers, being five hundred miles away [at school], were not readily available
as vehicles for ambition. Being at hand, I became the focus of all the
aspiration for achievement that had fueled both parents' prodigious energies.

This was a form of attention that Jill did not want.

In December 1944, when she was ten, Jill's adored father died in a
perplexing accident on Coorain; although no one verbalized the suspicion of suicide, privately the conclusion was hard to avoid. Mrs. Ker,
"somehow a ghost of herself," resolved to stay on at Coorain. In the
continuing drought, however, and in the face of death duties and other
crippling costs, she began to fall apart. The primary unwitting target
of her anguish was Jill.

Finally, Mrs. Ker was persuaded to give over the care of Coorain to
managers, and in August 1945 the diminished family settled in Sydney.
For Jill, this move was to prove both wrenching and liberating, the
beginning of a years-long, frightening journey to responsibility and
independence. "I . . . refused to pack any toys or dolls. I knew that
in most important ways my childhood was over."

During the next decade, Jill became socialized into traditional
schooling and city life and became more sophisticated regarding her
country's status in the world. It was a difficult progression, one
marked by her shyness, her mother's deterioration into depression and
bitterness, and Jill's fight against the rigid social mores that disallowed
ambitious women paths for self-fulfillment. Of particular concern to
her were her mother's increasing isolation and the world's perception
of Australia as a colonial backwater.

In Coorain the roots of Jill's essential values and capabilities had
been put down. In Sydney, she bloomed into an independent being, an
attractive and appealing young woman, and an impressive scholar.

As Jill's world vision increased, so did family pressures. A stunning
blow was the death of her golden brother Bob, at age twenty-one, in a
car accident. "He had been like the sun in my universe, and most of
my aspirations at school and in my daily life had centered on winning
his approval. Now there were not just my father's wishes to be carried
out in his absence, but Bob's too." This event caused Jill to lose
temporarily her capacity for emotional response: "intellectual tasks
. . . gave little pleasure. . . . I was haunted by the knowledge of my
mother, alone at home. I often came in to find her just sitting gazing
into space."

It took years—until Barry, Jill's surviving brother, defied his mother's wishes and took his own path, and until Jill came to understand
that her mother's unhappiness was not Jill's responsibility—for the

young woman to be able to start breaking free from her mother's controlling nature and serious emotional problems. Mrs. Ker's reactions to her daughter's individuation were varied and contradictory, at once admiring and envious, proud and raging. As Jill completed college, began the then unorthodox job for a woman of teaching history at the college level, and experienced a range of warm friendships and romances, she nevertheless all the more determinedly pursued the "world [she] really belonged in."

In the early 1960s, to pursue advanced history studies at Harvard, Jill left her native country, her friends, and her family to reach out for her own place—"a rite of passage which was both a sentence and a release. . . . I comforted myself with the notion that wherever on the earth was my final resting place, my body would return to the restless red dust of the western plains."

The strength and beauty of Jill Ker Conway's wonderful descriptions of the Australian bush prove that, although Jill left Australia and created her own unique place in the world as a respected history scholar and a longtime president of Smith College, her early environment, both natural and cultural, remains an essential and immutable part of her. All of *The Road from Coorain* is absorbing. Her observations of her world as she matures are acute; her conclusions about Australian and world history are compelling; and the reader can empathize with many of the agonizing reflections she finally must face about her role in her family and her society. Yet it is the power of her early past that constitutes the particular charm of this autobiography (whose sequel many will await anxiously). The book is a reminder that however people may grow and change, however they may achieve their special ways of living and being, the individuals and places from their childhood are part of them forever.

Lisa M. Clyde

THE RUSSIA HOUSE

Author: John le Carré (1931–   )
Publisher: Alfred A. Knopf (New York). 353 pp. $19.95
Type of work: Novel
Time: The present
Locale: London; Moscow; Leningrad; Maine

A British publishing executive, his lovely Russian counterpart, and a vision-ary Soviet scientist become pawns in a ponderous game of glasnost-era espi-onage, played out among the Soviet, British, and U.S. spy bureaucracies

> Principal characters:
> B. S. "BARLEY" BLAIR, a British publishing
>   executive
> KATYA ORLOVA, a young Soviet woman employed by
>   the State publishing house
> YAKOV SAVELYEV ("GOETHE"), a Russian scientist
> HARRY PALFREY, a legal adviser to British
>   Intelligence, and the narrator

John le Carré's latest venture is another finely crafted tale of spying: an espionage fable for the age of *glasnost*. The story begins at a trade show in Moscow, on a late summer's day. Niki Landau, a British citizen and Polish expatriate, is approached by a Russian woman; her nametag identifies her as Katya, an employee of the Soviet State pub-lisher October. Katya seeks Scott Blair, the representative of the firm Abercrombie & Blair. Upon being told by Niki that Blair has not attended the show, she importunes Landau to take a manuscript to Blair for publication. Katya hands over three notebooks and leaves.

Niki is streetwise, and so able surreptitiously to bring the notebooks back to his hotel. He examines the books and finds the first to be filled with nonsensical polemic ravings. The second and third, however, contain recognizably scientific drawings. Niki accurately assesses their importance and takes action to smuggle the books out of Russia and back to London. On returning, unable to locate Blair, he attempts to turn the books over to British Intelligence.   Various Whitehall min-istries fob him off, until an astute official puts him in touch with the Russia House, as the branch of intelligence dealing with the Soviet Union is familiarly known.

The Russia House, led by Ned (all of the spies are known only by their first names, except Harry Palfrey, the narrator and legal voice of the Russia House), put Niki through a series of interrogations for his troubles. After shrill and affected questioning from Walter, nerveless and hostile questioning from the American, Johnny, and a final admo-nition from the ambitious and secretive Clive, Niki signs the Official

Secrets Act as directed by Palfrey, and is ushered from the story as the prelude ends.

The agents now turn their attention to B. Scott "Barley" Blair. The notebooks have been scrutinized and seem to contain data showing that the Soviet missile program is beset with inaccuracy, incompetence, and an unpreparedness previously unsuspected. Blair is, therefore, a crucial cog, as he is the only connection with the woman Katya and the mysterious writer of the books, code-named Bluebird. They track Blair to Lisbon.

Barley Blair is an upper-class Englishman living the life of a wastrel. His marriages have failed and he plays at his occupation as publisher, drunkenly drifting in and out of unsatisfying relationships. Yet he has a keen mind and a natural resilience that sees him through his first round of questioning by Ned, Walter, Bob (from the CIA), and Clive.

It so happens that at an earlier book fair in Moscow, Barley had encountered an enigmatic Russian with the nickname Goethe. Barley and Goethe traded anecdotes, ideas, and dreams throughout a drunken night. Goethe, stirred by Barley's grand flights of rhetoric, announced his intention to finally take action against the foolish militarists within the USSR. Barley has not thought of this until now, when it appears that Goethe is Bluebird. The spies decide that Barley is genuine, but they must know if Bluebird is, too, or a clever Soviet trap. They enlist Barley to be their contact. Impressed by Goethe's follow-through on his intention, Barley agrees. After a rapid training program, he goes to Moscow.

In Moscow, Blair calls Katya and identifies himself. Katya checks with the mysterious Goethe, who is pleased that Blair has come. Katya and Blair meet; he is struck by her beauty and poise under pressure. According to plan, he grills her, eliciting details about both Goethe and herself. The details about Goethe are reported to Barley's masters, who are able to identify the Russian as one Yakov Savelyev, a well-placed rocket scientist. Barley keeps to himself the details about Katya, fueling his growing admiration for her and her courage. Goethe wishes to meet with Barley in Leningrad. The spies, the "gray men," decide that Barley should take this next step. More information is needed before Bluebird can be pronounced genuine.

As Barley travels to Leningrad, the Americans arrive in force at the Russia House. Their approach is bureaucratic and heavy-handed. Ned is wary of them, Clive is eagerly fawning, and Walter is removed entirely. In Leningrad, Barley meets Goethe, who is strained, yet excited at the thought of publication of the notebooks. Barley is able to extract some additional information from Goethe before the meeting ends. Barley returns to London for debriefing.

Before this can occur, Barley disappears. There is panic at the Russia House and paranoia among the Americans. The spymasters discover that Barley had also vanished from surveillance for several hours in Leningrad. A frantic manhunt finally tracks Barley down, playing his beloved saxophone at a friend's wake and contemplating the state of his unfulfilled life. The Americans will brook no more nonsense; they retreat with Barley, Ned, and Clive to a private island off the coast of Maine.

At the island, Barley undergoes a grueling interrogation, aimed at verifying his reliability and, more important, assuring the Americans that Bluebird and his notebooks are not lies. Ned tries to convince the Americans of the genuineness of both Barley and Bluebird, and of the need for haste. Ned sees a distancing in Barley, as if they are losing him somehow. Barley is subjected to a lie-detector test, and the results of the test and of the interrogations become caught up in three days of political jockeying in Washington. At last, they receive the word: Barley and Bluebird are pronounced genuine. The Americans assume full control of the operation and plan to send Barley back to Bluebird with a shopping list of questions that will fully expose the Soviet missile secrets. Ned's misgivings continue.

In Moscow for the final time, Barley and Katya meet again. Barley is by now very much in love with her. She has been in contact with Goethe; there are elements of the contact that seem unusual, but she shrugs them off. Barley is more concerned, but conceals his fear from both Katya and his masters. The appointed means for the two of them to contact Goethe is with a phone call; the call devastates Katya as Goethe tells her through code signals that he has been caught by the KGB. Katya and her children are in danger, so Barley decides to take action.

The spymasters watch their operation proceed toward what they believe will be a remarkable coup. As the bureaucratic machinery of the Americans propels events forward, only the ever-cautious Ned realizes, by studying Barley's actions, that something is seriously amiss. He is ignored.

As Barley goes through the motions of the American plan, he makes his own plans. He receives the shopping list of American questions, and the rendezvous with Bluebird is set up. Barley walks into the building for the meeting. Observers see the "OK" signal given. Nothing happens. Barley has disappeared.

In the ensuing internal inquest, heads roll and fingers point, and the spymasters rewrite the history of the case to make it into a triumph. They observe Katya living a normal life, and a newspaper report from Russia mentions the sad death of a scientist. Years later, Palfrey finds

Barley living a quiet life in Lisbon, and hears the entire story: how Barley bargained the American shopping list in exchange for safety for Katya and her children. Now he awaits her emigration to the West. He is prepared to wait forever, and he is content.

John le Carré has again written a richly textured novel that is successful at many levels. *The Russia House* is a riveting spy novel, with requisite twists and details of spycraft for which le Carré is famous. The interrogation scenes are particularly fascinating, as the questioner and the questioned reveal themselves through the give and take of relentless cross-examination.

The Russia House is a quiet and rewarding love story, as Barley and Katya must cross cultural and political barriers, and at the end risk everything to find each other. As for a happy ending, the possibility remains open, but unclear.

The book is a warning against the real danger of unchecked bureaucracy. The massive machinery of British and American intelligence enclaves threatens the very values it is charged to protect, in an attempt to justify the existence of such organizations in a world where they seem archaic and unnecessary.

Finally, it is a fable about taking control of one's life and actions. Each of the three protagonists, Goethe, Katya, and Blair, takes active steps to control his or her own destiny: Goethe, by writing the notebooks; Katya, by risking everything for love of both men and for her own beliefs; and Barley, who reverses the useless direction of his life and finds contentment in doing so. In emphatic counterpoint, Palfrey reveals piecemeal how his own failure to take action at a critical point in his life has left him lonely and embittered, and the failure of the spies to act or react at the key juncture causes the operation to fail.

Le Carré weaves his themes deftly and subtly, his language both simple and artful. His characters are all memorable, no matter how brief the appearance. The spy aficionado will be delighted with the book, while the reader searching only for a powerful and well-written novel should be equally impressed. *The Russia House* adds significant luster to le Carré's already enhanced reputation.

Hank Stewart

THE SATANIC VERSES

Author: Salman Rushdie (1947–)
Publisher: Viking Press (New York). 547 pp. $19.95
Type of work: Novel
Time: The present, with flashbacks, mainly to the recent past
Locale: Bombay; London; and points between and beyond

Two Indian actors survive the midair destruction of their jet and fall gently to earth, only to discover that they have become pawns in an epic, ancient struggle that profoundly affects their lives, their bodies, and the world around them

Principal characters:
GIBREEL FARISHTA, a Bombay movie star whose strange visions suggest that he is the archangel Gabriel
SALADIN CHAMCHA, an Anglophilic Indian actor who finds himself growing goat hair and horns
JUMPY JOSHI, Saladin's friend
PAMELA CHAMCHA, Saladin's wife, Jumpy's lover
ALLELUIA "ALLIE" CONE, Gibreel's lover, a mountain climber

The jumbo jet *Bostan*, destroyed by a terrorist bomb, rains its ruined insides upon the predawn sea near the shores of England. Amid the wreckage of their plane and its passengers two men tumble from the sky, singing, arguing, unharmed but a bit dazed: Gibreel Farishta, Bombay superstar famous for his portrayals of various deities in lavish Indian productions, and Saladin Chamcha, a London actor whose myriad voices have made him ubiquitous on radio and television. As they pass through the cloud cover, the dreamlike pace of their fall vanishes, replaced by the sensation of plummeting fatally earthward from a great height. Terrified, the two men clutch at each other. Saladin, nearly suffocated by a sudden will to live, finds himself commanding Gibreel to fly and sing, which the other does, absurdly and with great vigor. The pair decelerate, accompanied by a flapping of arms and a strange song that emerges in a language neither understands.

Later, Gibreel will remember the sea parting for them as they floated ever more slowly toward it; Saladin will insist that their survival was simply a wild stroke of luck. To resolve this dispute, the narrator of *The Satanic Verses* offers this statement: "I know the truth, obviously. . . . Chamcha willed it and Farishta did what was willed. . . . Of what type—angelic, satanic—was Farishta's song? Who am I? Let's put it this way: who has the best tunes?"

This narrator has more important plans for Saladin and Gibreel than seeing them die over the English Channel. No sooner have they washed ashore on a snowy beach than unusual things begin to occur.

The fastidious Saladin, a man who bitterly rejects his Indian heritage, sprouts horns on his forehead and thick hair on his legs; his feet become cloven hooves. Gibreel, an extravagantly Indian product of the brash, chaotic Bombay streets, can no longer control the boundary between his strange and insistent dreams of being the archangel Gabriel and waking reality. On occasion, a soft golden light can be seen emanating from behind his head. From the outset, these changes cause a deep rift between the two; the police arrest Saladin and beat him savagely, but they do not touch Gibreel, leaving him to watch silently as Saladin is taken away.

Saladin's life becomes a surreal nightmare. Escaping from custody, Saladin ends up surreptitiously established in the attic of the Shaandaar B&B, a restaurant and rooming house for illegal immigrants. The ethnic proprietors of the Shaandaar, the Sufyans, represent precisely the kind of people Saladin disdains, and their kindness toward him only increases his misery and feelings of alienation. While Saladin hides his growing horns, his friend Jumpy, who brought him to the Shaandaar, moves into Saladin's house and his bed. The passionate affair between Saladin's wife, Pamela, and Jumpy had begun the night they heard the news of the *Bostan* explosion and continues despite Jumpy's guilt and Pamela's hysterical refusal to accept the bizarre but miraculous reappearance of her husband.

The secret, steady progress of Saladin's transformation into a satanic figure proceeds in tandem with a growing unrest in Brickhall, the ethnically mixed London neighborhood he unwillingly inhabits. Rumors of occult rituals practiced by police and a manhunt for the "Granny Ripper" terrorizing the area awaken latent hostility between civic authorities and unruly citizens. As Saladin sprouts a tail, much to the delight of the Sufyans' teenage daughters, a cloven-hooved devil invades the dreams of the locals, rapidly becoming a symbol of revolt against oppression and persecution.

In another part of the city, another transformation wracks Gibreel, player of gods and betrayer of his friend Saladin. The dreams that have chased Gibreel since the night he left India now begin to spill into everyday life. When Gibreel sleeps, he dreams of the prophet Muhammad kneeling below him in a cave, asking for divine revelation from the archangel Gabriel. Hovering above the prophet, feeling like a stage actor who has forgotten his lines, Gibreel hears a voice issue from his mouth in response to Muhammad's impassioned questions. He cannot resist the force of Muhammad's desire to know, to recite, and it is this force, and not anything within or beyond Gibreel, that articulates the answers the prophet seeks.

In addition to these dreams, different, equally disturbing visions enter his life after the *Bostan* explosion. Rekha Merchant, a married woman who had recently thrown her children and herself off of her high-rise apartment building when spurned by Gibreel, appears on a flying carpet, cursing and taunting him. Rekha's threats to make his life miserable take shape in insidious forms: just as in his dreams of Muhammad, Gibreel finds that the desires of others unleash in him unpredictable powers.

Haunted by these visions, Gibreel sets out for London, determined to find Alleluia Cone, the mountain climber he left India for, the woman he is convinced is the love of his life. He spends an entire day rushing wildly around the city trying to escape Rekha and her carpet, only to fall, defeated and exhausted, on a park path as Allie approaches through the dusk. Although this reunion temporarily discourages Rekha, Gibreel's dreams do not abate. He dreams one, and then another, each unfolding over several nights, each casting him as the archangel Gabriel appearing to someone seeking divine guidance. The fact that he is conscious, within the dreams, of being Gibreel Farishta, movie actor, does not prevent the driven, fanatical figures from expecting, desiring, forcing revelation or action from their reluctant angelic apparition. When these dreams become as real to him as his affair with Alleluia, Gibreel begins seriously to consider that he might indeed be the archangel Gabriel.

Across town in the attic of the Shaandaar, Saladin's body grows ever larger and more alarming. Confronted by the undeniable physical evidence of his demonic transformation, Saladin finally submits to his condition. In his rage he searches for someone to blame, and finds the face of Gibreel taking shape in his mind. Gibreel allowed him to be arrested and humiliated. Gibreel, his life seemingly untouched by his fall to earth, has even publicly denied his presence on the doomed *Bostan*, claiming that he missed the flight, that nothing strange occurred, that he is ready to resume his film career.

The night that the target of his hatred at last becomes clear in Saladin's mind, his body sheds all pretense of humanity, and the Shaandaar begins to rumble and shake with the weight and horror that bursts out of the attic. The Sufyans' fearless daughter, Mishal, and her lover, Hanif, smuggle the monster to the Hot Wax Nightclub, where wax effigies of Establishment politicians are ritually melted every night. In the morning, after a night of terrifying screams and crashes from the empty club, the lovers hesitantly open the door. Lying asleep on the floor, surrounded by broken furniture and the puddled remains of all the waxworks, is Saladin, naked and entirely human.

Gibreel's progress, if less spectacular, is equally frightening. The visions of Rekha and Muhammad and the others continue, and Gibreel often wanders the streets for days without food or shelter, seeking to work miracles and reliving his newly remembered archangelic past. Every time he reaches out his hand to save a soul, or steps into traffic certain that he towers above the buildings and cars, he is punched or run over or simply mocked. The ever-widening chasm between his own reality and that of the rest of the world leads him to the brink of sanity, and, after several breakdowns, he undergoes psychiatric treatment for paranoid schizophrenia. Determined to pick up his career, he commits himself to a series of movies about the archangel Gabriel, with plots drawn from his own dreams.

At a movie-industry party he encounters the recovering Saladin, whose anger is aroused once more by Gibreel's heavily sedated, lackluster greeting. Drawing upon the still large reserves of hatred and evil within him, Saladin sets out to destroy Gibreel's life as he imagines Gibreel to have destroyed his own. For weeks he calls Gibreel and Allie, always in a different voice, repeating intimate secrets Gibreel has told him and reciting limericks designed to convince the ever-jealous actor of Allie's nonexistent infidelity. He succeeds, and Gibreel once more takes to the streets, giving himself over wholly to his visions. The night that the city erupts into the ethnic violence that has been building for months, Gibreel comes upon the burning Shaandaar just as Saladin rushes in, trying vainly to save the Sufyans. Suddenly realizing that it was Saladin whose voices have destroyed his love and his sanity, Gibreel runs after him, determined to wreak vengeance. Inside, he finds Saladin unconscious on the floor and, looking at the face of his enemy at his feet, chooses to save Saladin.

More that a year later, Saladin returns to India to the deathbed of his father, leaving his formerly pristine English life in shambles behind him. Pamela and Jumpy had died the night of the rioting, victims of a mysterious arsonist who torched the Brickhall community center while the two were there copying documents that had been gathered as proof of the occult practices of the police and of the racial persecution that had sparked the violence. As Saladin watches the decline of his father, he discovers a bond that the pride and bitterness of both men and decades of estrangement have been unable to shatter. After his father dies, Saladin, now returning to his given name of Salahuddin, realizes that he has taken the first steps toward regaining his past, reconciling himself with his Indian identity.

He stays, briefly, in the house of his childhood, and it is here that the raving Gibreel finds him. Farishta's return to India has forced his visions into fatal confrontation with the outside world; Alleluia Cone, brought by a well-meaning friend to the apartment of her former lover in the Everest high-rise complex, has fallen to her death from the top of the building. Gibreel, babbling wildly to Salahuddin, swears it was Rekha's idea to take Allie to the roof and that Rekha pushed Allie; he never would have, he loved her. Gibreel looks at Salahuddin, produces a gun, puts the barrel in his own mouth, and pulls the trigger.

The Satanic Verses represents a stunning display of narrative power. Rushdie challenges conventional concepts of time, space, language, and narrative development, creating a work that belongs as much to the great Eastern tradition of nested fables as it does to the Western novel. The interlocking sequences of Gibreel's extended dreams provide much of the material that has placed this book at the center of an international controversy, for it is here that Rushdie deals directly and irreverently with the prophet Muhammad and the foundations of Islam. These passages serve as a rich counterpoint to the contemporary sections, particularly for Western readers with some knowledge of Islam and the history of Eastern literature; for a Muslim, there is little latitude for either interpretation or enjoyment.

Saladin and Gibreel act out a version of the endless struggle between good and evil, but the narrator makes it clear that they are acting on his personal, satanic, stage. The magical realism that pervades the novel accentuates the unsettling, ambiguous power the narrator possesses and is strongly reminiscent of García Márquez and other Latin American authors. Rushdie's utter command of language enables him to sustain this delicate balance between the acceptable and the unacceptable, the believable and the incredible. The proper English of Saladin, the infectious dialect of Bombay, the languages of disenfranchisement, of exile, of transformation, of power and vulnerability, of death and rebirth—all these voices fill this work and give it life and power. *The Satanic Verses* demands much of its audience, and offers in return an astonishing, fantastical journey.

Nancy M. Seybold

SAYING GOODBYE: A MEMOIR FOR TWO FATHERS

Author: M. R. Montgomery (1938–   )
Publisher: Alfred A. Knopf (New York). 256 pp. $18.95
Type of work: Memoir
Time: 1904–1981
Locale: Montana; California; England; Scotland; Japan

A personal and historical account of the lives of journalist M. R. Montgomery's father and father-in-law

Principal personages:
M. R. MONTGOMERY, the author and narrator
MAURICE RICHARD MONTGOMERY, the author's father
LEE MITSUYOSHI WATANABE, the author's father-in-law

Saying Goodbye is a moving homage to two important yet apparently dissimilar men in the life of M. R. Montgomery: his father and his father-in-law. Both men were in their graves before the author was moved to explore their lives, hoping, he writes, that "if I could place them in their proper context, I could, somehow, reconcile them to each other, and to us." Montgomery leads the reader chronologically through the quite remarkable lives of these two men, who met only twice. "I hope only to tell enough for each of them, so that, if you follow me, there is some alignment of their repose."

The journey begins in northern Montana, a place that has "the look of a land that has been abused by a capricious god." Montgomery's father, Maurice Richard Montgomery, was born in 1904 in Chinook on the Milk River in northern Montana. The author's vivid descriptions of the land and the people and the culture in this part of Montana where his family lived and his father worked, are revealing. In some respects his father's life was like that of other men then: he worked, had a family, and was independent and lonely. Yet, his father was a civil engineer who built bridges, dams, skyscrapers, and airfields. He was also involved in overseas naval operations during World War II.

The relationship between father and son was distant. The elder Montgomery did not disclose to his son a great deal about his job or the war, nor did the younger Montgomery ever ask many questions. "I think my father didn't talk much about the navy and the war simply because it hurt."

In his quest for an understanding of his father, Montgomery visits the Fort Peck Dam in Montana, the construction of which his father had been involved in with the Army Corps of Civil Engineers in the 1930s. He was assistant engineer, second in charge of the spillway channel for one of the largest earth-filled dams in the world, making it possible for him to raise two children relatively well during the Great Depression.

The descriptions of the shantytowns that sprang up around the Fort Peck City to support the dam workers are brilliant. Photographer Margaret Bourke-White documented the dam and the nightlife in surrounding towns for *Life* magazine's first cover story in 1936. Bourke-White, who arrived in high heels, had borrowed Montgomery's father's shoes to wear while she photographed the bridge structure.

His father saw political events worsening in Europe and anticipated the U.S. entry into World War II. He applied for a commission in the Navy Civil Engineers Corps in 1936. The senior Montgomery's records show that his initial application to the Navy was rejected because he had only half of the usual 24 molars in his mouth. However, he entered the Navy reserves as a lieutenant that year, after he promised to have dental work done. This abhorrence of dentists is a trait the younger Montgomery claims to have inherited.

Fortunately, his father was not in Fort Peck at the time of the "big Slide" of 1938, when the upstream end of the dam slid. His father had been worried about such a catastrophe. He told his nine-year-old son that the slide was caused by "the dam's simply being filled too fast, making it waterlogged and unstable." When Montgomery visited Fort Peck, he found those complaints in official memos written by his father.

In 1940 his father, at age thirty-seven, was commissioned into the navy. A year later he was sent to Great Britain on special assignment. Montgomery reports that his father was excited to be going to his ancestral home of Scotland. But, "more than the satisfaction of being a naval officer and practicing his profession, my father had a sense of being a key player in what he must have seen as the first move in a most audacious plan to come to the aid of Great Britain, to begin America's war against Hitler."

He helped build two naval bases in Rosneath, England, and an oil pipeline in Scotland. Montgomery believes that, toward the end of his term there, his father had come to the realization that the United States was playing games with Great Britain while setting up a base from which to invade North Africa. By this time, he had assumed command of the operation working to complete the naval bases and pipeline.

Although the family was separated for two years, Montgomery believes that his father was happy in Great Britain. "When I think of my father today, more often than not I imagine him in Scotland. It was such a perfect match between the demands of a practical job and a very practical man, all suffused with the patriotic glow of wartime urgency."

Montgomery says that the dislocation of his family was nothing compared to that of his wife's family, ethnic Japanese who were living in California when the Japanese bombed Pearl Harbor in December 1941. They escaped the concentration camps that followed a wave of anti-Japanese sentiment because his father-in-law, Dr. Lee Mitsuyoshi Watanabe, was able to teach Japanese at the Navy Oriental Language School in Colorado.

From his home in a small fishing village in western Japan, Watanabe became the first Japanese to graduate from Stanford University and its medical school. Both of Watanabe's parents were dead by the time he was twelve. He was considered too intelligent to remain an orphan. His teacher worked to arrange his immigration to the United States where he was adopted by a Japanese family who had moved from their village to California. He paid for his education by selling aluminum cookware and working as a houseboy in San Francisco.

When Watanabe graduated from medical school in 1932, he was one of the few Western-trained Japanese physicians in California. He first worked as a doctor in Fresno and then in San Jose, where he assumed the role of a leader in the large Japanese population there. When the family left California that year, Watanabe tried to practice in Illinois and Colorado but he was rejected because of his citizenship status. He ended up in Boulder teaching Japanese language and culture to navy cadets. Nevertheless, he missed practicing medicine.

That same year, Montgomery's father returned from Scotland. Here the gap between father and son became noticeable. The father had missed some important events in the child's life. "Among other things that might have contributed to what amounted to a distance between my father and myself was that somehow I wasn't exactly the way small boys might be . . . ." Montgomery was a slight young boy who had a speech impediment and was nearsighted. Unfortunately, his father was a busy man and had no time to play ball or relax with his son.

In 1944, Watanabe was accepted as a doctor in Salt Lake City, which had a large Japanese population, while the senior Montgomery went to Manila on assignment with the navy's Seventh Fleet to survey airfields there. A navy document states that the senior Montgomery had been in charge of planning and loading supplies to send the Australians to invade Borneo; he returned home in 1945.

As a young man, the author spent six summers and two full years working for his father's construction company. "My father and I reached a kind of amicable truce, over the years." After his father's death from cancer in 1981, Montgomery felt "compelled" to go to England and Scotland to find pieces of his life to see what he had seen and meet people he had met. While there, he discovered quite a few important navy documents about his father as well as America's intentions at that time. He learned that many of the places his father worked or stayed at had been destroyed. Nor were there a lot of old timers around either, some forty years later. He did meet a couple who knew his father and called him "a lovely man."

Not surprisingly, author M. R. Montgomery devotes the majority of *Saying Goodbye* to recounting his father's life. The stories of both fathers reveal the obvious differences between them but also point out the similarities between two strong men who loved their families and professions in wartime.

Montgomery, a journalist for the *Boston Globe*, had to rely on sources other than his memory to write much of this book. It is heavily littered with accounts provided by people who knew his father, official documents, photos, and historical background to give a better sense of time and place. In fact, the author unearthed some rather important navy documents that make for enlightening reading.

At times Montgomery provides the reader with too much detail about such technicalities as highways and building methods, but his skill as a reporter and writer serves him well. With graphic descriptions of barren Montana, the wartime effort, geological surveys, and the inner workings of government, Montgomery provides the reader with lessons in American history as well as engineering, as he undertakes his personal journey into the past.

It is clear that the author "needed" to find his father to better understand their relationship as well as his own life. "I went all that way and he was still dead," Montgomery laments, yet in many ways he has succeeded in bringing his father to life again in these pages.

Sheryl Jean

SECOND CHANCES: MEN, WOMEN AND CHILDREN A DECADE AFTER DIVORCE

Authors: Judith S. Wallerstein
Sandra Blakeslee
Publisher: Ticknor and Fields (New York). 329 pp. $19.95
Type of work: Social science
Time: 1971 to the present
Locale: The United States

An examination of the impact of divorce, a common outcome of marriages in the United States that continues to influence the lives of all family members many years after the event

Approximately one-half of all marriages in the United States end in divorce, and a significant minority of middle-class American children experience the divorce of their parents. The short-term effects of divorce have been studied extensively, but there is little research as to its long-term impact upon parents and children. Psychologist Judith Wallerstein and science writer Sandra Blakeslee have teamed up to produce such a study and have found that adults and children of divorce continue to be profoundly affected. The effects cut across generations because the children must confront the failure of their parents' marriage as they enter relationships of their own. Too, while some of the parents learn from their mistakes and go on to make the best of their "second chances," others suffer a permanent drop in their standard of living or fail to construct another healthy adult relationship. Many parents lose contact with their children altogether, and others who remarry are divorced a second, third, or fourth time. Wallerstein follows sixty such families over a period of ten years, interviewing each family member at the time of the divorce and at intervals of one, five, ten, and (for some) fifteen years. From those interviews, the authors present three "representative" families—the Moores, the Burrelles, and the Catalanos (fictitious names)—and supplement their accounts with statistical data and examples of other parents and children who have experienced the problems and opportunities created by divorce.

The story of Denise Moore illustrates what the authors term the "sleeper effect" of divorce. The pretty daughter of an upper-middle-class family, she seemed to adapt well when her parents split. Since her father, a doctor, continued to support the family, her standard of living did not suffer, and she remained unruffled in the face of her mother's depression and her younger brother's difficulties in school. After her freshman year in college, however, she fell apart. She could not continue a long-term relationship because her parents' difficulties had left her ill-prepared for commitment, and she had not resolved her anger at her father for leaving her mother and marrying a younger woman. Her father had done well, but her mother had suffered emotionally and never again established a successful relationship. Denise and other victims of the sleeper effect fear repeating their mothers' experiences.

The Moores had two other children, and each of them reacted in different ways. Ruth, the oldest, became her mother's helper and confidante. Like Denise, she fears relationships and harbors anger toward men, and she feels a responsibility for her mother, clearly the loser in the divorce. Sammy, the youngest, suffered immediately. His behavior in school deteriorated, and at the five-year mark, he went into therapy for several years. Fortunately, he received support from both parents, as well as from friends. He developed an interest in exotic animals and gained self-confidence. His grades improved, and at the end of the study he was preparing to go to college to study captive animal breeding. According to Wallerstein, boys between seven and nine, like Sammy Moore, suffer most at the time of the divorce. Many need therapy, although few get it, and their relationships with both parents often determine whether they will recover from the initial trauma.

Unlike the Moore children, whose economic circumstances changed little, the Burrelles endured a cross-country move and instant impoverishment. There seemed to be little obvious cause for the divorce between Betty and Dale Burrelle. Betty's mother had been killed in an accident a year earlier, and Dale complained that his wife had become impossible to live with thereafter. Although he had a well-paying job, Dale sent inadequate child support, and often the payments were late. Betty moved out of state to be near her family, but they offered little assistance. In the end, she took two full-time jobs, one of them involving dangerous work, and her children saw little of her. Betty is one of the majority of divorced women—those whose remunerative skills are few. They become dependent upon child-support payments that are irregular and inadequate; the result is a 73-percent drop in their standard of living and that of their children.

While Betty Burrelle was clearly a financial loser, she did gain self-confidence through her ability to support and raise her three children single-handedly. Her husband suffered little financially, but emotionally he was made poorer by the experience. He married again, and that marriage ended in divorce as well. Lacking day-to-day contact with his children, he made little effort to see them.

With parental attention lacking, the Burrelle children faced numerous difficulties and responded in drastically different ways. Steve, the oldest, longed for contact with his father and, at sixteen, went to live with him for a year. It was profoundly disillusioning (primarily because Dale was going through his second divorce), and Steve returned depressed about his future and with a low concept of his self-worth. He illustrates the large number of adolescent boys who fail to develop a good relationship with their father and who, as a result, never develop the confidence and self-esteem to become healthy adults. These boys turn out to be the most obviously troubled of Wallerstein's subjects; many of them turn to alcohol, drugs, and crime or, like Steve Burrelle, remain immobilized, unable to plan for the future.

Tanya Burrelle represents another pattern—that of the adolescent girl who is forced to "raise herself" because of the inattention or problems of her parents. Teenage girls whose lives lack structure tend to become promiscuous; they take advantage of their early freedom, but it gives them no happiness. Others fit the pattern of the "overburdened child," who must tend to parents who are mentally or physically ill and who sacrifice their own childhood. They have few friends and emerge from adolescence with few of their own needs satisfied and are ill-prepared to cope with adult relationships. Many children, however, seem to emerge virtually intact from the most difficult situations. One of them is Kyle Burrelle, Steve and Tanya's younger brother. Wallerstein examines factors that contribute to some children's resilience. They tend to be very young at the time of the divorce (Kyle was three), and of all the siblings, the youngest have a stronger relationship with the custodial parent. In intact families, the oldest child seems to occupy a favored position with the parents. In a divorced family, this tends to be reversed, with the oldest child the most burdened and the youngest the most favored and protected.

The experiences of the Catalano family illustrate the effects of divorce upon younger families and the impact of remarriage upon the children. Pregnant and married at eighteen, Rosemary left a relationship in which she feared for her safety. She finished school, and with a more mature concept of herself and her needs, she enjoyed a successful second marriage. She was clearly a "winner." Bob, on the other hand, failed to grow as a result of his experience. His child-support payments locked him into a low-paying job. Unable to continue his education or to commit to another long-term relationship, he drifted away from his children and ultimately left town in search of more steady work. Wallerstein observes that the younger the couple, the more likely it is for the woman to rebuild her life (Christina Moore, in her forties, was unable to do so) and the more likely for the man to stagnate both emotionally and occupationally.

Rosemary's remarriage had opposite effects on her two children.

Billy remained angry at his father for spending so little time with him, and he never accepted his stepfather. As a teenager, he began to drink heavily and to defy his stepfather openly. At the ten-year mark, he seemed likely to follow the pattern of the most troubled adolescent boys. Kelly, however, who was only two at the time of the divorce, became attached to her stepfather, virtually accepting him as her real father.

Wallerstein and Blakeslee consider other patterns, including new forms of joint custody and the repetition of violence in the relationships of children from abusive families. They conclude with recommendations, for parents and children, to soften the blow of divorce and to make the postdivorce adjustment easier. In particular, they emphasize the need for noncustodial parents to maintain their relationships with their children.

Wallerstein and Blakeslee do not argue that troubled marriages should remain intact "for the sake of the children," but they do point out the long-term legacy of divorce upon the second generation. Whether or not parents attain a fulfilling life the second time around, their children are the biggest losers, for they must deal with a situation not of their making and for which they often feel guilt and anger. Furthermore, the end of their parents' relationship generally leads to a disruption in, if not an end to, their relationship with at least one parent. In telling the story of divorce from the children's perspective, Wallerstein and Blakeslee give a voice to the most helpless members of the family; they ask parents to consider the children before making their decisions. Furthermore, they show that divorce is not a panacea for adults, either.

Sometimes divorce is unavoidable, and for those escaping physically or emotionally abusive relationships, the authors give some hope. Many adults do succeed the second time around. With adequate resources and support, children do overcome the mistakes of their parents and establish healthy relationships of their own. *Second Chances* is a cautionary tale, however, showing in vivid detail that divorce is not a crisis from which people recover easily.

Lyn Miller-Lachmann

THE SECOND SHIFT: WORKING PARENTS AND THE REVOLUTION AT HOME

Author: Arlie Hochschild (1940–   )
    with Anne Machung
Publisher: Viking Press (New York). 309 pp. $18.95
Type of work: Sociology
Time: The present
Locale: The United States

An examination of the dynamics within the increasingly common two-working-parent family, in the context of the family unit, the workplace, and U.S. society as a whole

As the number of women who work outside the home has increased over the last thirty to forty years, the percentage of married mothers who do so has more than doubled. The effects of the influx of women into the labor pool have been well documented from the viewpoint of industry and economics. Less studied has been the effect on the family of working parents. Arlie Hochschild's book looks at the ramifications of this modern stage of the industrial revolution.

The author finds that the revolution has stalled. Through extensive questionnaires and detailed series of interviews, she observes that the burden of the "second shift"—the housework and child-rearing that must be done to keep the family going—falls squarely (and unfairly) on the back of the working mother. This inequity persists to the extent that the average working mother works an extra month of 24-hour days every year. The focus of the book is on determining why such an unfair division of household labor occurs in some families, and why in others the burden is shared between husband and wife.

The forces behind the inequities in the division of the second shift act internally, within the family unit, and externally, in society in general. Outside the family, modern culture contributes to the stress on working parents in several ways. Society promulgates the myth of the supermom: the woman who "has it all"—career, husband, children, the looks of a model, and the energy of a dynamo. The worth of parenting is devalued: its tasks are underrated and unappreciated, its exigencies are ignored and trivialized. Finally, corporate America remains fixed on its gender-specific track—working women must conform to the classic male-dominated work pattern to succeed. Working mothers are seen as less committed, while working fathers are neither expected nor encouraged to extend their participation in parenthood.

Gender ideology is a person's set of beliefs about the role that the genders should play in the marriage. A traditionalist believes that the male is responsible for the breadwinning work while the female shoulders the responsibility for the care of the home and the children. An egalitarian feels that the housework and childcare should be shared, regardless of the wage-earning responsibility. A transitional gender ideology falls somewhere in between the two. Within the family, the individual parent's gender ideology and the harmony or clash with the partner's gender ideology play the major role in determining the division of the second shift.

Hochschild examines the interplay between gender ideologies in a series of case studies of families like the Holts, Nancy and Evan. Nancy is an egalitarian, strongly believing in her job and in the sharing of the second shift at home. Evan is ostensibly a transitional at worst, and yet he resists all of Nancy's efforts to increase his participation in the housework and childcare. He balks at Nancy's devising lists of chores, he lets laundry piles mount skyward when given this responsibility, and the attempt to split cooking fails miserably as Evan either forgets his turn or ends up taking the family out. Evan does not mind that Nancy pursues her career, but he does not give her any help at home. Nancy is naturally resentful of this.

Given these divisive forces within their marriage, how do the Holts cope? They devise a family myth, achieving an equilibrium by pretending that they divide the work down the middle. Evan's responsibilities are the garage (maintaining the cars, lawn mower, etc.), the basement (household repairs and tinkering), and the dog (feeding and the like). Nancy is responsible for everything else. The myth is that this "upstairs/downstairs" division of labor is equitable. Nancy accedes to this because a stable marriage ultimately is more important to her than an equal split of housework; the myth allows her to pretend that her husband shares the tasks, thus salvaging a fragment of her beliefs. Evan accedes to the arrangement because he essentially gets his way. Both are content, although they wonder why their son has sleep and behavior problems.

The Delacortes, Carmen and Frank, have also developed a family myth, but their marriage is the antithesis of the Holts'. Both are traditionalists: both feel that Frank should work and that Carmen should stay home and tend the kids. This option is not possible for them, because they need Carmen's income to survive. As for the work of the second shift, Carmen and Frank share the load. The paradox here is that their gender ideology is traditional, while in fact their marriage proceeds along egalitarian lines. Their own myth reconciles this discordance: Frank does not help because he thinks he should, but because Carmen is (supposedly) incompetent in some areas, such as cooking. Carmen plays the role of the helpless one, and Frank plays the role of gallant protector, thus enabling them to preserve their belief in their ideologies while economic reality prevents it in fact.

Other case studies reveal myriad permutations of both clashing and complementing gender ideologies and strategies, including the concept that couples exchange intangible "gifts" to balance disharmonies in the gender ideologies. Peter Tanagawa is transitional in that he supports his wife, Nina, in her desire to succeed at her career. He is, however, uncomfortable with the fact that she outearns him. It would be a further affront to his manhood were he to share the traditionally distaff role of childcare provider. In the complicated rationalizing within the Tanagawa marriage, Peter's "gift" to the marriage is that he graciously allows Nina to earn more, and out of gratitude, Nina assumes full responsibility for the second shift.

The Steins, on the other hand, Jessica and Seth, have a different response to the second shift: they transfer it. Initially, Jessica was willing to sacrifice her career to carry most of the weight; she wanted only a small amount of sharing from Seth. Seth instead threw himself even harder into his law practice; this was his "gift." Jessica has responded by adopting excessive career duties herself. With two sizable incomes, they pay a babysitter and a housekeeper to handle the home chores. The only cost is their marriage—they are now distant and aloof from each other to the point where they cannot be said to truly have a marriage anymore.

Not all of the case studies represent a failure to share. Both Michael Sherman and Art Winfield are full participants in the complete life of their respective families. Michael had to be cajoled, pushed, prodded, and finally threatened with separation before coming around, but the result is equal sharing and a very happy home life, balanced against a successful, if not spectacular, career. Art was a natural. The dual influence of a poor father and a wonderful stepfather showed him the way he wished himself to be. Art plunges totally into fatherhood and the second shift.

Still, Art Winfield and Michael Sherman are the anomalies, not the norm. The majority of men resist involvement in the second shift, leaving the majority of women to cope alone in one way or another. The ways in which the women cope range from forcing a change, overtly or covertly; to cutting back, either at home or at work; to "doing it all," often at the expense of physical and emotional health; to seeking outside help; to withdrawing from the struggle through separation or divorce.

The United States is at a point at which still more women will be entering the work force, and still more couples will be forced to address the issues raised by the conflict between career and home. The proper prescription for the country is a national profamily policy that acknowledges the realities of life in the late 20th century. This should include more opportunities for paternity leave, flexible work schedules, pay equity for women, job-sharing schemes, and a general revaluation of parenting and childcare. As external factors make it easier for families to cope, problems associated with gender ideologies will be easier to resolve and may disappear altogether. To do otherwise will perpetuate the stall in the industrial revolution.

If presenting the facts can be a controversial act, then Arlie Hochschild has produced a provocative and extremely controversial book on certain significant deficiencies in the "American Dream." With statistical evidence from her own studies and others', as well as the even more compelling truths revealed in the ten case studies that she presents in detail, she lays out a picture of social and economic inequity existing within the institution of the modern marriage. She prepares her case with clarity and extensive factual evidence, yet at the same time she avoids being judgmental toward individuals or groups. Just as society is the ultimate victim of the inequitable present, so, too, society is to blame for the current state of affairs. Similarly, society will be ultimately responsible for redressing existing wrongs or suffering the consequences should change not occur.

Hochschild's skill as a teacher is evident in her presentation of the material. This no unreadable sociological tome, but a fascinating mirror held up to society. *The Second Shift* is an important book for today, a book that should be read by all working parents who face the trials of the second shift, and by all couples preparing for marriage and childbirth. There are two futures prophesied by this book: one of a continuing stall to industrial progress, in which the United States is eventually bypassed by its foreign competitors; the other of a future of equality and progress in which the nation successfully moves toward its next stage of development.

Hank Stewart

SELF-CONSCIOUSNESS: MEMOIRS

Author: John Updike (1932–   )
Publisher: Alfred A. Knopf (New York). 257 pp. $18.95
Type of work: Memoir
Time: 1932–the present
Locale: Shillington, Pennsylvania; Ipswich, Massachusetts

Reflections of Pulitzer Prize-winning author and poet John Updike on the hidden insecurities of a small-town boy to whom success and fortune seemingly came easily

> *Principal personages:*
> JOHN UPDIKE, the narrator
> WES and LINDA UPDIKE, his parents

Like many well-known people, John Updike had humble beginnings. His grandparents moved to Shillington, Pennsylvania, a small farming community, in the early 1920s and purchased a "grand" house in which to retire. But the family fortune was lost in the stock-market crash of 1929, and his grandfather went to work on the town road crews.

John's father, Wes, taught at Shillington High School. He came from a poor family in Trenton, New Jersey, attended college on a football scholarship (his nose was broken more than once), and moved to Shillington when he married. Although he took civic pride in Shillington and taught Bible school on Sundays, he was belittled by his students, who often mimicked his nasal voice. He applied for membership in, and was turned down by, a local civic organization, a fact that John still remembers bitterly. John remembers his father as a defeated man, an outsider who never really fit in.

His mother, Linda Hoyer, held a master's degree from Cornell University. After teaching seventh grade for a few hours, she walked out of the school, never to return. She spent much of her time writing, and although none of her work was published, this activity also left a deep and lasting impression on her son.

John and his parents lived with his grandparents. Although he grew up during the depression and the early days of World War II, his memories of those days are always of having the things he most wanted —a Schwinn bicycle, a Flexible Flyer sled, a Jimmy Foxx fielder's glove—and the gift he had requested of Santa was usually under the Christmas tree. Yet his father insists that they were poor, and that he had to work on construction jobs during the summer to augment his meager teacher's salary. Other early memories are not unlike those of many who lived through that era: victory gardens, organizing scrap collections, flattening tin cans, and salvaging rubber for the war effort. The house and yard, with its walnut and cherry trees, flower gardens and birdbath, were the scenes of happy memories.

Like his mother, John developed psoriasis at an early age, and he spent the warm summer months sunbathing with her on an upstairs porch. Summer was the only season that the outbreaks could be held at bay, and the only time John was allowed the freedom of appearing "normal." The older he grew, the more upsetting his bouts with psoriasis became, as he struggled to keep this problem a secret. He would not participate in any sports events that would expose him, and he excluded himself from swimming at the YMCA with his friends; gym classes were pure torture. Eventually, he found something favorable about this affliction—he was excluded from the draft because of it.

Another tendency that became more than problematic was John's tendency to choke, inherited from his grandmother. He often disrupted meals by running out to the porch, tears streaming, choking. John vividly recalls the terror of having a cough-drop lodge in his throat, the mad race home gasping for air, dizzy and frightened, sure that he would never make it there alive. He was, of course, saved, but the problem occurred repeatedly, without warning, whether he swallowed something or not, and was another source of anxiety.

As though this was not enough to make anyone nervous and self-conscious, John had a stammering problem. He was popular and articulate, appearing in school plays, an active member of the debating team. He gave droll chalk-talks with aplomb. But when called upon to speak as part of his duties as class president, he would become tongue-tied, struggling to remember what he was trying to say while he tried to concentrate on keeping calm, speaking slowly, and forming his words carefully. (Many years later, John was to realize that this occurred only when he was in what he considered to be a "false position." When he was sure of himself, as when he went to readings of his works, the problem never came up.)

John eventually arrived at Harvard, outwardly the picture of a brilliant, confident young man eagerly beginning life on his own. Yet, inwardly, he arrived in terror, a young man full of the secret maladies he desperately hoped no one would discover—psoriasis, choking spells, and stammering. There is little mentioned about these years, other than a few references to incidents involving these painful afflictions that continued to act up from time to time.

John eventually married (a mysterious woman who remains nameless throughout the book) and fathered four children. He and his family moved to Ipswich, Massachusetts, and here John found a solution to the psoriasis problem. Every day, he would venture out to the seclusion of the sand dunes with his portable radio, to "hide from the world" and expose his tortured skin to the sun. He did this religiously, no matter what the weather or temperature, from April to November. And for most of the summer, he could escort his family around town clad only in bathing trunks, his skin glowing with radiant good health and adorned with a summer tan—just like the other natives. Life was good. John enjoyed the community and made many friends, and his afflictions finally were under control.

This period lasted for a while, but eventually the seasonal outings were not enough, and the psoriasis began to erupt in midwinter. Fortunately, John was financially able to go to the Caribbean for the necessary sunbathing, and this became his new routine, occasionally with his family, but usually alone for a week or two of sun and solitude each year. He soon became aware, however, that his skin was becoming resistant to the sun's healing power.

In 1974, when John was in his forties, he had to face the fact that his marriage was no longer working—that he had changed and was not happy with his life. This fact was brought home vividly after a series of serious asthma attacks and choking episodes—something he thought he had put behind him. When he finally realized what was causing these symptoms, he made the decision to end the marriage. He moved to Boston; the asthma cleared up; but much to his chagrin, he began stuttering again whenever he spoke with the children.

John's move to Boston, away from his summertime beach treatments, perhaps in addition to his guilt over the divorce, triggered a metabolic riot—a meteoric flareup of the psoriasis. And this time, his emergency trip to the Caribbean did not work. Completely despondent, John returned to Boston. But once again, luck was with him; he heard of an experimental program being conducted at Massachusetts General Hospital for the treatment of severe cases of psoriasis, and he applied for admission into the program. He was quite pleased with himself when he passed all the requirements and was allowed to participate. The medication and artificial light succeeded in making his skin the clearest it had been since kindergarten.

John takes an entire chapter to relate one of the most upsetting events that occurred during this time. One day he received a questionnaire in the mail from a British publisher who was surveying American authors on their feelings about the Vietnam War. The accompanying letter indicated that the results would be published if response warranted it; John hastily filled out the papers, stating his position and following up with what he considered possible solutions to the escalating twenty-year-old problem. Several months later, *The New York Times* published the article, using some of John's responses. For the first time, he was aware that he had taken an unpopular stance—a fact that startled and confused him. He was, and is, pro-American, and he took pride in that fact. He was "born and raised a Democrat," and considered himself a liberal; he had taken an active part in the civil rights movement. But he had also taken a trip to Russia with a group of authors and was appalled at the conditions there and in other Communist-bloc countries. Not all of his views were expressed in the article, nor was his solution mentioned. John felt that the article did not accurately reflect his position, and he was criticized by friends and by people he admired. It was a bitter experience for him, but it taught him to be more cautious when responding to unsolicited queries.

In a chapter titled "A Letter to My Grandsons," John very touchingly discusses those problems he fears they may face growing up in today's society. His two young grandsons, to whom the book itself is dedicated, are half black. John tries to warn them of the prejudice with which they may have to deal. He also presents them with a thorough genealogy, hoping to instill a pride for their rich heritage. And perhaps he tries to arm them with the fact that problems can be surmounted, as evidenced by the physical problems he faced and finally overcame.

A trip home to visit his mother in Plowville, Pennsylvania, and a rendezvous to retrieve luggage lost on the flight, allow John Updike an hour of solitude where he grew up. Here begin the reflections of a fifty-five-year-old man who seemed to progress easily from one achievement to another: from Pennsylvania public schools to Harvard, to the Ruskin School of Drawing and Fine Art at Oxford on a Knox fellowship; staff writer for *The New Yorker*; published poet and author of fiction, short stories, poetry, and children's books by his thirtieth birthday; and winner of such awards as the Pulitzer Prize for fiction, the National Book Award, the American Book Award, and the National Book Critics Circle Award. How then should this man come to publish a memoir entitled *Self-Consciousness*? Surely a life that could produce so much success must have been a privileged and easy one.

This memoir by John Updike vividly portrays a childhood haunted by the terror of psoriasis and stuttering, of asthmatic flareups, and of his uncomfortable stance of patriotism during the Vietnam War. Although each chapter is devoted to a problem John experienced both as a child and as an adult, his story weaves back and forth through time; the pieces are unified by these personal insecurities and childhood traumas, and by the ways in which he overcame them with maturity and a deepening spirituality.

Jeanne Larrivee

THE SHAWL

Author: Cynthia Ozick (1928–   )
Publisher: Alfred A. Knopf (New York). 70 pp. $12.95
Type of work: A short story and a novella
Time: The late 1930s to the present
Locale: Central Europe; Miami, Florida

Two tales of the pain of the Holocaust and the ways of coping with suffering

Principal characters:
>   ROSA, a half-sane former antiques dealer in her fifties, who lost
>   her child in a Nazi concentration camp
>   STELLA, Rosa's fortyish niece and companion in the camps
>   PERSKY, a retired factory owner in his seventies

The Shawl, just seventy pages long, collects two tales. They first appeared in *The New Yorker,* three years apart, and each appeared in *Best American Short Stories* and *O. Henry Prize Stories.* The author, Cynthia Ozick, essayist and short-story writer, often focuses on Jewishness. An Ozick story will frequently bring together a traditional Jew with an assimilated one, to thrash out their differences in ways that raise questions about God in the fractured modern world. In her essays, the author brings a strongly motivated and subtle moral sense to literary issues. She is a great admirer of the man she calls "the Master," the American novelist Henry James.

The title story of this tiny collection is brief. The action is simple, two short scenes with the same three characters. Rosa, a young mother, starved and cold, is seen in a forced march with her infant daughter, Magda, trying to feed at her dry breast. Stella, a teenager, jealous of Magda's free ride, trudges alongside.

Months later, all three Jews are in a concentration camp. Rosa has hidden Magda from the prison guards by wrapping her each day in a shawl and leaving her in the barracks. Rosa stumbles around the yard during daylight, as she is required to do, and returns to her hidden child each night. The baby lies silent and undiscovered. Indeed, she has never made a sound of any kind.

But now Rosa sees the child walking on rickety legs in the camp yard. Stella has unwrapped the shawl from the hidden child, for her own use. Disoriented, Magda has left the barracks and even begins to cry aloud for its mother. As Rosa watches, a guard picks her child up and throws her into the electric fence. Rosa has torn the shawl away from Stella, and stuffs it into her own mouth to keep silent. The scream welling up in her would identify her as the dead, forbidden infant's mother, and Rosa herself would be shot.

The trick works, and the young mother survives the camp. But now, in the novella "Rosa," she is "a madwoman and a scavenger." She lives in a residential hotel in Miami, sustained on tea and peas she can cook on her one-burner stove. She is a strong woman of fifty-eight, until recently the owner of a business in New York. One day she deliberately, ferociously destroyed her junk shop, smashing every item and the glass storefront. The authorities let her go free only on the condition that she leave town.

Rosa keeps to herself in Miami, seldom leaving her hotel. Finally, the filth of her sheets has driven Rosa from her squalid room, with a shopping cart full of blackened laundry, to walk in the punishing sun to the laundromat. An elderly gentleman, who lounges by the washing machines to meet women, expresses an interest in Rosa.

Simon Persky breaks the ice by noticing her accent. He, too, is from Warsaw, but he left in 1920. "My Warsaw isn't your Warsaw," Rosa tells him, without elaboration. She reluctantly lets him help her unload the dryer, and he chides her for being timid. "In Miami, people are more friendly," he says, "Nazis we ain't got, Ku Kluxers we ain't got. What kind of person are you, you're still afraid?" (Ozick has once again brought together a tolerant Jew and separatist one.)

Persky is not a twit, but he does take a relentlessly positive attitude. For instance, he boasts that when he lost his teeth, he did not have a single cavity. His salesmanlike friendliness brings Rosa back to thoughts of her genteel childhood, while she imagines the ghetto alley from which the Perskys sprang. When he asks her name, she gives it, but gives it as one does to an official: "Lublin, Rosa."

Persky admits that he comes to the laundromat to find ladies. When Rosa tells him the story of how she ended her business with a big hammer, Persky is unfazed. He has a wife who is crazy, committed to an institution, he tells his companion. Nonetheless, Rosa bolts; she says thank you and rolls her shopping cart back to her hotel.

She stops for her mail at the lobby desk and receives two letters and a package. Without opening the box Rosa knows that it is Magda's shawl. Rosa took it with her from the camps and recently asked Stella to send it down from New York. Rosa hurries through all the old people up to her private room. First she opens the letter from Stella. It announces that she has sent the shawl and upbraids Rosa for her craziness.

Rosa turns to her laundry. She counts it all to make sure everything is there. A pair of underpants is gone. She makes tea and worries. The thought comes to her that Persky has the underwear. She had seen him pick up something from the floor. Is he a pervert? Was he simply too embarrassed to return a lady's undergarment?

In a flurry Rosa returns to the second letter. She passed it by at first because it is one from a university, like many she has received, postmarked over and again as it sought her at her landlord's, at her niece's house, and now in Miami. This one is from James Tree, a Ph.D. at the Department of Clinical Social Pathology at the University of Kansas-Iowa. He wants to interview Rosa to verify a new theory of "repressed animation," an idea developed in the study of "survivors," meaning those who lived through the Nazi camps.

Usually Rosa flushes letters from universities down the toilet, but this one she burns. It is unusually fatuous, comparing the apathy of brutalized prisoners to the detachment of the Buddhist Eightfold Path, all in bloodless jargon. Rosa despises academic ghouls and their studies of other people's suffering. She hates the word "survivor." She believes that it is used to avoid "human being," and she has no tolerance for any evasion of humanity.

Then Rosa does something dotty. She sits at her table and writes a letter to her daughter, to a Magda who is now a professor of Greek philosophy at Columbia University. It is fluent and dense, witty and concerned with serious moral questions. "Motherhood—I've always known this—is a profound distraction from philosophy, and all philosophy is rooted in suffering over the passage of time." Rosa's thoughts ascend, but finally she snaps out of her writing trance and reflects that her whole letter is a lie. She turns to her package, Magda's shawl, but leaves it unopened. She tidies up, and goes out to look for her underwear. It is not on the floor of the elevator, nor in the hotel lobby. She searches the sidewalks all the way to the cafeteria where she noshed with Persky, without success. Rosa finds that the laundromat is locked for the night. Her search becomes a little unhinged, and she goes to a newsstand where Persky might have bought a paper and dropped her underwear. Rosa drops her pretense of reasonability entirely and goes to look for her underwear on the beach. She walks through a gate with a loose latch onto a private hotel shorefront. She stumbles over naked lovers in the sand and flees from them into the hotel itself because the gate to the street has locked behind her. In the lobby, she finds the hotel manager and scolds him. While shrieking at him, Rosa becomes convinced that Dr. Tree, author of the letter she burned, is staying at the hotel. She walks out of the hotel, warmed by her victory, and returns to her place, where she finds Persky waiting for her. She agrees to serve him tea, and after much prodding, even opens her sacred package. It is not Magda's shawl. It is a book, *Repressed Animation*, sent by Dr. Tree, the sight of which sends Rosa into an angry frenzy.

When she washes her face in the morning, Rosa finds the missing underwear stuck to her towel. She goes to the desk downstairs to have her phone reconnected. While she is there, she is given a registered package. This time, it is Magda's shawl. She is indifferent to it. She calls her niece Stella to complain about Dr. Tree and his book. She carries on incoherently about all that happened to her the previous day. As the conversation ends, Rosa wraps the handset of her telephone in Magda's shawl, as if it were a doll. Rosa imagines her daughter at sixteen, a golden beauty. Rosa writes Magda a letter in her head, telling her what it was like in the Warsaw ghetto. She tells about a streetcar line that passed through that miserable place, full of ordinary Polish shoppers staring at the Jews on the street. Rosa collapses emotionally as her letter ends. Then the phone rings. Persky is at the desk, asking if he can come up. "He's used to crazy women, so let him come up," Rosa tells the receptionist. Rosa takes the shawl off the phone, and notices that Magda has left her. Rosa's hallucination is shy, and runs from the new man in Rosa's life.

"Rosa" ends here, with Persky on his way up to continue his friendship with a woman who is only half sane. The inconclusive resolution is appropriate for the story, and for the book. The trauma presented in "The Shawl" is too painful, and the illness shown in "Rosa" is too profound, for any more definitely hopeful ending.

The Holocaust is a perennial subject for Cynthia Ozick. The suffering of the Jews under the monstrous inhumanity of the camps is a memory that possesses her characters. The story "The Shawl" is an evocation of that suffering, a benchmark notched at the beginning of the book to give a measure of the pain that is under discussion in the novella "Rosa."

In "Rosa," Ozick presents four human responses to this kind of suffering. The most attractive is Persky. He is a bundle of contradictory experiences that have prepared him well for the complexities of life. He is a practical man, a former factory owner, who is sympathetic to the impracticalities of human beings. His wife is insane, and he has realized that certain people have problems they must work through. He can listen to Rosa rave, he can point out where she is wrong, and he can keep coming back to her with kindness. Persky is the "mensch," the character who maintains that pain must be met with resolve and compassion. The optimism Ozick displays by presenting Persky is tempered by her choice not to make him a survivor of the camps. Ozick seems to be saying that Persky's attitude is the right one to adopt toward the effects of evil, but it is not an attitude that an actual victim of that evil can take.

Dan Duffy

SHOW YOUR TONGUE

Author: Günter Grass (1927–   )
Publisher: Harcourt Brace Jovanovich (San Diego). 224 pp. $34.95
Type of work: Travel
Time: The present
Locale: Calcutta, India

Günter Grass investigates his shame in the face of India's poverty

Show Your Tongue is a miscellany by the multitalented Günter Grass. In it the German novelist, acclaimed author of *The Tin Drum* (1959), presents an essay, a sheaf of drawings, and an ode, all reflections on a sojourn in India, where a theater produced one of his plays. *Show Your Tongue* is travel writing about an extended residence, rather than a journey. Most of it is drawn from a stay of six months in Calcutta, with trips to other Bengali cities on a variety of literary and political business. Grass visits a publishing house, helps with rehearsals of his play, opens an arts park, tours workplaces with other leftist authors. Grass writes about his drawing, and his drawings are covered with text from his essay.

The book's title refers to the traditional representation of Kali, goddess of change and destruction. She is typically rendered in her attitude upon discovering that she has tried to kill her spouse Siva. She sticks out her tongue to indicate shame. The volume's first drawing is a bust portrait of the goddess with a necklace of human heads. The title reads, "Kali Puja is announced"; that is, the feast of Kali is here. The next drawing shows the goddess, always with her tongue out, on her haunches by a pile of heads and coconuts at the edge of the city. All the drawings resemble the well-known grotesques of Ralph Steadman, blotty black-ink line drawings with documentary text from the same pen. The line is thicker than Steadman's, and clearly the monstrosities depicted are not caricatures.

There are ninety more pages of drawings of Calcutta's misery, the illustrations from Grass's sketchbook diary. They follow together after an equal length of diary text. The drawings are titled with the first line of writing that happens to be on them, and the title of the diary-essay itself is simply the first phrase of its first sentence.

"On the North Side of Calcutta" starts with a description of the part of town where Grass and his wife occupied a middle-class apartment. At an intersection of five streets there is an equestrian statue of the Bengali hero Subhas Chandra Bose. Also called "Netaji," he collaborated with all three Axis powers in an attempt to free India. For Grass, Netaji, a progressive whose nationalism led him to ally with the forces of reaction, symbolizes the separateness of India that is yet always influenced by the West.

Grass is accompanied by his wife, Ute, who is repelled by India. He reports the daily strain of their relationship by focusing on her reading. In the crowded train, in their apartment, wherever possible, she keeps her nose in the elegant, subtle, 19th-century novels of Theodor Fontane. Grass himself meditates on the aphorisms of the 18th-century savant George Lichtenberg. The very European nature of these refined authors makes strange India seem more real. The fact is that Ute and Günter have more in common with today's Calcutta than with the Germany of centuries past. Ute begins to read Urdu novels, and Günter moves on to the most contemporary German works, galley proofs sent by a literary colleague.

On one trip within the city, they visit the Victoria Memorial Museum. They hope to see "documentation of Calcutta's history as a city, of the Indian struggle for independence as well as that of the Bengalis." Instead they find a repository of colonial mementos: oil paintings, etchings, swords, and uniforms. The building itself is a monstrosity of stone and bronze. The Calcutta section of the museum shows only photographs, including one of Bose and one of Gandhi, without any mention that the two struggled along conflicting paths to national liberation. Grass invokes the novelist Fontane to comment on the historical vacuity of the exhibits, but the spirit of the old artist is drawn only to portraits of British officials, sons and daughters of those he knew during his exile to England. Worst of all for Grass, the museum is well attended by Indians, who all stop at the oil paintings of British victories. The Grasses leave the museum to visit a sociologist who studies the rickshaw pullers, and go home, where they collapse from strain.

Abroad in the mess of India again, attempting to discuss a factory neighborhood as a connected whole, Grass suggests that the viewer "ignore the misery—custom invites you to ignore it." Although Grass the tourist seems never to ignore the squalor of Calcutta, he does dampen his shame and horror long enough to discriminate among what he sees, to guess at causes and cures. The idle clerks snoring in the cramped and dirty offices are different from the legless beggar who takes alarm at a large tip and proudly shows his certificate of authentic disability. Grass never shows just a hovel or a dead beggar. He always notes some clues as to the origin and the future of what he reports.

Soon after the production of his play, Gunter and Ute leave India. Their trip, like the essay, was ruminative, without a clear purpose. No goal achieved, they simply depart. The essay ends. The reader turns the page to find another drawing of Kali, with a bag full of human heads. The images mentioned in Grass's travel notes are laid out in blotchy grays: the men with the net who fish minnows from the sewer, the charge of the sacred bulls, Kali looking over the factory district, one tent city or garbage dump after another. Most of the sketches carry Grass's scrawl, at once frantic and stunned in the face of what he draws.

The last part of the book, bounded at the end by four more sketches, is the title poem, "Show Your Tongue." There are twelve sections, of six or eight stanzas each. The verse takes phrases from the prose part of the book and relies on the historical background presented in the essay to present a distillation of what Grass learned in Calcutta.

The first section of the poem introduces the locale: India, black with bats, dripping with sweat, loud with radios and the cry of geckos. The second section shows the sheer complication of India. There are the masses who sleep on the streets, the rotting colonial buildings, all the useless plans to save the city that "lie in a pile like / garbage beside the road." In the face of all this, the next section ridicules dreams such as land reform, once a political program, now just a superstition "like remission / of sins, more water taps and ricksha licenses / more words like renovation and powdered milk." Reforms are made futile by the overwhelming bulk of humanity. The only transcendent value that survives is the "patience of poverty," the mystery that keeps the poor going.

Grass repeats this observation in the fourth section, about the traffic problem, where he evokes the overcrowded and crumbling streets and then points to a blind man jaywalking in perfect confidence through traffic. Grass is stunned by this, as he is stunned in the next section by the old disease of colonialism. He reviews the relics in the Victoria Museum and meditates on the nationalist Bose, the would-be dictator. What would have happened if he had "freed the subcontinent for Japan and turned / history east of the Suez upside down?" The poem goes on to emphasize that the direction of the future, even the state of the present, is as unknowable as the past that never came to be.

The sixth section discusses the city's garbage, seemingly another symbol of waste. But it si clean garbage, picked over by children for everything of use, converted by a few seasons of weather to fruitful soil. In a stinking garbage dump there is a school, where the children learn to write by copying the phrase "life is beautiful." But this inexplicable persistence of humanity is not something the poet can understand.

The next section discusses the mechanisms of the world that he knows about: the elections, the feast of Kali, and a flood. The election is a victory for communism, a spawn of Europe, and the floods came from ice melting at the faraway poles. The poet dreams a conversation with a rat, whose relations died in the flood, as all of Bombay may die in the fluctuations of international credit. The eighth section ruminates among the pains of India, the rickshaws, the roaming cattle, the crushing land debts, the money bearers, the money that stinks of sweat. "Too much, this is too much!" Grass resolves, "Hand over by bag."

The writer flees India, but his thoughts remain there. He shows corpses floating on the floodwaters, conjures the days of the Black Hole in 1756, the coconuts that remind him of severed heads. He describes the jammed train carriages, the burning funeral pyres on the Ganges, the Marxist politicians who persecute the city beggars.

Finally, the twelfth section resorts to dreams and visions to deal with Calcutta. The poet sees four brooms sweeping the city. He sees the city's monuments turned upside down, the Brahmans cleaning latrines, and Patience cutting off heads. Kali, the goddess of destruction, emerges, and the poet mimics her, sticking out his tongue. The poem ends, leaving a sense that the poet has observed the city and left it to the destiny of its own nature. Three drawings illustrate his last visions.

Show Your Tongue is about suffering in India: the miseries of the country's poor and the discomfort of the author on viewing them. It is an intimate work from a public man. He is troubled not simply by the fact of poverty, but also by the debris of human efforts toward a better world. In hinting that India is the trash heap of Western ideas, Grass gives both urgency and despair to the role of a compassionate intellectual. The book does not really develop ideas, but lays them out over and again, in journal form, in sketches, in a poem, with an attitude toward forms of expression that is mirrored in the author's position on the matter of the personal and the political: it's all of a piece. Confronted with his evidence, the reader can only agree that shame is the only feeling for a prosperous Westerner to entertain in the face of India. It is a special quality of Grass's shame that it is not entirely disabling. He continues his intellectual work and praises those he finds at work for a better India. An ethic of productivity lies behind the book, which is, if nothing else, a record of alert and vigorous attention to the world's human condition.

Dan Duffy

SKETCHES FROM A LIFE

Author: George F. Kennan (1904–   )
Publisher: Pantheon Books (New York). 365 pp. $22.95
Type of work: Memoirs
Time: 1927–1988
Locale: The United States; Europe; and Russia

*After a long career as statesman, historian, and author, George Kennan
provides a self-portrait through a compilation of diary entries covering more
than fifty years*

> *Principal personages:*
> GEORGE KENNAN, Foreign Service officer, historian, and author
> ANNELISE SOERENSEN KENNAN, Kennan's wife
> GRACE, Kennan's eldest daughter
> JOAN, Kennan's second child
> CHRISTOPHER, Kennan's son
> WENDY, Kennan's third daughter

At the start of his Foreign Service career, George Kennan began
keeping a diary ancillary to the official notes and papers that were
ordinarily a part of his work. Mostly, Kennan made notes and observations about the cities in which he lived and traveled, sometimes as
part of his work, or while on vacation and personal trips. His diary
entries would remind him of the particular places and events they
described, securing their place in the richness of his remembered experience.

In 1927, Kennan was vice-consul in Hamburg, Germany. His early
distaste for communism is evident, and he longs for a more idealistic
time. Kennan returned to Washington, D.C., in 1928, planning to resign from the Foreign Service, but was offered an assignment in Russia. Before taking his post as second secretary to the embassy in
Moscow in 1933, Kennan spent the intervening years in Berlin; Reval,
Estonia; and Riga, Latvia, training for this service. It was during this
period that Kennan met and married Annelise Soerensen and that the
first of the couple's four children was born. After his initial assignment
in Russia, Kennan returned to Washington and the State Department
until 1938, when he was stationed in Prague, Czechoslovakia. Kennan,
on hand for the Munich Crisis that changed the fate of Europe, writes:

> The world had taken final farewell, it seemed, of nearly everything that
> these monuments [in Munich] represented. Gone were the unifying faith
> and national tolerance of the Middle Ages; gone—in large measure—was
> the glamour of the Counter-Reformation, the outward manifestation of the
> wealth and power of Rome; gone indeed were the gay dreams of the empire

of Joseph II and Maria Theresa; the laughing voice of Vienna, the spirit of
Mozart.

With the outbreak of war in Europe in 1939, Kennan was transferred
from Prague to the embassy in Berlin. In July 1940 he traveled to The
Hague and to Paris to make contact with American personnel at the
embassies in those cities. He describes the condition of these two
cities under German occupation. Paris, in particular, he viewed as
having a spirit too fragile to withstand German domination. Kennan
remained in Berlin until Germany's declaration of war on the United
States in December 1941, when he and the rest of the embassy staff
were temporarily taken into custody by the Germans.

The war years 1942 and 1943 found Kennan stationed in Portugal.
In 1944, while in London, he was assigned as Averell Harriman's
deputy in Moscow. After this tour of duty in Russia, Kennan was once
again in Washington, where he served in several capacities, first at the
National War College, then as Director of the Policy Planning Staff in
the State Department and, later, as counselor of that department. He
remained there until 1950.

In March 1949, Kennan made an official visit to the U.S. and British
zones of occupied Germany. He returned to Hamburg, a city devastated by the war, where he had served earlier in his career:

> I felt an unshakable conviction that no momentary military advantage . . .
> could have justified this stupendous, careless destruction of civilian life
> and of material values, built up laboriously by human hands over the
> course of centuries for purposes having nothing to do with this war.

Although there were to be two more periods of ambassadorial service, the bulk of Kennan's career as a Foreign Service officer was
behind him. In 1950 he moved to Princeton, New Jersey, and began
devoting his energies to teaching and writing.

Kennan returned to the Foreign Service in 1952 (at the height of the
cold war) to take the post of ambassador to Russia. He conveyed to
State Department officials his view that the monolithic structure of the
Communist party regime and of the party leaders was not invincible
and that changes would take place. Kennan was expelled from Russia
after several months as ambassador, and John Foster Dulles, head of
the State Department, decided that Kennan's career in the Foreign
Service was over. Three years earlier, at the time he moved to Princeton, Kennan had felt that the major effort of his life had come to an
end and that nothing of consequence remained for him. This belief was
reinforced by the events of that year. Sadly, when Kennan left the
State Department (after twenty-seven years), the only person he found
to say goodbye to was a receptionist.

Although Kennan's career as a public servant had ended, his productive life was far from over. In the years after leaving the State Department, he distinguished himself as a historian, teacher, and writer. Winner of both the Pulitzer Prize and the National Book Award, among others, Kennan has written eighteen books on Russia and the Soviet Union, the nuclear question, and diplomatic history. He has taught at universities and colleges throughout the world, and in his diaries he has continued to record and reflect upon his extensive travels, including his many sailing vacations in the waters off Norway and Sweden.

When Kennan returned to Berlin in 1960, fifteen years after the war's end, he and a companion went to the theater in East Berlin. Returning to West Berlin he observed:

> All about us were the ruins of the great old buildings, semisilhouetted against the bright sky. And what ruins! In their original state, they had seemed slightly imitative and pretentious. Now they suddenly had a grandeur I had never seen even in Rome. . . . There was a stillness, a beauty, a sense of infinite, elegiac sadness and timelessness such as I have never experienced. Death, obviously was near, and in the air. . . . Here all the measureless tragedy of the Second War . . . had its perpetuation.

It is this elegiac note that becomes prominent in Kennan's journal writing and, it seems, in his life. Increasingly in his travels (and as he notes in his diary), Kennan finds more to lament regarding modern society, in both the United States and Europe. There is a touching moment in Yalta (in 1976) as Kennan listens to a Soviet guide drone on in the former palace where Churchill, Stalin, and Roosevelt met.

> My mind kept returning to the image of the coming-out ball, in May 1913, of the eldest daughter of the tsar . . . in this same palace. I could see it all in retrospect: the great French windows thrown open to the view of the sea; the smell of the roses and the perfumes; the brilliance of the candles and the uniforms, the many jewels, and the flowers in the doomed girl's hair, put up for the first time in honor of the occasion.

In June 1987 he returned to Moscow to chair the American delegation at a conference of Soviet and American historians. On this trip Kennan revisited Riga: "I was constantly obliged to remind myself that I was separated from many of the objects I remembered . . . by a vast intervening catastrophe, the Second World War. . . ."

There was a moment of some splendor for Kennan when in 1987 he attended a reception in Washington for Mikhail Gorbachev, and the Russian leader said, "Mr. Kennan. We in our country believe that a man may be the friend of another country and remain, at the same time, a loyal and devoted citizen of his own; and that is the way we view you." Kennan reflects that, if he cannot have this sort of recognition from his own government for his service in the Soviet Union, then it is fitting to have it at least from the one-time adversary.

Sketches from a Life is a testament to the life of a man of moral courage and devotion to duty. Yet in some ways George Kennan is a hard man to like. He seems to be carping continually about the faults of his country. But it is precisely because he loves his country, as he points out in the epilogue, that its imperfections strike him with greater force. *Sketches from a Life* is episodic; the element that holds it together is the consistency (one might say the relentlessness) of Kennan's view of what he wants for and expects from the United States.

Although he feels that there is much that is great in U.S. society, Kennan's view is that the United States of these last years of the century is essentially a tragic country. According to Kennan, the United States has vast natural and human resources that are rapidly being wasted. He feels that the dominant political force of the country has little understanding of or regard for the intelligentsia. Kennan acknowledges the pessimism of his view, but he feels as he does because he cares about what happens in the United States. Very often in this book, Kennan comes through as a person who keeps a professional distance between himself and those around him, yet he is a passionate man with a sweeping moral vision, both of which are difficult to ignore.

Louis Sasso

SPARTINA

Author: John Casey (1939–   )
Publisher: Alfred A. Knopf (New York). 375 pp. $18.95
Type of work: Novel
Time: The present
Locale: The fishing village of Galilee, Rhode Island

This novel highlights the culmination of the lifetime dream of Dick Pierce to become captain of his own fishing boat and details Pierce's motives, both conscious and unconscious, behind the dream

Principal characters:
 DICK PIERCE, fisherman, husband, father, lover
 MAY PIERCE, Dick's wife
 ELSIE BUTTRICK, Dick's friend and lover
 LARRY PARKER, Dick's "friend"

Dick Pierce was a forty-year-old fisherman who had lived all his life in Galilee, Rhode Island. His family used to own a substantial amount of land in Galilee, but over the years the land had been sold for one reason or another. By the time Dick's father died, there was only one acre left.

Dick returned from military service to his one acre of land, with no money to build a house. He never quite forgave his father for "squandering away" the family land. But Dick managed to build his house and lived there with his wife, May, and his two sons, Charlie and Tom. Dick had spent his life scrambling for money, working for others, barely eking out a living, having to set his lobster pots in the salt marshes close to home. All he owned was an eighteen-foot skiff. His anger and resentment and bitterness with life made him testy and taciturn. In fact, he often lost jobs because of his rudeness to customers.

Now, at age forty, Dick felt at the end of his rope. If he was ever to "make it," he had to achieve his dream: to own his own fishing boat. He had been building the boat of his dreams in his backyard over the last several years, spending every spare dollar and hour he had on it. It was as big as his house, over fifty feet long, with an eighteen-foot beam. He had decided to name her *Spartina*, in tribute to the beautiful salt-marsh grass. He now needed $10,000 to complete it, and he was running low on hope. The long struggle to build the boat was taking its toll not only on Dick, but also on May and the boys. May wanted the boat in the water by the fall because she could not bear the thought of going through the confining winter months with Dick and his bad moods. It was now early summer, and time was running out.

Dick was doing everything and anything to make extra money, including fixing up clambakes for the rich summer folks, making boat repairs, and doing other odd jobs. He even slipped into the bird sanctuary to steal clams one night. Another source of illicit money came through his acquaintance with Larry Parker. Parker always had his hand in some pie or another, and it usually involved a shady deal. However, Parker owned a small fishing boat, and he often took Dick along on fishing trips for lobster, swordfish, and red crab and cut Dick in on the earnings.

One day, while Dick was working at a clambake, he ran into Elsie Buttrick, an old neighbor and ex–rich kid whose family had bought some prime Pierce property years before. She worked as an officer for the Natural Resource Department, a game-and-fish agency. During a personal conversation with Dick that day, Elsie let him know that she was aware of his transgression into the bird sanctuary and subtly warned him off. Later in the day, she approached Dick about going out on Parker's boat with a friend, Schuyler, to film a swordfishing trip. Dick arranged for Elsie and Schuyler to go along on the next fishing excursion.

On that trip, Dick became aware that little Elsie Buttrick had definitely grown up. He also found her to be smart and warm and strong-minded. Yet he still viewed her as one of the spoiled rich kids who indirectly were responsible for the loss of his family lands.

Some days later, Dick and Parker went out swordfishing again. Out at sea, Parker retrieved a stash of cocaine. He offered Dick $5,000 to help him navigate the salt marshes for a prearranged delivery onshore. With some inner turmoil, Dick went along. He wanted his boat at any cost, even his freedom. Nevertheless, the delivery had to be aborted, and Dick and Parker were forced into the salt marshes to hide out from the law (including Elsie). As Dick lay hidden in the spartina, contemplating this dire turn of events, he realized that he had lost his self-esteem; he had become a desperate man.

Some days later, safely home, Dick ran into Elsie again as she bicycled home in the rain, and he offered her a ride. She made him lunch, and as the conversation flowed comfortably, she discussed a fantasy of hers: to have a child and share the responsibility with a friend. She would choose Mary Scanlon, a mutual friend of theirs, because she, too, was unmarried, and while Elsie worked days, Mary worked nights. Elsie thought it was a perfect dream. Dick, however, found this notion a bit amusing, and Elsie got indignant and ended up having a crying fit. Dick consoled her, and before either of them knew it, they were in each other's arms.

Over the next few weeks, Dick floated along in a fog as the affair with Elsie progressed. He still pushed to find extra work, but now he had Elsie to soothe his frustrations over the lack of funds for the boat, and to act as his confidante.

Finally, however, after a particularly rewarding swordfishing trip, Dick resolved to ask for a loan from a wealthy old lady, Miss Perry, a family acquaintance for many years. This was a momentous decision for such a proud man as Dick, but he felt that he owed it to May and himself. He simply must finish the boat. As it happened, Elsie was very close to Miss Perry, and before Dick was able to meet with Miss Perry, Elsie discussed it with her and secured the $10,000 loan for Dick. Elsie even loaned him an additional $1,000 herself.

Dick threw himself wholeheartedly into completing the boat, in a fever to get it launched. He was anxious to begin his "new" life as captain. He also came to the realization that his "new" life could not include Elsie and that their affair must end.

The night before the launching and christening of the boat, Dick went by Elsie's to invite her to the event, and to discuss the termination of their affair. But, in the midst of their conversation, Mary Scanlon arrived unexpectedly. She needed a friend to talk to after attending her father's funeral. They all shared a few drinks, Elsie invited Mary to stay the night, and Dick left. Wanting to finish his conversation with Elsie, Dick returned shortly to her house but stopped outside when he heard Elsie's and Mary's voices on the back porch. He eavesdropped and discovered that Elsie was pregnant with his baby. He slipped away quietly.

The next day, a good portion of the town turned out to attend the launching. May cracked a bottle of champagne, a gift from Elsie and Mary, against the hull and christened the boat *Spartina-May*. Dick went through that day in a haze of happiness.

Not more than a couple of days later, Dick learned that Galilee was in the path of a powerful hurricane coming out of the Caribbean. The harbor master recommended that Dick tie up safely outside the harbor. But first, Dick visited his insurance agent who warned him that the *Spartina* was not insured for another two days. So, rather than risk losing her, Dick decided to go out to sea to ride out the storm.

For three terror-filled days Dick battled the seas. In retrospect, he realized he could have lost his life, but he perceived that the *Spartina* was his life. Nevertheless, he made it home in one piece, welcomed back by May and the boys and some neighbors . . . and Elsie. Although the *Spartina* had survived intact, his house had sustained considerable damage. All in all, however, Dick was grateful: *Spartina*, his livelihood, was safe, and the house was insured!

A couple of days later, Elsie caught Dick out in the harbor on his boat and took the opportunity to tell him that she was pregnant and that she had unconsciously planned it. She did not hold him responsible and wanted to care for the child herself. She also admitted that *she*, and not Miss Perry, had loaned him the $10,000. Stunned, Dick in turn confessed he had "overheard" her tell Mary she was pregnant and that he would go along with whatever she had planned. He told her that he decided he had to tell May. Elsie told him her plan was to go down to Boston for the last months of her pregnancy, and, upon her return with the baby, she would tell townspeople that she had adopted the child. Dick agreed with her plan, and they parted, knowing they would always be good friends.

Dick waited for a few months until he told May, unwilling to relinquish his newfound peace until he felt ready. When he finally told her, she handled it with dignity and grace. Her only demand was that Dick contribute to the welfare of the child. He knew then that she could live with the situation, and he was grateful. Life would go on. He was, after all, master of his destiny.

John Casey has written a profoundly moving novel, *Spartina*, which describes how the character of Dick Pierce overcomes his flaws, ultimately revealing him to be a man of honor, a man of integrity. Casey has caught the essence of the simple man who has a dream that raises him above his own pettiness and selfishness. Casey writes so flowingly, he paints his scenes so vividly, that the reader hears the wind rustling in the spartina, smells and tastes the salty breezes, squints against the brilliant skies. Casey has created a character who is likable, but who has to fight to retain his dignity, his ethics, his morals. In short, he profiles a character who is wholly human. *Spartina* is a powerful story, one that will be well-received by a widely diverse audience.

Constance Clyde

THE STORYTELLER

Author: Mario Vargas Llosa (1936–   )
Publisher: Farrar, Straus and Giroux (New York). 246 pp. $17.95
Type of work: Novel
Time: 1953 to the present
Locale: Peru; Florence, Italy

A disillusioned Peruvian intellectual travels to Florence, where he sees a photograph of an Amazonian Indian storyteller that revives his fascination with the traditional storytellers and raises questions as to the fate of a former friend

Principal characters:
THE AUTHOR, a Peruvian intellectual
SAÚL ZURATAS, a disfigured Jew who becomes a storyteller in the Amazon jungle
MR. SCHNEIL, a North American linguist who studies the Machiguenga Indians
MRS. SCHNEIL, his wife, also a linguist
TASURINCHI, the Machiguenga god who breathes life into man
KIENTIBAKORI, the evil spirit in Machiguenga lore
KASHIRI, the moon in Machiguenga lore, seen as a destructive force

In a small art gallery in Florence, Italy, a traveling Peruvian intellectual, a nameless author, sees a collection of photographs taken in his distant country, among the Machiguenga Indians of the Amazonian jungle. Some of the faces look familiar, as the author had visited the same tribe three years earlier. One photograph, of a storyteller with his face shadowed, rekindles even earlier memories of a long-disappeared former friend. The author asks the gallery owner if he can meet the photographer to find out more about the people in the pictures. Instead he finds out that the photographer has died, a victim of a fever he contracted in the jungle.

The shadowy face of the storyteller reminds the author of his old friend Saúl Zuratas, whom he had known at the university almost thirty years earlier. Zuratas is a Jew, an oddity in Peru. His father moved to a small town after immigrating from Eastern Europe; he married a *mestiza* woman and forced her to convert. Young Saúl spent his early life in the town, then moved with his family to Lima, where his mother died soon afterward. Even more unusual than Zuratas's background is his appearance. Beneath a head of frizzy red hair, his face is horribly disfigured by a birthmark that covers one entire side. Because of the disfigurement, he is nicknamed Mascarita—the masked one. When he walks through the streets people block his path and stare; a few even make cruel remarks. Zuratas refuses to fight them.

His remarkably positive attitude toward his deformity shocks and amazes the author, who calls him an "archangel." The two become close—or at least as close as Zuratas is to anyone—and they frequently meet to discuss literature, as both have a passion for Kafka and Dante.

At the university, Zuratas drifts from his law studies, in which his father has enrolled him, into the study of anthropology. He becomes particularly fascinated by the small Amazonian Indian tribes who, in contrast to the Incas, hardly have been touched by Western civilization. He begins to study the Machiguenga Indians, who wander in small family groups through the jungle, on the run from the Mashcos, an enemy tribe, and from the white people, known as the Viracocha. From the Machiguenga, Zuratas learns that anger and hatred can destroy the universe, and so he tells the author not to be angry at those who tease him for his horrifying appearance. Even so, Zuratas becomes more and more outspoken in opposing not only those who seek to Westernize and exploit the Indians but also those who merely wish to study them. Having completed his thesis with highest honors, Zuratas refuses a generous fellowship to study anthropology in France. He tells his friends and professors that his elderly father is ill and needs him at home. Zuratas's anthropology professor doubts his story, and when the author confronts Zuratas to find the truth, his old friend evades his questions.

After graduating with a degree in literature, the author is invited to take part in a one-month expedition to the Amazon as part of the Summer Language Institute. Run by a North American couple, the Schneils, the Institute studies the language and culture of the various indigenous tribes, for whom it offers a literacy program. The Machiguenga in particular arouse his interest because of Zuratas's fascination with them and because of their wandering life-style. According to their lore, the Machiguenga fear annihilation if they stay in one place too long. Their life span is short, and they are highly vulnerable to illnesses brought by outsiders. They have no leaders, for they travel in groups of eight to ten, and they are dispersed throughout the Amazon, living in territory occupied by other tribes. Typically, deformed infants are put to death, for they are seen as the creations of an evil spirit. Finally, the Schneils tell the author of the Machiguenga storytellers, who travel the region with the tribe's folklore, news, and gossip and who can hold an audience spellbound for hours on end.

When the author next sees Zuratas, he describes his expedition with the Summer Language Institute. Zuratas launches into a tirade against the Institute, which he sees as the principal destroyer of the Amazonian Indian culture, worse than the missionaries, the mine owners, and the rubber merchants. That is the last time the two ever meet. The author leaves on a fellowship to study in Spain. Later he hears that Zuratas and his father have emigrated to Israel.

In Spain, the author tries to investigate the Machiguenga storytellers, but he can find little information. He interviews a Spanish missionary, who recounts Machiguenga tales of a Dantesque world, with seven levels from the highest heaven, Inkite, to the lowest hell, Gamaironi. In Inkite resides the god Tasurinchi, who breathes life into humankind (and for whom all men, in the absence of family and given names, are named). The chief resident of Gamaironi is Kientibakori, the evil spirit who creates deformed babies and is responsible for all that goes wrong in the world. On earth, the sun struggles for predominance with a vengeful moon, known as Kashiri. When the Machiguenga die, they are reborn, sometimes as humans, sometimes as animals, sometimes as combinations of the two, although, like Kafka's Gregor Samsa, with human consciousness.

The author tries to write stories about the Machiguenga storytellers, but his efforts end in failure. He becomes involved in a number of other projects over the next two decades, and his interest in the indigenous tribe wanes. In 1981, however, he is asked to produce a cultural program for Peruvian television, and one of the programs suggested to him is a twenty-five-year retrospective of the Summer Language Institute. The Schneils are planning to depart, and the program is slated to be a chronicle of their achievements.

Upon his arrival, the author sees a changed landscape. Most of the Machiguenga are living in villages now, with leaders who speak Spanish and have been trained as ministers. The Bible and other books have been translated into their language. Many of the Indians work for the mines or the plantations, or else tap trees for rubber. Only a few Machiguenga remain in the ever-shrinking jungle, wandering from place to place to escape the reaches of civilization. The author asks some of the Indians about their storytellers, but receives no answer, even though the Indians are willing informants about every other aspect of their lives. Have the storytellers died out, he wonders. He finally receives an answer from Edwin Schneil, who describes hearing a storyteller several years earlier; for him, it was an extremely unpleasant experience. The storyteller seemed to have been an albino, or rather, he had red hair and a face that was half-white and half-purple. He had initially refused to have Schneil listen because of his hatred for the Viracocha, and his stories, which went on all night, put Schneil into a trance that left him feeling ill for days.

The author returns to the city to find information on his former friend, who he thought moved to Israel a decade earlier with his elderly father. He discovers that Zuratas's father had died in 1960, and no one had any information on the son. In Florence, the author realizes the truth, that Zuratas had gone to live with the Machiguenga and had not only become one of them but had become the tribe's storyteller, maintaining its folklore and spiritually holding the tribe together. But in telling the Machiguenga's lore, Zuratas had in a sense become the creator of that lore, weaving into the traditional mythology elements from Dante, Kafka, the Old Testament, and tales from the Jewish Diaspora. And in a gallery photograph of the Machiguenga, the author sees that the storyteller's shadowed face is the discolored and deformed side of Zuratas's face.

Vargas Llosa juxtaposes his nameless author's narrative with the stories heard and told by the storyteller himself. In those stores, Tasurinchi represents a variety of Machiguenga men—a blind old storyteller, a medicine man, a sorcerer—as well as the god who battles Kientibakori for control of the earth. As the stories unfold, one after the other, the storyteller openly weaves in Kafka's transformation stories and elements of the Judeo-Christian mythology. The reader assumes that the stories are told by Zuratas, but the author himself has endeavored to write fiction based upon the Machiguenga storytellers. The stories may be Zuratas's, or they may be the nameless author's representation of Zuratas's life.

In either case, Zuratas emerges as a unique and unforgettable character, a Western intellectual who identifies so completely with the indigenous people that he gives up his comfortable life to join them. Despite his congenital disfigurement, he is accepted by them, and in fact they protect him by refusing to mention their storytellers to ethnographers. Perhaps as a Jew he is able to sympathize with the eternal wandering of the Machiguenga. Perhaps his disfigurement, and the Western world's reaction to it, has convinced him that he will always live in solitude, behind a mask that has ironically conferred to him a special power. *The Storyteller* is a fascinating novel, one that examines the origins and development of myth as well as the encounter between two separate and incompatible cultures.

Lyn Miller-Lachmann

THE TEMPLE OF MY FAMILIAR

Author: Alice Walker (1944–   )
Publisher: Harcourt Brace Jovanovich (San Diego). 416 pp. $19.95
Type of work: Novel
Time: The present
Locale: Africa; San Francisco; Baltimore

Three generations of black Americans help each other to understand their connections and responsibilities to each other and to their collective past

> *Principal characters:*
> ZEDÉ, a weaver of feather capes, who escapes from South America to San Francisco
> CARLOTTA, the daughter of Zedé
> ARVEYDA, a famous rock star, the husband of Carlotta
> SUWELO, a professor of history
> LISSIE, lover and friend of Suwelo's Uncle Rafe
> HAL JENKINS, Lissie's husband
> FANNY NZINGHA, the wife of Suwelo
> MISS CELIE, the grandmother of Fanny
> MISS SHUG, Celie's longtime friend

Shug Avery, the flamboyant and indomitable woman who teaches the abused heroine of Alice Walker's *The Color Purple* how to love, returns in Walker's new book, *The Temple of My Familiar*. Along with Celie, whose innocent and moving letters to God form the heart of *The Color Purple*, Shug raises Celie's granddaughter, Fanny Nzingha, in a house full of independent women who are not afraid to show their love for one another, a home full of music, art, and laughter. Toward the end of her life, Miss Shug writes her own gospel. Fanny, whose mother, Olivia, grew up among missionaries in Africa, becomes a missionary of Shug's idiosyncratic teachings, invoking Shug's philosophy in trying to change the world around her. "Helped are those who love and actively support the diversity of life; they shall be secure in their differences" and "Helped are those who *know*" are the two beatitudes that end "The Gospel According to Shug." These teachings pervade and shape *The Temple of My Familiar*, a complex novel in which extremely diverse characters search for their own individual ways of knowing themselves.

It is only fitting that some of the characters from Walker's last novel should turn up in *The Temple of My Familiar*, for the novel is about connectedness, memory, and familiarity. What unites the characters is their search for the past, their struggle to understand the lives of family members whose sufferings, or even whose existence, they may temporarily have forgotten. The novel opens with the story of Zedé

and her daughter, Carlotta. Through Carlotta's eyes, the reader learns
the story of her mother's childhood in South America. Her grandmother, also named Zedé, was a kind of "sewing magician." She
sewed together brilliant peacock feathers used for traditional festivals.
When the younger Zedé grew up, she became a teacher, but during
political upheaval in her country, Guatuzolan, she was arrested; Carlotta was born in prison. Eventually, Zedé and Carlotta manage, with
the help of a mysterious white benefactor, to escape to the United
States where they begin a new life in San Francisco. Zedé begins
sewing feathered capes, like the ones her mother had crafted in the old
country. When Carlotta delivers one of these capes to the famous
singer Arveyda, the two fall in love. Zede's response to Arveyda surprises her daughter: " 'It is as if you went out,' Carlotta's mother
sobbed after that first meeting, 'and brought your father home.' "
Carlotta never knew her father, who died before her birth. After Arveyda and Carlotta have been married for three years, Arveyda and
Zedé realize they are in love and leave together on a journey of discovery back to South America, leaving the embittered Carlotta to take
care of two children.

The next episode introduces Suwelo. He has been the lover of both
Fanny, at one time his wife, and Carlotta, his colleague at a college in
San Francisco. When he inherits the house in Baltimore that had belonged to his great-uncle Rafe, Suwelo begins a journey that will take
him back into Rafe's past and finally into his own, bringing him closer
to both Fanny and Carlotta at the novel's end. At his uncle's house,
Suwelo meets Hal Jenkins, an old friend of Rafe's from their childhood
on an island "'cross the bay from Charleston." They lived happily on
this island as the children of black laborers on the white-owned plantations. Hal married Lissie Lyles, the soul mate he had known all his
life. Lissie means "the one who remembers everything," and Lissie
does, as Suwelo gradually discovers. Miss Lissie, now a very old
woman who lives with Hal in Baltimore, remembers not only her past
in this life, but a seemingly endless string of lives, stretching back to
Africa, where she was captured by slave traders, and even further
back, to a time before men had taken away matriarchal power and
murdered the "Goddess." As the book progresses, Suwelo will learn
that Lissie was not always a black woman, but has also had lives as a
white man and as a lion. Lissie is the model for connectedness with
the past: "Some people don't understand that it is the nature of the
eye to have seen forever, and the nature of the mind to recall anything
that was ever known." Lissie is able to see what "man" has done to
women and to nature. Lissie had loved Rafe because he was the only
one who understood how many different people were within her. By

imparting the wisdom of her special gift to Suwelo, she enables him to understand the suffering of his parents and of the two women in his life, Fanny and Carlotta.

The danger of neither remembering nor respecting the past is expressed in Lissie's allegorical dream about the temple of her familiar. Her familiar, "what you might these days, unfortunately, call a 'pet,' " in Lissie's past and in her dream was a magical little companion, a beautiful bird who lived with her in her own personal temple. But Lissie grew proud and tried to control the little familiar by capturing it. The creature continually broke through any container she used. Finally, the familiar broke completely free and left Lissie, not with her own personal temple, but with a cold, stone building, in a different century from her own. Her only connection to the happiness of her past was the memory of "the beautiful little familiar, who was so cheerful and loyal to me, and whom I so thoughtlessly, out of pride and distraction, betrayed." Lissie seems to be educating Suwelo on the subject of freedom. With the help of Hal and Lissie, Suwelo learns that he can love Fanny without confining her in marriage (which she hates), and he learns to open himself up to the memory of his dead parents, whose misery he has successfully repressed for years.

Suwelo has felt estranged from Fanny, who demands a divorce but never stops loving him, in part because her own roots in Africa have become so important to her. On a trip to Africa with her mother Olivia (Celie's daughter), Fanny realizes for the first time that she has a father who is still alive. He is a famous political playwright named Ola who continues to criticize the government of his people, the Olinka, even after the blacks take control from the white colonizers. Fanny grows close to Ola, and after he dies, she bonds with his daughter by another marriage, Nzingha Anne. The two vow to continue writing subversive plays and to keep the spirit of their father alive. In addition to renewing her ties with Africa, Fanny is able, through therapy, to remember the white prejudice against her and her "grandmothers" Shug and Celie during her childhood in the American South.

Due to Suwelo's growing sensitivity under the influence of Hal and Lissie, and due to Fanny's understanding of both of her parents, the two are able to reunite while remaining free of the bonds of marriage and jealousy. At the end of the novel, Fanny and Suwelo have become friends with Arveyda and Carlotta, themselves reconciled after Arveyda's return from South America without Zedé. Carlotta is happier because she can visit her mother Zedé and her grandmother Zedé, both living in Mexico. Also, Arveyda is now content to stay with Carlotta and their children. Fanny and Arveyda become sexually involved, as do Carlotta and Suwelo, yet because they all have come to a mature understanding of themselves by confronting their pasts, they are able to give and take each other's love freely.

The Temple of My Familiar differs from *The Color Purple* in many ways. In her earlier work, Walker relied heavily on regional dialect to create atmosphere and character. In contrast, most of the characters in *The Temple of My Familiar* are well educated and, to varying degrees, assimilated. They are artists or teachers, and they all seem to speak in a similar, rather unrealistically literary way. Realism, however, is not the style or objective of this novel. There is no chronological narration, and many of the people and places have a mythic quality. Walker uses magic, but sparingly, as if trying to avoid the haunting magical realism so beautifully mastered by another important chronicler of black American experience, Toni Morrison.

Walker has managed to connect the lives of many individuals in her novel, and to portray the impact of each life on many others. Furthermore, she has attempted to show how past generations are able to influence the present and, through those few people with a magical gift like that of Miss Lissie, how past generations can literally speak to the present. One underlying strain of *The Temple of My Familiar* is the way in which art transmits culture and unites people. Zedé is a magical weaver; Arveyda is a seductive musician; Hal's father was a masterful woodcarver; Hal and Lissie are devoted painters. At one point, Arveyda has a revelation about his own mission as an artist: "Artists, he now understood, were simply messengers. On them fell the responsibility for uniting the world." Walker has certainly taken on a daunting task in imagining how the lives of so many black American individuals develop within history and in relation to an ongoing history of oppression. Her novel offers not just one but numerous utopian possibilities within a society plagued with racial prejudice and patriarchal domination. The connections between Celie and Shug, Hal and Lissie, Arveyda and Zedé stand as examples of love from which the younger generation of black and white Americans must learn if it is to prevent its own destruction.

Nancy E. Henry

THIS BOY'S LIFE: A MEMOIR

Author: Tobias Wolff (1945–   )
Publisher: The Atlantic Monthly Press (New York). 288 pp. $18.95
Type of work: Autobiography
Time: 1955–1961
Locale: Salt Lake City, Utah; Seattle, Concrete, and Chinook, Washington

Author Tobias Wolff recounts his childhood as he moved across country with his divorced mother to escape her violent boyfriend and ended up living in a small town with a stepfather who hated him

> Principal personages:
> TOBIAS WOLFF, a boy who overcame his troubled youth to become an award-winning writer
> ROSEMARY WOLFF, Tobias's mother, a woman convinced she would find good luck even as her life was marred by cruel men
> DWIGHT, Rosemary's second husband, who hated and abused Tobias
> ARTHUR GAYLE, Tobias's best friend in Chinook
> CHUCK BOLGER, Tobias's drinking companion
> MR. HOWARD, an alumnus who interviewed Tobias for admission to the Hill School
> GEOFFREY WOLFF, Tobias's older brother, a student at Princeton

Tobias lived with his mother following his parents' divorce. Over the next six years he neither saw nor spoke with his father and his older brother, Geoffrey, a student at Choate and then Princeton who wrote sophisticated and polished short stories. Tobias moved with his mother across the country as she tried to escape from Roy, her alcoholic, unemployed, and violent boyfriend. Rosemary first settled in Salt Lake City, where she hoped to become rich by finding uranium. Instead, she worked as a secretary. Roy found her there, moved in with them, and curried Tobias's favor by teaching him how to shoot and giving him a rifle as a birthday present. Tobias would skip school, stay at home with his loaded rifle, and enjoy the feeling of power he gained from the thought that he could shoot passersby. He never did shoot at a person, but enjoyed killing animals and hitting parked cars.

Several months later, Rosemary again moved with her son, settling in Seattle. This time Roy did not find them. Tobias, a poor student at school, channeled his energies into stealing candy and toys from stores. One day Tobias was caught at school carving an obscenity on a bathroom wall. His mother was summoned, but by the time she arrived, Tobias had convinced himself of his innocence and therefore was able to convince Rosemary that the school principal was unjustly punishing her son. Rosemary demanded justice for Tobias, and the principal relented.

Rosemary was concerned about her son's poor grades and delinquent friends. By now she was being courted by Dwight, a short, ugly, divorced father of three teenagers. Tobias "knew [his] mother would never let herself get tangled up in a mess like that." Tobias accompanied his mother on a Thanksgiving visit to Dwight's home in Chinook, a tiny company town in the Cascade Mountains of Washington. After Seattle, Tobias and his mother found Chinook boring. Nevertheless, Rosemary accepted Dwight's offer to let Tobias live with him and attend school in Chinook. Rosemary hoped that her son's behavior would improve away from his Seattle companions and under a steady male influence. If Tobias was happy in Chinook, his mother told him, she would quit her job in Seattle and marry Dwight.

Dwight treated Tobias with contempt and cruelty. He put his future stepson to work shelling thousands of chestnuts. The work cut Tobias's hands and stained them yellow, which provoked teasing from his new schoolmates. Dwight also forced Tobias to take on a newspaper delivery route, promising to hold Tobias's earnings for the future. (Years later, when Tobias finally left home, he learned that Dwight had spent all the money Tobias had earned.) Tobias refused to tell his mother that he was unhappy with Dwight, believing that his mother was ordained to marry that man and in so doing ruin both their lives.

Once she arrived in Chinook, Rosemary knew she had made a mistake. She was reluctant, however, to fail at marriage for a second time and remained with Dwight. He abused her as well as Tobias. The family went to shooting exhibitions where Dwight always missed the target and Rosemary often won first prize. After her success, Dwight would become sullen, stopping at bars on the way home until he was drunk and then driving recklessly on dangerous mountain roads.

At school in Chinook, and later at the high school in nearby Concrete (named for the factory that employed most of the locals and blanketed the town with concrete dust), Tobias again was a poor student and spent his time with the most troubled boys. His best friend was Arthur Gayle, like Tobias a gentle boy who pretended to be a bully. Occasionally, Tobias and Arthur fought, egged on by other students and by Mr. Mitchell, a teacher who loved fights and required students to list the right to bear arms as their "favorite amendment." Also in Tobias's circle were Chuck Bolger, son of a fundamentalist minister and the supplier of liquor to his friends, and Gerald Huff, who enjoyed discussing sex and later was faced with marrying a pregnant girlfriend.

On various occasions, Tobias tried to escape his stepfather. Dwight made Tobias join the Boy Scouts, and at Scout conventions in Seattle, Tobias dreamed of running away. Once Tobias brought eighty dollars he had accumulated by stealing from the homes of people on his newspaper route. Tobias's plan was thwarted, however, when he lost the money gambling at a fair next to the Scout convention. On another occasion, Tobias wrote to his maternal uncle, exaggerating the abuse he suffered from Dwight. The uncle wrote to Rosemary, offering to adopt Tobias, but Tobias decided that he did not want to lose his mother as well as his father, and so remained in Chinook.

Tobias did become attached to his step-siblings. Skipper spent his time rebuilding an antique car. Norma, who became an object of Tobias's sexual fantasies, married a nasty Seventh-Day Adventist named Kenneth who enjoyed baiting Dwight about his drinking. Tobias treated Pearl, an ugly and shy girl his own age, with kindness. Yet Tobias was continually angered by Dwight's favoritism to his own three children and wanton cruelty toward Tobias. Dwight refused to send in the final certificate to allow Tobias to become an Eagle Scout after years of effort to accumulate the necessary badges.

Finally, after four years in Chinook, Tobias telephoned his older brother Geoffrey at Princeton and told him of his plight. Geoffrey suggested that Tobias apply to prep schools for scholarships. Tobias was contacted by his father, who urged him to attend Deerfield, from which the elder Wolff had been expelled. Tobias did well on the standardized admission test, but he needed to submit a transcript and recommendations from teachers who hated him and coaches for whom he had never played. Tobias solved the problem by stealing blank transcript forms and school stationery. He invented a straight-A record for himself and wrote glowing recommendations from his teachers and coaches. Although he was rejected by Deerfield, Tobias was accepted at the Hill School. Mr. Howard, a Hill School alumnus who lived in Seattle, interviewed Tobias and later helped him with advice on what to expect at prep school and bought him an elegant wardrobe so that he would fit in at the elite school.

Once Tobias knew he would be leaving Chinook, he could no longer bear to live with Dwight. Rosemary arranged for Tobias to live with Chuck Bolger's family. Tobias was with Chuck when he was accused of getting poor Tina Flood pregnant. Fortunately for Chuck, several other boys were also involved with her. Chuck was saved from a choice of marriage or prison when Gerald Huff agreed to marry Tina. Wolff's memoir ends with Tobias and Chuck singing for joy at their respective escapes from Dwight and Tina. The happiness of that moment is not undercut by Wolff's brief overview of his years at Hill

School, from which he was expelled, and his later years as a soldier in Vietnam.

Wolff's memoir captures the sensibilities of a boy as he develops into a teenager. The reader views Rosemary and her boyfriends, as well as the other adults and children in Tobias's life, through the eyes of a boy. The reader empathizes with Tobias's anger toward Dwight and the other adult bullies in his life, and shares the young Wolff's concern for his mother's happiness and his desire to escape Chinook for the privilege of Hill School. Yet the narrator is Wolff as an adult, who adds to the boy's recollections an adult's understanding of the child. Wolff layers the memoir with suggestions of his mature realizations of his and his mother's motives at the time. Wolff even sees some of Dwight in himself when he becomes a father, and is ready to sympathize with, although not to excuse, Dwight and Rosemary's failings as parents.

The title of Wolff's memoir seems a purposeful contrast to *Boy's Life* magazine, which depicted the supposed idyllic lives of young boys. *This Boy's Life* is written in a vivid and realistic style. The reader is able to visualize all the houses and towns in which Tobias spent his boyhood. Images of the dark and damp Washington State forests accent the bleakness of Tobias's years under Dwight's domination. Yet, the memoir never becomes gloomy. Wolff's wit is felt in every recollection. The reader never loses awareness of the fact that Tobias Wolff survived his childhood, escaping with the capacity to write sympathetically about his experiences and those of his family, friends, and tormentors.

Richard Lachmann

TO ASMARA

Author: Thomas Keneally (1935–   )
Publisher: Warner Books (New York). 290 pp. $18.95
Type of work: Novel
Time: The present
Locale: Australia; England; the Sudan; Eritrea

An Australian journalist discovers the truth about the Eritrean rebellion and himself in the course of a journey to Asmara

> *Principal characters:*
> DARCY, an Australian journalist
> BERNADETTE YANG, his wife
> STELLA HARRIES, a BBC correspondent
> ROLAND MALMÉDY/MASIHI, a French cinematographer
> CHRISTINE MALMÉDY, Masihi's daughter
> MARK HENRY, an American aid worker
> PETRA, Henry's Somali fiancée
> "COLONEL" TESSFAHA, an Eritrean rebel leader
> MAJOR FIDA, a downed Ethiopian pilot
> DAVID BURRAPTITI, an Australian Aborigine, Bernadette's lover
> AMNA NURHUSSEIN, an Eritrean rebel

An Australian-born journalist named Darcy has disappeared while covering the rebellion of Eritrea against the Ethiopian central government. Although the fate of this journalist remains a mystery, it is a minor one when compared to the greater mystery of how an African war that has been going on for approximately a quarter of a century has received so little notice in the Western press—excepting the rock concerts staged to aid the starving.

The popular Western conception of the situation in Africa is characterized for Darcy by another television appearance of a rock star. The singer condemns the actions of the Eritrean rebels, who have supposedly ambushed and burned a convoy of famine-aid trucks. In an obvious parallel of Band Aid and USA for Africa, this singer has participated in a musical relief project called Worldbeat, and his anger against the Eritreans will translate into very bad press for their rebellion—just what the Ethiopians most desire.

Darcy becomes interested in learning the truth that lies beneath the slick media-presented surface of this incident. At the prompting of Stella Harries, BBC correspondent at Khartoum, Darcy meets the Eritrean leader "Colonel" Tessfaha, who is visiting London. He tells Darcy that it is an Ethiopian ruse to disguise shipments of armaments as aid convoys, hence the attack. When Darcy expresses sarcasm, since Tessfaha is scarcely an objective source of information, the colonel offers him the chance to come to Eritrea himself and observe an attack on a similar false convoy.

Darcy accepts and soon finds himself in the Sudan, awaiting transportation into Eritrea. In his company are an American aid worker named Mark Henry and a French girl named Christine Malmédy. Christine is in her twenties yet has the vulnerability of a child. She is the daughter of Roland Malmédy, better known to the natives as Masihi—"*He who expects the Messiah.*" Masihi is a cinematographer who has been immortalizing the Eritrean struggle for independence for years, while his family remained in France. It is almost as if the revolution were Masihi's mistress.

For some reason not immediately revealed to her companions, Christine has decided to come to Africa and seek out her father. This will be difficult, considering her total lack of survival skills for traveling in Islamic countries and the fact that she must seek out Masihi as he travels from place to place, strictly on the spur of the moment, through what is a war zone. Darcy immediately takes her under his wing, refusing to consider her as anything other than a child in need of help and protection.

Mark Henry has the familiarity with things African that Christine lacks. An agricultural student, Peace Corps veteran, and worker for Southern Unitarian Aid (SUA), he has done extensive work in many Third World nations. His connection with Eritrea is a tangled one. While in Ethiopia, he fell in love with a woman named Petra, a Somali who is now supposedly under house arrest in Addis Ababa. Henry explains that he is currently negotiating to get Petra an exit visa. As Henry tells about her, Darcy seems to recall Stella having mentioned the situation, ending with the chilling statement that the woman was probably already dead. Henry was himself exiled from Ethiopia when Haile Mariam Mengistu, leader of the Ethiopian government—the Dergue—had all SUA people expelled for giving aid to the Eritrean rebels.

The journey to Eritrea proves to be one of succeeding revelations, some involving Darcy's traveling companions, some touching the true situation in Eritrea, some merely his own flashes of awareness concerning his past. In Port Sudan they encounter an Eritrean-run clinic for the veterans of the rebellion. Here they see many young amputees, unembittered, who work assiduously at their studies. The theme of continuing education—grammar lessons in the teeth of the guns—is one that permeates the whole fabric of the rebellion.

While they are in Port Sudan, Henry tells Darcy that he has learned what set Christine off in search of her father: she has had an abortion. Darcy does not believe him and finds his attitude obnoxious. This conversation, however, leads to Darcy's giving Henry a very bowdler-ized version of his own marital status. The true story he reserves for himself.

In Australia, Darcy was married to Bernadette Yang, an Australian-Chinese woman he met while working as a volunteer lawyer for the Aboriginal Legal Service. After they marry, Darcy and Bernadette decide to devote themselves completely to helping the Aborigines on their own tribal turf, specifically in the settlement of Fryer River.

Here their marriage crumbles, for while Darcy is apparently ac-cepted by the tribal elders and allowed some participation in the rich mystic background of Aboriginal beliefs, Bernadette is shut out. Alien-ated, she complains to Darcy, who is too wrapped up in his own Third World experience to give her any support. Angered, Bernadette delib-erately flouts tribal taboos. When the elders demand that Darcy do something about her, he is unwilling to risk his precious new adoptive status even to defend his wife.

At last, Bernadette runs off with David Burraptiti, a citified Aborig-ine with a jail record. The shame of this incident makes it impossible for Darcy to remain in Fryer River. He now experiences the ostracism that drove Bernadette to desperation. When he tracks her down in a city and attempts a reconciliation, it is too little, too late. She has borne Burraptiti a child and is finished with Darcy. The story is re-vealed in installments throughout his Eritrean travels, which prompt Darcy himself to reflect on the many parallels linking Australia with Africa.

Another story interwoven with the saga of Darcy's trek to the battle-front is that of the captured Ethiopian pilot Major Fida. When his plane is downed by the Eritreans, he learns firsthand that the Dergue has lied about the supposed tortures he may expect at the hands of his captors. Prisoners of war are treated well. Darcy confirms this when he visits Fida, delivering a letter from his wife. What is more, since Fida is no longer of use to them, the Ethiopians behave as if he never existed. Disillusioned, he agrees to help Colonel Tessfaha on a raid against an Ethiopian airbase. Despite the fact that during this raid Tessfaha dies, many Russian-made aircraft are destroyed.

Back with Darcy's party, the three travelers meet the lovely and elegant Amna Nurhussein, an Eritrean woman for whom Darcy con-ceives a grand infatuation. She was once a prisoner of the Dergue, but she dismisses her experiences as minor torture—nothing worse than the beatings on the soles of her feet that left her only intermittently lame. Darcy fantasizes about how he might best approach Amna, whose natural elegance and Third World otherness simultaneously at-tract him and compel him to keep his distance.

Eventually, along the battle line called the Nacfa Front, Christine finds her father, Masihi. Their reunion is in no way awkward, which gives Darcy a stab of envy. Masihi immediately conscripts Christine as a member of his film crew, and she takes to it like a natural. Gone is the childish helplessness. She even takes Darcy aside and explains to him the full story behind her departure from France. She did not have an abortion, as she said to make Henry leave her alone. She did bear a child, but the baby died after less than a day, and she realized that she had nothing left to keep her in her old life. As for Henry, it is revealed that he has been placing electronic tracking devices at the various sites they have visited, so that Ethiopian bombers can target them. This was probably done in an attempt to buy the favor of the Dergue and win Petra's freedom. Henry is expelled from Eritrea.

The group proceeds to a rendezvous with the rebels' planned ambush of the arms shipment disguised as an aid convoy. They do not know that Tessfaha, who was supposed to meet them, has been killed. The night before the ambush, Masihi tells Darcy the truth about Amna: the Dergue tortured her horribly, to the full extent of their diabolic skills. Now the gulf separating the comfortable Western journalist and the African rebel is even wider; he cannot possibly comprehend all she has suffered and lost. To his mind, there is no way he can ever approach her.

The convoy arrives and is attacked. As has become the norm, there is little resistance from the conscripted Ethiopian troops. The rebels start to burn the trucks, then learn to their shock that the Ethiopians have second-guessed them. The trucks really do contain famine relief. Everyone plunges in to the attempt to salvage the convoy, including Amna and Darcy, who together leap into the cab of a burning truck and drive it away. The truck explodes. Amna's body is found, but Darcy's is not. His fate remains unknown.

Thomas Keneally has done an admirable job of showing the reader the modern equivalent of the 19th-century "romance of Africa" mystique. His Westerners view Third World people in terms of ideals, not as human beings. They cannot be troubled to learn the gritty truths behind the nightly news stories that present far too little of the situation for it to be really understood. Like Darcy with the Aborigines, and later with Amna, Westerners see the Third World as either in need of aid and pity, or removed to some untouchable mystic sphere that none can ever hope to penetrate.

Esther M. Friesner

A TURN IN THE SOUTH

Author: V. S. Naipaul (1932–   )
Publisher: Alfred A. Knopf (New York). 307 pp. $18.95
Type of work: Travel
Time: The present
Locale: The southeastern United States

*The author journeys through former slave states interviewing a cross section
of black and white Americans to probe the complexities of Southern identity*

Principal personages:
V. S. NAIPAUL, a London-based author

Jimmy, a New York artist, asks his assistant, Howard, what he
would do if he could not get a job. Howard says, "I would go home to
my mama." Naipaul's journey begins with this (to him) remarkable
and foreign notion of "home." He joins Howard on a visit to the tiny,
flat, Carolinian town of Bowen to explore the duality of this young
black man's rootedness and restlessness.

Later, visiting various sections of Atlanta, Naipaul hopes to meet
members of the black elite who reportedly run the city. But, for all its
glass and high-rise splendor, Atlanta seems lifeless and semiderelict.
A black leader wryly explains that political power without real wealth
is meaningless. In Forsyth County, Georgia (scene of a brutal racial
clash in 1912), Sheriff Walraven tells Naipaul that despite the freedoms
won during the civil rights movement, there are still no blacks in
Forsyth County. He describes the plight not of a race but of an under-
class—black and white—who, without job-training and opportunities,
will be forever locked in a losing struggle for power.

Naipaul travels to a hundred-year-old Appalachian settlement and
meets Esther Lefever, who runs the community and craft center. She
stresses the importance of identity: when you know who you are, you
can outlast the hostility of others. A religious scholar tells the author
that religious faith is the core of one's identity, especially in the South.
This is a view Naipaul will hear expressed again and again throughout
his travels.

Anne Siddons, a novelist, feels rooted and yoked to the South. She
tells Naipaul that racism is not about race but about power. Poor and
rural whites struggle to stay above blacks, whom they fear and hate.
For a white woman in the South, she adds, power means snaring a
man.

Visiting a theology school, Naipaul meets a woman who finds her
identity in being "part of the herd." Her family has lived in the same
house for 200 years. Her aunts speak of the Civil War as if it were

yesterday, showing off their old houses and period costumes. One student, a young man named Frank, moans that "the twentieth century is pouring over the mountain." He has found a new sense of community in theology school. In conversations with an Atlanta school-board member and a young mayoral candidate, both black, Naipaul observes that alongside the efforts of the black community to join the mainstream of America there is a longing for a solidarity, a community, that desegregation has taken away.

With its brisk tourist trade, historic Charleston stands in stark contrast to the black housing projects that border it. To Naipaul the blacks seem almost like squatters, although in this region they are as "old" as the "old families." He explores the South Carolina coastal forest with Jack Leland, a retired newspaperman. They tour Leland's family's plantation as Leland explains how early fortunes were made in indigo and then rice and cotton. Before the Depression, blacks and whites lived side by side; there was social separation but also respect.

When Naipaul visits the Confederate Memorial, he sees grief for the past as a kind of religion. Slavery and the Civil War left wounds that blacks and whites both bear. He is aware of Southerners' sense of heroism and of grand defeat. Tellingly, a historical essay by Herbert Sass evokes the romance and beauty of plantation life in 1850 but makes no mention of slavery. Marion Sass, the historian's son, tells Naipaul that he mourns for a past he never really knew, while resenting the North's crass commercialization of the South.

Leland drives Naipaul past "cracker houses"—homes for "poor white trash" and backwoods whites. The author meets Alex Sanders, a judge, who explains that in the Southern culture there is more to life than the moment. Family and God matter greatly.

In Tallahassee, Naipaul compares Caribbean blacks, a freed majority in their own land, to American blacks, a freed yet powerless minority in the world's most advanced economy. He recalls James Baldwin's urging blacks to make a "truce with reality." Naipaul wonders if blacks now need to make a truce with the irrationality surrounding them.

Bernyce Clausell, a Baptist pastor and social worker, like many in this book, laments the vanishing structures of the black family and church community. Granger is a white Baptist who dreads the advent of developers. Barrett, a thirtyish middle-class black relocating from the urban North, suffers both culture shock and loss, finding himself without minority status.

Booker T. Washington University in Tuskegee, Alabama, is Naipaul's next stop. Once a beacon of hope for newly freed slaves, it is now a slightly shabby campus in need of repairs. Even the elevator donated by Henry Ford is broken. Staying in the university dorm, Naipaul meets the oldest person on campus—a black musician who arrived in 1913 with $1.50 in his pocket. The university persists as a black sanctuary in a desegregated world.

In Jackson, Mississippi, Naipaul sees "shotgun houses" in black inner-city slums, street-corner prayer meetings, and much street life. A white woman, Ellen, tells him that the blacks have it so much better now: instead of being servants, they can work at McDonalds or a bank or a store. Naipaul finds the South steeped in nostalgia for its past. Louise, eighty years old, misses the forests and wildflowers of her childhood in the Mississippi delta. She believes that class divisions have more to do with behavior and seemliness than race or occupation. She likes living with blacks—she enjoys their warmth and humor.

Naipaul visits a catfish farm and observes harvesting and flavor testing. He meets Sam Hinote, who has built up the fish-farming co-operative, employing blacks and out-of-work farmers.

A young man named Campbell is one of the new conservative breed —very authoritarian. He is glad that his children fear him. Although he hates the church, he loves its values. Calling himself a "law-and-order, blood-and-guts guy," he describes for Naipaul the definitive Southern redneck. In a short meeting, Eudora Welty discusses the pioneer character of the redneck and the strong historical continuity in the South.

In Memphis, Naipaul visits Elvis Presley's Graceland and is struck by the abundance and extravagance of the place and the people. Obesity seems to him almost characteristic of the redneck. In Nashville he attends the Grand Ole Opry. Allen Reynolds, a music producer, shows Naipaul grocery bags full of tapes from musical hopefuls and describes country and western music as "white soul," the down-home music that unites poor and oppressed whites. Many call Nashville the buckle of the Bible Belt. Will Campbell, a Baptist minister, worries about the strain of fundamentalism that offers a "theology of certainty." He sees danger in a religion with an answer for everything.

Naipaul visits a Nissan plant in Smyrna, Tennessee, that combines a Japanese corporate structure with a Southern labor force. It seems to be a world unto itself—efficient and complete. Job security, new wealth, and economic revitalization will come at a price, however. Naipaul envisions the traffic, the tension, the crowds, and the crime that follow industrialization.

Before moving north to Chapel Hill, North Carolina, Naipaul deplores the insufferable heat of summer in northwestern Georgia. He muses that perhaps the Southern obsession with religion is like a life beyond the senses.

James Applewhite, poet and teacher at Duke University in Durham, shows Naipaul a tobacco field. As Jim tells it, this crop that gave the region its culture is now in commercial decline. Naipaul sees each stage of history as marked by small ruins to the landscape. Jim is attracted to tobacco for its impracticality; like art, it has a divine uselessness.

Naipaul discerns a completeness in his journey, which began with Howard on a black street and ended with Jim on a white street. The two Southerners are from different worlds but united by a common wound and a common hunger.

In V. S. Naipaul's first travel book, he wrote about the former slave colonies of the Caribbean and South America. His own grandparents were immigrants from India to the former slave colony of Trinidad, where he grew up. For his latest travel book, he says, he wished to explore the old slave states of the American Southeast. His is a journey of gentle curiosity and observation—a quiet, almost passive, meandering. His personal interest in family origin and historical pattern adds flavor and texture to his travel descriptions. The South he discovers is one that seems to move from crisis to crisis: the Civil War, Reconstruction, the Great Depression, the civil rights movement, agricultural decline.

Naipaul begins *A Turn in the South* with an interest in the issue of race but soon finds "that other South—of order and faith, and music and melancholy." His book portrays wounded people with a past they can neither shed nor regain. Naipaul's method of exploration is loose and open ended. Most meetings are serendipitous and most conversations desultory. Naipaul enters other people's lives briefly and intensely. He looks closely, with a visitor's fresh eye. He listens carefully, as an outsider, to what people say about who they are and what they want. This process reveals a cultural and geographical terrain rich with contradiction and stubbornly rooted in the past. In the end, Naipaul brings alive on the page the passion and pain of the Southern soul.

Wendy DuBois

WARTIME: UNDERSTANDING AND BEHAVIOR IN THE SECOND WORLD WAR

Author: Paul Fussell (1924–)
Publisher: Oxford University Press (New York). 330 pp. $19.95
Type of work: Social criticism
Time: 1939–1945
Locale: The United States; Europe; the Pacific area

An examination of the impact of World War II on common soldiers and civilians alike, as well as a description of the emotional and psychological atmosphere during the period of wartime

The outbreak of war in Europe in 1939 and its eventual spread to include Japan and the United States changed completely the way in which battles were fought. The Second World War also ushered in a degree of mechanization in warfare that had not existed previously. Yet even as German tanks swiftly and deftly crushed various European countries, the military establishment in both Britain and the United States clung to the notion of the usefulness of cavalry in battle. Only after the two nations were well into the struggle did thinking about this sort of thing change, and, supported by engineering and science, the war by its end bore little resemblance to the war as it had begun. Fussell points out that what was needed was a change in thinking regarding winning the war—subtlety, finesse, accuracy went by the board, and massive power became the factor that made all the difference in the outcome.

Initially, it was believed that precision bombing would carry the day. The B-17 Flying Fortress with its Norden bombsight was touted as the mightiest bomber ever, but by the war's end, 22,000 of the Allied bombers had been destroyed, along with 16,000 airmen killed. Flight crews had no control over wind, weather, and cloud cover, and the effectiveness of the enemy's antiaircraft flak had been severely underestimated.

The American troops who fought in the war were unprepared for what they were to experience. For most of them this was their first war. The United States had no real standing army, and the vast majority of troops, therefore, were "neophytes and amateurs, plucked from civilian life to engage in deadly on-the-job training." Simple fear can lead to a great many fatal errors. War relies on the young for their physical stamina and their innocence about their own immortality.

Soldiers in World War II were, according to Fussell, the epitome of anonymity. They were in effect interchangeable parts, and it is this factor of interchangeability that would be instrumental in the winning of the war. But soldiers, in wartime at least, hated being looked upon and treated this way. In wartime military life, a compound of hatred and fear finds expression in an idiom that implies contempt for persons and things as a matter of course. In this context, expletives take over and become the pattern of everyday speech. Within the wartime atmosphere there is a type of behavior referred to as "chickenshit," something that makes military life worse than it needs to be: "petty harassment of the weak by the strong; open scrimmage for power and authority and prestige; sadism thinly disguised as necessary discipline; a constant 'paying off of old scores': and insistence on the letter rather than the spirit of ordinances."

During World War II, escape for the ordinary soldier from absurdity, boredom, contempt, and damage to one's self-esteem was drink. One American soldier on Okinawa drank a fifth and a half of whiskey daily as the only way to go on killing. Once the war was over, he stopped drinking entirely. According to Fussell, "the canteens of those at the cutting edge [of the fighting] contained brandy, whisky, or gin almost as often as water." On the home front there was a lot of drinking as well—ostensibly to calm nerves. The front was one wartime place that was sexless. Soldiers were generally too scared, busy, hungry, tired, and demoralized to think about sex.

There was much typecasting by the military during the war. In the military world, rank and branch of service pegged individuals. For the military there were basically four groups in the civilian world: (1) females—wife, sister, mother, grandmother, as well as "agents of sexual solace'; (2) elderly men; (3) the very young; and (4) 4-F, or those physically unfit. As for the enemy, they were severely dehumanized and demeaned and were classified on a scale ranging from courageous to cowardly. The Japanese were considered the bravest but the most bestial (Americans hated the Japanese most). The Italians were looked on as the most cowardly but the most human, and the Germans ranked someplace between the Japanese and the Italians.

There was reluctance to talk about the purposes for which the war was being fought because, as Fussell reveals, there was no clear recognizable reason for the killing and maiming. It may have been, in part, because coming so close on the heels of the Great War of 1914-1918, the repetition of war was so demoralizing that no one felt it appropriate to focus on either making the war understood or explaining it. For most Americans the war seemed to be about avenging the attack on Pearl Harbor, and the reason that the European part had to be finished first was so that complete attention could be paid to the destruction of Japan.

During the war, raising and sustaining morale became all important, and morale itself developed into one of the unique obsessions of the Allies. Euphemisms came into regular and widespread use, and military officers such as MacArthur and Eisenhower had their own publicity officers. In some cases the truth was shaded and actualities tinted so that morale would be kept at a high level. War correspondents and radio broadcasters were actively enjoined by the military from reporting information that would be disturbing either to the troops or to those at home.

A tone of high-mindedness may have been manufactured to go along with the fighting of the war. It was as though the elementary logic of wartime requires the enemy to be totally evil and the Allies to be totally good. Fussell reports that for most Americans the war was looked on almost as a religious operation. (General Eisenhower, before the invasion of Normandy, called the undertaking "The Great Crusade.") At times it seemed as though virtue and not power would defeat the Axis. Almost anything was acceptable so long as it sounded sincere and patriotic and seemed to minister to the spirit of group self-satisfaction.

The various outlets of popular culture were spoken out with one voice in support of the war effort. Radio, popular music, and films presented a united front in maintaining a high tone regarding the waging of the war. The film industry, particularly, had an impressive effect, and in most cases, films spoke out with one optimistic voice. In many cases a particular branch of the service had the power to approve a screenplay or it would not cooperate in the making of a movie.

For the duration of the war there were many shortages of goods for civilians. In Britain, rationing and shortages were harsher than in the United States, but Americans supposedly took deprivation harder than their British counterparts. Americans were shocked by the shortages "because the 'frontier' aura of 'freedom' had governed for so long most Americans' imaginative and psychological relations with their peers. Visible possessions and conspicuous consumption had been the traditional signals of personal distinction . . . and now to be told by the government that one could not buy and exhibit [certain goods] was a heavy blow to the psyche."

Troops in World War II held the conviction that optimistic publicity and euphemisms had portrayed their experience falsely and that it would never be readily communicable. The real war, one of fear and death, was never fully conveyed to the people at home either in Britain or in the United States.

It is difficult to read this book and not come away with the feeling that Fussell has written a mean-spirited and carping study of what was really at work during the fighting of the Second World War. But Fussell states with clarity his reason for writing *Wartime*: "For the past fifty years the Allied war has been sanitized . . . by the sentimental, the loony patriotic, the ignorant, and the bloodthirsty. I have tried to balance the scales."

This book is an effort to demystify those aspects of the war which have been glorified. Most Americans never experienced the destructive horror of the war firsthand, and time has tended to gloss over the more devastating aspects of fighting. *Wartime*, whether talking about the common soldier's use of language or the bombing blunders of the Allies, makes real the fact that existence for the wartime soldier is, on the one hand, boring and lonely and, on the other, shadowed by the fear of having to kill or be killed.

In an earlier work, *The Great War and Modern Memory*, Fussell studied the British soldier's experience of trench warfare on the Western Front. He brings the same intensity to bear in this more recent study; the two works together form a useful and sobering treatment of the two major wars of the 20th century. War is not glorious; Fussell calls it stupid and sadistic. It is his intention that his readers not forget this.

Louis Sasso

WHAT AM I DOING HERE

Author: Bruce Chatwin (1940–1989)
Publisher: Viking Press (New York). 367 pp. $19.95
Type of work: Essays and short stories
Time: 1970s and 1980s
Locale: The world

A collection of essays and stories that take the reader to remote areas of the world to encounter individuals and cultures that enrich life on the planet

What Am I Doing Here is the late Bruce Chatwin's personal selection of his own stories, profiles, and travelogues. It reflects a lifetime's fascination with the beautiful and the bizarre, with the strange backwaters of history and the stories that create cultures. Best known for *The Songlines*, which achieved true insight into the lives and culture of the Australian Aborigines, and for travel books such as *In Patagonia*, Bruce Chatwin died in January 1989 of a rare fungus of the bone marrow contracted on his travels in a remote region of China.

In the section entitled "Strange Encounters," Chatwin's talent for combining imagination with his extensive experience as a traveler to the world's most remote regions is well illustrated. "A Coup—A Story" penetrates to the heart of African politics. In this story, the narrator, a tourist, is caught in a remote African country during a coup and is arrested with other Europeans. Upon his arrest, he begins to learn about the absurdity of African politics. It is unclear if the coup is really a coup, or if it is a "*coup monte,*" which means that the leader may have hired a planeload of mercenaries to shoot up the town. Those who join the revolutionaries are then easily identified as enemies and can be eliminated. In the meantime, the army can amuse itself by terrorizing both citizens and Europeans as well as settling old scores. At the end, when the narrator and others are released from many extremely uncomfortable and terrorizing hours in detention, it is unclear who staged the coup and what their intentions were. All that is known is that a new group has taken over the secret police and that the dictator knew about it all before it happened.

The tale "The Chinese Geomancer" seems in many ways as fantastic as "A Coup," but it is not fiction. In Hong Kong, Chatwin met a smartly dressed man who handed him a business card that read

LUNG KING CHUEN
Geomancer

Searching and fixing of good location for the burial of passed-away ancestors; surveying and arranging of good position for settling down business and lodging places, in which would gain prosperity and luck in the very near future

Mr. Lung was the man who had been chosen to choose the site for the new Hongkong and Shanghai Bank, the most expensive office building ever built. The business of the geomancer is to make certain, with the help of a magnetic compass, that a building is aligned to one or another of the "dragonlines" and shielded from dangerous crosscurrents. Without clearance of this sort, even the most Westernized Chinese gets nervous about building construction. As unbelievable as it seems, locating a building by this method usually brings it into harmony with its environment, and this new bank is beautifully sited to take advantage of Hong Kong's best features. What Mr. Lung refuses to discuss is how the bank, a typically rectangular modern building, can bring good luck, when Chinese belief prescribes that dragonlines are curved and only curved buildings have good *feng-shui* (the Chinese phase for these relationships).

The section "Friends" contains a significant essay on Kevin Volans that explains Chatwin's views about the nature of human beings and their innate restlessness. Chatwin relates humankind's migratory nature to its speech and songs. He believes that *homo sapiens* made long seasonal journeys interrupted by a period of settlement, a "lean season" like Lent. The men were hunters and the women gatherers, but one of the purposes of the journey was to "talk their way through the problem of inbreeding," and their first language was in song. Songs were used not only to win mates and prevent aggression, but also to guide these migratory people on their journeys. In Chatwin's opinion, it is the highest of arts.

"Encounters" is the theme of the fourth section. The most impressive of these encounters is found in "Werner Herzog in Ghana." Herzog is the German movie director with whom Chatwin shared an interest in the relation of Aboriginals to their land and the "sacramental aspects of walking." They also shared the "belief that walking is not simply therapeutic for oneself but is a poetic activity that can cure the world of its ills." Herzog summed up his position in the stern pronouncement: "Walking is virtue, tourism deadly sin." In 1974, Herzog tested his faith in the power of walking by walking from Munich to Paris in the dead of winter when he heard that Lotte Eisner, the guiding spirit of the German cinema and his mentor, was dying. By the time he reached her apartment she had recovered; she went on to live another ten years.

Section five is devoted to "Russia." The most incisive of the Russian essays is "George Costakis: The Story of an Art Collector in the Soviet Union," which allows Chatwin to discuss the significance of art and its relation to politics. At the time of the Russian Revolution, there were two artistic camps in Russia. "In one camp were the Futurists.

As the old order tottered, they had conducted a war of nerves against middle-class morality and taste. They saw themselves as a wrecking-party which would unhinge the future from the past." Their art was primarily abstract, and they came primarily from "good" families. The Bolsheviks were tougher and more serious, and their view of art different. In their opinion, the serious artist "must merge in with the masses and do nothing to affront the taste of the common man. That taste was bound to be traditional." Lenin saw the need to broadcast the Revolution in simple, traditional images. Lenin's authority was challenged by Alexander Malinovsky, who believed in creating a new *Proletcult*, which would be experimental and modern. The Futurists attached themselves to Malinovsky. They chose the wrong man and got on the wrong side of Soviet history.

Chatwin makes another valuable point in this essay on Costakis. He observes that "authoritarian societies love images because they reinforce the chain of command at all levels of the hierarchy. But an abstract art of pure form and colour, if it is serious and not merely decorative, mocks the pretensions of secular power because it transcends the limits of this world and attempts to penetrate a hidden world of universal law." In addition he points out that anarchic peoples hate and destroy images. The shattering of images is a revolutionary act. In revolutionary Russia, the people did not want to shatter, but rather possess, the old images. They desired the monumental architecture, opulent decoration, and gilt-framed pictures of the rulers of old Russia. As Lunacharsky said, "The People too have a right to colonnades." It is also to be remembered that the purpose of the Socialist Realist style that replaced the discarded Futurism was to inspire the people to heroic acts, and the only way of doing that is to make people look more heroic than they really are—to create kitsch.

Section six, devoted to "China," contains a number of insightful points. One is that Chinese civilization, like most of the great early civilizations, was based on harnessing the rivers for agriculture, and this task required backbreaking labor by unfree workers. It is Chatwin's contention that the Great Wall was built less to hold out the barbarians than to hold in the Chinese who would be attracted to the freedom of the nomadic life. Since almost all of history has been written by sedentary men, Chatwin is one of history's few advocates of nomadism. He finds the act of wandering purifying and believes that "much of what the ethologists have designated 'aggression' is simply an angered response to the frustrations of confinement." He points out that "a crying child is a very rare sight on a nomad caravan." Despite their violence, Chatwin sees nomads as far freer and happier than "civilized" persons.

In the remaining five sections, Chatwin explores more worlds and examines more people. Perhaps the most interesting of these (earlier) essays is "Donald Evans," about a young American artist who died in 1977. Evans painted postage stamps and with them created his own world. What Chatwin finds significant about his work is the belief that it expresses the best aspirations of the "drop-out generation . . . the flight from war and the machine; the asceticism; the nomadic restlessness; the yearning for sensual cloud-cuckoo-lands; the retreat from public into private obsessions, from the big and noisy to the small and still."

Like Donald Evans's, Bruce Chatwin's distinctive voice will be missed. Neither man was a great artist, but both created new worlds out of the old. While Evans looked into himself and created a miniature world, Bruce Chatwin looked out into the far corners of the planet to find a large vision of a better world. For Chatwin, this better world would be one in which a person would have the freedom to move, to explore, and to express the whole of his or her individual personality. It would be a world in which all humans would be regarded as equal and no culture would be seen as superior to another. It would be a world more like African than European music. It would be free and alive and grow by addition rather than subdivision. *What Am I Doing Here* is a fine expression of this vision.

Christine Brendel Scriabine

WHEN HEAVEN AND EARTH CHANGED PLACES: A VIETNAMESE WOMAN'S JOURNEY FROM WAR TO PEACE

Author: Le Ly Hayslip (1949–)
     with Jan Wurts
Publisher: Doubleday and Company (Garden City, N.Y.). 368 pp. $18.95
Type of work: Memoirs
Time: 1949–1986
Locale: Vietnam

A Vietnamese-American tells of her life as a peasant in Vietnam during the war, of her eventual escape to a new life in America, and of her return to Vietnam as an expatriate tourist in 1986

> *Principal personages:*
> LE LY HAYSLIP, the narrator, the sixth child of her family
> HUYEN and PHUNG TRONG, her parents
> HAI NGAI, Le Ly's sister, the eldest
> BA XUAN, a sister, the second child
> BON NGHE, a brother, the third child
> LAN, a sister, the fourth child
> SAU BAN, a brother, the fifth child

Le Ly Hayslip was born in 1949 in Ky La (now called Xa Hoa Qui), a small village near Da Nang in central Vietnam. In ordinary times Le Ly, her parents, and her five brothers and sisters would have spent their entire lives tied to the demanding yearly rounds of the peasant rice farmer. Vietnam was, however, seething under French colonial rule, and Ky La, like other villages and towns in the middle of the country, swirled in the crosscurrents of the Northern guerrilla war for independence and the Southern colonial retaliation. Moroccan mercenaries periodically came looking for soldiers and sympathizers of the Viet Minh (the Communist revolutionary movement of Ho Chi Minh). One of the earliest recollections of Le Ly is her mother's story of the Moroccans' gang rape of a neighbor and dismemberment for sport of her frantic husband. The Viet Cong (the reorganized Viet Minh) were by contrast fellow Vietnamese, kind to villagers, and very persuasive propagandists for the Communist cause.

There were those who remained loyal to the government in Saigon (where the French were succeeded by a "republic" to be backed by U.S. forces), but the majority of houses in Ky La had tunnels underneath for hiding Viet Cong (VC) soldiers, and Le Ly herself became a VC lookout. Idealistic, fearless, Le Ly was winning local fame for her exploits—villagers sang a song to honor her—when her accidental presence near the flushing out and killing of a VC soldier was turned into a circumstantial case of betrayal of the revolution. The two VC cadres assigned to carry out her death sentence in the jungle raped her instead. This "ruined" her for marriage, shattered her perception of heroic war, and refocused her energies: "From now on, I promised myself, I would only flow with the strongest current and drift with the steadiest wind."

Resigning herself to mere survival amid the treacheries of war put her on the same footing as the villagers who now shunned her from fear for their own lives. Her family, too, was being sundered by the war. Her older brother Bon Nghe had gone north to Hanoi in 1954 following the Viet Minh victory over the French. Sau Ban, her other brother, on reaching military age also joined the Viet Cong but was killed by an American mine. Of her three sisters, the eldest, Hai, wound up working as a domestic in Saigon to support herself and her daughter, Tinh, after her husband failed to return from Hanoi. Ba Xuan had a delicate relationship with the family because of her marriage to a government police officer. Lan became a "Saigon tea girl" catering to American servicemen in Da Nang.

Le Ly was only fifteen on her arrival in Saigon in 1965. Her mother, rescued at the very last moment from a VC death sentence, and Le Ly, still on the VC death list, had fled Ky La with other refugees for the relative safety of the city. Hai, already in Saigon, with great caution, because of VC spying, found her sister and mother a place as servants for a wealthy manufacturer. Within months, Le Ly's girlish infatuation for their master, Anh, had led to a passionate night in the servants' quarters and pregnancy.

Thus began the estrangement from her past that would bring a new life in the United States. There is a recurring phrase in her story—"fate or luck or god"—a summation in a sense of her changing philosophy of life. Anh's son was born in Da Nang, where Le Ly was staying with her sister Lan. The U.S. base at Da Nang soon became her source of livelihood: first as a seller of souvenirs; then as a marijuana dealer; and finally, for an irresistible 400 U.S. dollars that might mean escape from Vietnam, a hooker for a day for a departing GI afraid of contracting diseases from the "regulars."

Finding an American to marry as a way out of Vietnam became an obsession. One prospect, Red, seemed sincere and got her a job at a hospital but soon thereafter tried to turn her into a go-go dancer to enhance his reputation among his buddies. Another almost killed her in a drunken spree. Edward Munro, the one Le Ly *did* marry, an aging civilian construction contractor, treasured her, brought her to California, and fathered two more sons before his death in 1973 of emphysema.

Le Ly's story is only half told, however, in the events of her early life in Vietnam. The other half, interspersed with these memories, is the poignant account of her return to Vietnam in 1986 "to find out what happened to my family, my village, my people, and to the man I loved who had given me my first son." The Socialist Republic of Vietnam was going to be different from the Vietnam of memory, but knowing this hardly prepared her for the reality. Saigon had changed "from a bejeweled, jaded dowager to shabby, grasping bag lady in less than a decade." Anh had been reduced to a lowly worker in his factory since its takeover by the Communists, but her girlhood "prince" welcomed her warmly into his home and escorted her everywhere during her stay. The tight grip of the Communist security system kept her family in terror of being caught associating with an American (Le Ly suddenly realized: "My god—by coming here I've endangered them all!"), but one by one her haggard relatives showed up at her niece Tinh's house near Da Nang, the windows closed and the door bolted as soon as possible each time. Her brother Bon Nghe was a Communist bureaucrat and, as such, somewhat guarded at first in greeting his "American" sister. Her sister Hai was back living with their mother in Ky La, barely subsisting from the sale of snails collected in the swamp. Le Ly noted sadly Hai's pathetically thin hands, muddy bare feet splayed like a duck's, and face as lined and crusty as dried sod.

Le Ly almost had to be introduced to her mother, so shriveled was she by the brutal life since liberation. After a tentative start, their conversation grew warm and lively. There was, of course, much to catch up on. "I was near death twice, did you know that?" said her mother, "Once from a dog bite! Yes! Packs of stray dogs ran everywhere in those days [after liberation]." Her mother spoke without a trace of bitterness, recalling the Buddhist maxim that one word of forgiveness brings back nine gentle favors. Besides, "*troi dat doi thay* —heaven and earth changed places!" and North or South, Republican or Viet Cong, everybody suffered. Le Ly ached with desire to do something to ease her mother's life.

The close control of her travel as a *Viet Kieu* (Vietnamese expatriate) allowed only five precious days in Da Nang near her family. Moreover, the authorities claimed even some of that time. There was a dinner with two party officials eager to get her views as an American on a wide range of subjects, from the attitudes of Vietnamese refugees in the United States to the MIA issue. Her dream of setting up clinics for the homeless and rural poor (Victims of War Centers to be supported and staffed by American Vietnam veterans and volunteer medical personnel) was going to require making political contacts in Saigon before her departure.

The one thing that would have crowned her visit, however—a return to Ky La—was denied her. An obligatory tour of the countryside in a chauffeured car passed within a mile of the village. Le Ly got the driver to stop where the trail went off to Ky La by pretending carsickness, but Anh, who was accompanying her, thwarted her impulse by reminding her of the consequences for her mother and sister. As the plane taking her back to Saigon circled Da Nang and banked for the South, the familiar mountains and rivers raced by the window. Suddenly there in the jungle was the tiny village of her birth: "For a glistening instant, Ky La dances before my eyes, then vanishes into memory."

In an epilogue the author proudly mentions the beginning of work on another of her Vietnam clinics, this one in Ky La.

The recent surge of interest in the Vietnam War has several sources, such as fading memories of the national trauma and the curiosity of a generation too young to have experienced the reality. So far, however, the focus has been on the tragic cost in American lives of a glaring misjudgment by American policymakers. The Vietnamese, particularly those who found refuge in the United States, have only slowly begun to tell their side of the story.

When Heaven and Earth Changed Places is one of the best of these revelatory accounts. Part of the credit must go to Jay Wurts, an Air Guard pilot during the Vietnam War, whose collaboration with Le Ly Hayslip has resulted in an unsparing recall of terror and suffering tempered by a surprisingly lyrical style. Notably, the alternation of stories about her childhood and her family in those days with the details and impressions of her return trip, which in other hands would certainly have produced confusion, has been so skillfully accomplished as to seem utterly logical while heightening the dramatic impact of both. As events unfold, however, linking people and places would have been facilitated by an index, and the lack of one is unfortunate.

By portraying herself with total and refreshing honesty, Le Ly Hayslip eludes classification as a glamorizing seeker of publicity. But her story *was* intended to draw attention to her humanitarian efforts to improve relations between her native and adopted countries and heal the wounds of war. Hayslip enjoins the reader to wish that "luck or fate or god" furthers her noble cause.

Adrienne Suddard

WHY DID THE HEAVENS NOT DARKEN?:
THE "FINAL SOLUTION" IN HISTORY

Author: Arno J. Mayer (1926–   )
Publisher: Pantheon Books (New York). 492 pp. $27.95
Type of work: History
Time: The 1930s and 1940s
Locale: Europe

   *Mayer's reappraisal of the Nazi Judeocide, stressing its place in the histor-
ical context of 20th-century European history rather than its unique qualities*

Arno Mayer, who was born in Luxembourg and is currently a professor of European history at Princeton University, was prompted to
write *Why Did the Heavens Not Darken?* when he began to think about
the fate of his maternal grandparents. Although the rest of his extended
Jewish family fled Luxembourg ahead of the invading Nazis, his maternal grandparents refused to leave. In 1943 they were transported to
Theresienstadt, a relative oasis in the German concentration-camp
system. Despite her advanced age, his grandmother survived. Her fate
made him aware that

> the impact of the Jewish catastrophe was not altogether democratic, in that
> the odds for survival were unequal. Throughout much of the Continent,
> including Luxembourg, Yiddish-speaking, unprosperous, politically con-
> servative, and religiously Orthodox Jews had a considerably smaller
> chance of remaining alive than more assimilated, privileged, and less reli-
> gious Jews.

Answering the obvious question of "why?" led Mayer into writing this
major revisionist history of Hitler's campaign of Judeocide.

Mayer rejects the use of the term "Holocaust" to describe the Nazi
Judeocide for a number of significant reasons. The first is that he
believes that the term has significance only in Jewish history and that
the meaning of catastrophe is much wider. Further, he argues that a
holocaust is a unique event, while the Judeocide of the 1940s was only
unprecedented in terms of size.

To rethink the Judeocide of the 1940s, Mayer believes that three
steps must be taken. The first is to discard the vantage point of the
cold war and to see clearly the interconnection between anticommunism and anti-Semitism in the Nazi ideology, the treatment of the
Jews, and the conduct of the war in Eastern Europe. The second is to
set firmly the Judeocide in the historical context of the time, more
specifically in the German drive toward the conquest of *Lebensraum*
in the East and the thwarting of this drive by the Russian armies.
Third, he conceptualizes three developments—the Nazi regime, the

Eastern campaign, the Judeocide—as integral components and expressions of the "General Crisis and Thirty Years War of the twentieth century."

Europe's Jewish population has classically been made the scapegoat for national and social problems. When the plague ravaged Europe, Jewish communities were attacked as the source of infection. The same process operated in much the same way in post–World War I Europe. As Europe lost world dominance and the power of traditional elites was eroded, a new kind of secular, cynically manipulated anti-Semitism was grafted onto a resurgence of old-fashioned, theologically informed, and unforced Judeophobia. The right used this newly grafted product to restore, maintain, and purify the established order. To the new fascists and to the old right, Jews were the chief carriers of social and cultural subversion and the masterminds of political revolution. The identification of many Russian and Eastern European Jews with the Soviet regime and the large number of Jews in the middle ranks of the Soviet Communist party intensified this identification. Many Europeans also saw them as symbols of modernity, and as such, they threatened not only traditional elites but also many of the petty bourgeois who were threatened by the modernization of the economy and society.

Germany became the chief agent of this new Judeophobia for a number of reasons. In the 20th century, Germany grew into the hub of a chronically and dynamically unstable capitalist world economy and the European balance of power. "This dual centrality was all the more crucial because Germany was also saddled with more severe internal strains and stresses than any other major European power. The tensions stemming from the contemporaneousness of institutions and mentalities rooted in vastly different historical periods became particularly explosive" when exploited by the National Socialists. To the enraged Germans, Hitler became a prophet.

From his reading of *Mein Kampf*, Mayer postulates that while anti-Semitism was an essential tenet of the Nazi worldview, it was neither its foundation nor its principal or sole intention. "Anti-Semitism was one of several central creeds of an essentially syncretic ideology, the others being social Darwinism, the geopolitics of eastern expansionism, and anti-Marxism." In Nazi ideology "the Jew" becomes the symbol of the enemy—modernism, parasitic capitalism, Marxist subversion. He becomes an easily identifiable single enemy.

When the Nazis came to power, their first objective was not the persecution of the Jews. The first concentration camps were founded to hold Hitler's political enemies—Communists, Social Democrats, and politically active Catholics. With the removal of the parties of the left, Germany's Jewish population lost its chief political defenders, and many politically active Jews began to leave Germany. Book burning, the harassment of individuals and businesses by groups such as the SA (or brownshirts), and restrictions on Jews in the professions prompted many others to leave. Government policy seemed to be to push the Jewish population out gradually. Government persecution was stepped up in 1935 when the Jews were de-emancipated and denied all civil, political, and legal rights.

By 1938, Hitler's maneuvers to rid Germany of its Jews had not been very successful (only 30 percent had left), and his policies of expansion were resulting only in bringing more Jews into the Reich. So in the summer of 1938, the first synagogues were demolished, and in November the famous Crystal Night occurred. Synagogues and Jewish businesses were destroyed, Jews were beaten on the street, and between 20,000 and 30,000 Jewish men were arrested and roughed up. The purpose of all of this was to promote emigration. Many left.

The problem was that as prosperous and socially integrated German Jews left, German expansionism led to the takeover of areas with large less-assimilated Jewish populations. When Germany went to war with Poland, thousands of individual Jews were murdered by squads of SS troops, the Nazis' paramilitary arm, but no program for the systematic elimination of the Jewish population was in place. In fact, the concentration camps held mostly Polish prisoners of war who were used for forced labor. The first Nazi Jewish policy in Poland was focused on pushing some Jews toward the Eastern frontier and the ghettoization of others. In the ghettos, Jews could be kept on short rations and their labor exploited. The price they had to pay for life was laboring for the German war effort. This policy remained fairly intact until the German advance was halted in Russia.

It is Mayer's contention that the policy of Jewish extermination was forged in the Nazi rage against their defeats on the Eastern front and in their growing need for war production. The Jews became the objects of the rage against the defeats by the Russian armies because in the Nazi mind they personified the evils of "Judeobolshevism." The only argument among the Nazi leadership centered on whether using Jews to labor for the Reich should be the first priority or if the elimination of Jews should be the first priority. For the most part, Jews who could work were worked to death. Those who could not work were quickly eliminated. The eventual elimination of European Jewry became German policy in 1943.

The greatest tragedy for world Jewry was that this policy of extermination was decided upon at a time when the Germans controlled the heartland of European Jewry—the old Russian Pale of Settlement in western Russia and eastern Poland. Not only were Jewish populations sent to the camps, but many were also summarily eliminated as potential partisans or because they were in the way of the war machine. The Nazi extermination of the Jews was aided by the largely anti-Semitic local populations. Some joined SS killing squads while others joined random pogroms and killed Jewish neighbors before the Nazis had the opportunity.

When large segments of Western Europe's Jewish population began to be sent to the camps, there were few protests. This situation can be attributed partially to anti-Semitism, partially to the fact that great numbers of Europeans were being forced into labor in Germany—and many saw little difference between what was being done to them and what was being done to the Jews—and partially because most of the Jews being sent east were not native-born citizens and were not highly assimilated. At least 40 percent of all France's foreign-born Jews perished in the camps, compared to about 10 percent of all French Jews.

The basics about life and death in the camps are well known. In the last chapters of the book, which focus on this subject, Mayer has little new to add.

Mayer's real contribution in *Why Did the Heavens Not Darken?* is his presentation of a new framework in which to view the Holocaust. While some may object that putting these events into the larger context of the history of this century detracts from the human and religious significance of the destruction of Eastern European Jewry, it is certain that this larger framework allows the reader to understand the interrelationships between the Nazi Judeocide and modernization that previously were not clear. It also calls for a reexamination of the crucial nexus between anticommunism and anti-Semitism. His revised appraisal of the place that anti-Semitism played in Nazi ideology and actions is convincing. These are important historical issues; and this is an important book. No scholar in the future will be able to discuss World War II or the Judeocide of the 20th century without taking it into account.

Christine Brendel Scriabine

WILLIAM FAULKNER: AMERICAN WRITER

Author: Frederick R. Karl (1927–   )
Publisher: Weidenfeld and Nicolson (New York). 1,131 pp. $37.50
Type of work: Biography
Time: 1897–1962
Locale: Oxford, Mississippi

A biography that focuses on the people and the events that helped shape William Faulkner into a Nobel Prize–winning author

> Principal personages:
> WILLIAM CUTHBERT FAULKNER, American novelist
> MAUD BUTLER FALKNER, his mother
> ESTELLE OLDHAM FAULKNER, his wife
> META CARPENTER, his longtime lover

William Faulkner was born on September 25, 1897, in New Albany, Mississippi. A few years later, his family moved to Oxford, Mississippi, where Faulkner would live for most of his life. His father, Murry C. Falkner, was a man's man, big and beefy. William Faulkner, short in stature and slight in build, received little attention from Murry, who did not think much of his son's chosen profession, considering it an unmanly vocation for a Southerner. In time, Faulkner added the "u" in his last name to differentiate himself from his father and the rest of his family. Like his father, however, Faulkner began drinking early in life. It was his domineering mother, Maud, however, who headed the Falkner family. She believed in her son and encouraged him to become a writer. She was his staunchest supporter throughout his life.

William Faulkner was a self-destructive, adversarial individual who frequently drank himself into oblivion. He also was known for falling into sudden and complete silences. He suffered debilitating bouts of depression throughout his life, interrupted by monumental alcoholic binges. Faulkner fictionalized his past to create a more dramatic self-image. He claimed that he had been injured in combat during World War I, supporting this story by sporting a limp and a cane for years afterward. In reality, after having been rejected by the U.S. Air Corps for being too slight physically, he spent five months as a recruit in the Royal Air Force in Toronto and was discharged without seeing any combat. Always prickly and insecure about his size, Faulkner compensated by pursuing dangerous hobbies. He began flying planes in the early days of rudimentary instrumentation. One of his brothers, Doug, was killed flying a plane. Faulkner also took up horseback riding, choosing horses too powerful for him to handle properly and, consequently, suffering many injuries from falls.

Faulkner could also be very charming when he wanted to be. His seriousness about and devotion to his writing earned him the lifelong loyalty and admiration of his colleagues, including Howard Hawks, the Hollywood director; Bennett Cerf, his publisher at Random House; and Saxe Commins, his editor at Random House. Faulkner, who was thirty-five years old before he ever made a decent living, became the sole support not only of his wife and children, but also of his mother and several other members of his extended family.

Estelle Oldham was Faulkner's childhood sweetheart. Her family, one of the true aristocratic families of the Old South, rejected him as unsuitable for their daughter. Estelle ended up marrying another member of the "bluebloods," Cornell Franklin, but the marriage failed after ten years. During that time, she began drinking and using drugs to escape her unhappiness. In June 1929, a few months after her divorce from Franklin, Estelle Oldham and William Faulkner were married. Estelle was quite emotionally unstable, as evidenced by her suicide attempt during their honeymoon. Their union was never a happy one, although it endured until Faulkner died in 1962. Estelle brought a daughter, Victoria, and a son, Malcolm, to the marriage. She and Faulkner produced two daughters, one of whom died in infancy, and Jill, born in 1933. All three children left home as soon as possible to escape the drinking and squabbling of their parents.

After the birth of Jill, the Faulkners permanently ended their sexual relationship, and he began a series of extramarital affairs with younger women. Faulkner had a dualistic view of women, as either whore or madonna. All of his friendships with women were based on his need to be admired, to bolster his innate insecurity, and to be mothered and supported through his frequent alcoholic episodes. So while he became their mentor, they, in turn, became his nurses.

Faulkner started his writing career composing "stylization" poetry. In later years, Faulkner's poetry changed from stylization to flat realism. After a long apprenticeship as poet, he wrote his first novel in 1925. With the publication of *Soldiers' Pay*, Faulkner discovered the satisfaction of being paid for his work. At this point he joined the ranks of his contemporaries—including F. Scott Fitzgerald, Ernest Hemingway, and John Dos Passos—and his years as a struggling novelist began. He began writing in earnest, stopping periodically to indulge in a binge to fortify himself. Faulkner wrote several short fiction stories to make ends meet. He was an inconsistent short-story writer, but he was able to earn enough to support himself while he worked on his novels.

Faulkner's great middle-career novels, such as *Sanctuary* and *Go Down, Moses*, demonstrate his fatalism: the individual goes through stages that are predestined. *As I Lay Dying* was Faulkner's favorite novel. He stood for antimodernism, a true Southerner. He preferred pastoral themes because he viewed urbanism as destructive of individual values. In his best works, however, Faulkner became an American, not only a Southerner. *Absalom, Absalom!*, completed in 1936, is considered the peak of his fictional achievement. Regarded by many as the greatest American novel, it describes the fullness of American failure: the Civil War.

Faulkner was not afraid of controversy, as evinced in one of his most significant racial themes: in the face of injustice, the good man is silenced by intimidation. This view ultimately caused Faulkner to be ostracized from his hometown and, indeed, throughout the South. But still, a true child of his environment, Faulkner felt that the white man was the black man's best friend and provider. Nevertheless, racial equality remained a burning issue for Faulkner.

In 1932 he began working sporadically in Hollywood as a screenwriter. This style of writing gave Faulkner poor writing habits over the years, but he earned a great deal of money there. Although he detested the commercialism of Hollywood, there were some positive results: he made a living, he temporarily escaped his unhappy home life, and most important, he received great exposure in Hollywood.

Then, in 1950, Faulkner received the Nobel Prize for Literature. Not only was this a great honor, but it completely changed and improved his life. With receipt of the Nobel Prize, his financial problems were finally over. The award also resulted in worldwide recognition that gave Faulkner an entrée into the world of the glamorous and rich, and he began traveling extensively. Although he was no longer writing much, he received several other awards, including the Howells Medal for distinguished fiction from the American Academy of Arts and Letters; the National Book Award for his third and final volume of short fiction, *Collected Stories*; and France's prestigious Medal of Honor. In 1955 he received a second National Book Award for *A Fable*, a novel about an egalitarian democracy, a just society, a theme close to his heart. He had spent many years working on this piece.

In his remaining years, Faulkner divided his time between Oxford and Charlottesville, Virginia, where he was writer-in-residence at the University of Virginia. He also went on diplomatic missions for the U.S. State Department, traveling to places such as Brazil and Venezuela. His most important mission was to Nagano, Japan, in 1955. His final work, *The Reivers*, was written in 1961 and published shortly before his death. On July 6, 1962, William Faulkner suffered a fatal heart attack. He is buried in Oxford, Mississippi.

William Faulkner: American Writer is the richly interpretive work of the respected biographer Frederick Karl. Karl demonstrates considerable insight into Faulkner's works, many of them complicated and ambiguous. Karl obviously put an enormous amount of research into this book; he conducted many interviews with some of Faulkner's close friends and relatives. Karl offers abundant details in his analysis of both Faulkner's life and works. He provides a clear picture of the impact of Faulkner's life events on the quality and power of the novels of the author known as the "Balzac of America"—Faulkner represented his own Southern heritage as well as that of the nation. Karl shows great sympathy for the man and captures Faulkner's burning need to communicate his special vision of the world. Through that view, Faulkner revealed the man who disguised his inner self behind alcohol and silence. The biography is a thought-provoking book on one of America's most profound and distinguished writers.

Constance Clyde

WONDERFUL LIFE: THE BURGESS SHALE AND THE NATURE OF HISTORY

Author: Stephen Jay Gould (1941–   )
Publisher: W. W. Norton and Company (New York). 347 pp. $19.95
Type of work: Science
Time: The beginning of life to the present
Locale: Primarily Canada's Yoho National Park and the Smithsonian Institution in Washington, D.C.

> *The recent reinterpretation of the Burgess Shale upsets the common notion of evolution as a ladder of progress and suggests the possibility that luck is largely responsible for the presence of human beings today*

Principal characters:
> DR. CHARLES D. WALCOTT, the discoverer of the Burgess Shale, who shoehorned the Burgess animals into conventional categories
> PROFESSOR HARRY WHITTINGTON, the paleontologist responsible for reinterpreting the life of the Burgess Shale
> DEREK BRIGGS, the assistant to Whittington who was responsible for studying what Walcott labeled "bivalved arthropods"
> SIMON CONWAY MORRIS, the assistant to Whittington who was responsible for studying what Walcott labeled "worms"
> DESMOND COLLINS, an employee of the Royal Ontario Museum and the discoverer of *Sanctacaris*

The Burgess Shale is located in Yoho National Park, far up in the Canadian Rockies. Ten feet high, less than a city block long, and 8,000 feet above sea level, the Burgess Shale was formed about 530 million years ago when a catastrophe of some sort—more than likely an underwater mud slide—buried dozens of creatures, producing the most bizarre animal fossils ever found. This small limestone quarry, discovered in the early 20th century, contains more varieties of life than can currently be found in all modern oceans. The discovery and diversity of the Burgess Shale, and what it reveals about the past and the improbability of human evolution, is the subject of *Wonderful Life* by Stephen J. Gould.

Gould takes his title from the Frank Capra film *It's a Wonderful Life*, which he considers both a symbol and the finest illustration of the main theme of his book: contingency. The particular scene that Gould has in mind is that of George Bailey's guardian angel showing him what life would have been like if George Bailey had never been born. The replay of past events yields an entirely different outcome, demonstrating the power of apparent insignificance in history. This theme of contingency, according to Gould, is demonstrated by the evidence of the Burgess Shale, which contradicts the traditional view of the progress of evolution and of predictability in the history of life. Gould says that the "pageant" of evolution is "a staggeringly improbable series of events, sensible enough in retrospect and subject to rigorous explanation, but utterly unpredictable and quite unrepeatable. Wind back the tape of life to the early days of the Burgess Shale; let it play again from an identical starting point, and the chance becomes vanishingly small that anything like human intelligence would grace the replay."

Gould begins by discussing the two traditional attitudes that the Burgess Shale challenges: the cone of increasing diversity and the ladder, or march, of progress, usually depicted with an ape on the far left gradually transforming into modern man on the far right. Gould gives many examples, some humorous, of the pervasive view of evolution as a march of progress rather than adaptation to changing environments, a wrong-headed concept directed toward reinforcing a comfortable view of human inevitability and superiority.

The author then goes on to place the catastrophe that created the Burgess Shale on a geologic time scale as occurring soon after "the 'Cambrian explosion,' or first appearance of multicellular animals with hard parts in the fossil record. . . . As the only major soft-bodied fauna from this primordial time, the Burgess Shale provides our sole vista upon the inception of modern life in all its fullness." Gould then gives evidence why a mud slide created this one small quarry containing anatomical disparity far exceeding the modern range throughout the world.

In 1909, Dr. Charles D. Walcott discovered the Burgess Shale. Walcott managed to collect 80,000 specimens for the Smithsonian Institution. Under the auspices of the Geological Survey of Canada in the mid-1960s, Professor Harry Whittington collected more specimens. The greatest "field work" occurred, however, in Washington in 1973, "when Whittington's brilliant and eclectic student Simon Conway Morris made a systematic search through *all* the drawers of Walcott's specimens, consciously looking for oddities because he had grasped the germ of the key insight about Burgess disparity."

The reconstruction of the Burgess Shale by Whittington and colleagues is recounted in five acts. Act 1 begins in the early 1970s with the most common organism in the Burgess Shale and the first that Walcott had found: the *Marrella splendens*. Although *Marrella* was not a conventional trilobite, Walcott had placed it in the class Trilobita, order previously unknown. Another Burgess animal, the *Yohoia*, had been placed among the branchiopods. In examining these Burgess organisms, Whittington discovered that Walcott's photos of the specimens were sometimes retouched, arousing his suspicions about the true placement of these Burgess organisms.

In act 2, Whittington presented his first reconstruction of *Opabinia*, the most puzzling of all Burgess arthropods, to the annual meeting of the Palaeontological Association in Oxford in 1972. His drawing of the five-eyed creature showing a frontal nozzle with a terminal claw brought a round of puzzled laughter. Based on his discovery that the Burgess fossils were three-dimensional objects with top layers that can be dissected away, Whittington dissected the two-inch long *Opabinia* and discovered not only that was it not an arthropod, but that it "belonged nowhere among the known animals of this or any former earth."

In act 3, Whittington took on two student associates: Simon Conway Morris, in charge of Walcott's "worms," and Derek Briggs, responsible for studying what Walcott labeled "bivalved arthropods." These students documented the same pattern of strange and unique anatomy found in *Opabinia* throughout the Burgess fauna, including the bizarre *Hallucigenia*. Just as important, they found modern prototypes establishing that the Burgess Shale is of ordinary Cambrian fauna and not some failed experiment with no connection to the origin of later life.

Whittington's classification of *Naraoia* as a trilobite, despite its soft body and carapace of two valves, takes up act 4. It proved that the basic Burgess pattern—anatomical disparity beyond the range of later times—applied at all levels, even the lowest level of disparity within major groups of a phylum.

Act 5 relates the ongoing saga of Burgess arthropods as being "uniquely specialized" rather than the traditional "primitively simple." Desmond Collins made, according to Gould, the most remarkable discovery of the 1980s in *Sanctacaris* ("Santa Claws"), "the first known member of a line that eventually yielded horseshoe crabs, spiders, scorpions, and mites." *Sanctacaris* completes the presence of the four great arthropod groups within the phylum in the Burgess Shale. Gould returns to his main theme, saying,

> I challenge any paleontologist to argue that he could have gone back to the Burgess seas and, without the benefit of hindsight, picked out *Naraoia*, *Canadaspis*, *Aysheaia*, and *Sanctacaris* for success, while identifying *Marrella*, *Odaraia*, *Sidneyia*, and *Leanchoilia* as ripe for the grim reaper. . . . The history of multicellular life has been dominated by decimation of a large initial stock, quickly generated in the Cambrian explosion. The story of the last 500 million years has featured restriction followed by proliferation within a few stereotyped designs, not general expansion of range and increase in complexity as our favored iconography, the cone of increasing diversity, implies.

Gould speaks instead of a grab-bag model of evolution, in which major features of each new lineage arise separately from a grab-bag of latent possibilities common to all. Ultimately, in this grand lottery, those which survived did so as a result of contingency, pure luck. "Replay the tape a million times from a Burgess beginning, and I doubt that anything like *Homo sapiens* would ever evolve again."

Chapter 4 examines the traditionalism in Walcott's political, religious, and social beliefs; his attitude toward organisms and their history; and his approach to the particular problems of the Cambrian that account for his shoehorning of the Burgess fauna into conventional classifications, despite evidence to the contrary. "Walcott read life's history as the fulfillment of a divine purpose guaranteed to yield human consciousness after a long history of gradual and stately progress. The Burgess organisms had to be primitive versions of later improvements, and life had to move forward from this restricted and simple beginning." In fact, Gould claims that humans are a detail in Darwin's scheme, not a purpose or embodiment of the whole.

In the last chapter, Gould gives actual examples as proof of the operation of contingency. He contrasts the fates of the two phyla sharing the invertebrate body plan of a worm, and the fates of birds versus mammals. Gould also suggests seven possible worlds that might exist today if the lottery had not gone the way it did. Gould ends his book with perhaps the most important Burgess animal, *Pikaia*, a chordate, the first recorded member of humankind's immediate ancestry, "the direct connection between Burgess decimation and eventual human evolution."

To claim that this is a fascinating and important book seems almost unnecessary. It is also at times rambling and difficult. Gould's references to popular culture that allow the eyes to rest from the scientific terms are like the necessary and unrevealing shards that one must sort through to find the prize fossil. This book, more than any of Gould's others, relies heavily on illustrations, and the drawings of the Burgess fauna emphasize the anatomical uniqueness of these fascinating creatures, most of which are less than three inches long. The position that the human race is the result of a series of unlikely accidents is certainly controversial. What is most striking about this book is that Gould makes that position seem inevitable.

Charles Agvent

WORKING DAYS: THE JOURNALS OF "THE GRAPES OF WRATH," 1938–1941

Author: John Steinbeck (1902–1968)
Editor: Robert DeMott (1943–   )
Publisher: Viking Press (New York). 180 pp. $18.95
Type of work: Journal
Time: 1938-1941
Locale: Los Gatos, California

A record, with intimate detail, of the conception and genesis of The Grapes of Wrath, *including the aftermath of its publication and its huge yet controversial success*

> *Principal personages:*
> JOHN STEINBECK, the novelist, winner of the Pulitzer Prize for *The Grapes of Wrath*
> CAROL HENNING STEINBECK, Steinbeck's wife, editor, typist, and confidante
> ELIZABETH OTIS, Steinbeck's trusted literary agent
> THOMAS COLLINS, a migrant-camp administrator and Steinbeck's chief guide into the world of the Okies
> PARE LORENTZ, a documentary filmmaker whose visual style strongly influenced the structure of *The Grapes of Wrath*
> PASCAL "PAT" COVICI, the writer's longtime editor and literary conscience
> ED RICKETTS, a marine biologist, author, friend, and spiritual partner
> GWYNDOLYN CONGER, a singer whose affair with Steinbeck led to marriage

John Steinbeck wrote *The Grapes of Wrath*, winner of the 1940 Pulitzer Prize and one of the most enduring American novels, in one concentrated burst of activity from June to October of 1938. Throughout the time he was creating his greatest work, Steinbeck faithfully recorded his progress and the obstacles he faced in a revealing journal that he described as "an attempt to map the actual working days and hours of a novel." The result, published for the first time in *Working Days: The Journals of "The Grapes of Wrath,"* is a daily account of the reclusive author's continual striving toward artistic fulfillment.

Steinbeck rediscovered the journal during Christmas week 1950 while sifting through memorabilia. He sent it to his longtime editor and literary conscience Pat Covici with a letter that read in part:

> Very many times I have been tempted to destroy this book. It is an account very personal and in many instances purposely obscure. But recently I reread it and only after all this time did the unconscious pattern emerge. It is true that this book is full of my own weaknesses, of complaints and violence. These are just as apparent as they ever were. What a complainer

> I am. But in rereading, those became less important and the times and the
> little histories seemed to be more apparent. . . . I had not realized that so
> much happened during the short period of the actual writing of *The Grapes
> of Wrath*—things that happened to me and to you and to the world.

By the time of the journal's first entry in February 1938, Steinbeck
had published a string of best sellers, including *Of Mice and Men* and
The Long Valley. His own harshest critic, Steinbeck was not convinced that his success was earned and constantly struggled with fears
of inadequacy. He also was repulsed by the public side of fame, particularly the requests for money from the laborers whose cause he es-
poused. In his first entry of the journal he writes, "I'm tired of living
completely tired. I'm tired of the struggle against all the forces that
this miserable success has brought against me. I don't know whether
I could write a decent book now. That is the greatest fear of all."

The "decent" book, of course, did get written, and although the
section of the journal containing the ninety-nine entries that chronicle
the creation of *The Grapes of Wrath* does not reveal much that was
not previously known about the novel, it does say a lot about the
various upheavals in Steinbeck's life, his feelings about his magnum
opus, and his daily work habits.

Most entries begin with general remarks about the weather, friends,
politics, or a number of other topics. Then Steinbeck approaches the
day's work, as in Entry 15:

> Now, concerning work. Today used cars, people and methods of selling,
> and hustle, profits, trades [Ed.—Chapter 7]. I think I can make it. Must be
> good, general and fierce. It will be just one day's work. A short chapter.
> Must get the sense of the yard in it. Must get the sense of cheating in it.
> Cars, trucks, trailers. Well here goes. Got her done and I think it's all right.
> Feel good about it anyway.

Steinbeck also had many occasions not to feel good about his progress on the novel. A number of entries begin with remarks such as
"Yesterday was a bust," or "Demoralization complete and seemingly
unbeatable," or even "This book has become a misery to me because
of my inadequacy." These feelings of hopelessness were not new to
Steinbeck. He had recorded similar notes of insecurity and self-loath-
ing in the ledgers he kept while writing *Of Mice and Men* and the
stories in *The Long Valley*. His solution to his temporary bouts of
paralysis of will lay in his regimen of discipline, which resulted in his
writing an average of 2,000 words a day, sometimes under very trying
circumstances. The connection between discipline and Steinbeck's
singleness of vision and commitment to his art is evidenced in Entry
49: "Every book seems the struggle of a whole life. And then, when it
is done—pouf. Never happened. Best thing is to get the words down
every day."

The role that Steinbeck assigned to discipline in his work is perhaps most clearly conveyed in Entry 13:

> The failure of will even for one day has a devastating effect on the whole, far more important than just the loss of time and wordage. The whole physical basis of the novel is discipline of the writer, of his material, of the language. And sadly enough, if any of the discipline is gone, all of it suffers.

Steinbeck faced many distractions, from the noise of the washing machine to his infrequent visitors (including Charlie Chaplin); the many letters requesting new material, money, and endorsements; the drawn-out closing on his new ranch. "Problems pile up so that this book moves like a Tide Pool snail with a shell and barnacles on its back." Sometimes the problems overwhelmed Steinbeck, and his regimen would break down, as when he missed a week because his first wife, Carol, had her tonsils out. Steinbeck piles word upon word in an effort to get back to the book until he reaches a crisis point of tension: "Wish I could control the jumping jitters though. Time to make the break and another try now. Time for it. I made it." Many of the entries in this journal have this same rushed, breathless quality to them, almost as if they were written impatiently in shorthand. Steinbeck had his sights set on the end, and nothing, not even sickness, could keep him from his destination. In Entry 100, the final journal entry during the actual composition of *The Grapes of Wrath*, he says, "I seem to have contracted an influenza of the stomach or something. Anyway I am so dizzy I can hardly see the page. . . . Finished this day—and I hope to God it's good."

The final section of his journal, comprising twenty-three entries, covers the years 1939–1941, the aftermath of the publication of *The Grapes of Wrath*. For Steinbeck it was a time of unforeseen financial success and chaotic emotional upheaval. The anticipated unfavorable response to Steinbeck's novel from the corporate agriculture industry also brought unexpected vicious rumors and threats of reprisal. Steinbeck became increasingly depressed and withdrawn, and this final segment of his journal is tinged with guilt, paranoia, and an ominous sense of fatality.

The arrival of twenty-year-old Gwyn Conger in his life offered Steinbeck the choice "between a settled existence of domestic attachment and financial security on the one hand, and an exciting life of uncertain future but passionate feeling on the other." Steinbeck chose the latter, but he was unable to escape from the guilt he felt over Carol's unhappiness.

The journal ends shortly after Steinbeck plunged into the writing of a book much different from those which came before it, *Sea of Cortez*. With the world massed for war and Steinbeck's inner life in conflict, editor Robert DeMott says he "turned to the oceanic tide pool not as a replacement for the world of men, but rather as a place to heal his vision, to begin again at the bedrock of observation. It was not the *subject* of the tide pool that captured his attention so much as the liberating *process* of observing it, a process that required baptismal immersion in its eddying currents." Three days into writing his new book, Steinbeck, confused and despairing, records his last journal entry:

> I don't seem to have the knack of living any more. The clock is running down, my clock. This book has to be written. It should be good. I think it is my book. Maybe those people who say that I should never deal with thinking subjects are correct. I don't know. It is impossible to say. Now the sun is gone again. Haven't heard from Carol. I hope she isn't feeling so lonely as she was. She was so low. I think I'll leave this book now.

Those who enjoyed Steinbeck's *Journal of a Novel*, his daily log for his 1952 novel *East of Eden*, will likely find this book somewhat disappointing. The entries in *Working Days* were not written to be read but to help Steinbeck warm up to the day's chores and to regulate his discipline. That does not mean, however, that one cannot find value in these brief, punchy, almost claustrophobic entries. Steinbeck's working through his daily struggles is occasionally fascinating, and every now and then the journals give a glimpse of relief as well as of the solid writing: "Oh! Lord, how good this paper feels under this pen. I can sit here writing and the words slipping out like grapes out of their skins and I feel so good doing it."

Editor Robert DeMott has done a fine job of arranging and introducing the entries. His copious notes bring to light many of the private allusions and public references found in the journal and make one's way through it much more enjoyable and fluid than it would otherwise be.

Charles Agvent

THE WRITING LIFE

Author: Annie Dillard (1945–   )
Publisher: Harper and Row (New York). 111 pp. $15.95
Type of work: Essays
Time: The present
Locale: Cape Cod; the Pacific Northwest; Virginia

A firsthand account of the working life of a writer, drawing from the wisdom of literature, art, nature, and humankind

For Annie Dillard, author of several critically acclaimed books, writing can be exhilarating, but it is also hard work. In *The Writing Life*, she describes the craft of writing through a series of brief essays based on personal experience and keen insight. She draws from a range of sources, from William Faulkner to inchworms to alligator wrestling, to bring her observations to life. The passages are loosely grouped under seven chapter headings, introduced by quotations from literary greats such as Goethe, Plato, and William James.

The early passages focus on the process of writing and rewriting, as well as on the pains taken at each stage. Dillard likens the pen to a miner's pick or a woodcarver's gouge, digging a path across the page that may or may not lead to the "real subject." As the work progresses, she observes, it may arrive at a completely new place, rendering the earlier work weak and unusable. Dillard admits that it is the beginning portion of the work, often containing the main hook, that must be jettisoned.

The decision to delete certain portions of a manuscript is not easy. She compares the situation to that of a photographer she once knew who refused to delete a mediocre photo from his portfolio because he had climbed a mountain in order to shoot it.

Readers of her autobiography *An American Childhood* will not be surprised that Dillard, a passionate insect and rock collector as a young girl, uses nature to illuminate the secrets of a writer's struggle for the perfect words. She has found in the inchworm an ideal simile for the writer. After inching its way along a blind path, the ugly, "absurd" inchworm often finds itself panicking at the edge of a blade of grass: "Its back pair of nubby feet clasps the grass stem; its front three pairs of nubs rear back and flail in the air, apparently in search of footing." Hours later it manages to maneuver itself onto another blade of grass, destined to repeat the same ordeal. But if it perseveres long enough, it will eventually emerge as a moth.

False trips up dead-end grass blades are common occurrences in the writing life. Often, the writer must begin again. Dillard explains that "this is why many experienced writers urge young men and women to learn a useful trade."

According to Dillard, it takes two to ten years to write a book. While she is in awe of authors such as Faulkner who wrote books in as little as six weeks, she realizes that such cases are rare. A novelist's work is as difficult as a biographer's. The time and effort it takes to amass research for a biography is no greater than the time it takes a novelist to fabricate "solid worlds that answer to immaterial truths."

Several sections of the book emphasize the setting for a writer's place of work, a factor of no small importance to Dillard. She prefers a study with the romanticism often associated with great writers, but there is a twist. She writes *The Writing Life* from a tiny shed on Cape Cod, set among the pine trees and warblers. Yet it is stocked with the latest high-tech computer, photocopier, air conditioner, and heater. There is no view, since she avoids workplaces that are appealing. Another requirement is that the study be separate from her main living quarters.

Another study took the form of a carrel in a college library with yellow cinderblock walls and a window overlooking a tar-graveled roof, a parking lot, a hilltop with grazing cows, and a lively softball field, all of which quickly became a distraction. She took to playing softball with the boys in the afternoons; she just happened to own a mitt. But one day she shut the blinds for good to concentrate on her work. To remind her of the outside world, she hung up a large picture she had drawn of the view.

Sometimes writing was slow for Dillard: "Even when passages seemed to come easily, as though I were copying from a folio held open by smiling angels, the manuscript revealed the usual signs of struggle—bloodstains, teethmarks, gashes, and burns." Following a daily schedule enabled Dillard to work effectively. A schedule, "a scaffolding on which a worker can stand and labor with both hands," was adopted by many great writers, such as Ralph Waldo Emerson, who took long walks as part of his writing routine. Jack London was said to have written daily after only four hours of sleep. During her stint in the library study carrel, Dillard worked the graveyard shift; she believes that the absence of dawns and sunsets affected her writing.

Another study was an uninsulated cabin on a island in Puget Sound. Life there was isolated and cold. Dillard attempted to chop her own wood, the sight of which amused her neighbors. She was reminded of Henry David Thoreau's claim that his firewood warmed him twice, since he chopped it himself. For the same reason, Dillard's firewood froze her twice. She spent a great deal of time cutting a small amount of wood, and whatever heat the wood generated in the fireplace went straight up the chimney. Later, the knack of cutting firewood came to her in a dream: to aim not for the wood but past it, directly to the chopping block. Dillard uses this as another metaphor for good writing, aiming not for individual words but for the end itself.

Dillard is surprised by the strong materialistic side of writing. She once believed that all that was required was a pen, paper, and a lap. But even tiny sheds and study carrels are not always adequate to complete the job. "Sometimes you need a warehouse," she says. She once spent many hours "rewriting" drafts by laying out pages across a twenty-foot conference table, juggling and weeding bits to get the order right. It was exhausting labor.

Preparation for writing is as arduous as the act of writing itself. Dillard compares it to the task of an Aztec maiden, undergoing a series of purification rites before being sacrificed to a volcano god. To help prepare for writing, she drinks boiled Colombian coffee in large doses, just enough to reach the narrow therapeutic window between the greatest efficacy and toxicity. She washes dishes, observes birds, smokes cigarettes. Then she might pick up a manuscript from the day before and begin reading, making minor changes in a word or phrase, then adding a sentence or two. Before she knows it, she is writing! As soon as she is conscious of this fact, her concentration is disrupted, and it is time for a break. At the end of the day, it is not uncommon for her to mark the strained new sentences that constituted her day's work for deletion.

In several passages, Dillard makes some observations about what creates successful writing. She believes that a writer can excel not in writing what he loves best, but by writing about the special things he alone loves. The more idiosyncratic the better. Examples might include writing about winter in the summer, or about a prairie from a study in New York City, all with the utmost fervor. She believes that one must like sentences in order to really enjoy writing, as a painter loves the smell of paint. It is necessary to study and appreciate other writers' works, and use them as models.

Dillard often sees her writing as taking on a life of its own, well out of her control. She notes that sometimes part of the book "simply gets up and walks away," against the writer's conscious wishes. She compares this phenomenon to that of a sea starfish that, for no apparent reason, breaks off one of its legs, or rays. Presumably, another, stronger ray regenerates in its place.

In another instance, Dillard likens writing to a dying friend she must sit up with during visiting hours, offering comfort and hoping for improvement. At other times, the work is a lion difficult to tame. And if it is neglected for a day or two, it reverts to its wild ways and becomes more fierce.

In an exaggerated account underscoring the uncontrollable nature of her work, she describes a strange occurrence. One evening, soon after she left her study, following a day of writing, her typewriter erupted in sparks, smoke, and flames. Twenty minutes later the commotion subsided. She could do nothing but watch.

An artist friend of Dillard, Paul Glenn, shared with her his view of the uncontrollable nature of his painting. He illustrated his recent lack of progress with a story of a local island man in a rowboat who was taken out by the tide as he struggled to tote a log that was floating out in the channel. It took the man all night to bring in the log—he had to wait for the tide to change in his favor. Paul concluded that in matters of art, one must persevere until the tide turns.

Although writing often can take on a life of its own, for Dillard the process is engaging and exhilarating. She compares a writer to a Seminole alligator wrestler. There is conflict and danger; sometimes it can even end in death.

In the book's final pages, Dillard takes this notion of a writer's courage a step further in her story of a stunt pilot. Dillard had grown attached to one outstanding pilot because he elevated his maneuvers to the level of art and pushed its limits. She discovered him one day at a local air show. His moves were like music or air sculptures, or like those of a gymnast. The line created by his plane in the sky was like the highly expressive pen lines of illustrator Saul Steinberg. The plane did tailspins, figure eights, hammerheads, and pirouettes. "He was pure energy and naked spirit. . . . it split the bulging rim of the future along its seam. It pried out the present."

Dillard was so impressed that she persuaded the pilot to take her up with him. The exhilaration she felt, doing barrel rolls and defying dangers of nearby mountains, reminded her of the enormous chances one must take in order to write well. It was actually a painful experience for the pilot, but Dillard sensed that he was too caught up in his art to notice. Years later, Dillard learned that the stunt pilot had crashed during a performance for King Hussein. Apparently, he had pushed the limits of his art just a little too far.

Annie Dillard's brief account of the writing life is an inspiration to all writers and anyone who wants to excel at a personal endeavor. Through anecdotes from her own experiences, analogies to nature, and connections with literature and art, she vividly illustrates the struggles of a serious writer.

Only Dillard could successfully compare the sensation of writing to "the sensation of spinning, blinded by love and daring. . . . of rearing and peering from the bent tip of a grassblade, looking for a route," or equate it with the lethal dangers of alligator wrestling or stunt aviation. Yet she convinces the reader that these are the risks a writer must take. In this book, she takes such risks and emerges unscathed.

Dillard takes writing very seriously. It is not fun, but hard work. Rewards lie in perseverence, passion, and dedication to her work. The greater the risks, the greater the rewards. Dillard reveals that the goal of a writer should be to probe life's deepest mystery and illustrate beauty. In *The Writing Life*, she has masterfully succeeded.

David M. Kennerley

CUMULATIVE AUTHOR INDEX
1971–1990

(Figures within parentheses indicate years; other figures indicate page numbers.)

CUMULATIVE AUTHOR INDEX—1971–1990

IV

CUMULATIVE AUTHOR INDEX—1971–1990

CUMULATIVE AUTHOR INDEX—1971–1990

CUMULATIVE AUTHOR INDEX—1971–1990

CUMULATIVE AUTHOR INDEX—1971–1990

VIII

CUMULATIVE AUTHOR INDEX—1971-1990

X

CUMULATIVE AUTHOR INDEX—1971–1990

CUMULATIVE AUTHOR INDEX—1971–1990

CUMULATIVE AUTHOR INDEX—1971–1990

CUMULATIVE AUTHOR INDEX—1971–1990

CUMULATIVE AUTHOR INDEX—1971–1990